D1539368

INDUSTRIAL FIRE PREVENTION AND PROTECTION

INDUSTRIAL FIRE PREVENTION AND PROTECTION

Thomas H. Ladwig

VNR VAN NOSTRAND REINHOLD
New York

Copyright © 1991 by Van Nostrand Reinhold

Library of Congress Catalog Card Number 90-47492
ISBN 0-442-23678-6

Manufactured in the United States of America

Published by Van Nostrand Reinhold
115 Fifth Avenue
New York, New York 10003

Chapman and Hall
2-6 Boundary Row
London, SE1 8HN

Thomas Nelson Australia
102 Dodds Street
South Melbourne 3205
Victoria, Australia

Nelson Canada
1120 Birchmount Road
Scarborough, Ontario M1K 5G4, Canada

16 15 14 13 12 11 10 9 8 7 6 5 4 3 2 1

Library of Congress Cataloging-in-Publication Data

Ladwig, Thomas H.
    Industrial fire prevention and protection / Thomas H. Ladwig.
        p.   cm.
    Includes index.
    ISBN 0-442-23678-6
    1. Industrial buildings—Fires and fire prevention.   I. Title.
TH9445.M4L33   1990
628.9'2—dc20   90-47492
                                                             CIP

To
Mary, Paul, Greg, and Russel without whose support and understanding this book would not have been possible.

CONTENTS

PREFACE

This book was written to serve a dual purpose role as a text and as a reference. As a text, it is intended as a basic introduction to the field of fire protection. The student of engineering, fire protection, or safety will find this text useful. As a reference, this book will serve the individual in business and industry who has responsibility for fire prevention and fire protection.

Fire prevention is sometimes implicit in fire protection. This will cause the title of this book to be misleading to some. I consider prevention activities to be of the utmost importance in the industrial loss control program. Fire prevention is a necessary part of the industrial safety and housekeeping program. It is unfortunate that these areas are frequently neglected. If the reader gains nothing more than an awareness and understanding of fire prevention, then this book will have been worthwhile. This is why I have chosen to emphasize prevention rather than include it in fire protection.

REFERENCE

During my 20 years as a safety professional I have supported various sized organizations. I have, like others in the field, also been responsible for firesafety. The scope of responsibilities of the safety professional, especially in smaller organizations, is not clearly defined.

Usually, fire protection is included in the responsibilities of the safety professional as a part of the broad loss control function. With no formal education or training in fire protection, these people must rely on assistance from public fire departments and insurance companies. The National Fire Protection Association is also available with information and assistance. For these safety professionals, this book provides a basic broad brush of the field of industrial fire protection. The person in industry for whom this book is intended will benefit from its simplicity, its examples of fire losses, and its relationship to the overall loss control program.

Many aspects of fire protection have been covered from characteristics of fire to fire suppression systems. I have attempted to emphasize industrial firesafety problems with examples of industrial fire losses.

Fire protection has been related to the other loss control functions of safety, industrial hygiene, and environmental affairs. I have tried to identify where there may be conflicts between these fields.

Two chapters have been devoted to hazardous materials and hazardous materials emergencies. This is an area that is taking on increased importance to the firesafety person as well as safety and health personnel and plant management.

TEXT

The second purpose of this book grew out of the 10 years that I have spent teaching undergraduate safety students at the University of Southern California. I have felt the need for a textbook that will prepare the college student for this area of his or her career in industrial safety. The student will learn the basics of fire prevention and protection.

The textbook provides the industrial safety engineer with an understanding of fire prevention and protection and the ability to recognize and evaluate potential fire hazards. Chapter 15, Loss Prevention Resources, was written to provide further resources for fire prevention and protection problems that are beyond the capabilities of the person who is charged with firesafety responsibilities.

ACKNOWLEDGMENTS

Acknowledgment and appreciation must be extended to the many friends, associates, and organizations who have helped to make this work possible.

The National Fire Protection Association provided many of the reference materials and has been very generous with permissions. The very complete library at NFPA headquarters in Quincy, Massachusetts was very useful, and the librarians were very friendly and helpful.

Factory Mutual Engineering Corporation also provided many of the references and was very generous with pictures.

My employer, Hughes Aircraft Company, Space and Communications Group provided me the opportunity, support, and encouragement to practice firesafety.

Special appreciation is extended to my friends and associates who helped with review, encouragement, and criticism in this endeavor, including the following: Jim Ballinger, Nick Brovko, Bob Bush, Jim Daneker, Ted Ferry, Bob Katson, Tony Luca, Louis Sotis, and Homer Wallace.

Finally, I must thank Janet Blaske and Martha Scarbrough for typing help and preparation of diagrams.

1
INTRODUCTION TO INDUSTRIAL FIRE PROTECTION AND PREVENTION

HISTORICAL NOTES

Since the beginning of recorded history, there are accounts of fires destroying homes and cities, forests, and farmlands. As society changed from craftsman to industrial, fires took on far greater importance. Factories were built in towns which once supported agricultural activities or towns were built to support factories which were located to take advantage of local resources such as lumber or minerals and flowing streams to provide energy. Towns grew to cities, shops grew to factories, and factories congregated into industrial centers. The concentration of population around industrial centers and concentration of activities to support industry created fire hazards and life safety problems. Thus as it has been from the beginning, fire has always been both a benefit and a problem for man.

On October 8, 1871, on the same day and almost the same hour as the Great Chicago fire, a fire in northeastern Wisconsin killed 1,500 people and devastated 2400 square miles of pristine forest. Lumbering and wood related industries on both sides of Green Bay were destroyed. The Peshtigo Fire, as it was called, was one of the worst forest fires in history. However, because it was overshadowed by the Great Chicago fire, it received little publicity.

Peshtigo, on the Peshtigo River, was a town that was built to support industry. Peshtigo was the site of the country's largest woodenware factory. The surrounding countryside was dense forest that supported a burgeoning lumber and wood products industry as well as fur trapping activities. Agriculture was growing in the cleared forest lands in the area. The population of Peshtigo was swelled by crews working on the Chicago and Northwestern Railway which was constructing a line from Fort Howard, through Peshtigo to support the lumber industry and the factory and the iron mines in upper Michigan. 1871 was an unusually dry year and conditions were favorable for the inferno that was to follow. During this period of growth in northeastern Wisconsin, there were extensive lumbering operations to support the woodenware factory and the

1

construction of Peshtigo and other small communities and construction of the railroad right-of-way.

The exact cause of the Peshtigo fire is unknown. It is reported by Father Pernin, the parish priest in that area, that firesafety was not a high priority among the hunters, lumberjacks, railroad workers, and farmers. There had been numerous smaller fires during the weeks prior to October 8, which residents and factory workers had successfully mobilized to fight. As was the practice in those days, other fires were allowed to burn as long as people and property were not in jeopardy. U. S. Weather Bureau data that was collected on October 8, 1871, shows a storm system centered over the central portion of the United States that produced conditions that intensified both the Peshtigo and the Great Chicago fires.

Although fire watchers were posted and barrels of water were strategically placed around the factory, the dry conditions and the high winds produced a fire storm that was so intense that there was no possibility to save anything. The fast-moving fire caught many victims before they could flee. People who did survive did so by wading into the Peshtigo River and continuously splashing water on their heads for five hours.

In his account of the fire, Father Pernin describes phenomena that we now recognize as typical fire characteristics. Imagine how many lives would have been saved if current knowledge and technology had been available. It may not have been possible to stop the firestorm once it developed, but the hazardous conditions would have been recognized and steps taken to prevent it. The unsafe practice of allowing small fires to burn would have been stopped. The smaller fires would have been extinguished before they could combine to produce the conflagration.

Fire, Energy and Enemy

In the United States, as in the rest of the world, fire was quickly harnessed to generate energy for industry. At the same time, numerous catastrophes were reported when fire got out of control. Factories were built to support the industrial process with little regard to fire prevention or life safety. Now a fire could devastate a factory and eliminate the investment of the owner and the jobs of all of the employees. With the development of assembly line production, the factories became larger, as did the warehouses to support the assembly lines. The larger factories and warehouses led to greater fire protection problems and greater losses when fire did occur.

The results are well documented in history in such industrial tragedies as the blaze at the Triangle Shirtwaist Company factory in New York. The lives of 146 garment workers were lost on March 25, 1911, when fire roared through this building with its high fuel load and insufficient exits.

The Triangle Shirtwaist factory was typical of those in the garment district at the time. It was located on the top three floors of a 10-story building, much higher than the 75 feet that the New York City Fire Department could reach. This building was built during 1910 and 1911, and was termed "fireproof" because it was equipped with noncombustible features such as protected cast iron columns, steel girders, beams, and tile arch floors. But there was no sprinkler system in the building to protect the high fuel loading consisting of piles of clothing and wooden work benches and chairs. There was inadequate exit capacity and no evacuation plan. Doors to exit stairways were locked, as was the custom, and other stairways soon became impassable due to the fire. At the time of the fire, New York City had no laws requiring fire drills, fire escapes or sprinkler systems in factories. It was a common practice for management to lock exit doors so that employees leaving the floor could be monitored. This tragedy, like so many others, led to legislative changes to improve worker safety and activity by the National Fire Protection Association which was 15 years old at the time. The Safety to Life Committee was formed in 1913 by the National Fire Protection Association. This committee was to originate the *Life Safety Code*. In 1918, the National Fire Protection Association published a pamphlet entitled "Safeguarding Factory Workers from Fire." This pamphlet and others as well as the activities of the Safety to Life Committee were some of the activities generated by the notable loss-of-life fires which had occurred.

Development of Fire Insurance Companies

Some of the first fire fighting forces were organized by factory owners in order to protect their investments. In the Great Peshtigo fire, factory workers were organized into bucket brigades and water barrels were prepositioned around the factory. But the fire brigades did not stop the fire losses that were occurring so the next logical step was for factory owners to pool their resources to form insurance protection.

Factory Mutual.   The Factory Mutual System, a world authority in loss control, had its foundations in a group of New England textile mill owners who banded together to pool their resources in order to cover losses. In 1835, industrial fire losses were increasing, especially in the textile mills located in the New England states. The insurance companies that were active at the time spread fire losses among all of their insureds. There were no allowances, and consequently no incentives, for factory owners to practice firesafety or to incorporate firesafe construction. Zachariah Allen, a prominent Rhode Island mill owner, requested an insurance premium reduction after installing a fire pump and other protection in his mill. Instead of a reduction, his premiums were increased to reflect the high losses in the rest of the industry. Soon after this increase, Allen met with a group of mill owners and formed a mutual fire insurance company known as Manufacturers' Mutual Fire Insurance Company. This was later to become Allendale Mutual Insurance Company. The mill owners demonstrated that losses and insurance premiums could be minimized by maintaining good fire prevention practices. From the start, Manufacturers' required regular fire inspections for member mills, a practice that continues today. Rhode Island Mutual Fire Insurance Company was added in 1848. To further add to the resources of the group, the Boston Manufacturers Mutual Fire Insurance Company was formed in 1850 and the Arkwright Mutual Insurance Company was added in 1860. So, by 1860, there were four mutual companies in the system which gave the system greater stability and the capability to handle greater losses.

Zachariah Allen's concept developed into a successful mutual protection system that has not only survived for over 150 years, but it has made vast contributions to the field of fire research, prevention, and protection. The Allendale, Arkwright, and Protection Mutual Insurance Companies in partnership with Factory Mutual Engineering and Research embody Zachariah Allen's principles and continue to be the world leader.

Industrial Risk Insurers.   Another major insurance organization to be developed about this time was Industrial Risk Insurers. To meet the needs of a developing industrial America, 11 insurance companies formed the Factory Insurance Association (FIA) in 1890. FIA was formed specifically to write property insurance on large facilities that had incorporated sprinkler protection. A year later, the Western Factory Insurance Association (WFIA) was formed in Chicago to underwrite midwestern properties. When the National Fire Protection Association was founded in 1896, FIA and WFIA were founding members. To meet the needs of America's growing industry, FIA expanded inspection services and broadened their coverage to include business interruption, sprinkler leakage, and windstorm. Following World War I, FIA continued to expand its services and coverage to meet the needs of American industry.

In 1932, the Pacific FIA was founded. By 1935, the insurance in force through the three associations totalled more than $6 billion. In 1943, due to the surge in production and the demand for loss prevention and control, the three associations—FIA, WFIA, and PFIA—merged. After the merger in 1943, a fire safety laboratory was founded for training purposes.

In 1975, the Factory Insurance Association and the Oil Insurance Association merged to form Industrial Risk Insurers (IRI). IRI is a capital stock company backed by the resources of more than 40 member companies. It provides total loss prevention and control programs for its insureds.

Development of Firesafety Institutions

Out of the fire-caused losses to life and property that plagued early industrialized America, three new institutions were formed to develop firesafety standards and practices aimed at stopping the catastrophic losses. These institutions included Factory Mutual Laboratories, Underwriters Laboratories (UL), and the National Fire Protection Association (NFPA).

Factory Mutual Laboratories was founded in 1886 to develop and approve sprinkler designs and other loss prevention devices. Underwriters Laboratories was founded in 1894, to test devices, systems, and materials to determine their relation to hazards to life and property. The NFPA was founded in 1896. Its purpose, at that time, was to standardize the design, installation, and maintenance of sprinkler systems.

Codes and Regulations Evolve From Tragedies

Historically, the United States has experienced too many tragic fires like the Triangle Shirtwaist Company. Most of these unfortunate experiences led to changes in the codes concerning fire and life safety. For example, in 1942, a fire in the Cocoanut Grove Night Club in Boston claimed the lives of 492 people. This disaster focused attention upon the importance of adequate exits and related firesafety features, and it resulted in changes to the Building Exits Code which was the forerunner to the *Life Safety Code*. Other changes including a new and revised section of the Building Exits Code were developed after three fatal hotel fires in 1946. A number of fatal nursing home fires in the 1950's through the 1970's led to legislation requiring nursing homes that receive federal funding to comply with the *Life Safety Code*.

In the 1970s, a series of devastating explosions occurred in the grain handling industry. These explosions resulted in an intense effort by the Occupational Safety and Health Administration and firesafety professionals to legislate stronger controls for this and other industries that generate potentially explosive dusts.

UNITED STATES FIRE LOSSES

Table 1-1 shows some of the more tragic fires and explosions that have occurred in the United States between 1930 and 1987. The decreasing severity of the incidents over time seems to indicate that lessons are being learned from these incidents.

Unfortunately, however, the lessons learned seem to have slowed. The NFPA's reported fire loss in the United States in 1988 indicates that the United States has been stuck on a plateau of about 6000 civilian fire deaths per year since 1982. This plateau occurred after a steady decline in fire deaths over the previous five years.

The most significant fire loss problem in the United States is, and always has been, in residential occupancies. This fact is true in terms of fire deaths and property loss. Residential occupancies include one and two family homes (in-

Table 1-1.   U.S. Fires and Explosions That Killed 50 or More Persons in Nonmining Structures and Vehicles. 1930–1987

DATE	INCIDENT	DEATHS
21 April 1930	Ohio State Penitentiary, Columbus, Ohio	320
18 March 1937	Consolidated School, New London, Texas	294
23 April 1940	Rhythm Club dance hall, Natchez, Mississippi	207
12 September 1940	Hercules Powder Company plant, Kenvil, New Jersey	52
5 June 1942	Elwood Ordnance Plant, Joliet, Illinois	54
28 November 1942	Cocoanut Grove night club, Boston, Massachusetts	492
7 September 1943	Gulf Motel, Houston, Texas	54
6 July 1944	Ringling Brothers and Barnum Bailey Circus tent, Hartford, Connecticut	168
20 October 1944	East Ohio Gas Company, Cleveland, Ohio	136
5 June 1946	LaSalle Hotel, Chicago, Illinois	61
7 December 1946	Winecoff Hotel, Atlanta, Georgia	119
4 April 1949	St. Anthony's Hospital, Effingham, Illinois	74
17 February 1957	Katie Jane Nursing Home, Warrenton, Missouri	72
1 December 1958	Our Lady of the Angels School, Chicago, Illinois	95
31 October 1963	Indiana State Fairgrounds Coliseum, Indianapolis, Indiana	75
23 November 1963	Golden Age Nursing Home, Fitchville, Ohio	63
9 August 1965	Missile silo, near Searcy, Arkansas	53
28 May 1977	Beverly Hills Supper Club, Southgate, Kentucky	165
21 November 1980	MGM Grand Hotel, Las Vegas, Nevada	85

Reprinted with permission from *Fire Journal* (Vol. 82 No. 3). Copyright © 1988, National Fire Protection Association, Quincy, Mass. 02269.

cluding mobile homes), apartments, hotels, and motels. The annual fire loss reports issued by the NFPA demonstrate that year after year, 75 to 80 percent of all fire deaths occur in residential occupancies. Similarly, 60 to 65 percent of all structural property fire losses have occurred in residential occupancies. Figure 1-1 provides further statistics that illustrate the current fire loss problem in the United States.

After residential property losses, the next highest fire loss experience in the United States is in the combined areas of stores, offices, industrial, and storage occupancies followed by public assembly, institutional, special structures, and educational. NFPA records for 1987 show these occupancies as accounting for about 16 percent of all building fires in the United States, and they account for about 30 percent of all of the property losses.

The data for large-loss fires which are reported by the NFPA demonstrate a need for more preventive and protective activities in the area of fire prevention. Large-loss fires are those in which the loss exceeds $5 million. In 1987, there were 49 such fires, almost double the number in 1986. These large-loss fires accounted for 13.8 percent of the estimated dollar loss for all fires in 1987. There was automatic fire suppression equipment present in only one-half of these fires. In most of these cases, there were deficiencies that rendered the fire

Fires
Fires attended by public fire departments increased from 1986 by 2.6% to 2,330,000.
There were 551,500 fires involving residential properties or 73% of all structural fires.
There was a decrease from 1986 in fires in structures of 5.3% to 758,000.

Fire Deaths
Civilian fire deaths decreased by 0.7% to 5,810.
Residential fire deaths, at 4,660, accounted for 80.2% of all fire fatalities.

Property Damage
Property losses increased from 1986 by 6.7% to $7.159 billion.
Structural fires caused 87% or $6.226 billion, of all property damage.
Residential properties accounted for 61%, or $3.699 billion, of all structural property loss.

Incendiary and Suspicious Fires
There were 105,000 structural fires that were deliberately set, or are suspected of having been set accounting for 25% of all structural property loss.

Figure 1-1. Selected 1987 United States fire statistics. (Reprinted with permission from *Fire Journal* (Vol. 82 No. 3) Copyright © 1988, National Fire Protection Association, Quincy, Mass. 02269).

suppression equipment ineffective. In only about one fourth of the cases was automatic detection equipment present. It is apparent that U.S. industry is not following its increases in property values with a comparable increase in fire prevention and protection activities, and more attention must be devoted to this area. It is also possible that more active fire prevention and protection programs in industry would increase employee awareness levels, and not only bring about a reduction in industrial fire losses, but also contribute to reducing the high residential fire death and property loss rate.

INDUSTRIAL FIRE PREVENTION AND PROTECTION

Before proceeding to the topic of industrial firesafety, it is necessary to explain the title of this book. In normal usage, the term fire protection is understood to include both prevention and suppression activities. In fact, as used throughout this book, the term is used in just that context. Fire protection, then would include those activities and equipment that are intended to prevent fire and explosion from occurring by controlling the causes of fire and those that are intended to detect and extinguish fire. Prevention activities play a big and very inportant role in the industrial firesafety program. It was necessary to emphasize prevention by including the word in the title.

INDUSTRIAL FIRE PROBLEM AREAS

There are a number of indications of the types of fire problems that plague American industry. These indicators, including fire loss experience, large-loss fire experience, and source of ignition data have been used as the basis for this book, and they can be used as emphasis areas for the industrial fire prevention and protection program. These emphasis areas, when combined with the unique fire hazards of the particular industry, can form the basis for the industrial fire prevention and protection program.

Fire Loss Experience

A review of industrial loss experiences generated by property loss insurance carriers and the NFPA show frequent high fire losses in oil refinery and storage operations, operations involving flammable and combustible liquids, and storage occupancies.

Oil Refinery and Storage.   The United States has experienced a number of spectacular and high loss oil refinery and storage fires throughout its history. In 1955, Standard Oil Company (Indiana) suffered a fire at its Whiting Refinery that burned for eight days. In 1956, the McKee Refinery of Shamrock Oil and Gas Company near Amarillo, Texas, had a major fire that killed 19 people. The fatalities occurred when a 500,000-gallon spheroid tank containing a mixture of pentane and hexane exploded. More recently, in 1983, a fire in a catalytic cracking unit in an Avon, California refinery resulted in a $49 million loss. In July, 1984, the rupture of a monoethanolamine absorber column in a Romeoville, Illinois, refinery resulted in a $127 million fire. In Torrance, California, a potassium hydroxide propane treater in a refinery hydrogen fluoride-alkylation unit exploded and caused a $15 million fire on November 24, 1987.

Flammable and Combustible Liquids.   Fires involving hydraulic and lubricating oils in industrial processes have been another high source of industrial fire loss in recent years. Many hydraulic fluids that are used have a high flash point, resulting in a tendency to pass them off as being firesafe. However, the flash points are determined under laboratory conditions and do not take into account conditions of high pressure and high temperature that occur in usage.

Some examples of industrial fires involving oil include a 1986 fire in Harrisburg, Pennsylvania, that resulted in a $65 million loss to a manufacturer of high quality turbine blades for aircraft. This fire was caused when the oil level in an electronic discharge machine (EDM) got too low. In this machining process, a high amperage electrical arc is generated between electrodes, which are submerged in a tank of dielectric oil, to perform high tolerance cutting. When the oil level dropped below the arcing, overheating occurred which led to ignition of the oil and the devastating fire.

On September 8, 1988, a Virginia chicken processing plant suffered a $10 million loss when cooking oils overheated.

Figure 1-2. Oil refinery fires have been a dramatic part of the United States fire experience. (Photo: Mike Mullen)

Overheating. In the above flammable and combustible liquids fires and other industrial fires, a frequent form of ignition is the failure of temperature controllers, resulting in overheating. Another frequent example occurs in plating and heat treating operations. A submersible heating element is frequently used to heat a liquid in a tank. To compound this hazard potential, the tank is frequently constructed of a plastic material. Fires often occur when the liquid level falls too low or the thermostat fails and overheating occurs.

Storage Occupancies. Another fire problem to hit American industry in the late 1970s and continuing into the 1980s was an increase in large warehouse fire losses. Some of the major causes of these losses have been the result of increased hazardous materials storage, inadequate sprinkler density, and improper arrangement of storage. Warehouse fire protection will be discussed in greater detail in Chapter 13.

Figure 1-3.   The result of an overheated submersible heater in a polyethylene platting tank.

Sources of Ignition

Another approach to identifying fire loss problem areas in industry is to look at ignition sources that have been reported for industrial fires. Knowledge of the most common sources of ignition for industrial fires will provide a basis for the fire prevention program for the person who is responsible for the fire prevention and protection program. This information can be used to conduct an evaluation of the industrial facility to determine the highest ignition risk area on which to concentrate fire prevention activities.

Probably the best source of information about fire ignition sources in industry is the property loss insurance industry. Figure 1-5 shows the causes of fires and explosions based upon data compiled by Factory Mutual Engineering Corporation over the period 1983–1987. Those ignition sources are described in the following sections.

Electricity.   The most frequent source of ignition in industrial fires is electricity. This is probably not difficult to understand when one stops to think about the widespread use of electricity in every business and industrial operation. Electricity provides the energy by which most industrial processes are performed. It is used in heating systems, lighting, controls, mechanical operations data processing, and telecommunications. A large industrial property may have

Figure 1-4. Warehouses present a severe fire challenge which have resulted in some large-loss fires. (Photo Alan Simmons)

many miles of electrical wiring used to carry electricity from the sources to the areas of use.

Smoking. Fires caused by the misuse of smoking materials is the second major source of ignition in industrial fires and the number one cause of fire for all fires as reported by the NFPA. Newspaper reports of residential fires are frequently encountered where the cause is listed as ''misuse of smoking materials.'' Many of these incidents have been the result of smoking materials dropping into upholstered furniture and producing a smoky and toxic smoldering fire. There has been extensive research into fire resistive furniture cushioning and covering material to try to address this problem.

Incendiarism. Deliberately set, or incendiary, fires, have become a multibillion dollar problem in the United States. Industry has not escaped the problem as evidenced by the fact that arson, the crime of setting an incendiary fire,

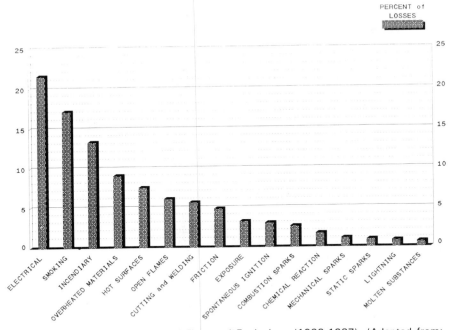

Figure 1-5. Causes of Industrial Fires and Explosions (1983-1987). (Adapted from: Factory Mutual Publication P8610. 1988. ''Ignition Sources: Recognizing the Causes of Fire.'' Factory Mutual Engineering Corporation)

is the third greatest source of ignition in large-loss industrial fires. Arson is usually thought to be for profit and insurance fraud and, in fact, most of the attention has been focused upon this type. However, the experts say that the chief motives behind arson are psychological. The Law Enforcement Assistance Administration reports that vandalism accounts for 42 percent of all arson fires, revenge accounts for 23 percent, pyromania 14 percent, and arson for profit for only 14 percent of the arson fires.

Overheated Materials.   It is surprising that overheated materials is not a greater source of ignition in large-loss industrial fires. There are many industrial processes that involve the heating of materials to include:

quenching	heating
degreasing	drying
dipping and plating	baking
cooking	

In most of these processes, combustible production materials or products are heated. If overheating occurs, the materials may ignite or produce flammable vapors that are subsequently ignited. In many other operations, the heated materials may not be combustible, but the container or surrounding materials are combustible and subject to overheating and ignition. For example, in plating operations such as in the manufacture of printed circuit boards, the plating solution may be corrosive, necessitating a plastic tank. These solutions are frequently heated using an immersion heater. Fires have occurred when the solution level drops to the point where the immersion heater is exposed and the walls of the tank are ignited. In this type of operation it is important to use, and frequently check, low liquid level sensors that interrupt power to the heater in the event that the liquid level drops to the point where the heater may be exposed.

Hot Surfaces.   Closely related to overheated materials, as a source of ignition, are hot surfaces. This category includes those instances where heat is carried by conduction from the surfaces of electrical heating equipment, piping, boilers, furnaces, ovens, dryers, flues, and ducts into adjacent combustible materials. Other losses in this category include the hot surface of an incandescent light bulb, soldering tools, and hot plates.

The best protection against this category of ignition is to recognize the existence, or possible existence, of hot surfaces and provide adequate safeguards such as insulation, cooling, and separation of hot surfaces. Automatic controls and alarms and training of operators are also important preventative measures.

Open Flames.   There are many instances of open flames in industry which have the potential to cause fires. Open flames include portable torches, cigarette lighters, matches, salamanders, space heaters, and roofers' tar kettles. Additionally, open flames at the burners of power boilers, dryers, ovens, and furnaces have caused significant numbers of fires and explosions.

The best protection against open flames as a source of ignition is to avoid the use of open flames wherever possible. When open flames must be used, they should be closely supervised. Fuel burners should be properly designed, installed, operated, and maintained. Adequate controls should be installed and operators should be properly trained.

Cutting and Welding.   Cutting and welding operations occur frequently as part of manufacturing, construction, and maintenance operations. Fires that are ignited by cutting and welding result from sparks or globules of molten metal that are generated. These sparks or molten metal may fly, fall, or roll into combustible material and start a fire. It is important to shield these operations and check the surrounding areas during and after to ensure that there are no smoldering materials. There have also been fires caused by heat from cutting and welding operations being carried by conduction to adjacent combustible materials.

Friction. In industries involving moving machinery, there is the inherent possibility of friction generating sufficient heat to ignite combustible materials. Friction is generally the result of inadequate maintenance procedures. Friction generates excessive heat when parts are loose, worn, or misaligned and when there is inadequate lubrication.

Obviously, a good safeguard against friction as a source of ignition is a good maintenance program that includes regularly scheduled preventive maintenance procedures and lubrication programs.

Spontaneous Ignition. As described in Chapter 2, spontaneous ignition is a phenomenon that results in the ignition of combustible solids by the action of internal heating caused by an exothermic reaction. Under confined conditions, when the heat that is generated cannot be dissipated, ignition can occur. Spontaneous ignition is common in agricultural products that are stored with too much moisture, allowing bacterial oxidation to occur. Spontaneous ignition also occurs in industry with substances such as linseed oil, animal oils, vegetable oils, and other oils of low volatility. Storage of damp bituminous coal and charcoal is also susceptible to internal heating.

As is so important in all other areas of fire prevention, the most important safeguard against spontaneous ignition is good housekeeping. The buildup of rags and other debris that are contaminated with animal or vegetable oils must be avoided. Storage of coal, charcoal, and organic materials should be carefully monitored to ensure that moisture levels are low and that heat does not build up.

Combustion Sparks. Ignition has been caused by sparks generated from fuel-burning equipment such as furnaces, boilers, incinerators, and industrial trucks in numerous industrial fires. When spark emitting equipment must be used in the vicinity of combustible materials, such as the industrial truck that is used in a warehouse, the equipment should be equipped with spark arresters.

Exposure. Ignition of buildings often occurs when they are exposed to fire from an adjacent building or brush or accumulations of combustibles. It has been a common practice in industry to store unused equipment, pallets, and other combustibles outside and adjacent to buildings. Also poor housekeeping practices sometimes result in accumulations of combustible debris adjacent to buildings. These materials offer ideal kindling for arsonists or for stray sparks.

The best protection against exposure ignition is to avoid the accumulation of combustibles near buildings. Where the exposure is another building, a blank firewall or exposure sprinklers can provide protection.

Chemical Reactions. Chemical reactions occur in many industries. While most of them are a planned and necessary part of the manufacturing process, fires and explosions can occur if these reactions get out of control. Other fires and explosions can occur when operator error or equipment malfunction allow incompatibles to react or when unstable chemicals decompose. In chemical processing, explicit written procedures are necessary and they must be followed by well-trained operators. Equipment must be well designed and maintained and must have appropriate safety controls.

Mechanical Sparks.   Mechanical sparks are created when steel tools or metal debris are struck. These sparks can be over 2000 degrees Fahrenheit. Metal debris that is mixed with combustible materials during processing can lead to fire or explosion. This material, sometimes known as "tramp metal," has been the cause of explosions in grain and other food and chemical processing operations. Industries that are susceptible to "tramp metal" use magnetic separators and screens to remove metal prior to grinding and other operations that might generate sparks.

In operations where flammable gases and vapors may be present, either non-metal or nonsparking alloy hand tools should be used to prevent generating mechanical sparks.

Static Sparks.   There are numerous industrial operations that generate static sparks, and they frequently occur where readily ignitable atmospheres are present. Static electricity is generated when electrons move between two objects that are in contact with one another. An electrical charge is produced when the objects are separated. If the charge is great enough, it will jump, as a spark, to an object that is grounded or that has a different charge. Static sparks can contain sufficient energy to ignite flammable vapors, dust in suspension in the air, and flammable gases. In industry, static electricity is generated by conveyor and power belts, rollers and reels, the flow of flammable liquids, and the movement of dust and other finely divided particles through enclosures.

Molten Materials.   The high temperatures that are inherent in molten metals and glass are obvious sources of ignition in industrial fires. Equipment malfunctions and deterioration are common causes of spillage that results in losses in these industries. Additionally, the introduction of moisture into these systems, or when the molten materials are spilled into areas containing moisture may result in a steam-expansion explosion.

These operations can be protected through frequent and thorough inspections and tests of the equipment and through the avoidance of combustible construction in or around areas where molten materials are present.

Lightning.   Direct lightning strikes and lightning induced power surges in electrical circuits have resulted in the ignition of fires. In areas of the country that are subject to frequent lightning strikes, buildings and operations must be protected. Lightning protection involves the use of grounded masts or rods that extend above the building or equipment to carry the lightning current to ground. Major electrical equipment, such as transformers, motors and generators should also be protected by surge protection equipment. Extremely hazardous operations such as explosives work and fuel transfer operations should be suspended when electrical storms are threatening.

FIRESAFETY REGULATIONS

There are many sources of regulations that are intended to regulate firesafety in industry in the United States. The federal regulations are generally secondary to some other purpose such as employee safety and health or control of hazardous materials. State and local regulations are generally more specific to firesafety in the form of building codes and fire prevention codes.

Federal Regulations

There are no federal regulations governing fire prevention and protection in the industrial sector which compare in magnitude or which are as comprehensive as the safety and health regulations in the Occupational Safety and Health Act (OSHAct). While OSHA does include some firesafety rules, and safety rules that have ancillary benefits to firesafety, their primary focus and emphasis on compliance activities are in the area of industrial injury/illness prevention. There is also some Environmental Protection Agency legislation that affects firesafety programs with regard to hazardous materials (Chapter 11). Department of Transportation regulations (Chapter 11) deal with the transportation of hazardous materials including packaging, labeling, and placarding. Most of the other fire safety requirements in industry come from the adoption of consensus standards and codes at the state and local level.

Occupational Safety and Health Act.   The firesafety rules contained in OSHAct relate to employee safety and health. OSHA has adopted extensive portions of the *National Electrical Code* and the *Life Safety Code*. OSHAct also cross-references a large number of NFPA standards as national consensus standards. As in other areas of regulatory development, OSHA has responded to the areas of greatest need or highest accident cause factors. Following a number of serious dust explosions and fires in grain handling facilities in the 1970s, OSHA responded with rules for that industry. More recently, OSHA recognized the need for rules to protect emergency response personnel who deal with hazardous materials incidents. 29 CFR 1910.120, Hazardous Waste Operations and Emergency Response was issued as an interim final rule in 1987, to protect emergency response personnel, whether they are municipal fire fighters or in-plant industrial personnel.

Superfund Amendments and Reauthorization Act (SARA) of 1986. Title III of SARA is referred to as the Emergency Planning and Community Right-to-Know Act (EPCRA) of 1986. Title III includes requirements for emergency planning and notification, community right-to-know reporting, and toxic chemical release reporting. SARA has as much application to the firesafety professional as to safety, industrial hygiene, and environmental compliance.

Department of Transportation. The Department of Transportation (DOT) has been regulating the transportation of hazardous materials for many years. Many DOT regulations are intended to reduce the fire hazards involved with this activity. Specific areas of coverage include packaging, labeling, and placarding.

State and Local Regulations

Most of the model codes that apply to public safety and health were developed in the private sector by volunteer groups such as the Southern Building Code Congress International and the Building Officials and Code Administrators International. This system plays an important role in our society by providing the public with reliable safety standards at a reasonable cost. This system also provides for nationwide uniformity in our standards which fosters the efficient flow of commerce. Privately developed model codes and standards are attractive to governmental entities as a source of state and local law because of the consensus system by which they were developed. Local and state legislatures do not have the resources or time necessary to produce their own codes. When model codes are adopted, the governmental body may incorporate some changes to reflect local needs and requirements, but for the most part, the codes are adopted as is.

Consensus standards and model codes, by their nature, prescribe a minimum level of protection. When conflicts arise between building and fire codes, it is often the result of varying definitions of what actually constitutes minimum protection. Most fire safety legislation comes from state and local authorities who adopt NFPA standards or other model codes such as the Uniform Fire Code or the *Standard Fire Prevention Code* as their municipal fire code. This has led to some disparity between municipalities with different codes being adopted, different amendments incorporated, and, due to delays in the legislative process, older editions being used.

Building Codes. The building codes that are used in the United States include the *National Building Code,* the *Standard Building Code,* and the *Uniform Building Code.* These codes are further described in Chapter 15.

The building codes deal with the construction, alteration, addition, repair, removal, demolition, use, location, occupancy, and maintenance of all buildings and structures. Interesting enough, the majority of the provisions of the building codes apply to firesafety. There are other building codes such as the electrical code, mechanical code, and the plumbing code which also contain provisions related to fire protection and firesafety. Building codes may also reference NFPA codes and standards as well as Factory Mutual Engineering and Research Standards.

Fire Prevention Codes.   Fire prevention codes regulate the hazards of fire and explosion associated with the storage, handling, and use of hazardous substances, materials, and devices and hazardous conditions associated with the use or occupancy of buildings or premises.

While the requirements for exits and fire extinguishing equipment are found in the building codes, the maintenance of these items is covered in the fire prevention codes.

The fire prevention codes that are used in the United States include the *Uniform Fire Code* and the *Standard Fire Prevention Code*.

National Fire Protection Association (NFPA) Codes and Standards. The NFPA codes are the largest, most democratic, and accessible voluntary standards in the world today. They are used by all levels of government and industry, from institutions and laboratories to installers, designers, insurance representatives, and scientists. They are formulated and maintained through NFPA committees composed of highly qualified professionals and organizations. These codes have been described by some as the ''cookbook'' to firesafety. They contain hands-on experience, practical solutions, legal legitimacy, and references to supporting sources.

Insurance and Code Requirements

American business and industry responds to insurance and code requirements under the belief that these requirements will bring about the best protection available for people and property. This is due to managements' lack of understanding or expertise in the area of fire prevention and protection. There is, therefore, extensive reliance upon the fire insurance carrier and code compliance to show the way and to provide adequate fire protection.

Francis L. Brannigan has been a longtime fire protection professional. He is a well-known fire safety instructor and has served on many technical committees. One of Brannigan's great myths of fire protection is ''it is insured, they don't want to lose money, therefore it must be okay.'' It must be remembered that the insurance company is primarily concerned with protecting the property of the insured, to protect its investment. Life safety, for example, is not a primary concern of the property insurance company, although some ancillary benefits may accrue from compliance with insurance company recommendations.

There is no way that insurance can cover all of the losses that occur when a company is devastated by fire. The loss of property, inventory, employees who may no longer be available when the operation recovers, and customer relations caused by late and missed deliveries can never be fully insured.

Code compliance is another area that some managers assume provides adequate fire protection. All too often, facilities are designed "to code," with little consideration to other factors such as future use and occupancy of the facility. Another one of Francis Brannigan's myths in fire protection is "it meets code therefore it must be safe." Brannigan goes on to say, "look at what *can* happen. Codes are a reaction to what *has* happened." How many major fires have occurred where many of the causative factors were not in violation of applicable codes? To be sure, in the investigation of major fires, there are frequently many code violations discovered which were responsible for the fire and amount of loss. But, lessons are also learned which emphasize the need for changes or additions to the codes.

The MGM Grand Hotel fire in Las Vegas on November 21, 1980 grimly supports this observation. A major factor in this fire was the fact that most of the hotel was not sprinklered. Sprinklers were not required by the local code which was in effect at the time.

The May 4, 1988 fire in the First Interstate Bank building in Los Angeles, California is another example. The First Interstate Bank Building was built in 1972, when the applicable codes did not require installation of a sprinkler system. In 1974, the City of Los Angeles changed its code to require sprinklers in high-rise buildings. However, it did not make the requirement retroactive. It is ironic that at the time of the fire, there was a $3.5 million project in process to install sprinklers in the building and it was 90 percent complete. As a result of this fire, the City of Los Angeles amended its code again to require sprinkler systems in older high-rise buildings.

It is up to the staff people who are charged with responsibilities for fire prevention and protection to look beyond the codes at what can happen. They must sell improvements to the responsible management and obtain professional help when necessary. There is an abundance of professional fire protection assistance available to assist the staff person who has limited training (Chapter 15).

INDUSTRIAL FIRE PROTECTION CONSIDERATIONS

The science of fire protection is constantly changing. Consequently, the industrial fire prevention and protection program must also change to not only take advantage of the improvements in technology, but to avoid fire hazards that are created by changing technology. Different kinds of industry will generate different program needs as do external factors such as geographical location and environmental compliance.

Complexity

The whole function of industrial fire prevention and protection is becoming increasingly complex and technical. From site selection to design, construction, occupancy, and daily operations, fire prevention and protection considerations are more important than ever. There are increasing environmental considerations that affect fire protection decisions in addition to the compromises that are sometimes necessary with the industrial process personnel. It has long been recognized that many industrial chemicals are flammable, and special procedures and equipment are required for their safe use. Alternatively, flammable materials were replaced by less flammable materials. For example, Stoddard Solvent and chlorinated hydrocarbons have been incorporated to replace more flammable industrial solvents.

It was also recognized that many of the solvents that were utilized by industry presented unacceptable health and environmental hazards to employees. Solvents such as benzene, 2-ethoxyethanol, and trichloroethylene were replaced by safer materials whenever possible. More recently, it was learned that many industrial solvents contribute significantly to air pollution and there are currently very active campaigns to control these emissions through legislation. Some solvents such as methyl isobutyl ketone (MIBK) and toluene are photochemically reactive. They react in sunlight to produce ozone in the lower atmosphere. Ozone is listed in the National Ambient Air Quality Standards (NAAQS) as a criteria pollutant. The Federal Clean Air Act requires the Environmental Protection Agency (EPA) to establish ambient ceilings for certain criteria pollutants. Ozone was one of six criteria pollutants for which the EPA established ambient levels of air quality necessary to protect public health.

Ironically, there is a layer of ozone in the stratosphere that is necessary to maintaining the ecosystem on earth. There are other solvents and industrial chemicals known as chlorofluorocarbons (CFCs) that are ozone depleters. These chemicals migrate to the stratosphere where they degrade the ozone layer that protects the earth from ultraviolet radiation. Table 1-2 shows the fire, health, or environmental hazards of some common industrial solvents.

Of equal importance are the needs of the industrial process. If chemicals are to be replaced to mitigate health hazards, fire hazards, or environmental effects, the new chemical must still meet the requirements of the industrial process. These activities require close communications and coordination between the process engineers, environmental engineers, industrial hygienists, and fire prevention and protection personnel.

STAFFING

The limited regulatory emphasis on fire protection at the federal level has resulted in a shortage of fire protection engineers in industry. Certainly, when

**Table 1-2. Fire, Health, and Environmental Hazards
of Selected Solvents.**

MATERIAL	FLASH POINT[1]	TLV[2]	PHOTOCHEM REACTIVE[3]	OZONE DEPLETION[4]
Acetone	−4	750		
Benzene	12	10		
2-Ethoxyethanol	232	5		
Ethyl alcohol	55	1000		
Hexane	−7	50		
Isopropanol	53	400		
Methanol	52	200		
Methylene chloride	None	50		
Methyl isobutyl ketone	64	50	Yes	
Toluene	40	100	Yes	
1,1,1-Trichloroethane	None	350		Yes
Trichloroethylene	None	50	Yes	
1,1,2-Trichloro-1,2,2-trifluoroethane	None	1000		Yes
Xylene	90	100	Yes	

[1] Flashpoint—The temperature (F) at which a liquid produces sufficient vapors to form an ignitable mixture in air. Source: NFPA 325M-1984. *Fire Hazard Properties of Flammable Liquids, Gases, and Volatile Solids.* National Fire Protection Association.
[2] TLV–TWA—The time-weighted average concentration (ppm) for a normal 8-hour workday and 40-hour work week, to which nearly all workers may be repeatedly exposed, day after day, without adverse effect. Source: *Threshold Limit Values and Biological Exposure Indices for 1988-1989.* American Conference of Governmental Industrial Hygienists.
[3] Photochemically reactive—Those chemicals that react, in the presence of sunlight, to produce ozone.
[4] Ozone depletion—Those chemicals that react with and break down ozone in the stratosphere.

compared to the numbers of safety engineers and industrial hygienists that have been generated by OSHA, the shortage of fire protection engineers becomes apparent. The inclusion of some fire safety in OSHAct and the fact that many safety professionals have cross-training and experience in fire prevention and protection has helped to provide firesafety to American industry. In many cases, because of the firesafety in OSHAct and the close relationship of safety to firesafety and loss control, the safety person in the industrial plant is given responsibilities for fire prevention and protection. It is important for whoever has this responsibility, to not base the entire fire prevention and protection program on OSHA, but have access to and use other fire safety resources (Chapter 15). Frequently, only very large companies have fire protection engineers. Some companies maintain fire suppression units, but no capability for engineering fire protection and prevention into facilities and processes. The vast majority of industry assigns fire protection to the suppression unit (if they have one) or, as an additional duty, to the safety office, plant engineer, or plant manager. This book is intended for the person who is not a fire protection engineer but has the responsibility for fire prevention and protection.

This book is primarily about industrial fire prevention and protection. It is not intended to address strictly industrial occupancies, but it will cross standard occupancy definitions to include hotels, businesses, and storage occupancies. In most cases, the personnel responsible for safety and firesafety in these occupancies are similar in needs and experience to their industrial counterparts. This book is intended to be general enough to address firesafety concerns in different occupancies.

In order to ensure the success of the fire prevention and protection, the program must be integrated into the total loss control program of each operating unit. This book will relate fire prevention and protection to safety, industrial hygiene, and environmental compliance activities and their involvement in the overall operations of the company.

The success of the program, like any of the others, rests heavily on not only management support, but also upon the amount of communications that takes place between the safety/firesafety, facilities, materials and processes, operations, and management personnel within the facility and the insurance company and local jurisdiction outside the facility.

Emphasis Areas

Throughout this book, emphasis has been placed on activities to minimize fuel load, eliminate sources of ignition, and formulate emergency actions that are planned and rehearsed. Emphasis will also be placed upon facility and equipment design and construction that incorporates fire prevention charateristics and protects life and property when fire does occur. All too often in the past, these activities occurred after the fire loss.

Proper design and construction for fire protection should proceed under the assumption that fire is going to occur and that other factors will be involved that will contribute to the extent of the damage. This book will also stress the importance of preventive maintenance programs that continuously monitor the condition of fire protection equipment. Finally, thorough training of all employees in fire prevention and protection is to be emphasized. In most of the fire investigations reviewed or conducted by the author, people who were involved have made mistakes. These mistakes either contributed to the cause of the fire or enhanced the effects of the fire. There is a need for training, for sound fire prevention programs that teach people basic fire prevention measures and how to react when fire does occur. But, training and prevention programs are not enough. When the ignition sequence is initiated, trained people may not be present or may be unable to respond. Therefore, systems, facilities, and equipment must be automatic and foolproof.

SUMMARY

As long as people have been organized into societies, they have suffered pain, death, and property loss from fires. Fires have destroyed farms, forests, towns, and cities. The industrial community has been no different from the rest of society with apathy and over-reliance on insurance and code requirements to safeguard employees and property. History is full of examples of spectacular and devastating industrial fires.

While tragic fires have resulted in new and improved codes that are intended to safeguard lives and property, the firesafety community must convince management of the need to exceed code requirements in order to achieve firesafety.

There is a shortage of trained and educated fire protection engineers in the industrial community which results in over-reliance upon code compliance, insurance requirements, and municipal fire suppression.

The area of industrial fire prevention and protection is becoming more complex as industrial technology evolves. There are increasing trade-offs due to conflicting needs with safety, industrial hygiene, environmental compliance, and material and processes interests that add more pressure to the person responsible for fire prevention and protection.

The following chapters will provide the basics of fire prevention and protection, information on program development, and resources for further assistance for the person who is charged with program responsibility.

The goal of the industrial fire protection program then is fire prevention and fire protection. Fire prevention includes those activities and equipment that are intended to prevent fire and explosion from occurring by controlling the causes of fire. Fire protection includes those activities and equipment that are intended to detect and extinguish fire, reduce losses, safeguard human life, and preserve property.

BIBLIOGRAPHY

Brannigan, F. L. 1986. Fire Loss Management. Paper presented at the AFCMD Safety, Occupational Health and Fire Protection Conference, 6–8 October 1986, at Albuquerque, New Mexico.

Chapman, Elmer F. 1988. High-Rise: An Analysis. *Fire Engineering* 141(8):52–61.

Code of Federal Regulations. 29 CFR 1910.154-165. 1987. Occupational Safety and Health Administration, Department of Labor. Washington, DC.

Cote, Arthur, and Bugbee, Percy. 1988. *Principles of Fire Protection.* Quincy: National Fire Protection Association.

Hall, John R., Jr. 1988. Fire Deaths Have Reached a Plateau Throughout North America. *Fire Journal* 82(5):39.

Factory Mutual System, 150 Years of Innovation. 1985. Norwood, MA: Factory Mutual Engineering Corp.

Fire Protection Handbook, 16th ed. 1986. Quincy: National Fire Protection Association.

The History of IRI: A National Resource. Hartford: Industrial Risk Insurers.

Karter, Michael J.. 1988. U.S. Fire Loss in 1987. *Fire Journal* 82(5):33–44.

Karter, Michael J.. 1989. U.S. Fire Loss in 1988. *Fire Journal* 83(5):24–32.

Lyons, P.R. 1976. *Fire in America.* Boston: National Fire Protection Association.

Naden, Corinne J. 1971. *The Triangle Shirtwaist Fire.* New York: Franklyn Watts Inc.

NFPA Fire Analysis Division. 1988. The Deadliest U.S. Fires and Explosions of the 1900s. *Fire Journal* May/June 1988: 48–54.

Pernin, Reverend Peter. 1971. The Great Peshtigo Fire. Madison, Wisconsin: The State Historical Society of Wisconsin.

Standards for Safety. 1989. Underwriters Laboratories, Inc. Northbrook, Ill.

Taylor, K. T., and Norton, A. L. 1988. Large-Loss Fires in the United States During 1987. Report by the National Fire Protection Association Fire Analysis and Research Division. Quincy, MA.

Threshold Limit Values and Biological Exposure Indices for 1988–1989. 1988. Cincinnati: American Conference of Governmental Industrial Hygienists.

Uniform Fire Code, 1988 Edition. Whittier, California: International Conference of Building Officials and Western Fire Chiefs Association.

2
CHARACTERISTICS
AND BEHAVIOR
OF FIRE

The science of combustion is very complex, and there have been many books written, at various technical levels, on the subject. There are ongoing studies into the characteristics and behavior of fire being conducted by universities, insurance-oriented laboratories, government agencies, fire protection equipment manufacturers, and many other groups. It is necessary to constantly incorporate the results of these studies into the codes and standards that govern all aspects of fire prevention and protection. Many times, an unusual industrial operation will generate a research project to develop appropriate fire protection. Too often, in the past, changes in fire protection have been the reactions to disastrous fire experience rather than as a result of proactive studies. For example, after a series of high loss warehouse fires, research was conducted on the proper protection for high-piled storage, storage of high fire load materials such as plastics and aerosols, and for various rack configurations. The research activity is an attempt to proactively develop improvements in the science of fire protection and is one piece of the of the loss control puzzle. For the purpose of industrial fire protection, an understanding of the basics of the combustion process will enable the reader to understand methods to ''prevent'' ignition and to ''protect'' or mitigate fire damage by controlling or extinguishing the fire when it does occur.

An understanding of the characteristics and behavior of fire is essential to understanding the rest of this book and the whole process of fire prevention and protection. With an understanding of the fire tetrahedron, for example, facilities and operations can be planned so that the chance of the tetrahedron components coming together is minimized.

With an understanding of the characteristics and behavior of fire, industrial and business management personnel will be able to relate better to advice and requirements of municipal fire authorities and fire insurance personnel.

FIRE TRIANGLE

For many years, fire was described by the fire triangle. This simple description of fire says that three things are required for fire to occur including oxygen, a fuel, and heat of ignition. These three components, which are common to the fire tetrahedron theory that follows, are described as making up the three sides of a triangle. Oxygen is normally available in the air in sufficient quantities for combustion to occur. A fuel source is required to react with the oxygen. A fuel is usually, but not always, a carbon-based material that is consumed, or partially consumed, in the combustion reaction. Hydrogen gas is an example of a fuel that is *not* carbon based.

Finally, since the fuel and oxygen will only react at a high temperature, a source of heat is required to cause the reaction, or ignition, to occur. For the reaction to be self-sustaining, or continue without the presence of an outside ignition source, there must be sufficient fuel and oxygen, and it must react at such a rate that it produces its own heat of ignition to sustain the reaction (Figure 2-1).

It is necessary to have a complete understanding of these three components and their interaction in order to understand the combustion process.

Fuel

Very simply, fuel is defined as anything that will burn. From the fire triangle, we can see that oxygen is also necessary. When fuels react with oxygen, they are oxidized. In the presence of heat, this oxidation reaction is the burning process, or combustion. There are many substances, with a wide range of ignition temperatures, which will burn in the presence of oxygen. Fuels are classified chemically as follows.

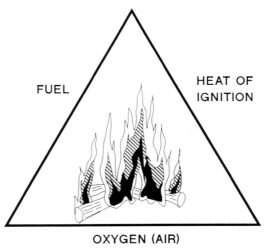

Figure 2-1. The fire triangle is represented with fuel, oxygen, and heat of ignition making up the three sides that are necessary for combustion to occur.

Carbon-Based and Other Readily Oxidizable Nonmetals. The most common fuels are carbon-based materials. Also included in this class are other readily oxidizable nonmetals such as sulfur, phosphorus, and arsenic.

Hydrocarbons. Compounds that are rich in carbon and hydrogen such as methane (CH_4), ethane (C_2H_4), and propane (C_4H_{10})are hydrocarbon fuels.

Compounds Containing Carbon, Hydrogen, and Oxygen. Fuel materials that contain carbon, hydrogen, and oxygen include alcohols, aldehydes, organic acids, cellulosic, and lignin (wood and vegetable materials).

Metals. Many metals and their alloys including sodium, potassium, magnesium, aluminum, zinc, titanium, zirconium, and uranium are classed as fuels.

Fuels may be solids, liquids, or gases, however, combustion occurs only with fuels in the vapor or gaseous state.

Oxygen

Because it is so readily available in the atmosphere, oxygen is the most difficult portion of the fire triangle to control in fire prevention. Ambient air is made up of about 21 percent oxygen, 79 percent nitrogen, and small amounts of other "rare" gases such as argon, xenon, krypton, and neon. This amount is adequate for most fuels to burn. Different fuels require different amounts of oxygen in order to burn. For example, wood requires 4 to 5 percent, acetylene requires less than 4 percent, and hydrocarbon fuels require greater than 15 percent oxygen. As you can see, there is ample oxygen in the air to react with these fuels.

The air is not the only source of oxygen. Oxygen is also available, chemically, in some compounds called oxidizers. Oxidizers are very important considerations in the study of fire because they can provide additional oxygen to the reaction. Some common chemical oxidizers include: hypochlorates, oxides, peroxides, and of course, oxygen gas. In areas where oxidizers may be present, extra caution is required, because an oxygen-enriched atmosphere will cause combustible materials to ignite more readily, spread flame faster, and burn more vigorously. Oxygen-enriched atmospheres can occur where chemical oxidizers are present or gaseous oxygen, such as might occur near a leaky oxyacetylene welding system. Oxygen and chemical oxidizers react vigorously with hydrocarbon-based materials and the reaction can generate sufficient heat for ignition to occur.

The amount of oxygen that is available and the rate at which it is available will have an effect upon how completely the fuel reacts. As the combustion reaction proceeds, oxygen is consumed from the immediate environment. If the environment is closed and the flow of oxygen is restricted, the nature of the reaction will change and incomplete combustion will occur. If the fire environment is sufficiently closed so that the consumed oxygen cannot be replenished, the fire will go out.

Restricting the ventilation to a structural fire is not a good means of fire control because the environment cannot be controlled sufficiently. When incomplete combustion takes place because of an inadequate supply of oxygen the fire produces carbon monoxide and other flammable gases. This can create an extremely dangerous situation if these flammable gases are produced in an oxygen-restricted fire and then oxygen is suddenly introduced. An explosion can occur when these heated and flammable gases suddenly have a source of oxygen as is the case if a door is opened. This explosion of unburned hot flammable gases is referred to as backdraft.

Heat Of Ignition

To complete the fire triangle, heat energy is required to initiate and sustain the chemical reaction between the fuel and the oxygen. The amount of heat energy required varies with the type of fuel. Solids and some liquids have to be heated to the point where they decompose or vaporize sufficiently to give off enough flammable vapors and gases to form an ignitable mixture in air. This thermal decomposition of solids is referred to as pyrolysis and in liquid fuels it is vaporization. Flammable gases require no decomposition energy because they are already in a form that is capable of combining with the oxygen in the air. Figure 2-2 demonstrates this relationship of the physical state of the fuels.

For this discussion, the ignition of solid fuels will be considered. In Chapter 3 and 4, ignition of the various forms of fuels, solids, liquids, and gases will be discussed in more detail. In initiating combustion, the process of pyrolysis is endothermic, or, heat is absorbed by the fuel from the source of ignition. Initially, as heating of solid fuels takes place, moisture is given off. As further heating takes place, combustible and flammable gases and vapors are given off. When there are enough gases to form an ignitable mixture in air, ignition is possible. Then the reaction turns exothermic, or heat is given off. This is the ignition temperature, the minimum temperature to which the substance in air must be heated in order to initiate self-sustained combustion. At the ignition temperature, the combustion reaction is self-sustaining in that it requires no

Figure 2-2. The physical relationships of the fuels. Solids and liquids must be thermally decomposed before they can form an ignitable mixture with oxygen. Fuel gases can mix directly with oxygen.

further heat input from an outside energy source. It is producing and recycling heat produced by its own reaction. The ignition temperature is dependent upon the size, shape, and density of the fuel and the availability of air or oxygen. The ease of ignition is dependent upon the ability of the fuel to be sufficiently heated to decomposition to the point where enough flammable vapors are produced to form an ignitable mixture in the air.

Spontaneous Ignition.   Spontaneous heating is a phenomenon that can occur in gas, liquid, and solid fuels. It involves the combination of materials with oxygen which evolves heat. In its most common usage, spontaneous ignition refers to the ignition of combustible solids by the action of internal heating caused by an exothermic reaction. Under confined conditions, when the heat that is generated by a slow oxidation reaction cannot be dissipated, ignition can occur. It is a complex situation. Air is required for heat producing oxidation to occur, but too much air will cause the heat to dissipate before ignition can occur. Spontaneous ignition is common in agricultural products that are stored too moist, thus allowing bacterial oxidation to occur. Storage of damp bituminous coal and charcoal is also susceptible to internal heating. Spontaneous ignition also occurs with materials that are of animal or vegetable origin such as linseed oil, animal oils, vegetable oils, and other oils of low volatility. Rags and clothing that contain these oils such as painters would generate are a serious source of spontaneous ignition. Clothing should be cleaned or hung in an area where there is adequate air circulation to dissipate any heat that might be generated. Rags should be stored in a self-closing metal container.

A less common, but equally important form of spontaneous ignition occurs as the result of a violent chemical reaction of certain chemicals with air or water. Phosphorous is an example of a material that ignites when exposed to air. Another form of spontaneous ignition occurs when sodium metal comes into contact with water.

Ignition sources are many and varied but they are basically anything or process capable of generating the temperatures required for ignition of an appropriate fuel/oxygen mixture.

Oxidation Reaction

What has been described is, very simply, an oxidation reaction in which the fuel and oxygen react in the presence of heat to produce heat and other products of combustion. The reaction occurs when the three sides of the fire triangle are present in the proper amounts. The reaction can take place very slowly as in spontaneous ignition, or it can occur explosively under some combinations and conditions that will be discussed later. The combustion reaction can be shown very simply, as follows, using methane as the fuel:

$$CH_4 + 2O_2 \rightarrow CO_2 + 2H_2O + Heat\uparrow$$

The methane and oxygen react in the presence of heat to produce carbon dioxide, water vapor, and heat. This is a simple reaction and it assumes ideal conditions and amounts of oxygen and fuel. The carbon dioxide, water, and heat are what we call products of combustion. In addition to these, impurities or other elements in the fuel will produce other products of combustion which will be discussed later.

Oxidation is a chemical reaction that takes place with oxygen, or when a substance combines with oxygen. The rusting of metal when exposed to the oxygen in the air is an example of a slow oxidation reaction. Another example of slow oxidation is the oxidation of sugar by yeast cells to produce alcohol. Oxidation reactions produce heat. An exothermic reaction is one that gives off heat. In the case of rusting metal and the action of yeast, the reaction, and consequent production of heat, is so slow that heat production is of no consequence (except maybe for the brewer who has to control temperatures very carefully). If finely divided iron, such as steel wool, is exposed to excess oxygen, the rate of the oxidation process can be increased to the point where the evolution of heat is a factor and flaming occurs. In the oxidation reaction that we call combustion, the reaction takes place rapidly and the evolution of heat is a factor. The heat that is evolved in this reaction becomes the ignition source to sustain the fire. A definition of fire, then, is as follows: Fire is a rapid, self-sustaining oxidation process resulting in the evolution of heat and light. Fire is rapid oxidation, not the slow oxidation of metal or organic materials. Fire is self-sustaining; it produces heat which decomposes and vaporizes additional fuel to perpetuate itself. A final characteristic of fire is that it produces excess heat and light which are given off as products of combustion.

Reduction Reaction

The antithesis of oxidation is reduction, or a reaction involving the removal of oxygen from a substance containing oxygen. In fire science, this reaction is important because when combustion and consumption of available oxygen occurs in a closed environment, reduction reactions take place. When there is insufficient oxygen available, incomplete combustion takes place, and carbon monoxide, a reducing agent, is produced. In addition to carbon monoxide being a toxic gas, it is flammable and highly reactive. Carbon monoxide may be explosive in a fire situation if it builds up and oxygen is suddenly made available as when a door is opened or a window broken. Carbon monoxide is usually present in fires and it will be covered in our discussion of products of combustion.

THE CHAIN REACTION

The fire triangle described three components that are necessary for fire to occur. The combustion reaction using methane as the fuel and yielding carbon dioxide and water appears to be very simple; however, it is really only an abbreviation of a very complex series of chain reactions. It was found that these chain reactions must take place for fire to occur and the interruption of the chain reactions would result in the extinguishment of the fire. Therefore, the simple fire triangle had to be expanded. The component that makes up the fourth side when the fire triangle is expanded to a tetrahedron is the chain reaction (Figure 2-3).

As discussed earlier, combustion is a chemical reaction. The chemical bonds that hold fuel molecules together are broken, resulting in free radicals. These free radicals with an unpaired electron, or broken bond, are highly reactive. They proceed to react with other molecules, causing additional broken bonds and free radicals. Some of the free radicals recombine with others, forming new molecules, some of which are with oxygen, forming carbon dioxide and water. Because the bonds that hold the fuel molecules together are stronger than the bonds that hold the carbon dioxide and water molecules, there is excess energy left over from this reaction. This excess energy is given off as heat resulting in

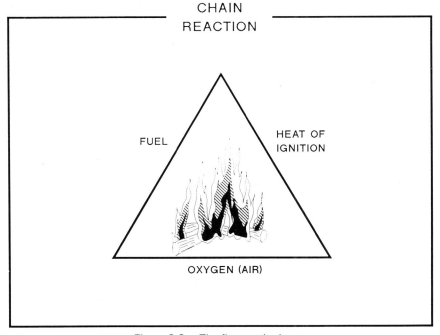

Figure 2-3. The fire tetrahydron.

what is known as an exothermic reaction. In the simple example of the combustion of methane used earlier, the carbon atom is bonded to four hydrogen atoms. In the presence of heat, the chemical bonds are broken, releasing the four hydrogens as reactive H radicals. These radicals react with oxygen molecules causing the bonds of their two atoms to break and they are either released as O radicals, or an oxygen atom may bond to a H radical to form an OH radical. While these radicals are short lived, they play an important role in the consumption of the fuel. They are constantly being regenerated and consumed in a series of chain reactions. The combustion of methane does not begin to describe the numerous reactions that are taking place in the candle flame where more complex fuels are involved. A structural fire is infinitely more complex, with the many different fuel sources and their various atomic components reacting with one another in the presence of heat and drastically varying amounts of oxygen. These reactions are all taking place in the flame portion of the fire and are known as gas-phase combustion. The apparent flicker, or dancing, of the flames is the movement of the reactions seeking additional oxygen or fuel vapors. These reactions must take place for fire, or flame, to exist.

Anyone who has ever used charcoal to barbeque knows that not all combustion reactions involve flames. Some combustion takes place in the glowing or smoldering phase.

GLOWING COMBUSTION

Glowing combustion is usually associated with carbonaceous materials, or char, such as charcoal, or materials like wood that produce a char. While these materials will produce flaming combustion, the involatile char will remain and continue to burn slowly. The char must be porous to allow oxygen through to the combustion zone, but it also produces a barrier to contain sufficient heat to maintain the reaction. Combustion will only continue as long as heat is conserved at the reacting surface. All backyard barbequers have used this theory to cool the fire by spreading the coals apart so that less heat is shared between the reacting surfaces. If the coals are spread far enough apart, the combustion process may stop.

Smoldering, or glowing, combustion is typically a cooler reaction than flaming combustion. The cooler burning temperatures are the result of the restricted oxygen flow which also results in less complete combustion than flaming combustion. Less oxygen availability also results in the production of more products of combustion. There have been many unfortunate instances where people have attempted to heat poorly ventilated structures using charcoal grills. The glowing charcoal produces more carbon monoxide because of the poor circulation of oxygen in the combustion zone. With inadequate ventilation, dangerous levels of carbon monoxide are produced.

HEAT TRANSFER

At this point in the discussion, a simple fire exists producing carbon dioxide, water, heat, light, and maybe other products of combustion. Now the fire must be sustained. It takes heat to vaporize liquid and solid fuels into combustible gases that can mix with oxygen to form an ignitable mixture. Gases are already in a form capable of mixing with oxygen and require no heat energy input. So, flammable gases only have to form an ignitable mixture in air and have an ignition source present to burn. Liquids and solids, on the other hand, need heat energy to convert them to a form capable of mixing with air. In the case of liquids, this process is called vaporization. The liquid is converted to a vapor which, when it forms an ignitable mixture in air and an ignition source is present, will burn. In the case of solid fuels, thermal decomposition, or pyrolysis, must occur to produce gaseous fuels capable of mixing with air (refer to Figure 2-2). With the simple fire triangle producing heat (Figure 2-4), it is necessary to get some of this heat back to the fuel to sustain the fire. There are three methods of heat transfer which facilitate this process and are necessary to the study of combustion. The three methods of heat transfer are conduction, convection, and radiation.

Conduction

Conduction is the transfer of heat through solid objects. Heat is conducted very readily through metal, which is a good conductor. Wood, on the other hand, is

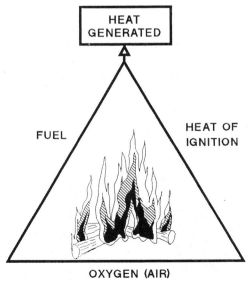

Figure 2-4. The combustion reaction generates heat as one of the products of combustion.

not a good conductor. In a structural fire situation, heat is transferred, by conduction, through steel beams, metal conduit, wires, and ducts and may spread from room to room by this means. Since steel is such a good conductor of heat, it is also very susceptible to heat damage. This fact is an important consideration in building design and construction.

Convection

Convection is the transfer of heat through air or through a fluid. Heat is mixed in the air or fluid through movement, or buoyancy currents. Convection is the mechanism that carries heat up the chimney from the fireplace. In a building fire, air that has been heated by the fire expands and moves away from the fire and primarily upward. As the heated air rises it carries with it smoke, gases, and other products of combustion. The hot air spreads out along the ceiling and may result in lateral spread of the fire at the ceiling. As it expands, the hot air also forms pressure and forces its way through doors, air ducts, and any other openings carrying with it the smoke and gases.

Convected heat is the primary mechanism of fire spread in a structural fire. There is a tremendous movement of hot air through convection up and away from a fire (heat always travels to cooler areas). As the hot air moves away from the fire it heats up more fuels and it also carries flammable gases away from the fire to areas where they may have more oxygen for ignition.

Radiation

Radiation is the transfer of heat by electromagnetic waves similar to visible light. In the earlier example of glowing combustion, the heat that sustains the charcoal fire is radiated heat. If the charcoal is spread out, there will not be enough radiated heat to keep the combustion process going and the fire will go out. In a high-rise fire where flames are burning out of a window and extending up the side of the building, radiated heat has been known to ignite materials through the windows in the floor above. Radiated heat from a building fire can spread from building to building (this is called an exposure fire).

Heat Transfer and Combustion

Once ignition has taken place, heat feedback is necessary to sustain the fire. This is accomplished through varying degrees of conduction, convection, and radiation (Figure 2-5). The rate of burning and flamespread is dependent upon the amount of heat that is fed back into the fuel. This is demonstrated by the charcoal example. When the charcoal pieces are close together, they will burn hotter and faster because they share heat to enhance pyrolysis. More practically,

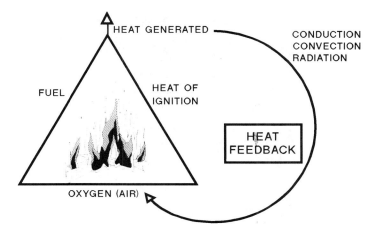

GREATER FEEDBACK INTENSIFIES FIRE

Figure 2-5. Heat feedback is necessary to sustain combustion. Some of the heat that is generated by the combustion reaction is necessary to heat additional fuel to sustain the reaction.

in the warehouse situation, where aisles separating stored materials are narrow, or are used for storage, fire will be able to spread more readily and may be able to exceed the capacity of the sprinkler system.

Another simple way to look at the combustion and heat transfer process is through the burning candle (Figure 2-6). The candle very simply demonstrates the combustion process and the physical phenomenon of heat transfer. Although the candle flame looks very simple, it is really a series of complex reactions with all of the different elements in the wax reacting in the presence of air and heat. When the candle is ignited, a small pool of wax melts and forms at the base of the wick. This pool must be present, as well as a sufficient length of wick, for the candle to ignite. The liquefied wax is drawn up the wick by capillary action, where it is vaporized by the ignition source and burns. When the ignition source is removed, the candle continues to burn because conducted and radiated heat continues to maintain the pool of melted wax. The melted wax continues to flow up the wick where it is vaporized by the intense heat of the flame, mixes with the oxygen in the air, and burns. Excess heat from this process is released through convection and radiation, while most of the fuel is melted by conducted heat and some convected and radiated heat. Looking very carefully at the flame, one can see that the colored portion of the flame does not touch the wick or the wax, but it seems to be suspended slightly above. This is where the oxygen from the air is diffusing into the heated vapors of the wax and forming a combustible mixture. Most of the light comes from the upper portion of the flame from the carbon particles that have been heated to incandescence and entered the combustion process with oxygen from the air. At the

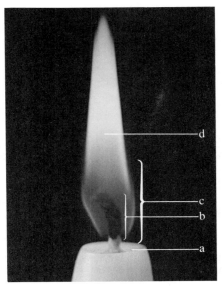

Figure 2-6.   Combustion in the candle flame. (a) Heat of the reaction melts wax forming a liquid pool. (b) The liquid wax is drawn up the wick by capillary action where it is vaporized by intense radiation from the reaction. (c) Vaporized fuel diffuses through the reaction zone where it reacts and various molecules and fragments are emitted. (d) Carbon particles are generated and, forming soot, become incandescent. (Photo: Charles Uebele)

tip of the flame, most of the carbon particles have been consumed and the products of combustion, primarily water and carbon dioxide, are emitted.

At this point, it is easy to visualize how the combustion process is enhanced or diminished by the arrangement of the fuels. If the fuels are arranged so as to improve heat feedback, the fire will increase, if the fuels are spread apart, the fire will decrease.

Flashover

In a structural fire, if conditions of heat feedback are favorable, a very dangerous condition known as flashover may occur. When fire occurs in a closed space, heat and smoke are carried by convection currents to the ceiling. The ceiling heat, which may reach temperatures of 800 to 1200 degrees Fahrenheit, is reflected back down into the room. This process results in the heating of all of the combustibles in the room to their ignition temperature. Flashover occurs when there is a sudden and dramatic simultaneous ignition of most of the combustible materials and gases in the room or space. This is, obviously, very dangerous for fire fighters, or anyone, who might be in the area.

Flashover will depend upon a number of factors including the amount of confinement of the space, the distance between the ceiling and the base of the fire, and the area of the floor. If the space is too confined, the fire will smother itself for lack of oxygen. If the ceiling is too high, the heat will be dissipated and cooled by the entrained air before flashover conditions can be reached. A large floor area and low ceiling will enhance flashover conditions by overcoming the confinement limitation.

One can visualize the potential for flashover occurring in the large open office arrangements that are so common. These spaces normally contain concentrated groupings of combustible work areas in a large open space that has a low ceiling.

Heat Measurement and Temperature

Temperature is the measure of how hot, or cold, something is. An important fact to remember in fire science is that heat always flows from higher to lower temperatures and that hot air rises. This is readily apparent in the study of heat transfer by convection. Convected heat is rapidly carried up and away from the fire as it moves to cooler air. The movement of heated air also carries away smoke and gases.

Temperature. Temperature is commonly measured in degrees Fahrenheit or Celsius (Centigrade). Both temperature measurements are related to the melting of ice and the freezing of water at 1 atmosphere of pressure (14.7 psi or 760 mm mercury). On the Fahrenheit scale, ice melts at 32 degrees and water boils at 212 degrees. On the Celsius scale, ice melts at 0 degrees and water boils at 100 degrees.

Heat. Heat is a form of energy and, as such, is measured in terms of work accomplished. Water is also the medium for defining heat units. The calorie is the amount of heat required to raise the temperature of 1 gram of water 1 degree Celsius at 15 degrees Celsius (59 degrees Fahrenheit). The other unit of heat measurement is the British thermal unit (Btu). A Btu is the amount of heat required to raise the temperature of 1 pound of water 1 degree Fahrenheit at 60 degrees Fahrenheit. For our purposes, the most commonly used term for heat measurement is the Btu. This term will be discussed later in this book in the discussion of fire load in terms of Btu/ft^2 and the discussion of the extinguishing properties of water in terms of the number of Btus absorbed by water.

PRODUCTS OF COMBUSTION

During the combustion process, certain products are produced as a result of the many complex reactions that are taking place. These are termed products of combustion and they include heat, light, smoke, and fire gases.

Heat

Heat is always present as a product of the combustion process. Besides the heat that is necessary to sustain the fire, there is excess heat that is given off. The amount of heat that is released during complete oxidation or combustion is referred to as the heat of combustion. Heat of combustion is expressed as heat per unit of mass. The rate and degree to which heat is evolved is dependent upon a complex set of variables including the type of fuel and amount of available oxygen and the rate at which it is supplied. Although heat of combustion is used in calculating fuel loads, it does not necessarily reflect the fire hazard of a material because it does not consider the rate of burning or the rate at which this heat is generated.

Heat is necessary to start and sustain the combustion process; it is also damaging to life, structures, and equipment. Its effects upon the human body are well known and documented. Burns produce one of the most painful and severe traumas to the body imaginable.

In terms of heat, the comfort zone of humans, between 60 and 80 degrees Fahreinheit is really quite narrow. Higher temperatures can be tolerated for short periods of time. The highest that the human body can tolerate is about 290 degrees Fahrenheit but only for about 5 minutes. Above 300 degrees, the skin can be irreversibly injured.

The respiratory system is more susceptible to heat than the body. Temperatures exceeding 120 degrees Fahrenheit taken into the lungs can cause a decrease in blood pressure, and the effects of moist heated air is worse. Heated air that is inhaled can cause fluid buildup in the lungs (edema) which, if extensive enough, can lead to death by asphyxiation.

It is a common misconception that heat is the principle danger to people in a fire. It is now well known from autopsies of fire victims that the primary cause of death is inhalation of carbon monoxide or other toxic fire gases.

Thermal damage to property is another obvious effect that is caused by the heat byproduct. Heat will cause warpage, distortion, and melting of many materials.

Light

The light, or flame, of a fire is a result of the gas-phase reaction. Light is generated by particles that have been heated to incandescence and entered into the combustion process with oxygen in the air.

Smoke

Smoke is a complex mixture of very fine solid particles, condensed vapor in the form of small droplets or aerosols, and gaseous compounds. Smoke is formed in almost all fire situations and is the result of incomplete combustion. The composition of smoke will vary depending upon the available fuels and the degree of combustion taking place. The degree of combustion taking place is dependent upon many factors as discussed previously. A hot burning fire with plenty of oxygen will burn "cleaner" because more of the decomposition products that produce smoke are being consumed.

Smoke is responsible for nonthermal fire damage. During a structure fire, convection currents carry smoke throughout the building. Its constituents, many of which are corrosive and electrically charged, will coat the surfaces of walls, floors, and equipment. The resulting nonthermal fire damage includes chemical reactions (corrosion), electrical shorting, discolored surfaces, and unpleasant odors.

Fire Gases

Fire gases are sometimes discussed as a component of smoke. For the purpose of this discussion, they will be included separately. There are many different gases produced in the combustion process. The types and quantities vary depending upon a complex series of reactions involving the fuels, temperatures, and duration of exposure at high temperature. During the combustion reaction chemical bonds are broken and new compounds are formed. It is important to note that for a fire gas to be produced, elements of its chemical structure must be present in the fuel. For example, under normal circumstances, hydrogen cyanide (HCN) would not be produced by burning methane (CH_4) because there are no isocyanates (OCN) in methane. Hydrogen cyanide is found only in combustion products of polymers containing OCN groups such as polyurethanes and acrylonitrile polymers.

Many of the fire gases are corrosive and toxic, they have varying effects, and they are of serious concern to the fire safety professional.

Physiological Effects. In the presence of fire, smoke, and fire gases, peoples' capacity to survive is dependent upon their age, physical and mental fitness, reaction time, education, and many other factors over which they may have little or no control. Death due to fire is a complex event that results from many different factors including oxygen deficiency, irritant and toxic gases, and destruction of tissue due to heat.

One of the effects of fire is the depletion of oxygen. Normal oxygen content of the air is about 20.9 percent. OSHA has established a minimum safe oxygen concentration of 19.5 percent for workers. People can exist at this level with no ill effects. Below 19.5 percent, oxygen deficiency begins to effect humans. At about 15 percent oxygen concentration, muscular skill is diminished, at 10 to 14 percent people would still be conscious but judgment would be impaired, and at 6 to 10 percent collapse and loss of consciousness would occur.

Some of the fire gases are irritants and some are toxic. Some have no smell, others destroy the sense of smell or are narcotic or anesthetic, blunting the victim's judgment and awareness of discomfort. Some of the irritants are swallowed, resulting in nausea and vomiting.

Smoke can impair visibility and impede a person's ability to escape. The irritant nature of smoke and some of the fire gases may divert the victim's concentration from escape. Other fire gases act to impair the victim's motor and/or judgment capabilities, causing confusion and disorientation.

Irritant materials may breach the lungs' natural defenses, making it more difficult for oxygen to reach the cells. The nasal passages and bronchial tubes are lined by a mucous membrane and cells containing cilia that help to move mucous and particles up and away from the lungs. Corrosive fire gases will damage the mucous membrane and the cilia, causing tissues to swell and weep. As the linings of the trachea and bronchial tubes break down, smoke particles are allowed to penetrate deeper into the respiratory system. These particles, fluid, and damaged tissue, accumulate making it more difficult for oxygen to reach the cells of the lungs. If this situation is prolonged, asphyxiation may result.

Toxic Effects of Fire Gases.   In the description of fire gases that follows, Threshold Limit Values–Time-Weighted Averages (TLV–TWA) as listed by the American Conference of Governmental Industrial Hygienists (ACGIH) are provided. These values reflect the time-weighted average concentration for a normal 8-hour workday and a 40-hour work week, to which nearly all workers may be exposed day after day without adverse effect. They are provided here as an indication and comparison of the degree of hazard that the fire gases present. Some of the more common fire gases include the following:

Carbon dioxide—CO_2 was discussed earlier in this chapter as a common product of combustion of carbon-based fuels. Besides being an asphyxiant, carbon dioxide has the effect of stimulating breathing. In a fire situation, this causes an increase in the rate of inhalation of other fire gases that may be present. The ACGIH TWA for CO_2 is 5000 ppm.

Carbon monoxide—CO is not the most toxic of the fire gases, but it is always the most abundant in a fire situation and is responsible for most of the fire fatalities. CO is a product of incomplete combustion of carbon-based fuels and is most predominant in poorly ventilated fires. It would be produced in copious amounts in a structural fire after much of the available oxygen has been consumed and as radiated heat is pyrolyzing other combustibles in the vicinity of the fire. As expected, less CO is produced in a flaming fire than one that is smoldering, such as smoldering combustion of porous materials such as polyurethane foam. The ACGIH TWA for CO is 50 ppm.

Sulfur dioxide—SO_2 is an irritant to the mucous membranes of the upper respiratory tract. It is formed during the combustion of materials containing sulfur such as polyphenylsulfone. It has a characteristic sharp suffocating odor. There is some evidence that the effects of SO_2 are enhanced by airborne particulate matter such as smoke. The National Institute of Occupational Safety and Health (NIOSH) recommended standard for exposure to SO_2 is 0.5 ppm and the ACGIH TWA is 2.0 ppm.

Ammonia—NH_3 gas is irritating to the upper respiratory tract and is formed during the combustion of nitrogen containing materials such as polyamides (nylon), melamine, wool, and silk. NH_3 is used as an industrial refrigerant and it is occasionally encountered by fire fighters and industrial personnel during accidental leakage. NH_3 is also a flammable gas and when present in the atmosphere may present a fire and explosion hazard. The ACGIH TWA for NH_3 is 25 ppm.

Hydrogen chloride—HCL is a strong sensory and pulmonary irritant that is formed during the combustion of chlorine containing materials such as polyvinylchloride (PVC), chlorinated acrylics, and retardant materials. The federal standard and the ACGIH TWA is 5 ppm. At 75 ppm HCl is extremely irritating to the eyes and the upper respiratory tract. Since HCl is a strong acid, its production in a fire situation may result in extensive damage to equipment that is susceptible to corrosion.

Hydrogen cyanide—HCN is an extremely poisonous and a highly flammable gas which is produced during the combustion of fuels containing the cyanide ion such as wool, silk, polyacrylonitrile, nylon, and polyurethane, and when cyanide containing chemicals are combined with an acid. In states that use the gas chamber for judicial executions, a cyanide salt pellet is dropped into sulfuric acid producing HCN. HCN has a bitter almond odor. Like CO, HCN attacks the respiratory system which can lead to paralysis of the respiratory center. Exposure to HCN causes constriction of the throat, nausea, vomiting, and difficult breathing. Concentrations as low as 0.5 percent may penetrate the skin of exposed individuals. The ACGIH TWA for skin exposure to HCN is 5 mg/m^3.

Acrolein—CH_2=CHCHO is a toxic, flammable, unstable, corrosive, and ir-ritating material with a very powerful acrid and disagreeable odor. It is an irritant to the eyes, nose, throat, lungs, and skin. Exposure to CH_2=CHCHO vapors cause coughing, dizziness, headaches, irritation, stomach upset, pul-monary edema, cyanosis, and death. Its odor is detectable in concentrations as low as 0.05 ppm, intolerable in concentrations of 5.5 ppm, and perhaps fatal at levels of 150 ppm. CH_2=CHCHO is what makes people cough and react violently to exposure to wood smoke.

   CH_2=CHCHO is produced during the welding of metal that has been coated with surface protecting fluids, by internal combustion engines in a confined space, and by burning wood and wood products such as paper or cardboard and polyolefins. The ACGIH TWA for $CH_2{=}CHCHO$ is 0.1 ppm.

Phosgene—$COCL_2$ causes pulmonary edema. When exposed to sufficient quantities, an individual chokes to death. An exposure to 50 ppm $COCl_2$ may be fatal. $COCl_2$ may be produced during the open flame cutting of certain metals in the presence of chlorinated hydrocarbons. $COCl_2$ is also produced when halon fire extinguishing agents are exposed to heat. Most extinguishing actions using halon occur very rapidly and there is minimal production of $COCl_2$, however it is always important to ventilate areas where halon has been used on a fire prior to reoccupancy. The ACGIH TWA for $COCl_2$ is 0.1 ppm.

FIRE EXTINGUISHMENT

Now that the requirements for fire to occur are understood, it is pretty simple to come up with ways to extinguish the fire. It is merely necessary to remove one of the sides of the fire tetrahedron. The fire may be extinguished by cooling the fuel, removing the oxygen, removing the fuel, or inhibition of the flame (Figure 2-7).

Extinguishment by Cooling

Cooling the fuel reduces and stops the rate of release of combustible gases and vapors. In the case of solid fuels, pyrolysis is retarded and stopped. With flammable and combustible liquids, the temperature of the fuel may be lowered below its flash point (see Chapter 4, Flammable and Combustible Liquids). One of the most obvious means of cooling the fuel, particularly ordinary combustibles, to extinguish a fire is through the use of water. Water is readily available, easy to apply, and has excellent heat absorption capabilities. Various additives may be added to water to improve its use to meet different fire situations. A side benefit of water is that when it is applied to a fire and turns to steam, it dilutes ambient oxygen to further retard the fire. There is more discussion of water as an extinguishing agent in Chapter 8, Fire Protection Systems and Equipment.

Extinguishment by Oxygen Dilution

Oxygen dilution, as a form of fire extinguishment, applies only to gaseous oxygen in the air, and not where oxygen is available chemically.

Source: *Threshold Limit Values and Biological Exposure Indices for 1988–1989.* American Conference of Governmental Industrial Hygienists.

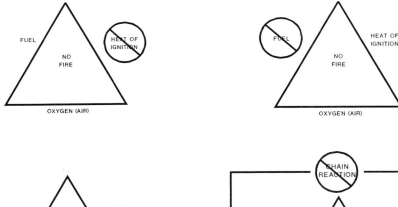

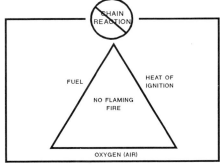

Figure 2-7. Removal of any part of the fire tetrahedron will extinguish the fire.

The most common extinguishing agent utilizing oxygen dilution as a means of fire extinguishment is carbon dioxide. Carbon dioxide is inexpensive, easy to store, and provides its own pressure for application to a fire.

Extinguishment by Fuel Removal

Fuel removal is one of the best fire preventative measures, minimizing fuel accumulations and separating fuel from ignition sources. But, once there is a fire, fuel removal is another method of extinguishment. Some examples of fuel removal as a means of controlling or extinguishing fire include the following:

If there is a fire in a tank of flammable liquids, the fuel (or liquids) may be pumped out of the bottom of the tank so that only a small amount of fuel remains which can be allowed to burn out or be extinguished by other means.

A fire involving a flammable gas may be extinguished if the gas supply can be shut off.

Fire breaks, or fuel-clear areas can be plowed in brush or forest fire areas to stop the spread of fire.

Piles of combustible materials such as wood chips or old tires can be separated to limit the amount of fuels available.

Housekeeping is a means of minimizing the amount of combustibles that are available as a fuel source for fire.

Burning metals can be covered with inert materials to separate the uninvolved materials.

Water soluble flammable liquids such as alcohols and ketones can be diluted with water to the point where they no longer give off enough flammable vapors to support combustion.

Wood materials can be coated or impregnated with a fire retardant material to minimize their availability to enter into the combustion reaction.

Extinguishment by Chemical Flame Inhibition

This form of extinguishment applies to combustion in the flaming mode only, and it involves the application of a chemical that chemically inhibits the chemical reaction by attaching to the reactive ions. The materials that are used to accomplish this form of extinguishment are commonly referred to as the "halons." The "halons" are halogenated agents, or, agents containing halogens. The halogens, fluorine (F), chlorine (Cl), bromine (Br), and iodine (I), are strong oxidizers. When they are chemically substituted for hydrogen in hydrocarbons to form halogenated hydrocarbons they are very efficient extinguishing agents. Apparently what happens is that when "halons" are applied to a fire, the heat of the fire breaks them down, releasing the halogens which have a strong affinity for the highly active free radicals O, H, and OH. Halons are a rapid and efficient form of fire extinguishment. In fact, they are so rapid that they can be used to stop an explosion in a flammable gas/air mixture after ignition has occurred.

The most common halons are Halon 1301, Halon 1211, and Halon 2402. The first digit of the number indicates the number of carbon atoms, the second digit the number of fluorine atoms, the third digit the number of chlorine atoms, and the fourth digit the number of bromine atoms. Therefore, Halon 1301 is bromotrifluoromethane $CBrF_3$, Halon 1211 is bromochlorodifluoromethane $CBrClF_2$, and Halon 2402 is dibromotetrafluoroethane $CBrF_2CBrF_2$.

SUMMARY

Fire is an oxidation process in which a fuel and oxygen react, in the presence of heat, to produce heat and other products of combustion. These three factors; fuel, oxygen, and heat of ignition make up what is known as the fire triangle.

Heat is a key factor in this reaction. It takes heat, with solid and liquid fuels, to decompose the fuel to the gas and vapor state. In this state, the fuel can mix with the oxygen in the air and be ignited by a source of heat energy. Air is not the sole source of oxygen to support the combustion reaction. Some chemicals contain oxygen in quantities that can support combustion. One of the byproducts of this simple reaction is heat which serves to continue the decomposition of the fuel and sustain the reaction. There is a fourth factor in this process which is involved in flaming combustion called the uninhibited chain reaction. The flames of a fire are actually a very complex series of chemical reactions.

A fire can be extinguished simply by removing any of the parts of the fire triangle, or, in the case of a flaming fire, interrupting the chain reaction.

The products of combustion include heat, light, smoke, and fire gases. Probably the most significant products of combustion for the fire safety professional are heat and the fire gases. Heat is transferred by the processes of convection, conduction and radiation. An understanding of these processes will help to understand the whole process of fire development and spread. The fire gases, many of which are toxic, are responsible for the majority of fire deaths that occur. Many of the fire gases are also flammable and will help to spread the fire.

BIBLIOGRAPHY

Friedman, Raymond. 1985. Some Unresolved Fire Chemistry Problems. In *Fire Safety Science— Proceedings of the First International Symposium*, eds. Cecile E. Grant and Patrick J. Pagni, pp. 349–359. New York: Hemisphere Publishing Corporation.

Cote, Arthur, and Bugbee, Percy. 1988. *Principles of Fire Protection*. Quincy: National Fire Protection Association.

Drysdale, Dougal. 1985. *An Introduction to Fire Dynamics*. Chichester: John Wiley & Sons Ltd.

Egan, M. David. 1978. *Concepts in Building Firesafety*. Toronto: John Wiley & Sons, Inc.

Fire Protection Handbook, 16th ed. 1986. Quincy: National Fire Protection Association.

Hamilton, Alice, M.D. and Hardy, Harriet L., M.D., F.A.C.P. 1974. *Industrial Toxicology*, 3rd ed. Acton, MA: Publishing Science Group, Inc.

Landrock, Arthur H. 1983. *Handbook of Plastics Flammability and Combustion Toxicology*. Park Ridge, NJ: Noyes Publications.

Lyons, John W. 1985. *Fire*. New York: Scientific American Books, Inc.

Sittig, Marshall. 1985. *Handbook of Toxic and Hazardous Chemicals and Carcinogens*, 2nd ed. Park Ridge, N.J.: Noyes Publications.

Threshold Limit Values and Biological Exposure Indices for 1988–1989. 1988. Cincinnati: American Conference of Governmental Industrial Hygienists.

Tuve, Richard L. 1976. *Principles of Fire Protection Chemistry*. Quincy: National Fire Protection Association.

3
THE FUELS

INTRODUCTION

As discussed in the previous chapter about the combustion reaction, it is known that fuels are reducing agents, substances that can reduce an oxidizing agent, losing one or more electrons to the oxidizing agent in the process. In the presence of an oxidizing agent, the fuel and oxidizing agent need energy (heat) to start the combustion reaction. Once started, the combustion reaction will continue until the fuel or oxidizing agent are exhausted, the heat energy is removed, or the reaction is chemically inhibited. This chapter will discuss the fuels as solids, liquids, and gases and the special hazards that they may present.

COMBUSTIBLE SOLIDS

Wood and wood-derived materials such as paper are the most extensively studied of the organic solids, and will be used as the example of combustible solids. Wood consists primarily of carbon, hydrogen, oxygen, and nitrogen. The two main components of wood are cellulose $(C_6H_{10}O_5)_x$ and lignin. Other components include: sugars, resins, tars, and mineral matter. The ash that remains after wood burns is a mineral and carbonaceous residue called char. This char formation actually works to slow down the combustion process by providing an insulating barrier between the exposed surface and the interior unburned portions of the wood. With this insulating barrier the thermal decomposition of the interior wood is inhibited and combustion is slowed.

Variables Influencing Ignition and Burning

There are four variables influencing ignition and burning of a combustible solid. They are the physical form of the material, its heat conductivity, the availability of oxygen, and the moisture content. These variables have an affect upon the rate of pyrolysis which affects both the initial ignition and the rate at which burning takes place. The rate of burning will affect the combustion products resulting from the reaction, since the duration and intensity of heat exposure will have an affect upon the many chemical reactions that are taking place.

Physical Form.   The physical form of the material will affect the rate at which ignition and burning occurs. For example, a block of wood is relatively difficult to ignite with a small ignition source such as a match. However, if the block of wood is shaved into small slivers resulting in more surface area exposed to the heat source, it can easily be ignited with a match. The relative density of wood prevents it from being a good fuel for glowing, or smoldering, combustion.

Polyurethane foam materials, on the other hand, are very porous and contain enough oxygen within the pores to allow them to smolder internally. Because of their porosity and large amounts of surface area exposed, polyurethane foams are easily ignited and present a severe fire hazard.

In fire prevention activities, it is very important to consider not only the type and amount, but also the physical form of the fuels that are present. When a combustible solid is stored, it is better to store it, if possible, in whatever form is the most difficult to ignite. Like the block of wood used as the example above, it is better to store it in block form than in shavings. In industrial fire prevention, it is important to consider the physical form and arrangement of the available fuels because this will have an affect upon the ease of fire ignition and rate of development of fire. A warehouse may be designed for the storage of materials of low combustibility with sprinklers that are appropriate to that storage. When the user decides that everything in the warehouse should be covered with plastic sheeting material, as has happened, the fire load in the warehouse will be significantly increased. It is very likely, in this example, that the sprinkler coverage would no longer be adequate.

The physical form of combustible metals is an important consideration for the firesafety person. In the machining of magnesium, for example, the magnesium chips or fines that are generated are readily ignited. Proper housekeeping in these operations is very important.

Heat Conductivity.   The heat conductivity of the material is a measure of the rate at which absorbed heat will flow through the mass of the material. Wood is a poor heat conductor, probably because of the air that is trapped in its cells. Remember the old classroom demonstration of heat conductivity in which you held a needle in a flame? Try this with a wooden toothpick. As wood burns, an insulating char is formed on the surface which slows the combustion process. In a fire situation, wood beams are structurally better than steel because of this difference in heat conductivity. Steel conducts heat and loses its strength very rapidly when heated, resulting in building collapse. But wood, on the other hand, maintains its strength longer because it is protected by the insulating char that forms on the surface. If, however, the wood is held together by steel bolts or metal structural members, heat will be readily transferred through the steel by conduction and will accelerate the failure of the wood in those areas.

Availability of Oxygen.   The availability of oxygen will influence the ignition and the rate of combustion of a fuel source. For virtually all compounds of carbon and hydrogen (hydrocarbons), or of carbon, hydrogen, and oxygen (organic, vegetable, and petroleum materials), the heat of combustion is dependent upon the availability of oxygen. The heat of combustion is a measure of the maximum amount of heat that can be released by the complete combustion of a unit mass of combustible material. The complete combustion of the material in this definition is dependent upon the availability of oxygen. If sufficient oxygen is available, the combustion process can proceed more completely, consuming more of the combustion products that might otherwise be given off as flammable gases and smoke.

Plastics are known for the high volume of smoke that they produce when they are involved in a fire. The reason for this is that during combustion, they consume oxygen at a greater rate than ordinary combustibles. Even in a normal air environment, the oxygen concentration in the combustion zone will not be maintained and incomplete combustion and a smoky fire result. Generally speaking, in the industrial environment, oxygen is readily available in the air. In some situations, there may be an abundance of oxygen available in the form of oxidizing chemicals. In these situations, a moderately combustible fuel and an oxidizer may form a dangerous combination. Therefore, storage and handling of strong oxidizers must be closely controlled, and they must be segregated from fuels.

Moisture Content.   The moisture content of combustible solids is one of the most important factors determining the ease of ignition and the burning rate of solid fuels once they are ignited. It takes a lot of thermal energy to convert the water to steam and then to drive it out of the combustible materials. Anyone who has ever attempted to light a campfire using wet or green wood can relate to the effects of moisture content. California brush fires and the great wildland fires of the summer of 1988 are testimony to the effects of low moisture. As wood is heated, there are insufficient flammable vapors for combustion until the water is converted to steam and cooked off. As wood is further dried, the moisture is replaced by air, which greatly enhances combustion if an ignition source is present. This characteristic may be utilized to our advantage by impregnating the air spaces in the wood with a fire retardant material to render it fire resistent.

Old wood in a structure can be much more readily ignited than new wood, because over the years the moisture has dried out. Wood that has been exposed to heat over long periods of time, such as wood that is near a steam pipe, also dries out and may be readily ignited.

From a fire protection standpoint, prewetting of wood through the operation of automatic sprinkler systems or hose streams serves to slow fire spread and contain a fire. Plastics, on the other hand, resist prewetting which results in a more severe fire hazard.

Ignition

Again, wood is used as the example of ignition of combustible solids. Ignition and burning of wood will occur only if it is heated to the point where combustible gases are released from the surface of the wood in sufficient quantities to support combustion. This process is known as pyrolysis, or the chemical decomposition of matter through the action of heat. As wood is heated, it initially gives off water vapor, carbon dioxide, and other noncombustible gases. As it is further heated and the amount of remaining moisture is reduced, the temperature of the wood increases. It gives off some water vapor and some carbon monoxide. At anywhere from 480 to 800 degrees Fahrenheit, the wood releases flammable vapors and particles in sufficient quantities for ignition and burning to occur.

The question might be asked about the almost 400 degree spread in the ignition temperature of the wood. The ignition temperature is dependant upon a number of variables.

The Specific Gravity. A dense wood, or one with a very small closely packed cellular structure has a higher ignition temperature, because it would be more difficult to cook out the moisture. Also, the remaining air spaces are smaller and would impede the flow of gases to the surface.

The Physical Characteristics. The size, shape, and moisture content will affect the ignition temperature of wood. The effects of moisture content on ignition have already been discussed. The size and shape is easily understood by anyone who has ever tried to light a campfire or fireplace with an inadequate supply of kindling wood.

The Rate and Period of Heating. A 2 by 4 inch piece of wood can be exposed to the 2000 degree Fahrenheit heat of a gas torch and probably not be ignited. The surface would certainly be charred, but this concentrated heat source would not heat enough of the wood and drive off enough of the moisture for pyrolysis to occur. But, it is known that wood will ignite at less than half of the temperature provided by the torch. It must merely be exposed at the lower temperatures over a large enough surface and for a sufficient period of time for the moisture to be cooked off and for pyrolysis to occur.

The Nature of the Heat Source. An intense but localized source of heat such as a gas torch may not ignite a piece of wood; however, a lower temperature and more widespread heat source may result in ignition. A building exposed to the radiant heat of a neighboring building fire may easily reach its ignition point and burst into flame.

The Air (Oxygen) Supply. As discussed with the fire triangle, oxygen is required for ignition to occur. If, for some reason, the oxygen supply is limited at the surface of the wood where pyrolysis is occurring, ignition will not occur.

Ignition sources can be anything that is capable of producing sufficient heat energy to initiate combustion of the exposed fuel. In industry, ignition sources are prevalent and varied as discussed previously in Chapter 1.

PLASTICS

The usage of plastics has increased tremendously since the 1960s. They are prevalent everywhere in society, in the home, office, factory, business, and means of transportation. Their prevalence in our lives, their burning characteristics, and the fire experience involving plastics has made them a major consideration in fire protection activities.

Burning Characteristics

The plastics are all combustible; they burn extremely hot producing very high ceiling temperatures; they melt and then flow and burn like flammable liquids; and they produce large quantities of smoke which is toxic and corrosive. These characteristics have been well documented by many fire tests and some highly destructive fire losses. Many of the plastics melt when exposed to fire and while burning drip into pools of flaming liquid which may flow and further spread the fire. The smoke that is produced when plastics burn is dense and thick. Initially, it radiates heat which accelerates flamespread, then as it thickens, it acts to hide the fire from firefighters. The toxic gases produced by burning plastics, as the gases produced by the combustion of any fuel, come from their components. Where the major primary fire gas of concern in fires was carbon monoxide, the compounds that make up plastics now contribute such others as hydrogen chloride, hydrogen cyanide, sulfur dioxide, and phosgene. For example, polyvinyl chloride (PVC) contains chlorine atoms which, in a fire situation and exposure to moisture, form hydrogen chloride (HCL) gas. HCL further combines with the available moisture in the air and moisture from fire suppression water to form hydrochloric acid. Polyurethane plastics contain isocyanate groups which, in a fire situation produce hydrogen cyanide (HCN). HCN is a particularly deadly gas which acts very rapidly, and at low concentrations, to bring about death.

Plastics have been responsible for many major fire losses, particularly where there has been no sprinkler protection, or when the amount of the plastics involved exceeded the ability of the sprinklers to control the fire. This occurs because plastics have a heat of combustion very close to that of gasoline. For example, the heat of combustion of both gasoline and polyethylene is about 20,000 Btu/lb, polypropylene is 19,800 Btu/lb, and polystyrene 18,056 Btu/lb.

Plastics in Major Fires

The prevalence of plastics in high-rise buildings is particularly critical to the firesafety professional. Plastics were a contributing factor to the rapid fire and smoke development in the MGM Grand Hotel fire in Las Vegas, Nevada on November 21, 1980. This fire resulted in the deaths of 85 people, the majority of which were the result of smoke inhalation. At least 61 of the victims died in the high-rise tower, far removed from the first floor fire. Some of the fuel load involved in this fire consisted of polyurethane-padded and vinyl-covered chairs and booths. The 68,000 square foot casino area included furnishings, contents, and interior finishes comprised of polyvinyl chloride, polyurethane, polystyrene, and methyl methacrylate.

In 1977, a fire devastated a 18.5-acre Ford Motor Company warehouse in Cologne, West Germany for a loss of $150 million. The sprinkler system was inadequate for the extensive amounts of plastic parts that were piled too high in this warehouse. The warehouse was built in 1962 when automobile parts were predominantly metal, and the sprinkler system was designed accordingly. When the fire occurred 15 years later, plastics were incorporated to a much greater extent in automobiles, and consequently, the warehouse was loaded with plastics rather than the metal for which it was designed. When the fire started, probably ignited by careless smoking, the sprinkler density was too low, and the sprinkler orifice sizes and temperature ratings were incorrect for the hazards present.

Plastics can be grouped into two major groups, thermoplastics and thermosets.

Thermoplastics

Thermoplastics are materials which, when heated, soften and flow and can be formed into any desired shape. Upon cooling, they harden but can be reheated and reshaped repeatedly. This process may be repeated as often as desired as long as chemical degradation has not occurred due to excessive heat.

Thermoplastics generally produce a more severe fire hazard than the thermosets because of their lower melting points and tendency to become melting, dripping flammable liquids.

Styrene Polymers. This group of thermoplastics include transparent polystyrenes and opaque high-impact strength copolymers based on styrene-butadiene (SB). Polystyrene (sold under the more familiar name "Styrofoam") is a familiar plastic foam that is used for insulation and packaging. Acrylonitrile-butadiene-styrene (ABS) is a common SB material that is used where strength, durability, and resistance to heat or solvents is required.

Decomposition products include hydrogen cyanide and complex completed materials due to the acrylonitrile, butadiene, and acrylic ester components.

The styrene polymers are considered to be severe fire hazards because of their common "expanded" or "foam" nature.

Polycarbonate. Polycarbonate is highly resistant to impact, may be self-extinguishing away from the ignition source, and melts only at high temperatures. Because of its strength, it is used for such things as hard hats and football helmets. The more familiar polycarbonate is "Lexan."

Combustion products of polycarbonate include aldehydes, ketones, and carbon oxides.

Polyolefins. This group of thermoplastics includes polyethylene and polypropylene materials which have numerous applications in industry. When exposed to an ignition source, they tend to soften and melt. When ignited, the fire gases and vapors smell of wax and paraffin, similar to a recently extinguished candle. One common usage of polyolefins is in plastic-type sheeting materials which may be of either polyethylene or polypropylene. Because of its configuration, plastic sheet materials produce a severe fire challenge. They are commonly used to drape equipment and to form temporary walls on construction projects. In this configuration they are perfectly situated, if an ignition source is present with plenty of available oxygen (air), to ignite and develop very rapid flamespread.

Polyvinyl Chloride. PVC is one of the most versatile of the thermoplastics in terms of range of applications. Rigid PVC is somewhat resistant to combustion because of the chlorine that is liberated as hydrogen chloride gas during heating. Hydrogen chloride interferes with the chemical reaction of flame, it dilutes the combustible gases that are given off, and a charred layer is formed on the surface of the PVC preventing further degradation by shielding the underlying polymer from oxygen and radiant heat. However, with further heating, the PVC burns and the evolution of hydrogen chloride continues.

A March 20, 1985 fire in a block-long warehouse in New Jersey containing 90,000 ft^2 of polyvinyl chloride waste demonstrated the severe fuel load and acid gases generated by this material. A rain shower during the fire resulted in "acid rain" from the hydrogen chloride gas in the smoke. The acid gases made it necessary for the Red Cross to evacuate more than 1000 area residents. Also contributing to the fuel load were the building's wood block floors which were soaked with machine oil from a previous tenant, a printing machine company. The 20-foot high, 3,000,000-ft^3 structure was totally destroyed. Contributing to the destruction was the fact that the building's sprinkler system was out of service. The fire took about 5 hours to control and resulted in the exposure of firefighters and area residents to hydrogen chloride from the burning PVC.

Fluorocarbon Polymers. There are numerous fluorine-containing polymers of which the most familiar is polytetrafluoroethylene (PTFE), or teflon. PTFE is useful because of its resistance to elevated temperatures. It decomposes at temperatures exceeding 500 degrees Celcius. At higher temperatures PTFE gives off toxic gases including hydrogen fluoride, perfluoroethylene, perfluoroisobutylene, and carbonyl fluoride. Of the thermoplastics, fluorocarbons present the lowest fire hazard.

Thermosetting Plastics

The plastics that are known as thermosets get their name from the fact that they are rigid and cannot be plastically formed even at elevated temperatures. They frequently incorporate filler materials to give them different properties.

Rather than melting and flowing when heated as the thermoplastics, thermosets char and decompose when exposed to flame. Because of the surface char that forms when exposed to flame, they generally are considered to be moderate to mild fire hazards.

Unsaturated Polyester Resins. These are the most widely used matrix materials in composites. They are widely utilized in commercial, industrial, and transportation applications. They are frequently mixed with glass fibers for reinforcement.

Phenolic Resins. Phenolics are formed from the reaction of phenol and formaldehyde. They are durable and heat resistant and are frequently used as electrically insulating plugs and utensil handles. Upon heating, phenolics form the char that is typical of thermosets, and their fire hazard can be further reduced by the addition of mineral fillers.

Composites

Composites are growing in importance in our lives, are being used more in industrial operations, and are important for the firesafety person to understand. They are not recognized as a severe fire hazard. Many components of composites are toxic, and their products of combustion are probably toxic.

A composite material can be defined as a macroscopic combination of two or more distinct materials, having a recognizable interface between them. Because composites are generally used for their structural properties, the definition can be restricted to include only those materials that contain a reinforcement such as fibers or particles supported by a binder (matrix) material.

Reinforcing Materials. Various reinforcement materials are added to a resin matrix of composites to provide strength to the cured material. The reinforcing materials are viewed as metallic structures, essentially as passive, load-bearing structural elements. For this reason, reinforcing materials are usually selected for strength, but heat, chemical, or solvent resistance may also be a consideration.

Glass fiber is a familiar reinforcing material which is widely used in industrial, consumer, military, and aerospace markets. Carbon fiber reinforced resin matrix composites are by far the most commonly used fibers in advanced composites. Carbon fibers offer excellent specific properties including modulus and strength, and they are readily available, inexpensive, and comparatively easy to manufacture.

Other reinforcing materials include aramid, other organics, boron fibers, fused silica, silicon carbide, alumina, and other ceramic fibers.

Matrix Materials.   Most of the matrix resins that are used today are complex, chemically reactive systems. Their purpose is to form a homogenous and continuous matrix or "glue" to hold the reinforcing materials in place. The matrix allows the transfer of loads to and between fibers and also protects them from chemical, physical, and mechanical damage.

Common matrix materials include polyurethane, polyester and vinyl ester, epoxy, bismaleimide (BMI), and polyimide resins.
Polyester and vinyl ester resins are the most widely used of all matrix materials. These resins are utilized mainly in commercial, industrial, and transportation applications. Epoxy resins and related chemicals are used far more than all other matrices in advanced composite materials for structural aerospace applications.

Fire Hazards.   The manufacture of composite materials involves complex chemicals and chemical reactions which present employee health considerations as well as the potential for emergencies (see also Chapter 12). There is little data concerning the combustibility of composites. It is difficult, if not impossible, to predict the components of thermal decomposition of the various composites described above. Decomposition products and concentrations will depend upon such things as temperature, recombination or subsequent reactions, products of incomplete combustion, and oxidant concentration. In general, products formed through thermal decomposition of these materials are toxic.

Foam Plastics

It is possible to obtain foams from practically any plastic, so many of the common foam plastics will be familiar names from the thermoplastic and thermosetting groups. Although the foamed plastics are either materials that are in either the thermoplastic or thermosetting group, they will be discussed separately here because of their importance to firesafety. Foams have a greater tendency to burn than their solid counterparts because they possess a high surface area per unit mass.

Polystyrene Foam.   The hazards of polystyrenes was described above. This material ignites readily at about 650 degrees Fahrenheit and softens and generates thick black smoke.

Polyurethane Foams.   Polyurethane foams, which include a whole family of flexible foam materials, are manufactured from two basic components, a polyol and an isocyanate. They have received extensive publicity because they are so much a part of our life style, and they have been involved in many fire deaths. The Los Angeles Times, for example, has described them as "a deadly and pervasive peril" that has the characteristics of "solid gasoline." There have been many attempts to treat polyurethane foams in their 30-year history to render them less combustible. However, even when treated, they are a combustible material, and, although ignition may be slower, they still burn. The author investigated an anechoic chamber fire in 1979, in which anechoic absorber material (polyurethane foam that has been impregnated with carbon to absorb electromagnetic energy) produced a raging fire that was, fortunately, controlled by a deluge sprinkler system. This material was advertised by the manufacturer as "Self-extinguishing by ASTM D1692-59T." Obviously, these tests did not represent real-life fire exposures. During the mid-to late 1970s, manufacturers developed polyurethanes with additives consisting of inorganic materials such as aluminum trihydrate which helped to retard combustion. These materials looked very promising in laboratory test conditions; however, in full-scale fire situations, they did not perform well. Factory Mutual Research Corporation conducted full-scale fire tests of treated anechoic absorber in 1980. In laboratory tests, this material appeared to be totally self-extinguishing. During the full-scale tests, using a standard wood crib as an ignition source, the material ignited and burned. In all fairness, the material took longer to burn and flamespread was greatly reduced, but the fact remains that the material is still combustible and it should be treated as such.

Phenolic Foams.   The principal application for these hard, brittle foam materials is as thermal insulation in buildings. They are less combustible than solid phenolics, which are already listed as mild hazard materials. The reason for this is that the cellular structure and low mass of the foam causes them to liberate volatiles at lower temperatures, leaving a stable carbonaceous residue.

FIBERS AND TEXTILES

There are increasing amounts of synthetic fibers and natural/synthetic fiber blends in our lives which are replacing the traditional natural fibers. The natural fibers are combustible, but they are generally less combustible than the synthetics. Natural fibers also produce about one-half of the heat of combustion of synthetic fibers. So, this change to synthetics and blends has resulted in an increase in the fire hazard of such things as drapery, carpeting, and clothing.

Natural Fibers

Natural fibers are generally combustible. Cotton is a common fiber found in both domestic and industrial use. Cotton consists of about 90 percent cellulose and ignites at about 400 degrees Celsius. When burning, cotton produces heat, smoke, carbon dioxide, carbon monoxide, and water. Another common natural fiber is wool. Animal fibers such as wool are mostly protein and high in nitrogen and are, therefore, more difficult to ignite. Wool ignites at about 600 degrees Celsius.

Silk is another natural material that is similar in combustion characteristics to wool. Silk is protein in nature, so its molecule contains large amounts of nitrogen. It is interesting to note that the self-ignition temperature of silk is about twice as high as most other naturally occurring combustible solids. Unfortunately, from a firesafety standpoint, silk has largely been replaced by synthetic fabrics.

Synthetic Fibers

Common synthetic fibers include acetate, nylon, polyesters, and glass fibers. Synthetic fibers are used in carpeting, clothing, bedding, and upholstery. Synthetic fibers, like plastics, are combustible, burn hot, and produce large quantities of toxic and corrosive smoke. Synthetic fibers are a particular concern to the fire protection professional, especially when used as a covering over combustible foam padding, and when used in buses, aircraft, schools, hospitals, and jails. In office environments, synthetic fiber material may be used in furniture, carpeting, and on temporary partitions and modular offices. These materials can greatly add to the fuel load of an area and increase the danger of flashover in a fire.

Fire Retardants

Methods for rendering combustible solids fire retardant or fire resistant include impregnation with inorganic salt materials and the application of surface coatings. Both impregnation and surface coatings act to restrict the combustion process by slowing the release of combustible gases and vapors. Inorganic salts have long been used as fire-retardant impregnants. They include ammonium, sodium, potassium or zinc in compounds with phosphate, borate, silicate, sulfate, or sulfamate. Intumescent coatings may also be applied to act as a barrier to pyrolysis. Intumescent coatings are paints that, when heated, swell to form a thick foamy insulating barrier to protect the material from decomposing. Intumescent coatings, like any coatings or fire-resistive paints, are subject to wear and chipping and, therefore they must be periodically inspected and reapplied if protection is to be maintained. It has also been reported that intumescent coatings are subject to weathering when exposed to very humid environments.

Whether impregnated or coated, the fact remains that the base material is still combustible and must be treated as such. This is an important concept. Wood and other combustible solids are frequently treated with fire-retardant materials and advertised as noncombustible or fire resistant. In many cases, small bench-scale tests have been quoted as proof that the material will not burn. And, in fact, fire-retardant treated materials generally perform very well in small bench-scale tests. But, the fact remains that the basic material is combustible and, given the right conditions such as a full-scale fire situation, they will burn. Allegations of fire retardancy and fire-proof characteristics should be closely scrutinized together with the proposed use of these "treated" materials. The bench tests and allegations of fire retardancy also fail to take into account the actions of building occupants and weathering. Many bench tests incorporate small point-sources for heating to ignition. In real use, though, exposures involving combinations of radiated and convected heat may be much greater. There is also a concern that water or exposure to high humidity will cause leaching of the fire-retardant materials.

Other coatings or additives, such as oil-based paint, preservatives, and insect repellents, may increase the combustibility and add to the toxic products of combustion of wood. All of these considerations must be evaluated by the user when purchasing and applying the materials.

LIQUIDS

Liquids, as fuels, include flammable and combustible liquids which will be discussed in greater detail in Chapter 4. Very simply, flammable liquids are those that at ambient temperatures will vaporize sufficiently to produce enough vapors to form an ignitable mixture in air. Combustible liquids are those that must be heated in order to produce sufficient vapors to form an ignitable mixture in air. The important point, here, is that liquids do not burn, their vapors burn. They must be vaporized, either by ambient temperatures in the case of flammable liquids or by an external heat source as is the case for combustible liquids.

GASES

The third state of matter besides solids and liquids is the gases. Gases are fluid substances that exist in the gaseous state at normal temperature (70 degrees Fahrenheit) and pressure (14.7 psia). The characteristic that separates gases from liquids which are also fluids is their vapor pressure. Gases are defined as fluids with a vapor pressure higher than 40 psia at 100 degrees Fahrenheit. The air that we breath is made up of a mixture of gases. In the gaseous state, the molecules of a material distribute themselves uniformly within the confines of a container. An important characteristic of a gas is the fact that it can be compressed. The compression of gases involves the three variables of pressure, temperature, and pressure. The relationships of these three variables are given by the gas laws (Figure 3-1). Gases are classified according to their physical properties and according to their chemical properties.

Physical Properties

Gases may be found in industry in either of two physical forms which vary depending upon the temperature and/or pressure at which they are stored. The two physical forms of gases are compressed gases and liquefied gases. Cryogenic gases are a type of liquefied gas with slightly different properties.

Compressed Gases. At normal temperature, a compressed gas exists only in the gaseous state under pressure. The pressurized form of compressed gases are those with an extremely low boiling point of around minus 150 degrees Fahrenheit. Compressed gases are stored in steel cylinders normally at anywhere from 25 to 3000 psi. Some gases are available and used at even higher pressures depending on the application.

Boyle's Law. The volume of a given mass of gas varies inversely with the pressure applied to it if the temperature remains constant.

$$V_2 = \frac{P_1 \times V_1}{P_2}$$

Charles' Law. The volume of a given mass of gas is directly proportional to the absolute temperature if the pressure remains constant.

$$V_2 = \frac{T_2}{T_1} \times V_1$$

Gay–Lussac's Law. The pressure of a given mass of gas is directly proportional to the temperature if the volume remains constant.

$$P_2 = \frac{T_2}{T_1} \times P_1$$

Where V_1 = initial volume V_2 = final volume
P_1 = initial pressure P_2 = final pressure
T_1 = initial temperature T_2 = final temperature

Figure 3-1. The gas laws.

Liquefied Gases.   The liquefied forms of compressed gases are those with a higher boiling point which may be anywhere from about minus 15 degrees to 32 degrees Fahrenheit. At normal temperature, but high pressure, gases exist in the liquid state. In order to achieve the liquid state, the pressure must be greater than the vapor pressure of the gas. Propane, butane, ammonia, and chlorine are common examples of liquefied gases. The liquid state is an economical way to store and ship gases because the vapor-to-liquid ratio for gases is very high. Propane has an expansion ratio of 270 parts of gas for every part of liquid.

Cryogenic Gases.   Gases that can be liquefied by cooling them to very low temperatures are cryogenic gases. These gases are defined by the National Bureau of Standards as a liquid having a boiling point below −238 degrees Fahrenheit. Cryogenic gases are maintained in the liquid state in their container under low pressure. Since they have an expansion ratio that is even higher than that of liquefied gases, special storage containers are required that allow gas that boils off of the liquid to escape. The difference between a cryogenic and liquefied gas is that the cryogenic gas cannot be maintained indefinitely in its container. Heat from the atmosphere will cause vaporization of the cryogenic gas and increased pressure within the container.

Nitrogen is an example of a gas that is frequently stored, shipped, and used as a cryogenic gas. Liquefied nitrogen is present in industry as an economical source of gaseous nitrogen and also when extreme cooling is required. As a liquid, nitrogen has a boiling point of −320 degrees Fahrenheit and an expansion ratio of 700:1 gas to liquid. Hydrogen (boiling point −423 degrees Fahrenheit) is a fuel gas and oxygen (boiling point −297 degrees Fahrenheit) is an oxidizer that is frequently stored, shipped, and used as a cryogenic. A major user of liquid hydrogen and oxygen is the space shuttle where liquid hydrogen is the fuel and oxygen the oxidizer which are the propellants that power the main shuttle engines.

Flammable Gases

A flammable gas is one that will burn in the normal concentrations of oxygen in the air. With flammable gases, there is no need for heat to pyrolyze or vaporize the fuel, since it is already in the gaseous state. All that is necessary for ignition is the proper gas/air mixture and an ignition source. The ignition temperature of a flammable gas is the temperature that is required to initiate combustion. Some examples of flammable gases include methane, propane, butane, hydrogen, and carbon monoxide. The most common uses of flammable gases are as fuels for heating, boilers, and generators. With the increasing concerns about air quality, flammable gases are becoming preferred as fuel because they burn much cleaner than the traditional fuel oils and coal.

Nonflammable Gases

Nonflammable gases are those that will not burn in air or in any concentration of oxygen. Some nonflammable gases will support combustion, however, and they must be treated cautiously when used or stored around flammable gases or combustible materials. These gases are the oxidizers and include such things as nitrous oxide, sulfur dioxide, and oxygen.

This category also includes gases that are inert, or those that are nonflammable and nonreactive. Inert gases include such things as nitrogen, helium, and argon. Also considered to be inert gases are carbon dioxide and sulfur dioxide. Only helium and argon are truly inert because they will not react with anything. Nitrogen and carbon dioxide will react with combustible metals.

Toxic Gases

Toxic gases are those that endanger life when inhaled, such as chlorine, hydrogen sulfide, sulfur dioxide, and carbon monoxide. Many of these and other toxic gases are used in, or produced by, industrial processes and are products of combustion, and therefore of great concern to the firesafety professional. Their existence or possible existence in an industrial process must be thoroughly evaluated, not only for fire, but also health and safety considerations.

Reactive Gases

Reactive gases are those that react with other materials or with themselves. Heat or shock may cause reactive gas molecules to rearrange themselves and produce heat. They may also form a reaction product which may be toxic. For example, fluorine reacts with organic and inorganic substances at normal temperature and pressure and produces flaming. Chlorine and hydrogen may burn when mixed.

Acetylene is frequently present in most industrial operations. It is a fuel gas that is used for cutting and welding metal. It is a reactive gas which, when exposed to heat and shock, can chemically rearrange and produce an explosion. For this reason, it is usually stored and shipped with a stabilizing substance. Acetylene is shipped and stored in a compressed gas cylinder and dissolved in acetone, much like carbon dioxide is dissolved in water in soft drinks.

Boiling Liquid, Expanding Vapor Explosion

The Boiling Liquid, Expanding Vapor Explosion, or BLEVE, is the primary hazard when a fire occurs during the transportation, storage, or use of liquefied fuel gases. A BLEVE is an explosion that occurs when a container holding a liquefied flammable gas fails when exposed to fire. Liquefied gases are above their boiling point at normal temperature. They will remain in the liquid state as long as they are kept under pressure. When the pressure is suddenly reduced to atmospheric because of a container failure, the stored heat in the liquid causes rapid vaporization and tremendous expansion into the gaseous state. If an ignition source is present, the rapidly expanding cloud creates the devastating explosion known as a BLEVE (See also, BLEVE in Chapter 10).

SUMMARY, IGNITION OF FUELS

To summarize, of the three forms of fuel, solids, liquids, and gases, only solids and liquids need to undergo thermal decomposition to achieve a vapor state where mixture with the oxygen in the air can take place. This concept was demonstrated in Figure 2-2. Solids undergo pyrolysis, or decomposition through the action of heat. In this process, the available moisture is cooked off and then the solid fuel molecules undergo thermal decomposition and become fuel gases without passing through an observable liquid phase. This process depends upon the size, shape, and density of the solid. When the fuel gases are of sufficient concentration to form an ignitable mixture in the air and an ignition source is available, combustion will occur.

Liquids undergo vaporization, or must be heated to sufficiently excite the molecules to overcome the surface tension of the liquid and be released to the air. This process must be sufficient to form enough vapors to provide an ignitable mixture in the air. Then, provided that an ignition source is present, combustion will occur.

Flammable gases, on the other hand, are already in the gaseous state and do not require thermal decomposition. All that is required is for sufficient quantities of the gas to be present to form an ignitable mixture in the air in the presence of an ignition source.

COMBUSTIBILITY TESTS

There are many tests for determining combustibility and other fire characteristics of materials. Tests range from, simply, using a match or bunsen burner to determine if something is ignitable, to very complex tests involving sophisticated laboratory equipment. There are currently tests available to determine all of the burning characteristics of materials. In the past, tests were ad hoc in nature. Combustion physics and chemistry were largely unknown. Tests were developed for a specific purpose, such as to pass a particular material and fail others. These tests were used by some so that their product could have a "fire-resistant" label. Many of these tests remain on the books and may be used by product suppliers to sell their product as "fire resistive." Therefore, it is important for those who recommend the use of "fire-resistant" materials to research the test methods cited to determine if the tests were appropriate for the material and for the intended use of the material.

Full-Scale Tests

Recently, testing has become more sophisticated. There are tests for all of the combustion process characteristics. The most useful type of test is the full scale fire test. The full-scale test presents the worst-case design scenario. Many materials that were thought to be fire resistant or noncombustible based upon small-scale tests have been demonstrated less than adequate for this rating in full-scale fire testing. Unfortunately, there are only a few laboratories in the United States that are capable of performing full-scale fire tests and the tests are very expensive.

Bench Tests

In most cases, it is not appropriate or feasible, to perform a full-scale test, and a suitable bench-scale test is necessary. Bench tests have three purposes. Bench tests may be used as a prediction of expected behavior in full-scale or real life situations. Bench tests can be used as quality assurance mechanisms in a manufacturing environment to ensure that products are being produced that maintain desired fire characteristics. Finally, bench tests can provide guidance in product development.

Much planning and study must go into the development of a realistic bench test. Recent examples have been the development of tests to determine the rate of heat release of upholstered furniture and the determination of time to flashover and rate of heat release for combustible wall cover materials.

It is very important to remember that bench-scale tests are merely indications of how a material will perform in a full-scale fire situation. Just because a material demonstrates fire resistance in the quality control laboratory does not mean that it will be fire resistant in use in the home or factory where it is exposed to many other hazards. A material that is fire resistant in the laboratory may not be fire resistant when ignited by other, more combustible, materials.

Fire Test Components

There are three major fire test components: ignition, flame spread, and burning and combustion product generation rates.

Ignition. The ease of ignition of a material is tested assuming an external source of heat or fire. Ignition may be tested using uniform heating or a concentrated heat source such as a bunsen burner. The bunsen burner is not a reliable test because it is difficult to predict. Some materials, such as some plastic materials, will shrink away from a heat source and may pass a bunsen burner test, but in actual fire exposure they may present a serious fire hazard. An example would be plastic sheet material that is used as a cover, drop cloth, or as drapery material. When exposed to a fire involving other combustibles, this material would be expected to contribute significantly to the flame spread and heat load. Additionally, the melting plastic material will produce a burning liquid fire. Other fire exposure factors such as radiant or convective heat sources must be considered.

Flame spread. The rating of the period in which material not yet involved in fire becomes progressively involved is called the flame spread. Flame spread may be thought of as continuous spreading ignition across the surface of a combustible material where the flames themselves provide the heat of ignition. This process has traditionally been characterized using the ASTM E 84 tunnel. This test method is for the comparative surface burning behavior of exposed building materials such as ceiling or wall surfaces. In this test, a 20 inch by 25 foot test sample is placed on the underside of the tunnel (called the Steiner tunnel, after the inventor). Gas burners are ignited at one end of the tunnel to simulate a fire exposure of about 1400 degrees Fahrenheit. Flame spread ratings are based upon the time that is required for flame to travel the length of the tunnel and are given compared to asbestos cement board which has a rating of zero and select grade red oak which has a rating of 100.

With the test data from E 84, a material may be classified by NFPA or UBC Class as follows:

FLAME SPREAD INDEX	NFPA CLASS	UBC CLASS
0–25	A	I
25–75	B	II
76–200	C	III

With these two materials as reference points, the test also provides ratings for "fuel contributed" and "smoke developed."

Although E 84 test results have generally showed performance similar to that observed during real building fires, it must be remembered that this test method is intended to provide only comparative classifications. It is a fairly large-scale test, with a 36 ft^2 test specimen, allowing for realistic fire involvement.

Limitations to the E 84 test are related to the orientation of the specimen in a horizontal ceiling position. Materials must be self-supporting in the ceiling position throughout the test. The test is not reliable for materials that may melt, drip, or burn away from the flame, or that may be completely engulfed in flame.

Burning and Product Generation Rates. A more accurate method than flame spread is that of measuring the mass loss rate of a specimen when it is fully ignited, with flame spread having covered its entire face. With this method, by using a cone calorimeter, heat release rates and combustion products can be measured.

SUMMARY

Fuels for the combustion process may be in the solid, liquid, or gas state. The actual combustion process takes place with the fuel gases and vapors in combination with oxygen in the presence of heat. This requires that solids and liquids first undergo thermal decomposition or vaporization. Gases are not required to undergo thermal degradation because they are already in a form that is capable of mixing with oxygen.

The ignition and burning of combustible solids is influenced by their physical form, heat conductivity, the availability of oxygen, and the moisture content.

The vast category of solid fuels known as plastics have become prevalent in all aspects of our lives. Consequently, plastics have been a major factor in fire loss experience. They are almost all readily combustible and they produce high heat, smoke, and toxic and corrosive gases.

Most solid fuels can be treated with fire-retardant materials to render them less combustible. It must be remembered that the basic material is still combustible. Given sufficient heat exposure, the material will burn. It is also possible for fire retardancy to lessen due to wear and weathering.

There are hundreds of tests available to determine burning characteristics of materials. There are three major characteristics that are determined through tests. They are ease of ignition, flame spread, and burning and combustion product generation rates. While small bench tests may be an indication of how a material will react in a real fire situation, full-scale tests present the worst-case exposure and are a better indicator. It is necessary for the fire protection personnel to research the tests that are cited and compare results to the material and its intended use.

BIBLIOGRAPHY

Angione, Charles. 1986. Plastics Warehouse Fire. *Fire Command* 53(1):38–41.

ASTM E-84-1987. Standard Test Method for Surface Burning Characteristics of Building Materials. Philadelphia: American Society for Testing and Materials.

Babrauskas, Vytenis. 1986. Fire Related Standards and Testing. Paper presented at Spacecraft Fire Safety Workshop, 20-21 August 1986, at NASA Lewis Research Center, Cleveland, Ohio.

Best, Richard, and David Demers. 1982. *Investigation Report on the MGM Grand Hotel Fire*, Las Vegas, Nevada, November 21, 1980. Boston: National Fire Protection Association.

Damant, G. H. 1988. Should Polyurethane Foam Be Banned? *Fire Journal*. May/June: 68–74.

Egan, M. David. 1978. *Concepts In Building Firesafety*. Toronto: John Wiley & Sons, Inc.

Fire Protection Handbook, 16th ed. 1986. Quincy: National Fire Protection Association.

Friedman, Raymond. 1985. Some Unresolved Fire Chemistry Problems. In *Fire Safety Science-Proceedings of the First International Symposium*, eds. Cecile E. Grant and Patrick J. Pagni, pp. 349–359. New York: Hemisphere Publishing Corporation.

Johansson, Olle. 1986. The Disaster at San Juanico. *Fire Journal* 80(1): 32–37, 93.

Landrock, Arthur H. 1983. *Handbook of Plastics Flammability and Combustion Toxicology*. Park Ridge, NJ: Noyes Publications.

Lyons, John W. 1985. *Fire*. New York: Scientific American Books, Inc.

Troitzsch, Jurgen. 1983. *International Plastics Flammability Handbook*. New York: Macmillan Publishing Co.

Tuve, Richard L. 1976. *Principles of Fire Protection Chemistry*. Boston: National Fire Protection Association.

4

FLAMMABLE AND COMBUSTIBLE LIQUIDS

A working knowledge of the safe use, storage, and disposal of flammable and combustible liquids is probably as necessary to the industrial firesafety professional as a thorough understanding of the life safety code. Flammable and combustible liquids are prevalent in almost all industries and many business and office occupancies. They represent unique hazards and have caused or supported many tragic fires. Flammable and combustible liquids may be used and stored safely as long as there is an understanding of their properties and a few rules are followed.

Also essential to the firesafety professional is an understanding of the definitions of flammable and combustible liquids, for it is these definitions that form the basis for the codes and the guidelines that provide for their safe use, storage, and disposal.

The majority of flammable and combustible liquids in use in industry fall in the categories of lubricants, hydraulic fluids, fuels, solvents, thinners, and paints. Compounding the decisions of the firesafety professional is the fact that these materials, and their safer counterparts, are increasingly regulated by environmental authorities. The fuels cause various forms of pollution when burned. Many solvents, thinners, and paints are referred to by the air quality authorities as volatile organic compounds (VOCs). Because of their high volatility, these materials readily enter the atmosphere where they contribute to air pollution. Some solvents, thinners, and paints are photochemically reactive, or they breakdown in the presence of sunlight to form ozone. Others, known as chlorofluorocarbons, react with and destroy the ozone in the earth's stratosphere. Therefore, the firesafety professional is faced with a dilemma; in some cases a liquid may be preferable because it is a combustible rather than a flammable liquid, but it may be environmentally undesirable. Compounding the firesafety/environmental dilemma is the fact that many of these materials are detrimental to employee health. The selection of industrial chemicals has become a complex activity involving the industrial hygienist, firesafety person, environmental engineer, and the process engineer. With an understanding of the characteristics and requirements for the safe use, storage and disposal of flammable and combustible liquids, the firesafety professional can incorporate proper equipment and procedural safeguards to use these materials when environmental and health concerns force the use of less firesafe materials.

TERMINOLOGY

There are a number of definitions that differentiate flammable and combustible liquids and describe the characteristics that make them hazardous. It is only through an understanding of these definitions that the safeguards that are necessary to store, use, and dispose of these materials safely may be understood.

Flash Point

The most important definition, which forms the basis for identifying and classifying flammable and combustible liquids, is flash point. Most materials cannot burn in the liquid or solid state. They must be broken down through the action of heat. In the case of solids, this thermal decomposition is called pyrolysis. In the case of liquids, vaporization, or conversion from the liquid to the vapor state is necessary. Flammable liquids, then, are those that vaporize at normal ambient temperatures. This vaporization must be to the extent that sufficient vapors are generated to form an ignitable mixture in air. The temperature at which this takes place is referred to as the flash point, the definition of which forms the basis for identifying and classifying flammable and combustible liquids. The flash point is the lowest temperature at which the liquid will give off enough vapors to form an ignitable mixture, which will momentarily flash across the surface of the liquid. A very general definition of a flammable liquid is one in which the flash point is less than 100 degrees Fahrenheit, or one which can form an ignitable mixture in air at or below normal ambient temperatures. A combustible liquid is one with a flash point between 100 and 250 degrees Fahrenheit, or one which can form an ignitable mixture in air with the application of heat.

Fire Point

Not to be confused with flash point, but related to it, is the fire point. The fire point is a temperature, usually about 5 to 10 degrees above the flash point, at which the ignitable mixture will continue to burn. Typically, at the flash point, if the vapor/air mixture is ignited, flame will only momentarily flash across the surface of the liquid and go out. At the fire point the temperature is higher and enough vapors are produced to support continuing combustion. For all practical purposes, though, the important definition, and the one that drives all of the requirements for flammable liquids is the flash point. The firesafety person is not concerned with this difference. If a liquid is at, or near, its flash point, it is considered hazardous and the safeguards discussed in this chapter must be employed.

Vapor Pressure

The molecules in a liquid are constantly in motion, but they are confined by the container and by the atmospheric pressure that is exerted on the liquid surface. Occasionally some molecules break through the surface into the air above the liquid. Sufficient numbers of these escaping molecules will result in pressure in a closed container. The motion of the liquid molecules and consequent pressure that they exert is called the vapor pressure, the pressure exerted by molecules in a liquid, when in equilibrium in the vapor space in a *closed* system. Vapor pressure is given in millimeters (mm) of mercury (Hg) or pounds per square inch (psi). As a reference, atmospheric pressure is 14.7 psi or 760 mm Hg. Vapor pressure is a very important consideration, along with flash point, in the study of flammable liquids, because it relates to the tendency of the liquid to vaporize and form ignitable mixtures. As discussed previously, liquids must be in the vapor state to form an ignitable mixture in air. A liquid with a higher vapor pressure will more readily form this ignitable mixture at the appropriate temperature.

Boiling Point

If the liquid is heated, the motion of the molecules, or volatility which relates to the ability of a molecule to escape into the air, is increased. This motion may increase to the point where the molecules overcome the atmospheric pressure. This is the boiling point, the temperature at which the vapor pressure of liquid equals atmospheric pressure. The fire hazard of a liquid is related to the boiling point. The lower the boiling point of a liquid, the greater the vapor pressure and therefore, the greater tendency the liquid will have to go into the vapor state. Since burning occurs in the vapor state, the higher the vapor pressure of the liquid, the greater is the fire hazard. The liquid molecules can also be released, or go into the vapor phase, should the surface pressure be reduced.

Flammable Limits

The concentration of a vapor/air mixture is generally given in percent by volume. With flammable vapors, there are concentrations in air below which the mixture is too "lean," or there are not enough fuel molecules to ignite, and above which the mixture is too "rich," or the concentration of fuel molecules is too great to ignite. Between too rich and too lean is a range of concentrations in which all mixtures are ignitable. This is the flammable range and the two limits are referred to as the upper flammable limit (UFL) and the lower flammable limit (LFL). All materials have different concentrations at which they form an ignitable mixture and different ranges of flammable limits. For example, gasoline has a very narrow range of flammability of from 1.4 to 7.4 percent (by volume). Older readers may remember how automobile carburetors were easily "flooded." The upper flammable limit was exceeded in the gasoline (vapor) air mixture going into the cylinders and the engine would not start. From a firesafety standpoint, this narrow range of flammability is beneficial. The possibility of ignition is limited to a very narrow concentration. The characteristic that makes gasoline so hazardous is its very low flash point of about −45 degrees Fahrenheit. This means that although the flammable range of gasoline is quite narrow, the LFL is very low, and at all ambient temperatures of most places on earth, it is at its flash point and produces ignitable vapor/air mixtures.

Specific Gravity

The specific gravity of a liquid is the ratio of the weight of the liquid to that of the same volume of water. In most cases, the specific gravity of flammable liquids is less than that of water which has a specific gravity of 1. Therefore, most flammable liquids float on water. Carbon disulfide is an example of a flammable liquid with a specific gravity greater than 1, and as expected, it sinks in water. This is an important consideration when the possibility exists that flammable liquids may be spilled into water, or burning flammable liquids may be spread over the surface of fire suppression water. The fact that most flammable and combustible liquids have a specific gravity of less than 1 and, therefore, float on water leads to a phenomenon known as boilover. For example, in a fire involving an open top tank of crude oil, there will be water or a water/oil emulsion at the bottom of the tank. As the crude oil burns and is heated, a heat wave, which may reach temperatures of 500 to 600 degrees F, travels down through the oil. When it reaches the water, an explosion will result from the quickly expanding steam/oil froth.

Probably the most serious loss of life from a boilover incident in an oil tank fire occurred on December 19, 1982 in Tacoa, Venezuela. After burning for over 6 hours and being declared under control, the tank containing approximately 3.5 million gallons of fuel oil #6 violently erupted into a boilover that killed more than 150 people.

Vapor Density

The vapor density is the ratio of the weight of vapors or gas to that of the same volume of air (air is 1). The vapor density of virtually all flammable liquids is greater than 1. Therefore, when flammable vapors are released into the air, they will tend to settle to low points. This is an important consideration when planning exhaust ventilation for flammable liquid storage areas. Additionally, the hazard of flammable liquids is increased because of the tendency of the vapors to spread out away from the liquid. Many fires have occurred when flammable vapors have spread from a "safe area" of liquid use to an ignition source such as an electrical appliance or the pilot light of a gas water heater. It is therefore necessary to evaluate all possible ignition sources in the area of flammable liquid use and to provide adequate low-point exhaust ventilation if the possibility of vapor accumulation and spread exists.

Ignition Temperature

It is important to note that the flash point and fire point require an external source of ignition. They are only the *temperatures* at which the liquid can form sufficient vapors to form an ignitable mixture. The ignition point or ignition temperature is the temperature at which the material ignites without an external source of ignition. If a beaker of liquid is heated over a bunsen burner and the vapors are prevented from reaching the flame, the liquid will spontaneously begin to burn when the ignition temperature is reached. The ignition temperature may also be referred to as the autoignition point or autogenous ignition point.

One must be very careful in designing processes and procedures based only on the flash point and ignition temperature. The flash point and ignition temperature are only observed phenomenon that occur under carefully controlled laboratory conditions. When the conditions or equipment are changed, the results may be entirely different. For example, hydraulic oil may be classified as a combustible liquid, and under normal test conditions, be very difficult to ignite unless heated extensively. But the conditions of use are, quite often very different from the laboratory conditions in which the flash point is determined. Consequently during normal usage, the oil may be at or above its flash point, or a breakdown in the system may result in a dangerous condition. Under high-pressure conditions, a small leak in the system will result in the oil being sprayed out in a fine mist which may, depending upon the pressure, encompass a wide area. In this form, it can be readily ignited when an ignition source is available. The resulting fire may burn torchlike, and because of the dispersion of the fuel in the air, produce a high rate of heat release.

Effect of Temperature, Pressure, and Oxygen Concentration

An increase in the temperature of the vapor/air mixture will result in an increase in the flammable limits as shown in Figure 4-1. For example, increasing the temperature 100 degrees Celcius will increase the UFL about 8 percent and lower the LFL about 8%. Similarly, an increase of atmospheric pressure raises

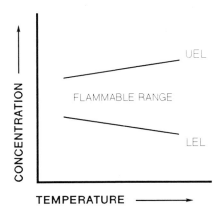

Figure 4-1. The effect of temperature on the flammable range.

the flash point and a decrease in pressure lowers the flash point (Figure 4-2). For example, in Denver, a flammable liquid will have a slightly lower flash point than it will in Los Angeles or New York. This is consistent with the earlier discussion of vapor pressure. As atmospheric pressure increases, it counters the vapor pressure of the liquid. This necessitates higher temperatures (flash point) to cause enough liquid to go into the vapor state to form an ignitable mixture.

An increase in the amount of available oxygen in the presence of fuel vapor will have a similar effect upon the flammable limits of the flammable vapor/air mixture (Figure 4-3). Oxygen-enriched atmospheres might be encountered in the industrial environment where chemical oxidizers are present or where gaseous oxygen is used.

For most industrial usage and storage situations, the variations caused by changes in temperature and pressure are negligible. A flammable liquid in Denver is still a flammable liquid in wherever else it is used, even if the flash point is slightly different. However, when used in an industrial process or confined in a closed system where unusual temperatures and pressures may be encountered, these characteristics become important considerations for the firesafety professional.

IGNITION SOURCES

While electrical causes are the most prevalent sources of ignition in industrial fires, many of the high dollar loss fires in recent years have involved flammable liquids either in the ignition scenario or as contributing factors following ignition. Flammable liquids have increased the severity of these fires by accelerating the spread or increasing the intensity. Chapter 13 contains some examples of warehouse fires that were significantly affected by the presence of flammable liquids.

The ignition of flammable liquid vapors can occur from a host of sources.

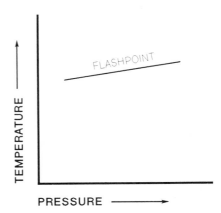

Figure 4-2. The effect of atmospheric pressure on the flash point.

When dealing with flammable liquids, it is normally best not to base explosion/firesafety on the presumption that all ignition sources have been excluded. In many flammable gas and liquid fires and explosions, the sources and forms of heat of ignition were never discovered. Nevertheless, reasonable measures must be taken to exclude all possible ignition sources. Where flammable liquids are present, it is best to assume that an ignitable mixture will occur and therefore there must be no ignition sources available.

Electrical Ignition

Electrical sources of ignition are the most common in industrial fires and they must certainly be controlled in areas where flammable or combustible liquids are present. There are primarily three sources of electrical ignition which are of concern. Electrical systems will cause excessive heat when overloaded and, in the case of flammable or combustible liquids, a fire will occur when this heat reaches the ignition temperature of the liquid. Sparks and arcing caused by breaks in conductors or short circuits may ignite flammable vapors. A third source of electrical ignition may be caused by the normal operation of electric heating equipment and appliances which, if improperly used, may exceed the ignition temperature of the liquid. There are four methods to avoid electrical sources of ignition in areas where flammable liquids are present. The first method, which is also the safest, is to eliminate electrical equipment from the hazardous area. This method should be employed wherever possible. When electrical equipment must be located in hazardous areas, it must be installed and used in accordance with the provisions of NFPA #70, *The National Electrical Code*, specifically Article 500. The second method is to employ what is known as explosion-proof equipment. When ordinary electrical equipment must be located in areas where flammable liquids may be present, adequate positive pressure ventilation from a source of clean air must be provided. This positive

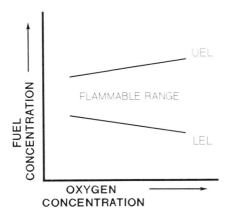

OXYGEN
CONCENTRATION

Figure 4-3. The effect of oxygen enrichment on the flammable range.

pressure ventilation is known as purging. The fourth method is to employ intrinsically safe equipment.

Explosion-Proof Equipment.   When it is necessary to locate electrical equipment in areas where flammable liquids are present, explosion-proof apparatus must be used. Explosion-proof equipment is enclosed in a substantial case that is capable of withstanding an internal explosion of specified gas or vapor which may be present due to leakage. The design of the case is such that normal operation of the equipment, or an explosion within the equipment will not ignite specific gases or vapors surrounding the enclosure by sparks or flashes (Figure 4-4). Finally, explosion-proof equipment does not produce enough heat externally to ignite a surrounding flammable atmosphere.

Positive Pressure Ventilation.   When ordinary electrical equipment is located in areas in which flammable liquids are present, it may be protected by purging, or supplying ventilation consisting of clean air or an inert gas to the equipment. This purge prevents the formation of an ignitable mixture of flammable vapors in the purged area.

   When purging is used as the means of protecting electrical equipment, it is important to safeguard against ventilation failure by providing automatic shutdown of the flammable liquid operation in the event of a failure of the ventilation system. As a minimum, alarms should be provided to alert the operator in the event of a ventilation system failure.

Intrinsically Safe Equipment.   One method of making electrical equipment safe for use in hazardous areas is to make it intrinsically safe. Intrinsically safe means that the equipment is not capable of releasing sufficient electrical thermal energy under normal or abnormal conditions to cause ignition of a specific hazardous atmospheric mixture in its most easily ignitable concentration. Intrin-

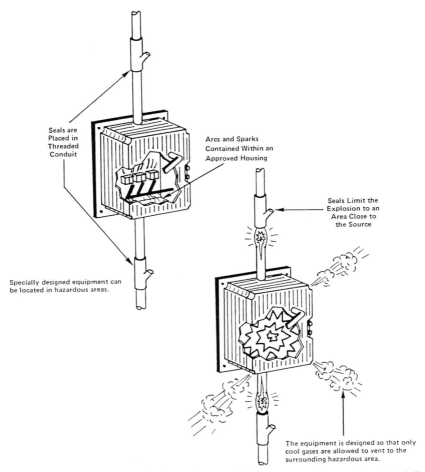

Figure 4-4. Explosion occurring in equipment that is approved for use in potentially explosive environments. (Source: U. S. Department of Labor)

sically safe equipment is, by definition, low power equipment. It is not applicable to power and lighting circuits, however it is well adapted for instrumentation and communications equipment where power use is inherently low.

Static Electricity.   Everyone is familiar with static electricity as a nuisance that causes shocks, unruly hair, clinging clothes, and other annoyances. In industrial operations involving the use of flammable liquids, static electricity is a potential fire ignition hazard.

When atoms of a piece of material contain as many electrons as protons, the material is said to be electrically neutral. Static electricity is caused by contact and separation of two materials, generally an electrical conductor and a non-conductor or two nonconductors. Separation of the materials results in a transfer of electrons resulting in the accumulation of a negative charge on one and an equal and positive charge on the other. During the transfer of flammable liquids, static electricity can build up on containers and people. If it is not safely equalized between two objects or transferred to ground, sparks can be generated which can be a source of ignition if flammable vapors are present. Methods to control static electricity include bonding and grounding. Bonding is a method of equalizing the electric charge on two conductive objects by providing an electrical path from one container to the other. When pouring flammable liquids from one container to another, as from a drum to a container, a bonding wire should be attached from the drum to the container. This prevents the buildup of static electricity and possible arcing from one container to the other. Grounding is a method for bleeding the electric charge to earth ground by means of a conductive wire attached from the container to earth ground. In the example above, the drum is "grounded" to earth ground to bleed off any electrical charge that is built up by the two containers.

Another method of reducing static electricity is by ionization of the air that is in contact with a charged body. Ionization of the air provides a conducting route through which the charge is dissipated. Air ionizers include a blower that blows air across a weak radioactive source such as polonium 210 to ionize the air. Humidification, or increasing the moisture in the air is another method for reducing static electricity. Relative humidity of less than 50% is conducive to the generation of static electricity. In areas where low humidity may contribute to a static problem, the humidity may be increased by humidifiers in the heating, ventilating, and air conditioning (HVAC) system, or by such simple means as wet-mopping floors.

Air ionization and humidification are methods of eliminating or minimizing the generation of static electricity. Bonding and grounding are methods of preventing its accumulation. In operations utilizing flammable liquids including pouring, pumping, spraying, or mixing, these static safety considerations are important. They must be incorporated into the design of the industrial equipment as well as in the development of the operating procedures. It is also important that operating personnel are trained in the hazards that are involved and procedures to conduct the operations safely. Preventive maintenance programs are also important to ensure that devices for the prevention and control of static electricity are functioning properly.

Catalytic Material

A catalyst is a material that accelerates a chemical reaction. A catalytic material may cause an exothermic reaction which results in ignition. The presence of a catalytic material may lower the ignition temperature of a flammable liquid. For example, the presence of metal oxides, or rust, may reduce the ignition temperature of a flammable liquid.

Auto Oxidation

The process of slow oxidation with accompanying evolution of heat which may lead to autoignition when the heat cannot be dissipated is known as auto oxidation or spontaneous ignition. Auto oxidation of liquids only occurs in those liquids with low volatility such as linseed oil, animal oils, and vegetable oils. Other, more volatile, liquids evaporate too quickly for the oxidation process to occur. The most common example of this form of ignition is oily waste, or rags that have been improperly stored. Oily waste may begin to oxidize and, over a period of time, heat will build up. If the storage of the waste is such that the heat is not removed by ventilation, the process may continue and heat build up to the point where ignition occurs. In areas where oily waste is generated, metal self-closing disposal containers should be provided.

Friction

Friction from rubbing or striking objects or defective equipment can result in heating or sparks that could ignite flammable vapors. Steel hand and mechanical tools such as hammers, shovels, and wrenches are likely sources of sparks. In areas where flammable vapors are possible, nonsparking tools must be used.

Compression

When gas is compressed rapidly, its temperature increases. Auto ignition of flammable vapors may occur if the temperatures resulting from compression exceed their ignition temperature. This is the principle on which the diesel engine operates. Diesel fuel which has a relatively high ignition temperature is sprayed into a cylinder and compressed to its ignition temperature.

CLASSIFICATION SYSTEMS

There are two classification systems that are commonly used to classify flammable and combustible liquids according to their degree of hazard. The reader should become familiar with the National Fire Protection Association (NFPA) and the Underwriters' Laboratories (UL) systems in addition to any local jurisdiction systems that may apply.

The NFPA classification system, as defined in NFPA 30, Flammable and Combustible Liquids Code, is based upon the flash point and boiling point of the liquid. Under this system, flammable liquids are listed as Class I and have a flash point below 100 degrees Fahrenheit. Remember, from the earlier definition, liquids are considered flammable if their flash point is within normal ambient temperatures. It is interesting to note that the upper flash point limits for Class I liquids in the NFPA system is higher at 100 degrees than the limit for highly flammable liquids in Great Britain which is 90 degrees. This is probably because of the lower expected ambient temperatures in Great Britain. The city of Los Angeles previously had its own classification system for flammable liquids. Again, because of higher ambient temperatures in southern California, the range of flammable liquids in this system included those with flash points up to 150 degrees.

The firesafety professional must evaluate the existing environment and establish unique requirements. For example, an industrial operation that is located in the desert and using kerosene (flash point 130 degrees Fahrenheit) may want to treat that material as a flammable liquid.

The NFPA system classifies flammable and combustible liquids as follows:*

Flammable liquids are in Class I.

Class IA are liquids with flash points less than 73 degrees Fahrenheit and with boiling points less than 100 degrees Fahrenheit.

Examples of Class IA liquids include acetaldehyde, ethyl ether, ethyl chloride, isoprene, methyl formate, pentane, and propylene oxide.

Class IB are liquids with flash points less than 73 degrees Fahrenheit and with boiling points at or above 100 degrees Fahrenheit.

Some examples of Class IB liquids include acetone, carbon disulfide, benzene, cyclohexane, ethyl acetate, 100 percent ethyl alcohol, gasoline, heptane, octane, toluene, and methyl alcohol.

Class IC are liquids with flash points at or above 73 degrees Fahrenheit and below 100 degrees Fahrenheit.

Some examples of Class IC liquids include styrene, methyl isobutyl ketone, isobutyl alcohol, turpentine, o-xylene, and amyl alcohol.

Combustible liquids are in class II or III.

Class II are liquids with flash points at or above 100 degrees Fahrenheit and below 140 degrees Fahrenheit.

---

*The NFPA classification of flammable and combustible liquids has been reprinted with permission from NFPA 30-1987, *Flammable and Combustible Liquids Code*, copyright © 1987, National Fire Protection Association, Quincy, MA 02269. This reprinted material is not the complete and official position of the National Fire Protection Association, on the referenced subject which is represented only by the standard in its entirety.

Some examples of Class II liquids include No. 1-3 fuel oils, kerosene, n-decane, hexyl alcohol, glacial acetic acid, and stoddard solvent.

Class IIIA are liquids with flash points at or above 140 degrees Fahrenheit and below 200 degrees Fahrenheit.

Some examples of Class IIIA liquids include aniline, benzaldehyde, butyl cellosolve, nitrobenzene, and pine oil.

Class IIIB are liquids with flash points at or above 200 degrees Fahrenheit.

Some examples of Class IIIB liquids include animal oils, ethylene glycol, glycerine, lubricating oil, quenching oil, transformer oil, triethanolamine, benzyl alcohol, and vegetable oil.

IA liquids are the ethers; they have high vapor pressures and are constantly trying to get out of their container. Therefore, containers for storing Class IA liquids require a vapor-tight seal. Class IB liquids which include gasoline and acetone are pretty well contained by a closed container. At normal room temperature molecular activity of the IB liquids is not as great as the class IA liquids. There are liquids such as the hydrazines with flash points listed as being at or slightly higher than 100 degrees Fahrenheit. In these cases, the reader must consider the individual applications to decide whether or not to treat them as flammable liquids.

Table 4-1 shows some common liquids, their NFPA classification, and the characteristics that determine their degree of hazard.

The Underwriters Laboratories (UL) Classification System is a comparative classification system that uses names and corresponding characteristics of a number of well-known liquids and a numerical rating as follows:

Ether class	100–110
Gasoline class	90–100
Alcohol (ethyl) class	60–70
Kerosene* class	30–40
Paraffin oil class	10–20

*Kerosene with flash point of 100 degrees Fahrenheit is the upper end of UL classification of flammable liquids with a class of 40.

This system* provides the degree of fire hazard on a numerical scale and in comparison with some well-known substances whose hazards have been established by field experience. The UL Classification System is used occasionally by manufacturers in the preparation of material safety data sheets (MSDS).

---

*Note: This material is reproduced, with permission, from Underwriters Laboratories Inc.'s Standard for Safety UL 340—"Tests for Comparative Flammability of Liquids," copyright © 1979 by Underwriters Laboratories Inc. Copies may be purchased from Underwriters Laboratories Inc. Publication Stock, 333 Pfingsten Road, Northbrook, Illinois 60062-2096.

Table 4-1. Fire Hazard of Various Materials.

MATERIAL	FLASH POINT (°F)	IGNITION TEMPERATURE (°F)	FLAMMABLE LIMITS		BOILING POINT (°F)	NFPA CLASS
			LOWER (%)	UPPER (%)		
Ethyl ether	−49	356	1.9	36.0	95	IA
Pentane	−40	500	1.5	7.8	97	IA
Acetone	−4	869	2.5	13.0	133	IB
Toluene	40	896	1.2	7.1	231	IB
Styrene	88	914	1.1	7.0	295	IC
o-xylene	90	867	1.0	7.0	292	IC
Kerosene	130	410	0.7	5.0	400	II
Acetic acid	103	867	4.0	19.9 @ 200°	245	II
Aniline	158	1139	1.3	11.0	364	IIIA
Nitrobenzene	190	900	1.8 @ 200		412	IIIA
Glycerine	390	698			340	IIIB
Ethylene glycol	232	748	3.2		387	IIIB

Source: NFPA 325M-1984. *Fire Hazard Properties of Flammable Liquids, Gases, and Volatile Solids.* The National Fire Protection Association.

AEROSOLS

Aerosols are defined as materials that are dispensed from their container as a mist spray or foam by a propellant under pressure. Either the product or the propellant may be flammable. There is dramatic evidence from tests and fire experiences that stored aerosol containers present a severe fire hazard. Two such major losses have occurred. On May 27, 1987, the Sherwin-Williams Warehouse fire in Dayton, Ohio and the June 21, 1982 K-Mart Center fire in Falls Township, Pennsylvania were both affected by aerosol containers. When exposed to a fire, aerosol containers rupture, releasing their contents which can burn as both a fireball and as a residual flammable liquid fire. The container may also rocket for great distances, trailing a tail of burning liquids. The rocketing containers spread the fire to uninvolved areas of the building, causing additional sprinkler systems to activate.

In the Sherwin-Williams Warehouse fire, fire fighters observed aerosol containers rocketing from the building for distances up to 200 feet. The flying aerosol cans actually made it unsafe for fire fighters to approach fire department water connections located at the side of the building.

In the K-Mart fire, when the fire involved palletized storage of petroleum-liquid-based aerosol containers, the sprinkler system was overwhelmed when rocketing cans spread fire throughout this and adjoining areas. Although the K-Mart Center was divided into four fire areas by 3-hour rated walls, some of

Figure 4-5. The aftermath of a warehouse fire involving aerosol containers. (Source: Factory Mutual Engineering Corporation)

the openings were not provided with fire doors. Instead, protection was provided by deluge water curtains designed to provide 3.0 gpm per linear foot of opening. During the fire, fire fighters in the building noted exploding aerosol cans going through the deluge curtain, trailing flaming contents behind them. In other areas, aerosol cans rocketed through the failed roof and ignited adjoining roof areas.

When fire spread is accelerated as in the K-Mart fire, it does not take long for more sprinklers to come on to the point where the system is overwhelmed.

Because of the hazards that are present when aerosols are exposed to fire, storage of these materials is very important. Large quantity storage should be in separate noncombustible rooms or buildings. Smaller quantities should be stored in enclosed noncombustible bins or, preferably, flammable liquid storage cabinets.

STORAGE OF FLAMMABLE LIQUIDS

Now that the basics of flammable and combustible liquids are understood, it is possible to apply this knowledge, to the characteristics and to the storage and usage of flammable and combustible liquids. The primary reference for the storage and usage of flammable and combustible liquids, and the basis for legal regulations is NFPA 30, *Flammable and Combustible Liquids*. The latest edition of the NFPA *Flammable and Combustible Liquids Code Handbook* is particularly useful because, not only does it provide the text of the code, but it provides explanatory information.

Allowable storage quantities of flammable liquids are provided by NFPA #30, and are generally based upon the hazard classification of the liquid. Some jurisdictions may modify the allowable storage quantities through locally adopted fire prevention codes. Therefore, it is important that one be familiar with the local storage allowances.

When received at the industrial plant site, flammable liquids may be in glass containers, metal cans, barrels, or bulk tanks. Flammable liquids should normally be ordered in nonbreakable containers, however, it is often necessary to order it in glass containers, particularly where liquids of high purity are required. It is then incumbent upon the user to properly store glass containers in a protected area such as a flammable liquid cabinet or a special flammable liquid storage room. All flammable liquids, regardless of the storage vessel, should be stored in flammable liquid cabinets or storage rooms whenever possible.

When used in small quantities, flammable liquids should be transferred from their shipping container to safety cans. A safety can is an approved container of not more than 5 gallons capacity. The purpose of the safety can is to control the flammable vapors and prevent an explosion if the safety can is heated. Safety containers are of substantial leak tight construction, have a spring-loaded self-closing cap, and a flash arrestor (Figure 4-6). The cap allows venting of vapors that may build up in the container at about 5 psig internal pressure. This venting of internal pressure prevents rupture or explosion of the container if it is exposed to a fire. The flame arrester screen prevents flame from flashing back into the container if the vapors should be ignited outside. A flame arrester is generally a wire mesh device that provides such rapid dissipation of heat from fire that vapor temperature on the inside of the can remains below the ignition point.

When flammable liquids are received in and dispensed from drums or portable containers, special precautions and attachments are necessary. For gravity dispensing, drum faucets are available that are self-closing and have built-in flame arresters (Figure 4-7). It should be noted that indoor gravity dispensing is not allowed by some jurisdictions, and in most cases Class I and II liquids are not to be dispensed by gravity. Drum vents are devices that relieve the vacuum that is created during dispensing and to vent pressures if the drum is exposed to fire (Figure 4-8).

Drum pumps are available for safer and more efficient dispensing from a drum. Because of the possible ignition hazards, it is not desirable to incorporate electrically driven pumps, therefore, hand-operated pumps are available that provide a simple and safe method of dispensing (Figure 4-9). The same safeguards are still necessary when using a drum pump, including bonding, grounding, and venting. Most flammable liquid drum pumps incorporate builtin venting capability and bonding is accomplished through the hoses which have integral bonding wires. However, a separate ground wire is still required.

Gas pressure may not be used to transfer flammable or combustible liquids unless the container has been specifically designed and approved for that pur-

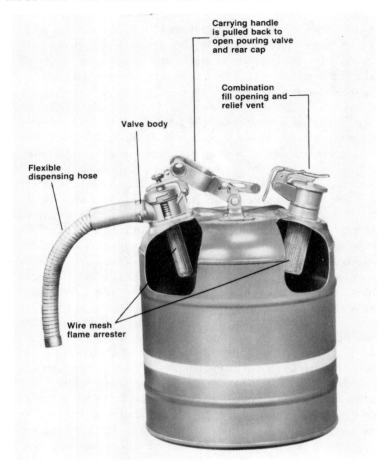

Carrying handle
is pulled back to
open pouring valve
and rear cap

Combination
fill opening and
relief vent

Valve body

Flexible
dispensing hose

Wire mesh
flame arrester

Figure 4-6. A safety can that is approved for use with flammable liquids. (Source: Justrite Manufacturing Company, Des Plaines, IL)

pose. Air or oxygen must not be used for this purpose. Instead, an inert gas such as nitrogen should be used. Class I liquids may not be transferred by gas pressure. Storage Cabinets–NFPA 30 describes design criteria for flammable liquid storage cabinets, and it allows both metal and wood cabinets for storing flammable and combustible liquids. Metal cabinets that meet the requirements of the code are readily available commercially and are preferred over wood (Figure 4-10). The criteria for cabinets is intended to provide protection for the stored materials from an external fire exposure. To be approved, flammable liquid cabinets must pass a fire test as described in ASTM E152-72 in which, following a 10-minute fire exposure, the temperature inside the cabinet does not exceed 325 degrees Fahrenheit.

Figure 4-7. A gravity flow faucet that is approved for use with flammable liquids. (Source: Justrite Manufacturing Company, Des Plaines, IL)

Metal cabinets must have double walls and be made of minimum No. 18 gauge steel. The cabinet must contain a minimum 2-inch pan, or containment capability, at the bottom to contain spills. The doors must have a three-point latch arrangement. In some jurisdictions the doors must be self-closing.

Most metal cabinets are provided with openings for venting purposes, al-

Figure 4-8. A drum vent plug that is used to vent pressures from the drum. (Source: Justrite Manufacturing Company, Des Plaines, IL)

Figure 4-9. A safety drum pump provides a safe method of transferring flammable liquids into smaller containers. (Source: Justrite Manufacturing Company, Des Plaines, IL)

though venting is not required for fire protection purposes. The vent opening is provided with a bung fitting which must be in place if the cabinet is not vented. If the cabinet is vented, it must be vented outdoors.

Most commercially produced flammable liquid storage cabinets are provided with grounding lugs. The cabinet is not required to be grounded for just incidental storage. However, if liquids are dispensed from containers within the cabinet, it must be grounded to complete the bonding/grounding circuit as described earlier in this chapter.

Commercially available cabinets are sized so as to not exceed the allowable storage quantities specified in NFPA 30. The Code allows a maximum of 60 gallons of Class I and Class II liquids per cabinet and not more than three cabinets in a fire area. Although, in an industrial occupancy, this may be exceeded if the additional cabinet, or group of three cabinets, are separated by 100 feet. This storage arrangement is sometimes necessary in a large manufacturing area, industrial warehouse, or ready stores area where more that 150

Figure 4-10. A flammable liquid storage cabinet provides safe storage for larger quantities of flammable liquids in small containers. (Source: Justrite Manufacturing Company, Des Plaines, IL)

gallons of flammable liquids are required in the fire area and the required separation distances are available.

STORAGE QUANTITIES

The allowable storage quantities for various occupancies of flammable and combustible liquids varies according the codes that are adopted by the local authority having jurisdiction.

Allowable storage quantities are based upon the type of storage containers and the use of the material. For example, allowable size glass containers varies from 1 pint for Class IA flammable liquids to 5 gallons for Class III combustible liquids.

Allowable storage in safety cans varies from 2 gallons for Class IA flammable liquids to 5 gallons for all of the other flammable and combustible liquids.

In all cases, quantities of flammable liquids for industrial operations should be maintained at the lowest amount necessary to maintain operations. But, in all cases, the amounts should not exceed that allowed by the code that is in force. When it is necessary to maintain larger quantities they should be in outdoor storage areas or specially protected separate storage rooms.

Generally accepted guidelines for storage of flammable and combustible liquids differ depending upon two categories, those areas where the containers may be opened and the liquids used and those areas where the containers are not opened such as merchandizing areas.

It is generally accepted that the following quantities may be stored in those occupancies where the containers will not be opened:

60 gallons of Class IA flammable liquids

120 gallons of Class IB flammable liquids

180 gallons of Class IC flammable liquids

240 gallons of Class II combustible liquids

660 gallons of Class III combustible liquids

These amounts will be relatively safe for storage. Amounts in excess of this must be stored in special storage rooms or outside storage.

It is generally accepted that users of flammable liquids in industrial occupancies may store, in the area of use, the following amounts:

In ordinary shipping containers a maximum of 25 gallons.

In flammable liquid safety containers a maximum of 50 gallons.

In flammable liquid storage cabinets a maximum of 60 gallons of flammable liquids each or 120 gallons of combustible liquid. There may be a maximum of three cabinets in a fire area. Where more than 150 gallons of flammable liquids are necessary, special storage rooms must be considered. Beyond that, sprinklers in the building and special construction must be provided. It should be emphasized that the storage quantities provided here are suggested safe amounts. The local authority having jurisdiction may have differing requirements. With this basic understanding of flammable liquids, it is possible to proceed to the safe guards that should be incorporated into building special rooms for the storage of flammable liquids.

Characteristics of Special Storage Rooms

A special room for the storage of flammable and combustible liquids should be of rated construction of 1 to 2 hours, depending upon the local code. NFPA #30 allows 1-hour construction for rooms of 150 ft^2 and 2 hours for rooms of 500 ft^2. Openings in the walls to adjacent rooms must have a minimum $1\frac{1}{2}$-hour door, and if any point in the room is greater than 15 feet to the door, a second exit may be necessary.

The floors of the storage room should be sealed with a minimum 4-inch curb provided so as to contain spills within the room. It may be desirable to provide floor drains, although some jurisdictions do not allow them. If floor drains are provided, they should drain to a safe place such as an underground tank or some other containment area.

Electrical service, if provided, should be rated for the materials stored in the room (explosion proof). Bonding wires and grounding points should be provided to ground containers in the room.

Ventilation must be provided in the form of either gravity or mechanical exhaust ventilation. The design of the ventilation must take into consideration the vapor density of most flammable liquid vapors. Most flammable liquids have a vapor density greater than 1, and they are therefore heavier than air. Exhaust and makeup air ducts must be located on opposite sides of the room and within 12 inches of the floor, so as to have air movement sweep across the floor.

BULK STORAGE OF FLAMMABLE LIQUIDS

Underground Storage Tanks

In the industrial plant, the safest and most economical method of storing bulk quantities of flammable liquids was in underground storage tanks. The principle fire hazard with this method of storage has been from leakage and overfilling which result in the accumulation of flammable vapors in the air pockets of conduits, tunnels, wells, vaults, and basements. With environmental considerations in the past several years, we have found that the underground storage of flammable liquids was not the most environmentally sound. It was found that the lifetime of steel storage tanks underground was not as long as anticipated, even with corrosion prevention equipment.

Underground tanks have been failing and causing contamination of the soil and groundwater at an alarming rate. Depending upon conditions, some steel tanks have failed in as little as 2 years. Leaks of underground tanks are usually not discovered or reported until there is a substantial product loss or visible surface contamination has occurred. Environmental damage that results from leaking underground storage tanks is difficult to assess and expensive to remedy. Underground is still the safest place to store flammable liquids but, with the necessary environmental safeguards, it is becoming a more costly method of storage.

Recent legislation requires the installation of positive leak detection systems in most underground storage installations, including the tank and associated piping systems.

Underground Tanks.   Different types of tank systems are available to overcome the corrosive effects of the soil and to provide a safer storage system. Tanks can be placed in underground, concrete-lined vaults to keep them away from the soil. This method also allows visual inspection of the tank for leaks and containment of any leaks or overfill that does occur. Depending upon the installation, a vault may present confined space hazards for personnel who may enter for inspections. Additionally, leakage or spills of flammable liquids may result in a fire or explosion hazard in the vault.

Other types of tanks and piping that overcome the corrosion problems include fiberglass, stainless steel, and steel-coated with fiberglass-reinforced polyester (FRP).

Leak Detection. There are various methods of determining if underground storage tanks are leaking, including inventory control, pressure testing, tank integrity testing, and monitoring equipment. Any loss detected at greater than 0.05 gal/hr is considered a leaking tank.

Inventory control is probably the least expensive, but it is also the least accurate of the detection methods. Inventory control requires the daily measurement of product levels and comparing this data to usage amounts. This method is inaccurate because of variation in the measurements caused by temperature fluctuations.

Pressure testing of underground tanks is not a satisfactory method because it is unsafe, and it may not indicate a leak that is below the surface of the liquid. Excessive test pressures have caused ruptures of the tank or piping and have forced liquid out through normal openings. If a leak is below the surface of the liquid in a tank, even a substantial leak may not cause a significant pressure drop during the test to indicate a leak. Leak detection devices are probably the most accurate method of continuously monitoring underground tanks. These include electronic sensor equipment that is placed in monitoring wells that are strategically placed around the tank and associated piping. These sensors monitor product vapors in the soil that result from a leaking tank. Electronic sensors can also be used between the walls of double-walled tanks and piping.

Bulk Plants

Bulk plants, or terminals consist of large storage tanks that receive, store, and blend liquids in bulk for subsequent redistribution via tank vessel, pipeline, tank car, or tank truck. The area of the bulk plant where trucks, cars, or vessels are filled are called loading racks. These operations have a severe static problem because of the high volume of liquids that are transferred from one vessel to another. Static is created as the liquid flows through pipes and hoses, and the rate of static buildup is related to the flow rate. When top-loading a vessel, it is important to keep the fill-spout below the level of the liquid. Preferably, the fill-spout should extend to the bottom of the vessel. Probably the most important safeguard during fill operations is proper bonding and grounding of the vessel and associated fill systems. Attaching bond and ground connections should be the first activity of any fill operation and detaching the connections should be the last activity upon completion of the operation.

Bulk plants also need a method to handle spills including dikes and proper sloping of the loading area away from the rack and vehicle to carry spilled product to a safer area.

Switch Loading. Switch loading is a dangerous practice that is forbidden by most codes. It produces a flammable mixture within the tanks during loading which may not be safeguarded by bonding and grounding. Switch loading is the practice of loading a Class II or III liquid into a tank or vehicle that has previously held a Class I liquid without completely draining and flushing the whole system. For example, if kerosene is loaded into a tank that previously contained gasoline, the residual gas vapors in the tank are concentrated and pass through the flammable range as the tank is filled. As a tank is being filled, static builds up on surface of the liquid and arcs across to the fill spout. If this occurs when the flammable vapors are in the flammable range, ignition will occur. The best safeguard is to dedicate vessels to only one class of liquid so that switch loading does not have to be performed. If switch loading must be performed, the total system must first be drained and flushed. The vessel may also be purged during the loading operation, but this is a costly operation.

SUMMARY

Flammable liquids are those that are capable of forming an ignitable mixture of vapors and air at normal ambient temperatures. The temperature at which a liquid gives off sufficient vapors to form an ignitable mixture is called the flash point. Generally, flammable liquids are those that have a flash point of 100 degrees Fahrenheit or less. Combustible liquids are those that must be heated to the point where they give off sufficient vapors to form an ignitable mixture.

The primary method of preventing flammable liquid hazards in industrial operations is to replace flammable liquids with combustible or noncombustible liquids wherever possible. This activity requires close coordination with health and safety, environmental, and process personnel to ensure that greater hazards are not created and that the resulting liquid is compatible with the industrial process. Where flammable liquids must be used, fire hazards are prevented by avoiding the build up of flammable vapors in the air and by eliminating, to the greatest extent possible, ignition sources. Concentrations of flammable vapors in the air are avoided by containment of the liquids in proper containers and by the provision of exhaust ventilation that takes into account the vapor density of the liquid. The most common sources of ignition in industrial fires are electrical. Where flammable vapors may be present, properly classified and approved electrical equipment must be used. Electrical equipment that meets these requirements may be either ventilated, explosion-proof, or intrinsically safe. Static electricity is another ignition hazard where flammable vapors may be present. During the transfer of flammable liquids from one container to another, the containers must be electrically bonded together and connected to earth ground.

Flammable and combustible liquids can be used safely if their characteristics are understood and incorporated into the procedures and equipment that is used to handle, store, and dispose of them.

BIBLIOGRAPHY

Assessing the Flammability of Aerosols in Warehouses. 1987. *Record* 64(3):4–10.

Best, Richard. 1983. $100 Million Fire in K-Mart Distribution Center. *Fire Journal* 77(2):36–42, 80.

Brodurtha, Frank T. 1980. *Industrial Explosion Prevention and Protection.* New York: McGraw-Hill, Inc.

Cooper, W. Fordham. 1978. *Electrical Safety Engineering.* Boston: Butterworth (Publishers) Inc.

Flammable and Combustible Liquids Code Handbook, 2nd ed. 1984. Quincy: National Fire Protection Association.

How to Handle Flammable Liquids Safely, 1985. Des Plaines: Justrite Manufacturing Company.

Isner, Michael S. 1988. $49 Million Loss in Sherwin-Williams Warehouse Fire. *Fire Journal* 82(2):65–73, 93.

NFPA 30-1987. *Flammable and Combustible Liquids Code.* Quincy, MA: National Fire Protection Association.

NFPA 321-1987. *Standard on Basic Classification of Flammable and Combustible Liquids.* Quincy, MA: National Fire Protection Association.

UL 340. July 30, 1979. Tests for Comparative Flammability of Liquids, Underwriters Laboratories Inc., Northbrook, IL.

Uniform Fire Code, 1985 Edition. Whittier, California: International Conference of Building Officials and Western Fire Chiefs Association.

5
BUILDING FIRE SAFETY

INTRODUCTION

In the past, major fires often burned across whole cities because of poor design, poor city layout, combustible construction, and general lack of understanding of fire prevention methods and fire protection. Some of the major urban fires include the Great New York fire (1935), the Great Chicago fire (1871), the Great Boston fire (1872), the San Francisco fire following the earthquake in 1906, the Baltimore fire (1904), and the Salem, Massachusetts conflagration (1914). These disasters brought about reforms in the existing codes and changes in construction methods and materials, width of streets and separation between buildings, and requirements for the provision of fire suppression systems. These incidents also brought about increases in "fireproof" construction, using concrete and steel. Unfortunately, this "fireproof" construction led to a false sense of security similar to the "unsinkable" Titanic. There was a lack of proper attention to fire prevention and protection. In order to save space and costs, basic life safety requirements were neglected. Sprinkler protection was not considered to be necessary. There was no attention paid to the combustibility of the contents, or fire load, that went into the buildings. Again, there were major fires that proved the fallacy of reliance upon "fireproof" construction such as the New York Parker Building fire in 1908 and Equitable Building fire in 1912.

As populations increased and space became more valuable, the number of high-rise buildings increased, and there was again too much reliance on "fireproof" construction and there were minimal considerations of overall fire-safety. Although the high rises were of noncombustible construction, few people realized the tremendous fire load created by occupant furnishings. There were also inadequate provisions for preventing fires from moving up through the chimney created by the high-rise structure. It was finally being recognized that there was a need for test procedures and standards to quantify the rating of "fire-proof."

As society became more consumer oriented in the late 1950s, large covered structures such as warehouses and shopping malls began to appear. Warehouses have become gigantic to accommodate the vast amount of consumer needs that are supplied through large discount department stores and shopping centers. In some cases, these warehouses have not been built with adequate fire protection for the fire load, or the fire load has changed from when the warehouse was built. The arrangement of flammables and combustibles has not been thought out properly. In the last several years, there have been a number of large warehouse fires including the Ford of Germany parts and accessories depot in Cologne West Germany, K-Mart Distribution Center in Falls Township, Pennsylvania, and the Sherwyn-Williams fire in Dayton, Ohio (see also Chapter 13).

Large shopping malls have grown in the United States in the past 30 years. Shopping malls are large complexes of stores and shops that are all enclosed in one structure. Problems presented by malls include the possibility of fire moving across the mall from one store to another by radiated heat. Store entrances frequently have no doors, just wire or metal grills which, in the event of a fire, allow smoke to spread among stores. Also, there is frequently a common attic, or plenum, through which fire can travel from one store to the next. This was the case in a $2 million fire loss in a shopping mall in Manitowoc, Wisconsin on July 4, 1987. This mall had combustible framing in the attic space above the ceiling level sprinkler system. The attic was not equipped with smoke detectors and the attic space was almost continuous throughout the complex. When fire occurred in an electrically lighted sign, it spread smoke and heat throughout the attic causing damage to most of the 14 retail stores in the mall. Because it is in a concealed space, this kind of a fire is very difficult for fire fighters to find and control; therefore, damage is invariably more extensive.

Codes and Standards

When discussing building firesafety, it is necessary to reemphasize the nature of building and fire codes. It must be remembered that codes are developed through the negotiations of various individuals and organizations who have different interests with regard to the resulting code. The codes that result are minimum requirements. For example, the *Life Safety Code's* purpose is "to establish minimum requirements that will provide a reasonable degree of safety from fire in buildings and structures." How comfortable does this make you feel, to know that you are working in a building that was designed and built to *minimum* requirements to provide a *reasonable* degree of safety? Codes are a reaction to what has happened. For example, after major fires of the past, the codes were changed to require, among other things, fire-resistive construction. It was thought that this would control the fire hazard. But, there was inadequate consideration given to building contents, automatic suppression systems, and other design and construction considerations. Fire-resistive construction may protect against structural collapse and may provide fire containment, but it will not provide smoke containment, life safety, or prevent property damage. Remember, noncombustible construction does not necessarily mean firesafe construction!

In 1973, The National Commission on Fire Prevention and Control concluded a 2-year study on the fire loss situation in America. The commission found, and reported in *America Burning*, upon the wide diversity and variability of codes and standards in the United States. These codes and standards, which are developed as models by various organizations, are not law until they are adopted, in whole or in part, by state or local jurisdictions. Therefore, different cities have adopted different codes and standards and different editions resulting in a wide disparity between jurisdictions. In order to win low-bid competitions, architects and builders generally submit bids based upon meeting the minimum code requirements. Consequently, many buildings are designed and built to minimum requirements, which are minimum standards to begin with! The commission recommended, in this regard, the following:

That all local governments have in force an adequate building code and fire prevention code or adopt whichever they lack.

That local governments provide competent inspector personnel, provide training for the inspector personnel, and require adequate coordination between the personnel involved with enforcing the building codes those involved with enforcing and the fire prevention codes.

That all model codes require smoke detection devices in all dwelling units, high-rise buildings, and all buildings where many people congregate. Model codes should also require that automatic fire extinguishing systems be installed in all high-rise buildings and all other buildings where many people congregate.

BUILDING FIRE HAZARDS

The fire hazards that must be considered in building design and construction include the thermal and nonthermal effects of fire. Thermal effects are produced by flame that produces radiant energy and convected and conducted heat. Thermal energy contributes to fire spread, damage to property, and injuries to personnel. Heat of fires results in about 25 percent of all of the fire deaths and many injuries that occur every year. Burns are one of the most traumatic injuries that people can endure.

Nonthermal effects are produced by smoke and the fire gases. Smoke can obscure the fire, making it difficult for fire fighters to find and initiate effective suppression activities. Smoke can also spread throughout a building, far from the fire where it can cause damage, obscure vision, make breathing difficult, cause injury to occupants, and contribute to feelings of panic. The majority of the deaths that occur as a result of fire are from the inhalation of the toxic gases that are produced.

Property is also affected by the nonthermal actions of fire. Many of the fire gases that are produced are corrosive and can damage contents, particularly electronics and communications equipment, within the building. Unburned fire gases, many of which are flammable, are carried throughout the building by convection currents. When not properly vented, they may reach a source of ignition and spread the fire.

OBJECTIVES OF FIRESAFE CONSTRUCTION AND DESIGN

It is the objective of firesafe construction and design to provide a building that is safe for people and property. The most important part of this objective for the firesafety professional is the safety of the occupants, or life safety. The building must resist ignition, and when ignition of the building and/or its contents does occur, the building must resist spread of the fire and the production of toxic products of combustion. Firesafety must be designed and built into each building. It must be a prime consideration from the first conceptual design to the last bit of construction prior to occupancy. The property owner is primarily concerned with property protection and continuity of operations. It is the duty of firesafety professionals to raise the level of awareness of the building owner of the need for design and construction considerations that achieve optimum safety for the building occupants and the fire fighters who may be called upon to enter the burning building. The building designer's top priorities include functionality, cost-effectiveness, timeliness, aesthetic appeal, and compliance with building and safety codes. It is unfortunate that code compliance is frequently the last of these priorities. It is up to the firesafety professional to elevate the level of importance of achieving more than code compliance.

To begin with, the firesafety professional will have to help the designer to determine who will occupy the building and what the occupants will be doing. For example, a hospital will differ in design and construction requirements from an office building; a warehouse will have different requirements from a manufacturing facility. The designer must know what the occupants will be doing while they are in the building. In a residential occupancy such as a hotel or apartment building, extra life safety considerations must be included. This has been demonstrated by the tragic experiences of the high fatality rates that occur in fires in these structures. The activity being conducted within the building is an important firesafety consideration for the designer. Special hazards involved with the occupancy such as hazardous laboratory or manufacturing operations must be identified and adequate protection must be incorporated early in the design process. Knowledge of the activity of the occupancy will provide the designer with an indication of the expected fire load, the combustible contents per unit floor area, which is usually given in terms of British thermal units per square foot (Btu/ft^2). The term fire load is commonly used to express the amount of combustibles in an occupancy.

In accomplishing this firesafe environment, property protection will also be achieved and continuity of operations will be ensured.

The prime considerations in firesafe construction and design are to achieve fire resistance, fire control, smoke and toxic gas control, and simplified fire fighting. Unfortunately, these optimum safety requirements cost more and are easily compromised during negotiations in the design phase of a structure. All too frequently, design requirements and economic considerations are placed before safety during design and construction. The only real protection is in the codes which, as has been pointed out, are minimum requirements and are never current with latest experience and state-of-the-art equipment.

Fire Resistance In Construction

After many years of unfortunate experience, the term fireproof construction has been replaced by fire-resistant construction. It is finally understood that there is no such thing as fireproof construction, only construction that resists the effects of fire.

Fire resistance refers to the ability of a building's structure and components to resist the effects of heat and flame. Fire-resistant construction includes considerations of ease of ignition and flame spread ratings of the building structure and interior including the walls, ceilings, columns, and floors. The flame spread rating is an index for a material of the rate at which fire will spread from the point of ignition to involve an ever-increasing area of combustible material. It can be considered as an advancing ignition front in which the leading edge of the flame acts as the ignition source. Flame spread in an upward direction will usually be rapid as convected heat accelerates burning by preheating fuel above the flames. Horizontal flame spread is less rapid because of heat being convected away from unburned material. Most of the heat that results in horizontal flame spread is due to conducted and radiated heat.

In addition to utilizing building structural materials and components that resist ignition and flame spread, fire-resistive construction also includes protection of the heat-susceptible structures of the building such as structural steel.

Building Materials and Construction

In Chapter 3, the various fire tests that are available to rate the fire safety of materials and the availability of test data were discussed. It was noted that it is important to ensure that the test that is cited for a certain material be compatible with and reflect the use to which the material is to be put. During considerations of building materials and construction it is necessary that applicable tests be reviewed. Again, it is important that tests are appropriate to the use or desired charateristics of the material or device.

The primary concerns with construction materials and building contents include such things as ignitability of the material, fuel contribution, flame spread, smoke contribution, and structural integrity. This information will help to predict the way a building fire will develop and spread.

Two important documents, in this regard, are the Underwriters Laboratories *Fire Resistance Directory* which provides hourly ratings for beams, columns, floors, roofs, walls, and partitions and the *Building Materials Directory* which contains listings and classifications for various building materials.

Fire-Resistance Directory. The UL *Fire-Resistance Directory* provides hourly ratings for beams, columns, floors, roofs, walls, and partitions. Designs for these structures which have been tested in accordance with E119 *Standard for Fire Tests of Building Construction Materials* are also contained in the directory. It also contains the names of companies that have qualified to use the ''Classification Marking'' of Underwriters Laboratories Inc. in connection with products or materials that have been found acceptable for use in the *Fire Resistance Directory.*

Building Materials Directory. The UL *Building Materials Directory* contains listings and classifications for various building materials that have been found to be in compliance with UL's requirements. These materials, and the companies that submitted them are qualified to use the Listing Mark or Classification Marking of Underwriters Laboratories Inc.

Structural Materials

Building structural materials must be able to support their structural loads during a fire. Structural failure, which can add to fire spread by eliminating barriers to the fire, can also result in building collapse and increased damage and can cause injuries to fire fighters. The primary building structural materials that are used, including wood, steel, and concrete, will be discussed here.

Wood. The size, shape, and moisture content of wood is important in determining its degree of fire hazard. As discussed in Chapter 3, heavy timber is a good structural material because it will withstand fire. When wood timbers burn

Figure 5-1. The familiar Underwriters Laboratories, Inc. logo which appears on listed products. (This material is reproduced, with permission, from Underwriters Laboratories Inc.'s Standard for Safety UL 340—"Tests for Comparative Flammability of Liquids," Copyright 1979 by Underwriters Laboratories Inc. Copies may be purchased from Underwriters Laboratories Inc. Publication Stock, 333 Pfingsten Road, Northbrook, Illinois 60062-2096.)

or are exposed to heat, a char is formed which has even better insulation properties than the wood. This insulation slows the thermal degradation of the wood and helps it to maintain its strength longer. Unfortunately, wood structures are normally held together using steel nails, bolts, plates, and hangers. These materials are particularly susceptible to heat from a fire and will lead to the early collapse of wood structural members. When a wood structure fails, it is liable to fail quickly, with little warning to fire fighters.

While wood structures may resist collapse longer when exposed to fire, this fact is of no use to fire fighters when the fire is in the concealed space above a suspended ceiling. In this situation, the structure can be weakened and collapse with little warning because the signs of stress are hidden from fire fighters. Additionally, the building occupant may have increased the fire hazard in this area by storing combustibles in the concealed space.

An example of this situation occurred in July 1988. Five fire fighters were killed while fighting a fire in an automobile dealership in Hackensack, New Jersey. The fire fighters were killed when the building's wood bowstring truss roof suddenly collapsed. Unknown to the fire fighters, the attic space of this structure had been used for storage of combustibles. The fire in this unprotected space burned for quite some time prior to discovery. With the high fuel load in the attic, the wood trusses burned through and part of the roof collapsed on the fire fighters with no warning.

The only real protection for wood structures is automatic sprinklers with particular attention to protecting all of the concealed spaces.

Steel. Steel is an excellent structural material, it is strong, relatively inexpensive, and it is noncombustible. Unfortunately, steel has three characteristics that are of concern under fire conditions including its loss of strength when heated, its coefficient of expansion, and its heat conducting characteristics.

Steel loses its strength rapidly when exposed to even modest fire temperatures. Above about 600 degrees Fahrenheit, mild steel loses its strength. The critical temperature for steel is about 1100 degrees Fahrenheit, a temperature which is easily achieved in most fires.

At this temperature steel will lose about 40 percent of its strength. Unprotected steel buildings will collapse rather quickly when exposed to fire.

Another important property of steel is its expansion when heated. At 1000 degrees Fahrenheit, steel will expand about $4\frac{1}{2}$ inches for every 50 feet of length. Expanding steel will result in distortion and collapse of walls. For these reasons, structural steel must be adequately insulated. Where structural steel is exposed, it should be protected with automatic sprinklers. Steel that is not adequately protected will fail earlier in the fire scenario and cause greater damage through building collapse and destruction of sprinkler piping (Figure 5-2).

The third characteristic is that steel is such a good conductor of thermal energy. Heat that is transmitted through steel can ignite combustible materials that

Figure 5-2. The characteristic distortion of collapsed steel beams and columns follow-ing roof collapse during a warehouse fire. (Source: Factory Mutual Engineering Corpo-ration)

are otherwise unexposed to fire, such as steel deck roof insulation and the con-tents of tanks and bins.

Concrete. Concrete is noncombustible and generally resists fire fairly well. But, like any other noncombustible material, concrete can be damaged by fire if it is exposed to enough heat for a sufficient amount of time. Spalling can occur when moisture within the concrete expands and causes cracks or chunks of the concrete to break off. Spalling can also occur due to thermal expansion of the outer surface in concrete under compression as in columns, walls, or prestressed structural members.

Reinforced and prestressed concrete has good fire-resistive qualities. Rein-forced concrete is reinforced with steel, usually rods that form a skeleton within the concrete. Concrete alone is strong only under compression loads. Steel pro-vides the tensile strength that concrete lacks. Both components must react to-gether under load. When one fails, the structure will fail. When fire causes spalling of the concrete, the reinforcing steel may be exposed, and the heated steel will lose its strength. The steel in prestressed concrete will lose approxi-mately 20 percent of its strength at 600 degrees Fahrenheit and it does not regain this strength when it is cooled.

In an April 14, 1989 Chicago fire, a seven-story industrial building suffered severe structural damage from burning tires. The fire originated in an adjacent combustible one-story warehouse which was used for the storage of old tires. Tires were also outside and throughout the first floor of the seven-story building. The fire involved the entire tire warehouse and quickly communicated to the first floor of the industrial building. The burning tires resulted in an intense fire that burned for several hours. The fire generated enough heat to cause failure in massive interior reinforced concrete columns. Spalling of the concrete exposed the steel reinforcing bars which resulted in the structural failure of the concrete floor slabs over the fire and progressive failure of the columns and floor slabs on the upper floors. After the fire, it was discovered that floors in the entire structure had either collapsed or sagged several feet.

Building Interior Materials

Many different materials go into the interior of the building which may either add to the fire problem or add to the fire resistiveness of the structure. Various forms of wood from paneling to wood-work to furniture may be incorporated. Wood, as a fire hazard, has been adequately covered in the previous section of this chapter and in Chapter 3.

Plastics are another group of materials that are increasingly used as building interior materials. They are lower in cost, light weight, and they have various aesthetic characteristics. However, they are very combustible. The fire hazards of plastics were adequately covered in Chapter 3.

Other building interior materials include glass, gypsum, and masonry.

Glass. Glass in windows, doors, and so on provides little resistance to fire. Not only does glass transmit radiated heat, but it will rapidly crack and break when exposed to the heat of a fire. Wired glass is somewhat more resistive and is required in windows that have a fire-exposure rating. Fire doors of $1\frac{1}{2}$-hour rating may have a glass window provided it is wired glass with less than 100 square inches in surface area.

The early failure of a glass partition was a factor in the spread of fire in the DuPont Plaza Hotel fire in San Juan, Puerto Rico on December 31, 1986. This fire started in a ballroom in combustible packaging materials including wood, cardboard, and foam plastics and spread through stored furniture, combustible wall coverings and ceiling, and a combustible partition. When flashover occurred in the ballroom a glass partition that separated the ballroom from the foyer failed, allowing superheated gas and smoke out into the foyer where more glass partitions failed, allowing the fire to spread into the lobby and casino areas.

Fiberglass is commonly used in most buildings as an insulation material and as fiberglass-reinforced plastic building products. Fiberglass does not burn and is an excellent insulator. Although the fiberglass is not combustible, when it is coated with a combustible resin binder, the final product is combustible.

Gypsum. Gypsum, also known as plaster, plasterboard, or drywall, has excellent fire-resistive properties. Gypsum contains chemically combined water. When it is heated, this water is released as steam, a process that absorbs a tremendous amount of heat energy.

Masonry. Masonry materials such as brick, tile, and sometimes concrete provide good resistance to heat and usually retain their integrity. There are a number of factors that makes the integrity of masonry structures questionable including the age and quality of the brick, the structural support provided, and the way the wall is used. The internal building structure will have an effect upon the masonry wall. Wood timbers will provide some support during a fire and unprotected steel will accelerate collapse of masonry structures.

A fire chief and three civilians were killed in a February 11, 1988 fire in Georgia when a brick wall fell on them. They were fighting a fire in a vacant warehouse of heavy-timber construction when the 20- to 30-foot-high wall collapsed.

FIRE CONTROL CONSTRUCTION

Fire control, or containment, is achieved through construction that resists the transmission of heat, smoke, and combustible gases to combustible materials outside the room or area of fire origin. Fire control construction is accomplished with fire barriers which are intended to restrict the spread of fire and subsequent damage. Fire barriers include walls, floors, and doors that are designed to meet fire-resistive specifications so as to provide varying duration of resistance to fire. Besides providing fire resistance, fire barriers must have structural stability so as to withstand collapse of ajoining fire areas.

By restricting the fire, fire barriers also help to control the number of sprinklers that operate on one floor. When too many sprinklers open in a large open area, water supplies can be depleted to the point where there is inadequate waterflow for the crucial sprinklers directly over the fire.

Fire control construction also includes the provision of automatic fire suppression equipment such as automatic sprinkler systems.

The greatest hazard to the integrity of fire barriers are openings. When not adequately protected, openings in fire walls for doors, windows, and conveyors, and penetrations for pipes and cables can negate the benefits of the fire wall. Usually, buildings are constructed with adequate fire barriers to provide protection for the contents and occupants. However, subsequent occupant modifications and remodeling can take place without adequate consideration for maintaining the integrity of the fire barrier. Penetrations through fire barriers must

Figure 5-3. Hazards of fire fighting near walls of questionable stability. All fire fighters escaped when this wall collapsed during a June 26, 1984, Los Angeles fire. (Photo: Al Simmons)

be avoided wherever possible. When penetrations must occur, they must be filled with a material capable of maintaining the fire resistance of the barrier, or protected by an approved device designed for that purpose. There are numerous kinds of firestop materials on the market for sealing the penetrations through fire walls and floors. They include putty, caulk, mortar, and bags of compound that expand when exposed to heat to seal an opening. As with other firesafety products, these materials should have appropriate approvals by local authorities or recognized fire protection laboratories.

The fact that the fire was not contained to the floor of fire origin was a significant factor in the May 4, 1988 fire in the 62-story First Interstate Bank Building in Los Angeles. This fire began on the twelfth floor, and before the night was over, it had consumed combustibles on the thirteenth, fourteenth, and fifteenth floor. The rapid vertical spread of the fire was facilitated by the glass curtain wall which allowed flames to extend externally and ignite combustibles through the windows on the floors above. Fire also spread through the 3-inch void that existed between the floor slab and the curtain wall of the building.

Compartmentation

Compartmentation is a method of confining a fire to the room or the area where the fire originated. It is an especially important concept in high-rise buildings when one considers that fire department efficiency decreases rapidly as a fire propagates vertically. Compartmentation will also help to contain the fire to a smaller area for a longer period of time, allowing occupants in the rest of the

Figure 5-4. On May 4, 1988, fire burned through four floors of the 62-story First Interstate Bank Building in Los Angeles. (Photo: Mike Mullen)

structure time to evacuate and fire fighters time to get to the fire before it is too big.

The goal of compartmentation is generally to segregate a space containing a higher hazard occupancy from the rest of the building. Examples of higher hazard occupancies that might be found within a building would include mechanical equipment rooms, trash rooms, restaurant kitchens, laboratories, and maintenance areas. Another goal is to protect the occupants of one space within the building from a fire in another space over which they have no control.

Compartmentation is accomplished by the provision of structurally sound and fire-resistive walls (fire walls), ceilings, and floors; the protection of all floor and wall openings; and the protection of all higher hazard areas.

It must be remembered that compartmentation is only as strong as the weakest link. One unprotected wall penetration or door with a malfunctioning closer can defeat the whole system and allow the fire to spread.

Compartmentalization was credited with confining a fire to the room of fire origin in an unsprinkled 11-story hotel in Tennessee. The 1988 fire, which occurred in a penthouse suite, was caused by an improperly discarded cigarette.

Fire Walls

The term fire wall is a loosely used term for a fire barrier wall. It may provide 2 to 4 hours of fire resistance. A true fire wall provides the required fire resistance and has no penetrations that are not adequately protected. A fire wall must extend from the basement and through the roof. It should extend above the roof to form a parapet. What some people refer to as a fire wall because it is a rated wall is really a fire partition. A fire partition separates fire areas within the building or floor of a building. A fire partition must extend from true floor to true ceiling.

A fire wall must be able to maintain its structural integrity if the walls and roof on one side collapse. It is too easy to assume that when a fire wall is present, an area is adequately contained. If there are any breaches or unprotected openings in the fire wall, its benefits will be negated. A fire is like water in a leaky bucket. It will find the holes and weaknesses and spread beyond the barrier.

American Society of Testing and Materials (ASTM) E 119 provides test methods for measuring the performance of walls, floors, and other building members under fire-exposure conditions. For various wall assemblies, the test standard evaluates the transmission of heat and hot gases, and load-carrying ability during the test exposure.

The K Mart Distribution Center in Falls Township, Pennsylvania was divided into four sections by fire walls that were not free standing and were not designed to maintain their stability in a fire. Additionally, some of the openings were not protected by fire doors, but they were protected by a deluge water curtain. The deluge water curtains were designed to provide 3.0 gpm for every linear foot of opening. When fire occurred in this warehouse on June 21, 1982, exploding and rocketing aerosol containers accelerated the spread of the fire through the openings and into other sections of the building. Even with functioning sprinkler systems and the quick response of the fire department, the inadequately protected openings and the early failure of the fire walls led to an uncontrollable fire. The 1.2 million ft² warehouse was totally destroyed for a loss of about $100 million dollars.

Maximum Foreseeable Loss Fire Walls

A Maximum Forseeable Loss (MFL) is an insurance industry term for the largest loss that may be expected from a single fire to a particular property. This term assumes the impairment of fire protection systems. When it is determined that the MFL is excessive, MFL fire walls may be used to subdivide the property to limit horizontal spread of fire. Normal applications would include situations where a very large building must be subdivided or where two buildings adjoin or are so close that they present an unacceptable exposure to one another. MFL fire walls normally must have a 4-hour fire-resistance rating, and they must be designed to maintain structural stability as well as fire resistance. There are four types of MFL fire walls that are named according to the way that they achieve their stability. They are the cantilever, tied, one-way, and double MFL fire walls.

Cantilever Fire Walls

These are fire walls that are entirely self-supporting without any ties to adjacent framing. Cantilever walls are built in the expansion joint in the framing, but they are not fastened to the building framing on either side.

Tied Fire Walls. These are fire walls in steel frame buildings that are tied into the building structure so that forces of collapse caused by the heating of the steel on one side are resisted by the unheated steel framing on the other side.

One-Way Fire Walls. These are fire walls that are tied to the steel frame on one side only. They are entirely independent of the frame on the other side. This type of wall is only effective when the fire is on the side that is not providing structural support.

Double Fire Walls. These are fire walls consisting of two one-way walls back to back. This method is useful when a building is constructed adjacent to an existing structure. Each building must have a one-way fire wall facing the other. Although each of these walls is required to have only a 3-hour rating, this is still a more expensive method.

Fire Doors

Fire doors are designed to protect the openings that are sometimes necessary in fire walls. As specified in NFPA 80, *Standard for Fire Doors and Windows*, fire doors are intended to restrict the spread of fire and smoke within buildings, whether from fire within or external. Fire doors must include arrangements for automatic operation in case of fire. Even with the provision of protection that is specified in NFPA 80, walls with openings have a lesser fire resistance than the intact wall. Fire doors are designed to protect the opening under normal conditions of use, with a clear space on either side of the opening. Poor housekeeping can result in obstructions that prevent the door from closing properly or combustibles that are stored too close to the opening, causing an excessive heat exposure in the event of a fire.

Fire doors are available in various ratings from 1/2 hour to 3 hours. They must be selected to have a rating that is appropriate to the wall that is being protected. Usually, a 3-hour fire door is used to protect a 3 or 4-hour rated wall, a $1\frac{1}{2}$-hour door to protect a 2-hour wall, and so on.

To keep fire and smoke from spreading, doors must be kept closed. Fire doors must be self-closing and the area around them must be maintained so that the door can swing freely and close completely. When it is necessary for a fire door to be kept open, smoke or heat-activated door closers should be incorporated to function when there is a fire.

The rating of fire doors is based upon the ASTM E 152 standard. While fire walls that are tested to ASTM E 119 are required to retard heat transfer through the wall, there is no such requirement for the testing of fire doors. ASTM E 152 does not evaluate the degree of control of the passage of smoke, heat, or other products of combustion through the door assembly. It is, therefore, important to maintain good housekeeping in the area of fire doors since radiated heat from a fire in the adjoining area could ignite combustibles that are placed too near the door.

The ASTM E 152 test methods provide for the exposure of a complete door assembly, including hardware and mounting fixtures, to a standard fire exposure for a specified period of time followed by the application of a specified standard fire hose stream. It is important to note that the hardware and mounting fixtures are tested with the door as a complete unit. It would not make sense to have an opening protected by a fire door when the fire could penetrate through the frame assembly, or if the hardware failed and allowed the door to open during the fire. It is also important to ensure that all components of the assembly are included when installing the door.

Fire doors are rated either by a letter which designates the opening protected, or by the hourly rating designation. NFPA #80, *Standard for Fire Doors and Windows,* refers to openings as Class A, B, C, D, and E according to the type and location of the wall. The following paragraphs provide the hourly rating of doors, the opening classification, and the types of locations that they are intended to protect:

A 3-hour fire-resistance rating is in a Class A opening. This is the highest rating for a door, and it is used in walls separating buildings or dividing a building into different fire areas. A 3-hour door is used to protect openings in 4-hour fire walls. In this application, two doors may be required, one on each side of the opening. The value of protecting openings in firewalls with two fire doors can be seen in Figure 5-5.

A $1\frac{1}{2}$-hour fire-resistance rating is in a Class B opening which is in 2-hour enclosures of vertical openings such as stairways and elevators. A 1-hour rated door may be used in this class if the vertical enclosure is rated at 1 hour.

A $\frac{3}{4}$-hour fire resistance rating is in a Class C opening which is in corridor and room partitions. They are for use with 1 hour corridor partitions.

Figure 5-5. The value of protecting a firewall opening with two fire doors. The building in the foreground was destroyed by fire. The adjacent building was saved even though the horizontal sliding fire doors on the near side of the wall failed to close. The fire doors on the far side of the wall closed and saved the building. (Source: Factory Mutual Engineering Corporation)

A $1\frac{1}{2}$-hour fire-resistance rating is in a Class D opening which is in exterior walls when the wall is only required to have a 2 hour rating.

A $\frac{3}{4}$-hour fire-resistance rating is in a Class E opening which is in an exterior wall that is only exposed to a moderate or light fire exposure.

There are basically four types of fire doors, swinging, horizontal and vertical sliding, and rolling steel (Figure 5-6). Swinging doors are the most common and need no description. They may be equipped with a closing device which causes the door to close and latch.

Horizontal and vertical sliding doors move horizontally or vertically on tracks and are provided with a counterweight. They are normally in the open position, and they protect large openings. They slide closed automatically when triggered by a detection device such as a fusible link or smoke detector. Rolling steel doors may be normally open in a housing located above the opening or they may be operated by hand, crank, or electric power. They close automatically during a fire when a fusible link releases a counterbalance allowing the doors to close by gravity.

Automatically operating fire doors must be tested periodically to ensure that they work properly. They are subject to malfunction for a number of reasons

Figure 5-6. A double fire door arrangement protecting an opening in a warehouse fire-wall. In front is a rolling steel door, on the other side is a horizontal sliding door. (Source: Factory Mutual Engineering Corporation)

including improper tension on springs, cables snagged in guides or on pulleys, bent or misaligned guides, inadequate lubrication, and dirt. Periodic maintenance is required to inspect for deficiencies that might cause malfunctions and to clean and lubricate moving parts. Then, the doors should be operationally tested at least once per year.

As in all other aspects of safety and fire prevention, housekeeping is important in the area around fire doors. Personnel frequently block doors open by piling boxes, crates or pallets in the doorway. The floor area around doorways should be striped and employees instructed not to place materials in the striped area. Combustible material that is stored too close to a closed fire door may be ignited should a fire occur on the other side. Therefore, storage practices should be carefully monitored.

It is important to note that although an exit door may be a fire rated door, not all fire doors are exit doors. Obviously, a rollup or sliding door would not allow free passage of personnel in an emergency. Only swinging type doors, which meet certain other requirements, may be used as exit doors. Exits will be discussed in more detail in Chapter 6, Life Safety.

CONTROL OF SMOKE AND FIRE GASES

The design and construction of buildings must incorporate methods to control the movement of smoke and gases or vent them away from exiting occupants. Smoke and gases must be controlled for life safety reasons, to limit fire spread, and for property protection. The most important reasons to control the movement of smoke and gases in a fire are as follows: for life safety by diverting smoke and toxic gases, to remove smoke and heat which will make it easier for fire fighters to advance, to control spread or direction of the fire, and to release unburned combustible gases before they acquire a flammable mixture.

It is known from experience that smoke and toxic gases are produced in great quantities in most fires and are responsible for most of the fire deaths. In many cases, people are killed by toxic gases far from the fire that produced them. A tragic example was the MGM Grand Hotel fire in Las Vegas on November 21, 1980. Although this fire occurred on the first floor, 61 of the 85 fatalities occurred on the sixteenth through the twenty-sixth floor. These people all died of asphyxiation secondary to carbon monoxide inhalation.

Many of the gases that are produced in a fire are flammable and are carried by convection currents to uninvolved areas where they contribute to the spread of fire. Therefore, the building must be designed and constructed to control the movement of smoke and gases to the greatest extent possible, particularly into means of egress, exit passageways, or other similar areas. This is accomplished through heating, ventilating, and air conditioning (HVAC) controls and through the protection of all openings in the building.

Besides the life safety aspects of smoke and toxic gas control, there are also considerations of damage to property and equipment. Smoke and fire gases are very corrosive and can result in severe damage to electronic equipment. In 1988, a small but very smoky fire occurred in a piece of equipment in a Carlsbad, California electronics manufacturing plant. Although the fire never progressed beyond the point of origin, smoke spread throughout the facility and caused almost $2 million damage, almost half of which was due to smoke.

Smoke behaves differently in high-rise buildings. In buildings with only a few stories, the influence of the fire's heat and convection air currents dictates the movement of smoke. In tall buildings, the movement of smoke and gases is affected more by the natural air movement in the building known as the stack effect. Also influencing the movement of smoke in the tall building are the expansion of gases due to temperature and influences of external wind forces. Smoke control and ventilation in all high-rise buildings are effected by pressure differentials which may vary from side to side and top to bottom. Smoke creates greater problems for escaping occupants and fire fighters than heat.

Stack Effect

In order to conserve energy, most modern high-rises are built tight, or with very few openings to the outside. Lacking the exterior venting, the movement of smoke and gases during a fire will be controlled by the normal air currents within the building. These air currents in the high-rise building produce what is known as the stack effect. The stack effect is characterized by a flow of air from the bottom to the top of the building. This occurs when the air inside the building is warmer than the outside air. When the outside temperatures are warmer than inside, the reverse will be true. The strength of this flow is affected by a number of factors including the tightness of the building, height of the building, temperature differentials, and wind levels and direction on the outside. There is a point in the building, usually about midway to the top and dependent upon the above conditions, called the neutral pressure plane. This is a point where pressure inside the building equals pressure on the outside. Below the neutral pressure plane the building pressure is less than outside and the predominant air flow is into the building. Above the neutral pressure plane the building pressure is greater and the predominant airflow is outward.

The smoke from a fire occurring on a lower floor of a building when the neutral plane is in the middle, will move up through any vertical openings and, unless vented, will collect on the upper floors. This is what occurred during the fire in the ground floor casino of the MGM Grand Hotel. On the morning of November 21, 1980, the temperature in Las Vegas was around 40 degrees Fahrenheit. In this situation, when outside temperatures are cooler, a normal stack effect is produced with the neutral pressure plane in the center of the building. Smoke and gases moved up through the 23-story hotel tower where 61 people died of asphyxiation secondary to carbon monoxide inhalation.

When fire occurs on a lower floor and there is exhaust ventilation from the top of the high-rise building, the neutral pressure plane will be raised and smoke accumulation on the upper floors should be lessened. When ventilation is provided at the fire floor or in a lower portion of the building, conditions will worsen. In this case the neutral pressure plane is lowered and smoke will accumulate on lower floors in addition to that which rises to the upper floors.

Wind Effects.   Basically, the windward wall has inward pressure and the leeward wall has outward pressure. Wind flow over the roof will also create a suction or negative pressure on the roof which may affect the movement of smoke.

High-Rise Smoke Control

Provisions for smoke control in the high-rise building must include a vertical shaft with dampers that would open on the fire floor and collect smoke and carry it to the roof. Exhaust fans may be required in the shaft and HVAC on the fire floor would have to be shut off to avoid spreading smoke to other parts of the building. In fact, smoke detectors are required in the HVAC systems of high-rise buildings to cause the system to be shut down in the event of smoke detection. In some cases, HVAC systems can be manually adjusted to help control smoke in a fire; however, most systems do not have the capacity to be the sole form of smoke control and other methods must be employed.

METHODS OF SMOKE AND GAS CONTROL

Methods to control smoke and gases include roof vents, curtain boards, dampers, smokeproof stairtowers, and HVAC system controls. These methods are used to alter the factors that would cause smoke to spread through the building such as stack effect, fire convection air currents, weather conditions, and mechanical air-handling systems. Essential to the control of smoke is proper building design and tight construction.

In a fire situation, smoke and hot gases rise to the ceiling and spread out. Smoke that is not vented rapidly builds up and lowers to the floor. Heat is reflected back down from the smoke layer and can add in establishing flashback conditions. The smoke makes it difficult for people to evacuate the area and difficult for fire fighters to begin effective suppression activities. When construction is not tight, smoke will seep through cracks and openings to other parts of the building and counter any other control methods.

Pressurization

The primary method of controlling smoke movement is by creating air pressure differences between building floors and/or areas. The intent is to create a negative pressure in the area of smoke generation so as to maintain a tenable environment for occupants to escape. Pressurization is difficult to attain, and the concept must be designed and constructed into the building. This means that attention must be paid to minimizing any openings such as cracks, construction joints, closed door gaps, and similar openings. Pressurization concepts must be designed in conjunction with building fire suppression systems.

Fire Suppression Systems.   An automatic sprinkler system is essential to almost all buildings. The sprinkler system and the smoke control system can complement one another. While the sprinkler system will control a fire longer and help to minimize smoke generation, the smoke control system will maintain a tenable environment along egress routes for escaping occupants and attacking fire fighters. Additionally, with a sprinkler system to minimize the size of the fire and the amount of smoke generated, the design requirements for the smoke control system will be lessened.

The smoke control system must be integrated with other systems such as when a gaseous fire suppression system is employed.

HVAC System Components

Some of the means that are available to control heat and smoke in buildings include ducts, fire and smoke dampers, smoke detectors, and active controls.

Ducts.   Ducts are used to distribute air throughout the building. Unfortunately, ducts can also transmit smoke and fire gases. Metal ducts may provide up to 1 hour of protection if the openings are properly protected. Should more than 1 hour of protection be required, fire dampers are necessary.

Fire Damper.   Fire dampers are devices that are tested and listed for use in HVAC ducts to restrict the flow of heat, smoke, and gases through ducts. Fire dampers close automatically when a fusible link device is activated by the heat of the fire. Fire dampers are required in ducts that penetrate or terminate at openings in walls or partitions that are required to have a fire resistant rating of 2 hours or more. When used to protect walls, partitions, or floors with fire resistance ratings of 3 hours or less, they must have a $1\frac{1}{2}$-hour rating.

Smoke Damper.   Smoke dampers are required in HVAC ducts which pass through smoke barrier partitions. They must function automatically upon detection of smoke by smoke detectors which are required to be in the system.

Smoke Detectors.   Smoke detectors are required in the HVAC system of high-rise buildings. They may be used in any building where it is necessary to prevent the movement of smoke and gases through the HVAC system to other parts of the building. They must be located in the main supply ducts, down stream of air filters or cleaners, and in the main return ducts prior to joining fresh air intakes. There are problems however, with air movement and dilution of smoke which make duct-mounted smoke detectors less effective. These problems will be discussed further in Chapter 7.

Controls.   Air distribution systems must have manual controls that are located so that the operation of supply, return, and exhaust can be stopped in an emergency.

Other Smoke Control Devices

Roof Vents.   Large open buildings such as factories and warehouses sometimes incorporate roof vents that open automatically when there is a fire. They are usually activated by heat from the fire. Roof vents are effective in venting smoke, gases, and heat. They may increase the severity of the fire by providing better ventilation. Although each situation must be reviewed separately, it is usually considered that the benefits of smoke vents outweigh the danger of increased fire severity. Vents release smoke and heat, reducing the likelihood of flashover and, particularly in large open buildings, allow fire fighters to approach closer to fight the fire.

The size and spacing of roof vents is dependent upon the anticipated heat release from the combustible materials in the building. Further guidance is provided in NFPA #204, *Guide for Smoke and Heat Venting*.

Curtain Boards.   In large single-story buildings with flat roofs, curtain boards are used to contain the horizontal spread of the smoke and hot gases. Curtain boards are partitions that extend vertically down from the underside of the roof and contain the smoke and gases in smaller areas that are equipped with roof vents.

SIMPLIFIED FIRE FIGHTING

All of the above characteristics, when properly incorporated into the building design and construction, will serve to simplify fire fighting. When life safety considerations are adequate so that the occupants are able to quickly evacuate themselves, the fire fighters will be able to proceed with fire suppression activities sooner. Fire-resistive construction serves to contain the fire and automatic sprinklers reduce the flame spread, making it easier to control when the fire fighters arrive on the scene. And finally, if smoke and gases are controlled, the fire fighters will be able to find the fire faster and will have a better atmosphere for suppression activities.

ELEMENTS OF BUILDING FIRESAFETY

Building firesafety will be achieved by designing for fire prevention, and designing to manage the impact (fire protection) when a fire does occur.

Firesafe planning begins during the early design review process and continues through building occupancy. The fire protection engineer must participate alongside all of the other professionals who are involved in the design effort. Each element must be considered from site planning through fire hazards of the building contents and expected activities of the building occupants. The bottom line of the planning and design effort is to carry out these activities with the idea that fire ignition is going to occur. During design, there are numerous design reviews by various municipal fire and building authorities, insurance representatives, and the owner's representatives. During the construction phase, there are numerous building inspections by these authorities. All of these activities are carried out in accordance with the applicable codes in effect for the jurisdiction. A higher degree of firesafety is possible only if the designer will go beyond the minimum requirements and the owner is willing to fund this additional effort. When this occurs and if everyone has done their job properly, a fire incident will be minor in nature rather than a catastrophe.

There are different phases that take place during the construction of a building including site planning, early design, design development, construction documents, construction, and occupancy. The firesafety professional must be involved in all of these.

Site Planning

Industrial site planning requires the involvement of all members of management and staff. Once a site has been proposed that meets the requirements of the occupancy, it must be evaluated by the staff personnel. One staff area that has required increased scrutiny in recent years is the environmental evaluation of the site.

An area that should receive increased scrutiny during the planning stage is the area of fire protection.

One of the first fire protection considerations in planning for a building is to ensure that the proposed building will fit on the site and still allow access for fire fighters. Some jurisdictions may have restrictions on height of building and type of construction. Ideally, the building would have adequate access on all four sides. The larger the building, the more important is access by fire fighters. Also, the higher the building, the more space that is required for access by aerial extension ladders. The maximum height that most fire departments can achieve via aerial extension ladder is 100 feet, or about the ninth floor of a high-rise building. As building access becomes more restricted, more reliance must be placed upon the internal fire prevention and protection characteristics.

Another consideration in site planning is to evaluate possible fire exposures to the proposed building. Radiant heat from a fire in an adjacent building or a brush fire may create a fire exposure. Where adequate separation is not possible from adverse exposures, exposure sprinklers may be installed to protect the exposed side, a barrier wall may be constructed, and wall openings may be eliminated from the exposed side of the building.

Water supply for fire fighting is another factor that must be evaluated very early in the planning stage. The adequacy of the municipal water supply in terms of size of mains and available pressure as well as the availability of hydrants must be evaluated. Auxiliary water supplies and booster pumps may be necessary on site to supplement and boost the pressure of the municipal supplies. At any rate, these needs must be identified during the site selection phase.

Early Design Phase

During this phase, the specifications for the building are established to include building type, height and area, interior finish, fire-resistance requirements for the structural members, and overall fire protection and life safety provisions. The applicable codes and standards are identified and the specific requirements outlined. Possible building code variances are identified at this time.

It is during this phase that total cost estimates are determined and dollar-saving compromises take place. The designer and owner are trying to hold down the costs, and all too frequently, firesafety provisions are subject to negotiation. This is an important but difficult time for the firesafety professional because the only support available is from the "minimum" code requirements.

Design Development Phase

During this phase, the actual design is taking place. As design proceeds, it becomes increasingly difficult to make changes that were not called out in the original specification document. Negotiations are conducted with building code officials concerning variances.

The firesafety person must stay close to the design effort and participate in design review meetings that take place during this phase.

Construction Documents Phase

During this phase, the designs are finalized and reviews take place by various authorities including the building code officials, insurance fire protection engineers, and the owner's representatives. Negotiations with the building code officials are completed. Final drawings and bid documents are prepared for submittal to contractors who will bid on various aspects of the construction. The firesafety person must review the bid documents for fire protection systems to ensure that firesafety requirements have not been altered and that the bidding contractors will know exactly what is required.

Construction Phase

During construction of the building, numerous site inspections take place by the building code officials, insurance fire protection personnel, and owner's representatives. These inspections are necessary to ensure that construction activities and materials used are as specified.

Final testing of the fire protection, life safety, and alarm systems take place during this phase.

Occupancy

Prior to occupancy, final inspections take place and occupancy permits are issued. But, the duties of the firesafety person do not end here. As the building is occupied, it must be ensured that operations and contents moved in are in accordance with the original plans.

Maintenance and testing programs for the building's fire protection and life safety systems must be established and occupants must be trained in their use.

OTHER BUILDING FIRESAFETY FACTORS

There are other factors to be included in the area of firesafe building design and construction that are covered in other chapters. Buildings must have means of detecting a fire, alerting both the building occupants and the fire department and providing communications for emergencies. These items are addressed in Chapter 7.

Many of the aspects that have been covered in this chapter are intended for life safety and, in fact, are code requirements. In Chapter 6 the subject of life safety will be addressed in greater detail.

Finally, the firesafe building will have provisions for fire suppression which must be considered during design, construction and occupancy. Chapter 9 will cover fire protection equipment and systems.

SUMMARY

The history of firesafe design and construction has progressed from so-called "fireproof" construction to "fire resistive" construction. It has been a difficult lesson, but it is finally understood that there is no such thing as "fireproof" construction. Only "fire-resistive" construction is possible and it does not ensure total protection for life and property. Fire-resistive construction is for the purpose of resisting the effects of the fire that would cause structural failure. Fire-resistive construction is intended to contain, or resist, the spread of fire. Fire-resistive construction does not specifically deal with life safety, smoke containment, or loss of the contents.

To achieve firesafe buildings requires the construction of buildings that incorporate fire resistance, fire control, and smoke and gas control. The achievement of these goals requires the building owner and designer to go beyond the codes and standards which are minimum requirements. It will cost more, in the beginning, to achieve these goals, but savings are possible in terms of life safety, property protection, and continuity of operations.

Fire prevention and protection does not end with the firesafe design and construction of a building, these are just the beginning. Modifications to the building and building support systems such as fire protection systems must be monitored to ensure that firesafety is not degraded. The building occupants and changing occupancies also must be monitored to ensure that the fire load in the building is not increased.

BIBLIOGRAPHY

America Burning. The Report of the National Commission on Fire Prevention and Control. Washington D.C. 1973.

ASTM E 119-88. *Standard Methods for Fire Tests of Building Construction and Materials*. Philadelphia: American Society of Testing and Materials.

ASTM E 152-81a. *Standard Methods of Fire Tests of Door Assemblies*. Philadelphia: American Society of Testing and Materials.

Best, Richard. 1983. Fire Walls that Failed: The K Mart Corporation Distribution Center Fire. *Fire Journal* 82(3):4, 83, 86.

Best, Richard L. 1982. Investigation Report K Mart Corporation Distribution Center Fire Falls Township, PA, June 21, 1982. Quincy: National Fire Protection Association.

Best, Richard, and Demers, David P. 1982. Investigation Report on the MGM Grand Hotel Fire Las Vegas, Nevada, November 21, 1980. Quincy: National Fire Protection Association.

Brannigan, Francis L. 1982. *Building Construction for the Fire Service*, Second ed. Quincy: National Fire Protection Association.

Broehm, K., and Herzog, C. 1988. $2 Million Loss Occurs in Shopping Mall Fire. *Fire Command* 55(8):18–22.

Cook, Brian M. 1986. Fire Doors: Closing the Gap. *Record* 63(5):11–17.

Cote, Arthur, and Bugbee, Percy. 1988. *Principles of Fire Protection*. Quincy: National Fire Protection Association.

Egan, M. David. 1978. *Concepts In Building Firesafety*. Toronto: John Wiley & Sons, Inc.

Fire Protection Handbook, 16th ed. 1986. Quincy: National Fire Protection Association.

Klem, T. J. 1988. The Hackensack Fatalities. *Fire Command* 55(10):27–28, 43–45.

Klem, Thomas J. 1987. *Investigation Report on the DuPont Plaza Hotel Fire*. Quincy: National Fire Protection Association.

Klem, Thomas J. 1989. Los Angeles High-Rise Bank Fire. *Fire Journal* 83(3):72–91.

Loss Prevention Data 1-22. 1985. *Criteria for Maximum Foreseeable Loss Fire Walls and Space Separation.* Norwood: Factory Mutual Engineering Corporation.

NFPA 80-1986. *Standard for Fire Doors and Windows.* Quincy: National Fire Protection Association.

NFPA 90A-1989. *Standard for the Installation of Air Conditioning and Ventilating Systems.* Quincy: National Fire Protection Association.

NFPA 92A-1988. *Recommended Practice for Smoke Control Systems.* Quincy: National Fire Protection Association.

Prendergast, Edward J. 1989. Fire Breaks Down Concrete. *Fire Engineering* 142(9):32–36.

6
LIFE SAFETY

In Chapter 5, Building Fire Safety, the design and construction methods to achieve life safety, property protection, and continuity of operations were discussed. This chapter will deal specifically with the life safety aspects of building and firesafety. The intent here is to insure that when fire or other emergency occurs, that people can quickly and safely exit the building or move to a safe area.

THE LIFE SAFETY CODE

The primary document to be used in life safety considerations is NFPA # 101, the *Life Safety Code*. The Life Safety Code grew out of the Building Exits Code which was first published in 1927 by the National Fire Protection Association. The code provides requirements that have a direct influence on safety to life in both new and existing structures. While the primary concern of the code is life safety, observance of the code requirements will result in ancillary benefits in personnel safety and property conservation. The code does not deal with fire prevention. It deals more with the assumption that a fire or other emergency is going to occur. When fire does occur, provisions must be in place to ensure that occupants receive adequate warning to escape and that there is an adequate escape route which is clearly marked and illuminated and is readily accessible so that the occupants can escape in a reasonable amount of time.

History is full of tragic examples of fires in which Life Safety Code violations have led to loss of life. In many of the historical examples, conditions that existed were to be recognized as contrary to life safety, and they resulted in changes to the Life Safety Code. In many fire deaths, and certainly in multiple death fires, investigations have revealed numerous code violations. Just as other advances in fire protection have resulted from lessons learned from disasters, so have advances and improvements in the Life Safety Code. For example, the Building Exits Code was changed extensively in the 1940s as a result of a number of fatal fires. In 1942, the Cocoanut Grove Night Club fire in Boston claimed 492 lives. Then, in 1946, there were three multiple fatality hotel fires. The LaSalle Hotel fire in Chicago claimed 61 lives, the Canfield Hotel fire in Dubuque claimed 19 lives, and the Winecoff Hotel fire in Atlanta claimed 119 lives.

These disasters prompted increased use and enforcement of the Building Exits Code. However, the Building Exits Code at that time was more of a reference document rather than a code that could be adopted into law. In subsequent editions, the code was re-edited and refined to become the Life Safety Code that exists today. The Life Safety Code is on a three-year revision cycle, with all modifications the result of extensive committee work by various technical subcommittees.

Most of the tragic fires resulting in high loss of life have not been in industrial occupancies. This is probably due to the health and safety laws that have been in existence since the early 1900s, and certainly to the Occupational Safety and Health Act of 1971 which contains numerous life safety provisions. There have, however, been loss of life incidents that resulted from Life Safety Code and OSHA violations in business, office, and industrial occupancies which could have been avoided. It is part of the job of the person charged with firesafety to ensure that these conditions do not develop.

This chapter is not intended to reproduce the Life Safety Code, but merely to highlight it and provide some examples that explain the requirements. The reader who has life/firesafety responsibilities is faced with numerous day-to-day considerations that require a basic understanding of the Life Safety Code provisions. For a more indepth presentation, such as that necessitated for building design and layout, the reader would be well advised to procure a current copy of the code or, better yet, a copy of NFPA's *Life Safety Code Handbook.* The *Handbook* contains the code plus easy-to-read explanations of the various requirements. The code is organized into seven chapters containing general life safety requirements followed by chapters containing modifications pertaining to each occupancy type. The occupancy specific chapters deal with special provisions and requirements that are unique to that occupancy, both for existing and for new construction.

OCCUPANCIES

The term occupancy refers to the use to which the building is to be put. The occupancy designation takes into consideration the activities that will take place in the building and the kinds of occupants who will be the primary occupants of the building. The occupancies that are addressed by the code are similar to occupancy definitions that are used by most building and fire prevention codes. The following are the occupancy designations with some examples:

Assembly. Includes theaters and movies, auditoriums, museums, exhibition halls, gymnasiums, bowling lanes, restaurants, church, dance halls, and bars.

Educational. Includes schools, universities and colleges, nursery schools, and child day care centers.

Health care. Includes hospitals, nursing homes, nurseries, and mentally retarded care institutions.

Penal occupancies. Includes jails, reformatories, and penitentiaries.

Residential. Includes hotels/motels, apartments, dormitories, lodging or rooming houses, and one and two family dwellings.

Mercantile. Includes supermarkets, department stores, shopping centers, and drug stores.

Business. Includes doctors offices, dentist offices, city halls, libraries, clinics, and general offices.

Industrial. Includes factories, laboratories, dry cleaning plants, power plants, pumping stations, laundries, gas plant refineries, and saw mills.

Storage. Includes warehouses, cold storage, freight terminals, bulk oil storage, parking garages, hangars, grain elevators, and barns stables.

GOALS OF THE LIFE SAFETY CODE

Probably the easiest way to understand the scope and provisions of the Life Safety Code is to discuss, in detail, each of the ten goals which appear in Chapter 2 of the code. OSHAct includes these goals as ''fundamental requirements'' under 29 CFR 1910, Subpart E, Means of Egress.

To Provide for Adequate Exits Without Dependence on Any One Safeguard

This statement is the basis of the Life Safety Code. It is to ensure, regardless of the type of occupancy or age of the building, that sufficient exits are provided to allow the prompt escape of the occupants in case of fire or other emergency. As in other firesafety subjects where it is not desirable to rely upon any one safeguard, the code specifies that life safety also should not be reliant upon any one safeguard. The basic requirement of the code is that there be at least two exits located remotely from one another. The remoteness of the exits cannot be overemphasized. This is so that a single fire will not simultaneously block all avenues of escape. The requirement for the number of exits is based upon the occupant load which is based upon the square feet required per occupant in the specific occupancy chapters of the code. These requirements are firm, regardless of other safeguards that are a part of the structure such as fire-resistant construction, sprinklers, alarms, and so on. The occupant load for an industrial occupancy is one person per 100 ft^2 of gross floor area. The requirement for a minimum of two separate exits applies also except for those areas with a total capacity of less than 25 people, located on a ground floor, and with a travel distance of less than 50 feet. High hazard areas must have at least two separate means of egress regardless of the occupancy.

As a comparison, the occupant load for an assembly area or where people are moderately concentrated such as a dining room or conference room is 15 ft^2 net floor area per person. This type of occupancy could very well exist in an industrial occupancy. In an industrial occupancy, the allowable travel distance to an exit may determine the number of exits required; in the assembly occupancy, the number of occupants will determine the number of exits. An assembly occupancy with an occupant load of greater than 1000 people must have at least four separate exits; an occupant load of from 500 to 1000 requires three separate exits; and an occupant load of 50 to 500 requires two separate exits.

In the Beverly Hills Supper Club fire which occurred in Southgate Kentucky on May 28, 1977, there were 2400 to 2800 patrons in the club at the time. This was about twice as many as it was designed to hold. The Cabaret Room was occupied by between 1200 and 1300 people which was about three times the safe occupant load for the floor space in that room. The capacity of the means of egress for the club, and especially the Cabaret Room, was also inadequate. The code requirement for an occupancy greater than 1000 is for four exits. One hundred fifty-nine people died in the Cabaret Room alone in this fire that claimed a total of 165 lives, making this the worst multiple-death building fire in the United States since the Cocoanut Grove night club fire in Boston in 1942.

To Ensure that Construction Is Sufficient to Provide Structural Integrity During a Fire While Occupants Are Exiting

The code requires that exits be enclosed along their entire length to provide protection from fire. This is accomplished through separation or construction that provides a designated level of fire resistance, by using interior finish within the exit which meets the code's requirements concerning flame spread and smoke development, and by maintaining tight control over openings into the exit enclosure which would allow penetration of fire and/or smoke. One of the contributing factors to the high loss of life in the Beverly Hills Supper Club fire was the interior finish of materials that exceeded allowable flame spread ratings. This facilitated the fire's rapid growth.

It is necessary to maintain tight control over openings into exit enclosures. As discussed in Chapter 5, openings are classified according to the expected fire exposure and doors are appropriately rated according to fire resistance as depicted in Table 6-1.

This provision can easily be nullified by the occupants and must be frequently monitored by the person who has the fire/life safety responsibility. In business and industrial occupancies, the occupants frequently store or place combustible materials in exit corridors. In a fire, these combustibles may become involved in the fire and result in a blocked exit path and destruction of the safe exit environment. In a December 13, 1977, fire in a girls' dormitory in Providence, Rhode Island, 10 students were killed when the exit corridor became untenable

Table 6-1. Classification of Wall Openings and Corresponding Door Fire Resistance.

OPENING	DOOR FIRE RESISTANCE (HOURS)
Class A	3
Class B	$1\frac{1}{2}$
Class C	$\frac{3}{4}$
Class D	$1\frac{1}{2}$
Class E	$\frac{3}{4}$

because of the fire. The students had placed combustible Christmas decorations on the walls and a live Christmas tree in the corridor. When the fire spread from the room of origin to the corridor, the decorations allowed the fire to spread throughout the corridor, making exiting impossible.

To Provide Exits That Have Been Designed to the Size, Shape, and Nature of the Occupancy

Not only must there be adequate numbers of exits for the occupants, but they must be appropriately sized. There are specific requirements for the width of exits based upon occupant load, as well as requirements that the size remain the same or enlarge nearer the termination. Also, it is fairly obvious that exits in hospitals and nursing homes, where occupants are confined to beds or wheel chairs must be appropriately sized to allow evacuation of these occupants.

A very basic requirement of the code is that exit doors must swing out, in the direction of travel. This is a fairly obvious requirement, but one that is easily overlooked with potentially tragic consequences. In the Cocoanut Grove fire 100 bodies were found stacked against a door that opened inward. An additional 200 bodies were stacked against a revolving door that had apparently jammed in the main entrance to the club. A more recent example occurred in the December 31, 1986 fire at the DuPont Plaza Hotel in San Juan, Puerto Rico which claimed 97 lives. One of the exit doors leading from the casino opened inward. Of the 97 fatalities, 84 occurred in the casino and the majority of these were in the area of this door.

When exit doors swing into a corridor, they must not obstruct more than half of the corridor. This requirement will prevent the door from interfering with people who are exiting through the corridor.

To provide exits that take into consideration the nature of the occupancy requires consideration of the hazards of the contents of the occupancy. The hazards of contents are defined by the code as low, ordinary, and high hazard contents. Low hazard contents are those of low combustibility in which it is expected that no self-propagating fire could occur. The only probable danger requiring the use of emergency exits in a building with low hazard contents will be from panic, fumes, or smoke, or fire from some external source. It should be noted that there are very few occupancies that can be classified as low hazard. There are very few that do not contain quantities of plastics, foams, wood, and other combustibles. Ordinary hazard contents are those contents that are liable to burn with moderate rapidity or to give off considerable volumes of smoke. In case of a fire in ordinary hazard contents, it is not expected that poisonous gases or explosions would result. Most industrial and office occupancies fall under this classification. High hazard contents are those which are liable to burn with extreme rapidity or from which poisonous gases or explosions are feared in the event of fire (Figure 6-1).

To Ensure That the Exits Are Clear, Unobstructed, and Unlocked

One of the most common code violations in business and industry is the tendency of the occupants to use the space in exit corridors and aisles and in front of exit doors for storage. Safety/fire safety inspections must ensure that these conditions are found and corrected. Training programs must ensure that all occupants are aware of the importance of maintaining clear and unobstructed means of egress.

LOW HAZARD CONTENTS
    Breweries
    Computer Centers (if no combustibles)
    Dairy Plants
    Light Machine Shops
    Meat Packing Plants

ORDINARY HAZARD CONTENTS
    Automobile Assembly Plants
    Computer Centers
    Electronic Assembly Plants
    Leather Goods Manufacturing
    Machine Shops using combustible oils and hydraulic fluids
    Offices

HIGH HAZARD CONTENTS
    Chemical Plants
    General Warehouses
    Grain Storage and Milling
    Painting Shops
    Paper Mills
    Refineries
    Rubber and Plastics Manufacturing

Figure 6-1. Classification of occupancies based upon the hazard of the contents. It should be noted that these classifications may vary based upon a physical review of the particular facility.

With regard to obstruction of exits, the code even goes so far as to specify headroom requirements. Ceiling height in means of egress cannot be less than 7 feet 6 inches and projections from the ceiling cannot be less than 6 feet 8 inches from the floor. There are also conflicts with security requirements which sometimes results in exit doors being locked. This occurred in the Cocoanut Grove Night Club fire in Boston in 1942, in which several exit doors were locked. Locked exits were also a factor contributing to the fatalities in the Beverly Hills Supper Club fire in 1977.

More recently, there is an increasing trend to install security bars and grills on the windows and doors of homes and businesses. This practice has resulted in numerous fire fatalities when the occupants have not been able to open the devices and rescuers have not been able to access the structures. Various security requirements in industry have also resulted in conflicts with the code. Solutions to these problems are being actively pursued by the manufacturers of door hardware. One device consists of a delayed response panic bar. When this bar is depressed, an alarm sounds, but the door does not release for 15 seconds. This delay allows time for security personnel to respond and apprehend unauthorized personnel, while still providing an approved emergency exit. Another problem with locking violations is the practice of installing deadbolts in addition to the normal lockset in the door. The code requires that exit doors be readily opened from the inside, without special knowledge, keys, or tools. A deadbolt may require the use of a key in both sides and is therefore not allowed. The latch or lockset must be easily and readily opened and its operation must be obvious such as a panic bar, door knob, or a simple one-motion latch. A dead bolt does not meet this requirement because it is a secondary device, in addition to the knob or latch, and it requires two-hand operation.

To Ensure That the Exits and Routes of Escape Are Clearly Marked So That There Is No Confusion In Reaching an Exit

Another common problem occurs when exit doors are not marked as such and doors that can be mistaken as exits lead into deadends. Exits must be clearly visible and conspicuously marked so that any occupant of the building will readily know the direction of escape from any point in the building. Doors or passageways which are not exits, or a way to an exit, but which may be confused with an exit must be clearly marked "not an exit."

In the Beverly Hills Supper Club fire, exits were inadequate, poorly arranged, and some were not properly marked. In theaters, in the past, it was common to find decorative curtains hanging in front of exit doors. Only knowledgeable people would know where the doors were. Even if there were an exit sign, the door would not be obvious.

The code is very specific concerning sign location, color, illumination, height, and width of letters. Basically, exits must be marked by an approved sign that is readily visible from any direction of exit access. No point in the exit access should be more than 100 feet from the nearest visible sign. Exit signs should be either red or green letters on matte white background. Illumination is required to be not less than 5 footcandles when the sign is externally illuminated. When emergency power is provided for the building, the lighting for the exit signs should also be on the emergency power system. There are some interesting exit devices on the market today which incorporate luminescent signs (to meet the illumination requirements) and luminescent disks or plates that contain directional arrows and which may be mounted at eye level or lower on the wall to provide direction when the lights may be out or smoke is obscuring vision. Some passenger airliners and theaters are now using floor-mounted light strips to aid in providing occupants with direction to the exits.

To Provide Adequate Lighting

There are provisions in the code for illumination of means of egress, even if there is a power failure. When fire occurs, it is very likely that a power failure will occur. Smoke will further obscure visibility. In many famous fires in history, lack of illumination has exacerbated the fatality rate. In the code, at least 1 footcandle of illumination is required at floor level throughout the three parts of the means of egress. Power must be provided from a reliable source, and there must be adequate redundancy so that the failure of a bulb does not cause any area to be in darkness. Battery-powered lights are allowable as an emergency source of light, however they must be self-charging and must be capable of maintaining light for $1\frac{1}{2}$ hour. Alternate power sources, such as emergency generators are allowed, but they must be capable of coming online within 10 seconds of the primary power failure. This is an obvious requirement when one considers how readily people could become confused, or even panic, in an emergency situation if the area were suddenly plunged into darkness.

To Ensure Early Warning of Fire

The code specifies requirements for notification of building occupants of the emergency situation so that they may begin to evacuate. Fire alarms must be of distinctive sound and loud enough to be heard in all parts of the structure. In industrial occupancies, the ambient noise levels must be taken into consideration in designing and testing an alarm system. It must be ensured that the alarm will be heard. It is also common, in industry, to have various alarm and signaling systems which have different meanings and which may have confusing tones. The emergency signaling system must be distinctive.

New occupancies must be reviewed to ensure that the emergency alarms can be heard throughout and above normal ambient noise levels. Periodic fire drills that incorporate all alarm systems are useful in evaluating the system and ensuring that occupants are familiar with the distinction between the evacuation alarm and other alarms and signals in the work environment. Some occupancies such as high-rise buildings even require public address systems in addition to the alarm signal so that occupants may be directed to safe areas and be given evacuation instructions.

The specific occupancy chapters detail which detection, alarm, and signaling systems are required. Chapter 7 of the code describes detection, alarm, and communication systems. Detection systems are discussed in this book in Chapter 7.

To Provide for Backup or Redundant Exit Arrangements

In the event that the fire or emergency condition blocks primary exits, the code provides for redundant exits. The code specifies that exits, where two or more are required, must be remote from one another. It was a common practice, in the past, to locate exit stairwells in the same area as the elevator shafts. When fires occurred in the area of the elevators, there was no other means of escape. This is referred to as a core-type building, when the elevators, stairs and service shaft are all in one central core. This is a less expensive form of construction, but it presents a real life safety problem to the life safety specialist.

The Rault Center Building in New Orleans was such a core-type building. When fire occurred near the core on the fifteenth floor in 1973, five women were trapped when heat and smoke prevented them from reaching either of the two stair towers which were located in the core. Four of the five women died when they all attempted to jump to the roof of an adjacent building. The Joelma Building in São Paulo, Brazil was another example of the core-type construction. In this building, there were 15 stories of offices located above 8 floors of open air parking. There was only one stairwell in the core of this building. This was just one of numerous deficiencies that led to the death of 179 occupants when this building was completely gutted by fire on February 1, 1974.

To Ensure the Suitable Enclosure of Vertical Openings

A vertical opening is any opening through a floor or roof. Vertical openings are important to life safety. When these are not adequately protected, they will allow the passage of smoke, gases, and fire to uninvolved portions of the building. A vertical opening may be a stairwell, elevator shaft, service chase, or merely a hole that has been drilled in the floor for the passage of wires. This later vertical opening is one of the most difficult to control in existing buildings where modifications may involve cutting through floors to install electrical or communications cabling. There is firestop material that can be used to reseal these holes, but these activities must be closely monitored to ensure that all such holes are identified and properly sealed.

Vertical openings that are part of the means of egress must be protected by appropriate enclosing walls and fire-resistant doors so as to maintain a protected passageway for exiting occupants. An example of unprotected vertical openings occurred in the MGM Grand Hotel Fire in Las Vegas, Nevada. In this building, unprotected seismic joint shafts and elevator hoistways contributed to smoke movement into and throughout the high-rise tower from the first floor fire.

On January 9, 1981, in Keansburgh, New Jersey, 31 people died in a boarding house fire because of unprotected vertical openings. On March 14, 1981, in Chicago, Illinois, 19 people died in a hotel fire because of unprotected vertical openings.

In some industrial occupancies, it is necessary to have unprotected vertical openings because of operations, processes, or equipment which require openings between floors. In this case, it is required that each floor that has unprotected openings must be provided with exits including fully enclosed stairways that allow occupants to safely escape.

Another exit component that protects vertical openings is the smokeproof tower. A smokeproof tower is a stair enclosure designed to limit the penetration of heat, smoke, and fire gases from a fire in any part of a building. Types of smokeproof towers include pressurized stairways, or the incorporation of a balcony or vestibule that is open to the outside. A pressurized stairway is just that; a stairway that is provided with fans which create positive pressure in the stairway. The pressure would keep smoke and gases from entering the stairway. The fans must be provided with emergency power to keep the stairway clear of smoke when there is a loss of commercial power. A balcony or vestibule is an area between the exit corridor and the stairway which is open to the outside. It allows smoke and fire gases to vent to the outside before entering the stairway. Smokeproof towers must be noncombustible enclosures with minimum 2-hour fire resistance rating.

To Make Allowances for Those Design Criteria That Go Beyond the Code Provisions and Are Tailored to the Normal Use and Needs of the Occupancy In Question.

Compliance with the code does not mean that other provisions for safety of persons using a structure, under normal occupancy, can be neglected. For example, compliance with the code does not mean that adequate means of egress are provided for people who are physically handicapped. The code recognizes that other provisions must be made for the handicapped and makes reference to ANSI A117.1, *Specifications for Making Buildings and Facilities Accessible to and Usable by the Physically Handicapped.*

Certain industrial operations may create hazardous conditions that require provisions that go beyond the code in order to ensure the life safety of the occupants. It is the responsibility of the safety/life/firesafety personnel to identify such conditions and to prescribe necessary life safety provisions. For example, chemical operations, refineries, and other high hazard occupancies will necessitate planning, training, special detection and suppression systems, and alarm systems to ensure that personnel can safely evacuate during an emergency.

MEANS OF EGRESS

In the discussion of life safety, it is common to loosely use the term exit for every portion of the way out of a building. The more proper term, and the one of which the exit is a part, is the means of egress. The means of egress is defined as a continuous and unobstructed way of exit travel from any point in a building or structure to a public way which consists of three separate and distinct parts including the way of exit access, the exit, and the way of exit discharge. The means of egress is the route that is required by a person to safely exit a building from any point in that building to a point outside at a place of safety. It includes the vertical and horizontal passageways which include doorways, corridors, ramps, stairs, intervening room spaces, and horizontal exits. The means of egress requirements are applicable to new and existing buildings as well as all occupancies.

Exit Access

That portion of a means of egress which leads to an entrance to an exit is the exit access. Exit access includes that area of the building through which the occupant must travel to reach the exit. It may include aisles, stairs, ramps, passageways, corridors, and doors. Maximum travel distances along the exit access are a consideration and are provided in the occupancy chapters of the code. Travel distances are measured from any point in the occupancy to the nearest exit. Allowable travel distances may be lessened in occupancies that have sprinkler protection. Sprinklers will usually control a fire for a longer period of time, allowing more time for the occupants to evacuate. For example, the travel distance for industrial occupancies is 100 feet for unsprinklered buildings and 250 feet for sprinklered buildings.

Exit

The exit is the portion of a means of egress which is separated from all other spaces of the building or structure by construction or equipment so as to provide a protected way of travel to the exit discharge. The simplest form of an exit is a door to the outside. The exit may be a corridor, ramp, or a stairwell when it provides a protected way of travel between the exit access and the exit discharge. A stairway exit includes the stair enclosure, stairs and landings within the enclosure, doors to and from the enclosure, and any exit passageway that is necessary to provide a protected path of travel from the enclosure to the street or open air.

The exit must be protected or enclosed so as to protect the occupants in an emergency. When the exit connects three or less stories, the enclosure must have a 1-hour fire resistance rating. When the exit connects four or more stories, the enclosure must have a 2-hour fire resistance rating. Openings into the exit enclosure must be protected by appropriate fire-resistant rated and self-closing doors. The only openings that are allowed are those that are needed to get into the exit from the normally occupied spaces of the building and the opening at the exit discharge.

Horizontal Exit. The horizontal exit is a special application that is worthy of discussion. It is a way of passage through a fire-resistant barrier from one area of a building, or an adjoining building, to an area of refuge on the same level. It is a method of providing exits in buildings with very large areas per floor. For example, when each floor of a multistory building has two stairways on opposite sides of the building, but the distance between the two exceeds the allowable travel distance to an exit, a horizontal exit may be appropriate. In this case, a fire door in a 2-hour fire-resistance rated wall that divides each floor could serve as a horizontal exit. This application would be much less expensive than incorporating a third protected stairway in the center of the building.

The Way of Exit Discharge

The exit discharge is the portion of the means of egress that is between the exit and a public way. The exit discharge is normally considered to be the point where the person transfers from the building to the outside, but it may also be inside the building where occupants exit an enclosed stairway and must traverse a lobby or corridor to the outside. It would not make much sense to have an exit discharge into a closed courtyard or an area that is too small to allow all of the exiting occupants to get safely away from the building. It is also not desirable to require the occupants to go back into the building in order to reach a public way. The code requires that passageways, at least as wide as the exit, be provided to allow all of the occupants to move to a place of safety away from the building.

A common problem that is created by evacuating people is that when they get outside, they stop and congregate around the exit. This can be a particularly severe problem in the evacuation of high rise buildings when people are not trained and directed to move away from the point of exit discharge. This is a problem that must be addressed through emergency planning, drills, and the assignment of monitors to direct people away from the exit discharge.

Other Means of Egress Components

There are many components that make up the means of egress system. It is essential that they all have the appropriate fire-resistance rating and be properly maintained. The failure of a single component of the means of egress could jeopardize the evacuating occupants.

Doors.   Doors are probably the most important means of egress component. They usually provide the entrance and exit from each portion of the means of egress. They are also one of the most frequently violated portions of the system.

There are three categories of doors that are of concern to the firesafety person because they act to resist the passage of heat and smoke including the non-fire-rated door, the fire door, and the smoke-stop door. The non-fire-rated door may offer some protection if it is closed, but it is not an acceptable part of the means of egress.

A fire door is one that has passed a standard fire test as defined in Chapter 5. Where a fire door is required, it should be self-closing. It is important to note though, that a fire door that is operated by a fusible link or other door-closing device is of limited value for exit purposes because quantities of smoke may pass through the door opening before there is sufficient heat to fuse the link. It is also important to note that not all fire-rated doors are acceptable as exit doors. This is obvious when the door is not easily opened, such as the case with a rollup or sliding steel fire door.

A smoke-stop door is one that is lighter than a fire door and is only intended as a temporary barrier to the passage of heat and smoke.

None of these doors can function as a part of the means of egress when it is open during the fire. This fact presents a reoccurring dilemma for firesafety personnel. In office areas, employees usually prefer to keep office doors open. When an office is located on an exit corridor, the code requires that the door must be closed. Another situation that occurs frequently in industrial operations is the placing of obstructions in and around doorways which will interfere with automatically closing doors and the passage of people. These items must be included in inspections by firesafety personnel and on checklists for others. To be included as a component of the means of egress, doors must meet certain minimum width restrictions. Doors must have a minimum clear width of 32 inches. Clear width means that the measurement must exclude any obstructions caused by the door, the door frame, or any door hardware.

Doors that are a part of the means of egress must also not exceed 48 inches in width. This requirement helps to avoid violating the ease of opening requirements. A door that is greater than 48 inches in width may be too heavy to open readily. Also, in a dark or smoke-filled environment, it may be difficult to locate the hardware to open the door when it is greater than 48 inches wide.

Doors must be readily opened from the inside and must swing in the direction of travel. There must be no locks, chains, deadbolts, or keys which require any extra effort or knowledge to operate. When it is necessary to lock an exit door, only approved panic hardware can be used. This is frequently a matter of controversy between security requirements and the Life Safety Code. It is up to the firesafety person to ensure that life safety requirements take precedence.

Stairs.   Another critical portion of the means of egress system is stairs. Stairs are frequently used parts of the system for nonemergency passage, and they are a common scene of accidents during normal usage. OSHAct recognizes this fact and has included requirements for fixed industrial stairs dealing with such things as width, angle of rise, treads, railings, and platforms. Since stairs are a part of the critical exit portion of the means of egress, it is also necessary that they receive considerable attention in the Life Safety Code. An accident during evacuation could result in injuries or fatalities. Likewise, should smoke and fire get into the stairway, the evacuation process will be affected. Therefore, the code addresses enclosure of the stairs as well as safety aspects that are similar to OSHA. Included in the physical aspects of stairs that are addressed by the code are such details as the size and shape of handrails. The code writers have recognized that exiting people need a conveniently placed handrail that is easy to grasp while using stairs. Exit stairs must be enclosed with the same level of fire resistance as other portions of the exit.

Occupant Load

The capacity of the means of egress is dependent upon the occupant load of the building, or the portion of the building that is under consideration. The total number of persons who may occupy a building or portion thereof at any one time is the occupant load. Again, specific load allowances are provided in the code in terms of square feet per occupant.

The occupant load is also a term that applies to considerations of means of egress. The capacity of the particular means of egress must be sufficient for the occupant load.

The occupant load for business and industrial occupancies is one person per 100 ft^2 of gross floor area. Most industrial occupancies do not come close to exceeding allowable occupant loads; however, special attention must be paid to more dense areas that may exist in an industrial occupancy such as offices, conference rooms, and auditoriums. As a comparison, the occupant load for assembly occupancies varies by the concentration of intended use from one person per 3 ft^2 in areas that are used as waiting areas, to one person per 100 ft^2 for a library stack area.

The occupant load is used to determine exit capacity, numbers of exits, aisle and corridor widths, and similar items using the unit of exit width.

Unit of Exit Width

Means of egress are measured in units of exit width of 22 inches. This width is considered to be the minimum space required for the orderly movement of a single file of people along a passageway. In the calculation of the capacity of components of means of exit width, the unit of exit width is used. For example, the allowable capacity per unit of exit width for Class A ramps is 100. This means that for every unit of exit width, or every 22 inches, a Class A ramp has a capacity of 100 occupants. A Class B ramp has a capacity of 75 for travel in the up direction and 100 for travel in the down direction. Stairways have a capacity of 75. For example, a stairway that is 44 inches wide will have a capacity of 150 persons. A floor of a building with an occupant load of 300 people would require a minimum of two such stairways.

The capacity of each component of the means of egress must be reviewed to determine if the capacity is adequate for the occupancy and that capacities do not deteriorate in any portion of the means of egress. Doors have a capacity of 100 people per unit of exit width in the above example. The doors at the bottom of each stairway must be at least 40 inches of clear width so that the stairway does not terminate at a door that has any less capacity than the stairway.

PSYCHOLOGICAL EFFECTS ON LIFE SAFETY

Human behavior during and following fires and other disaster incidents has been extensively studied and documented. Some of the recent high-rise fires have provided fertile grounds for extensive studies of the effects of fire on large numbers of people. It is important for the firesafety professional to understand the way that people respond in an emergency situation and design the life safety system to accommodate those behaviors. To a great extent, the Life Safety Code has done this and reflects those factors that will help all occupants to escape, regardless of their mental status. As further information is gathered from fire experience, changes have been made to the code to reflect the new data.

Human Behavior in an Emergency

In an emergency situation, approximately 25 percent of the exposed population assesses the danger correctly and takes prompt action. They become excited but feel little fear. Approximately 50 percent of the exposed population assesses the situation properly, but they are uncertain as to the actions to pursue. This group feels considerable fear, and they take no initiative on their own. They will follow a leader and obey orders and, with action, their fear diminishes. About 15 to 25 percent of the population perceive the situation imperfectly and require strong urging to respond to directions. One percent of the exposed population withdraws completely from the situation. They may become totally immobile or resort to some totally irrelevant activity. The elderly are particularly prone to unreasonable behavior such as refusing to leave, attacking the rescuer, or returning to the fire after having been taken to safety.

There is not much specific data on peoples' behavior in industrial fire situations. The closest similarities that have been experienced and studied are the ''place of employment'' emergency situations where the behavior of employees was differentiated from other occupants and studied. In the Beverly Hills Supper Club fire, for example, it was noted that waiters and waitresses continued to look after their customers during the emergency. They seemed to assume the responsibility for leading their particular group of customers to safety. One particular waitress only alerted customers in two rooms that she had been serving. She neglected customers in two adjoining rooms.

There is some data resulting from studies that were conducted following the Beverly Hills Supper Club fire, Las Vegas' MGM Grand and Hilton Hotel fires, and the Westchase Hilton Hotel fire in Houston, Texas. Although most of the data in these studies relate to the actions of hotel guests, some generalities may be made concerning how people would react in an industrial emergency. This information can be used in formulating industrial emergency action plans and in selecting employees for various emergency duties.

Initial Actions. It was found that evacuation of the building is not usually the first action of people in an emergency situation. Initial actions are those of validating the alarm, notifying others, and calling the fire department. There was also a difference in the actions of males and females which was observed in the Westchase Hilton fire. The initial actions of the males were those of fire fighting activities, preparing for evacuation, and the evacuation itself. Females, on the other hand, initially were concerned with information seeking, alerting others, and evacuating.

Supervisory Relationships. In studies that have been conducted in industrial or place of employment responses to emergencies, it was found that people tend to carry over their normal work activities and relationships into the emergency. Workers turn to their supervisors and managers for direction concerning when and how to evacuate. There is a tendency for the normal supervisors and managers to assert themselves in establishing response activities. In some cases, people followed their supervisor even though they thought the direction being given was in error. In other cases they refused to follow and elected a new leader. Maybe these cases were merely reflections of the normal supervisor/ employee relationships in these groupings. In any case, it would indicate that when evacuation plans are made and training is provided, the supervisors and managers should be the key individuals and receive training that allows them to continue their supervisory role in an emergency. Unfortunately, it is fairly common when establishing emergency evacuation plans, to designate staff members as the evacuation coordinators. Would it not make sense to designate supervisors and train them so that in times of emergency, their normal leadership role could just continue and they could lead the evacuation efforts? When other employees are designated as the monitors or emergency coordinators, there should be sufficient training and drills so that everyone recognizes these people as the leader in an emergency.

Irrational Behavior

Irrational behavior, or panic, has been used quite often by the media to describe behavior in an emergency. Studies have shown that panic, as defined, has rarely occurred in the large-scale disasters that have been studied. Panic is defined as irrational behavior brought about by excessive feelings of alarm or fear. Panic is caused by real or imagined danger and results in extreme and illogical activities that might be described as animalistic or self-destructive behavior to secure safety.

Although there are cases on record where panic has occurred and resulted in death (Iroquois Theater fire in Chicago in 1903 and the Cocoanut Grove Night Club fire in Boston in 1942), in most cases, panic is not present in the fire environment. In most cases of fire emergency, people do what they perceive to be the best under the circumstances. Investigators with more complete information, in retrospect, may consider such actions as irrational or panic motivated. What was reported as panic in the Beverly Hills Supper Club fire was actually, as described by the occupants, altruistic behavior.

At any rate, the use of the term ''do not panic'' in firesafety directives is probably as meaningless as the term ''be careful'' in safety directives. It would be far better to train people more completely so that they know what the proper response to fire emergencies should be. When people in the industrial environment are properly trained for various emergency situations that they might encounter, their actions in an emergency will be more conducive to life safety.

Convergence Clusters

Studies that have been conducted seem to support the tendency of people to group together. In fact, a term used to describe that action is convergence clusters.

The behavior that is described as ''convergence clusters'' was first identified in a report by John Bryan as behavior that was described by occupants of the Georgian Towers apartment complex in Silver Spring, Maryland, during a fire there on January 9, 1979. During this fire, occupants of the building who were stranded in corridors were taken into units that were not their own, either at their request or by the inhabitant's invitation, to take refuge from the smoke and heat. This type of behavior has since been observed in the MGM Grand Hotel fire in Las Vegas, and the Westchase Hilton Hotel fire in Houston, Texas.

The Fires.   The fire in the Georgian Towers began in a second floor apartment. By the time fire fighters arrived, flashover had occurred in the apartment and smoke had saturated the second floor corridor of both wings of the building. Smoke permeated above the floor of fire origin, and was especially heavy on the second, third, seventh, ninth, and eleventh floors.

The fire at the MGM was originally discovered in a restaurant on the first floor. It flashed over through the restaurant and into the casino, and the resulting smoke migrated to all the residential floors in the hotel through the building's seismic joints, stairways, elevator shafts, and air-conditioning systems.

The fire at the Westchase Hilton began in the early morning hours in a room on the fourth floor. Fire was confined almost completely to that room. However, smoke migrated to every floor above the fourth.

Similarities.   All three fires were major fires. They all occurred at night or in the early morning when most of the occupants were asleep. Fire alarms failed, therefore the occupants were alerted by other means. As a result, occupants became aware of the danger over an extended period of time. When they did, they perceived the fire to be severe and life threatening because smoke had already spread throughout the building.

Convergence Clusters.   All three fires resulted in the formation of convergence clusters of at least three people in units that appeared to be safer. In the MGM fire, clusters as large as 35 people were reported. People were either invited into the cluster by the occupants or they sought refuge and were apparently attracted by the presence of other people.

A common characteristic of the clusters was the absence of any previous personal, social, or professional relationships among the members. They seem to function as a mechanism for reducing the anxiety and tension that occupants felt when confronted with the life-threatening fire situation.

Members of the convergence clusters tended to concentrate their actions on information gathering, communication with one another and with officials, and reducing the smoke migration into the refuge area.

An understanding of convergence clusters is useful in designing refuge areas within large buildings such as high-rise buildings. People will go to a refuge area when it is an area that can be maintained tenable and has communications to the outside. Refuge areas, or compartments, would be a satisfactory alternative to total building evacuation. The phenomenon of convergence clusters seems to indicate that people would utilize such areas if they were provided.

HIGH-RISE LIFE SAFETY

A high-rise building is considered to be any building having floors used for human occupancy that are higher than 75 feet above ground level. Generally speaking, this includes buildings greater than 6 stories. In considering the life safety for high-rise buildings, all of the requirements presented in Chapter 5 and the first part of this chapter take on increased importance. Breakdowns in the safe design and construction of the high-rise building will intensify the effects of the fire on the building and the occupants. The design and construction practice of compartmentation is increasingly important in the high-rise building to contain the fire during the period that it takes fire fighters to reach the fire floor.

Deficiencies in basic life safety provisions are also magnified in a high-rise emergency. In the high-rise building, there is a whole new set of circumstances which create substantial challenges to the life safety specialist. Of major concern is the fact that a high-rise building may have thousands of occupants and may take hours to totally evacuate. Therefore, there must be adequate protected means of egress to protect the occupants while they are exiting. There must be emergency plans and occupants must have training in the implementation of these plans. Additionally, there must be refuge areas where the occupants can be safe when exiting is impossible or impractical. In the high-rise building, it is imperative that special consideration be given to provisions that allow occupants to move to safety; systems to control fire, smoke, heat, and gases; communications systems; and emergency preplanning activities.

Protected Means of Egress

Not only do means of egress need to afford protection for the occupants while they are exiting, there must be readily accessible fire and smoke-safe areas within the high-rise building where the occupants can take refuge or proceed to safety. Evacuation of the high-rise building may take an extensive amount of time, so means of egress must be adequately protected to maintain a safe environment throughout the evacuation. Refuge areas may be used to take some of the burden off of the means of egress and thereby allow fire fighters access to the stairs. Fire and smoke-safe elevators which can be manually controlled by fire fighters must be provided. When elevators are not available when there is a fire in a high-rise building, fire fighters will have to carry 40 pounds or more of hose and breathing apparatus up stairs. By the time they reach the fire, they may be too exhausted to fight it. An 18- or 20-minute delay between the alarm and the response by the fire department will generally mean the loss of all, or a large part of the average *low-rise* building. In *high-rise* buildings, it may take this long, or more for fire fighters just to climb the stairs once they get to the building.

Control of Fire, Smoke, Heat, and Gases

Because the nature of the high-rise building exaggerates so many of the basic principles of building fire safety, it is appropriate to review some previously covered areas.

Combustibles. The control of combustibles presents an unending problem in any occupancy, but the problem is intensified in the high-rise building. Most high-rise buildings contain business and office occupancies which contain combustible furnishings including large amounts of plastics. Combustibility of interior finish materials is also a factor. The specific hazards of combustible contents, such as plastics, wood, and foams have already been discussed. The trend in open office arrangements is also not conducive to fire control and separation of combustibles. Many older buildings do not have sprinkler systems or detection systems and a fire may burn for a long time before discovery and suppression efforts are initiated. There is a large quantity of combustible furnishings in most high-rise buildings. In the First Interstate Bank fire in Los Angeles on May 4, 1988, the fire was fed by heavy fuel loading including a vast array of computer and communications equipment. This fire involved an open office arrangement which allowed rapid fire development and spread.

A fire in the 15-story office tower at the Alexis Nihon Plaza in Montreal, Canada on October 26, 1986, destroyed one floor completely and heavily damaged five others for a total of about $80 million damage. This fire occurred in a typical office occupancy with fuel load including office furnishings, office equipment, filing cabinets containing combustible materials, shelves of books, and other combustible materials.

In many cases, there are communications and data cables strung through the plenums in office areas. A plenum is an air compartment or chamber to which one or more ducts are connected and which forms part of an air distribution system. Plenums are important to the discussion of life safety because they are part of the air-conditioning system and they may also contain combustible cables and wire insulation. The latest codes require all such wires and cables to be in conduit. This requirement is not retroactive and it will be many years before all cabling in plenums is protected. A fire in the plenum space will quickly spread smoke and gases throughout the building. Combustible insulation on these cables in the plenum can transmit fire through this very vulnerable system.

Faults in Building Fire Safety. Many of the problems of building design and construction are built in, but many more are created by further modifications to the buildings. Built-in problems include vertical flues in the outer walls between the outer skin and the floor slab such as existed in the First Interstate Bank Building in Los Angeles. These flues allowed the fire to spread upward to other floors. Another problem that allows the fire to spread upward is the lack of curtain walls under windows which prevent fire extension externally through the windows. The lack of fireproofing or soft and easily removed fireproofing in structural members will lead to their failure when exposed to fire. The floors in most high-rise buildings are intended to be fire barriers, making each floor a separate fire area. Individual floors are sometimes separated by fire walls. When buildings are modified to add power or telecommunications cables between floors or through fire walls, the fire integrity of these structures may be lost. In many cases, these holes are not filled with a fire stop material and a future fire could spread through the holes.

Sprinkler Protection. In the past, high-rise buildings have not had sprinkler systems installed for a number of reasons including those that have become so familiar. Agreements such as they are too expensive; the building is fireproof; it is just an office occupancy; there are no combustibles; and the code does not require sprinklers, and therefore they must not be necessary may sound persuasive but they are not sound.

The codes have been changed as a result in of several high rise building fires where the lack of sprinklers has resulted in high property loss fires and loss of life. Several hotel fires, including the MGM Grand and Hilton Hotels in Las Vegas resulted in increased requirements for sprinklers in high rise hotels. The First Interstate Bank Fire in Los Angeles accelerated requirements for retrofitting existing high rise buildings in that city with sprinklers.

It is noteworthy that there have been no major high rise building fires in buildings that had functioning sprinkler systems.

Heating, Ventilation, and Air-Conditioning Systems. Heating, ventilating, and air-conditioning (HVAC) systems have a significant impact on fire development and life safety in high-rise fires. In the early fire stages, fresh air provided by the HVAC system supplies oxygen to intensify the fire. When automatic controls are provided to shut down the HVAC system in the event of a fire but there are no provisions to close the air ducts, smoke can still travel through the building. The pressures developed by the fire will force smoke and gases through the air ducts throughout the building. This will affect people on other floors as they see, smell, or feel smoke. People are more likely to feel trapped in a high-rise building because windows cannot be opened. When fire occurs in high-rise buildings, it is essential that means are in place to control the movement of heat, smoke, and gases through the HVAC system. An adequately designed and installed HVAC system should provide the following important functions:

1. Protection of life by removing or diverting toxic gases and smoke from locations where building occupants must find temporary refuge or must travel to reach exits.

2. Improvement of the environment in the vicinity of the fire by removal of smoke and heat. This allows occupants time to travel to exits or areas of refuge and enables fire fighters to advance closer to the fire. Smoke can greatly delay the fire fighters in finding the fire and initiating effective suppression efforts.
3. Control of the spread or direction of spread of the fire by setting up air currents that cause the fire to move in a desired direction.
4. Dilution of the unburned, combustible gases that are produced by the fire before they reach an ignitable range and acquire a flammable mixture.

The building designer must be conscious of the important function of fire ventilation, and must provide effective means of facilitating venting. The capability of venting smoke and gases may include access panels, movable windows, skylights, or other means of readily opened spaces in case of fire emergency. Automatic systems should be in place in the high-rise building to pressurize exit stairways and elevator shafts.

Emergency controls on the mechanical equipment may also be effective in accomplishing the functions of fire ventilation. For example, it may be advantageous to ventilate the fire floor and pressurize the rest of the building. Each building is unique and will require a unique design and planning for the fire emergency.

Communications

Adequate means of communications is important in every building and, in particular, high-rise buildings. Public address systems are required in most codes for high-rise buildings. They are necessary to communicate with the building occupants to advise them of safe areas, alternate evacuation routes, and when and how to evacuate. Because they are so important to the life safety of the building occupants, speakers should be located throughout the structure and be loud enough so that they can be heard by all occupants above the normal ambient noise levels.

The communications system should originate in the building's central fire command center and it should be provided with emergency power in case of a power failure.

Like all of the other life safety systems in the high-rise building, the communications system should be tested periodically in addition to testing that occurs during the normal emergency evacuation drills.

Emergency Planning

Planning for the high-rise emergency should include a documented emergency preparedness plan, an emergency organization, and training for all building occupants.

Emergency Preparedness Plan.   The emergency plan must detail the makeup and duties of the emergency organization. It must detail the fire and life safety systems in the building. The most important function of the emergency plan is to detail the procedures to be followed for various emergencies and provide emergency notification instructions and telephone numbers.

Emergency Organization.   The building emergency organization must include floor monitors and area coordinators who have the responsibility to advise the people in their area of responsibility of actions to take such as routes to use. During an evacuation, floor monitors make sure that their floor is evacuated before they themselves evacuate. They are aware of handicapped people or others who may need special assistance, and they report this information to the fire fighters. When they evacuate, floor monitors report the status of their floor to the building coordinator or area monitor.

The emergency organization may include people with special duties such as helping in the command center, monitoring HVAC systems, and monitoring sprinkler systems.

Training.   To make the whole emergency evacuation system work, the building occupants must be trained regarding the systems that are in place to protect them and appropriate actions to take in an emergency. Training can include how to report an emergency, and how to operate manual alarm devices, building life safety systems, and equipment. Information regarding the building emergency organization, and other pertinent information concerning building emergencies should also be provided.

Additionally, periodic evacuation drills are an integral part of any emergency plan so that people are familiar with how the alarms sound and the routes of escape that are available to them. Occupants must also be instructed about refuge areas and how to protect themselves should it become necessary for them to remain in the building in a refuge area.

Joelma Building, São Paulo, Brazil.   The February 1, 1974 fire in the Joelma Building in São Paulo, Brazil was probably the most tragic example of fire in a high-rise building that did not have adequate life safety systems. Of the building's 756 occupants (only 601 worked in the office tower portion) 179 died. It was fortunate that the fire occurred during the summer vacation period, since there could normally have been as many as 1016 occupants in the building. Of the fatalities, 40 people jumped to their deaths. Thirty of these died after the fire had burned itself out. Ninety died on the roof and 49 died within the building.

The Joelma Building was a 25-story office building of reinforced concrete columns, beams, and floor slabs which was built in 1972. The second through the ninth floor was open-air parking and the rest of the building was office space.

Contents of the building were standard office contents with a fuel load of wood, plastic, polyurethane foam, and so on. There were individual electric window-mounted air conditioners in each office unit which presented an ignition source.

The water supply consisted of a 2000-gallon capacity roof tank that supplied a standpipe with a $1\frac{1}{2}$-inch hose on each floor. There were no fire department connections and the building lacked a sprinkler system. There were two soda acid fire extinguishers provided on each floor.

There were no illuminated exit signs, no emergency power or lights, no fire detection system, no manual fire alarms, or voice communication system. There was no smoke control or pressure system in the single 47.2-inch wide stairwell.

There was no emergency organization, plan, or procedure. Because of the lack of notification procedures, the fire department was not notified for at least 15 minutes after the fire was discovered.

The fire originated in temporary wiring that had been made to one of the air conditioning units on the twelfth floor. The maintenance man who made the temporary wiring connection had bypassed the circuit breaker panel and had not used shielded wire.

The fire quickly spread across combustible curtains, furniture, carpeting, and other interior furnishings. The fire ultimately spread throughout the building and consumed all of the combustibles. The one stairway quickly became blocked forcing occupants to the roof where some of them jumped to escape the heat and smoke.

This was a tragic example of how not to design and build a high-rise building. Given the physical characteristics of the building, there should have been management of the occupants to control combustibles and ignition sources and there should have been an emergency plan with procedures that established responsibilities, and training. The presence of any one of these would have helped to save lives.

SUMMARY

The Life Safety Code more than any other aspect of firesafety has developed out of tragedy. As hard lessons were learned, they were incorporated into the code which has developed into one of the most widely used of the NFPA's publications. The goals of the code, which have been incorporated by OSHA as fundamental requirements, provide the paradigm for life safety.

Life safety means that when there is a fire or some other emergency that requires people to vacate the building, that safeguards are in place to protect the occupants from fire, smoke, gases, and structural collapse while they are exiting. The code provides the requirements to achieve life safety, regardless of the type of occupancy. While the code is intended to provide safety to personnel, compliance with its requirements will have ancillary benefits for the property protection program.

To be effective, the Life Safety Code must not stand alone, but it must be supplemented by all of the other firesafety activities including fire prevention and fire protection.

BIBLIOGRAPHY

Best, Richard, and Demers, David P. 1982. Investigation Report on the MGM Grand Hotel Fire Las Vegas, Nevada November 21, 1980. Quincy: National Fire Protection Association.

Best, Richard L. 1977. *Reconstruction of a Tragedy, The Beverly Hills Supper Club Fire Southgate, Kentucky, May 28, 1977.* Boston: National Fire Protection Association.

Bryan, John L. 1985. Convergence Clusters. *Fire Journal* 79(6):27–30, 86–90.

Chapman, Elmer F. 1988. High-Rise: An Analysis. *Fire Engineering* 141(8):52–61.

Code of Federal Regulations. 29 CFR 1910.35-40. 1987. Occupational Safety and Health Administration, Department of Labor. Washington, DC.

Demers, David P. 1978, Ten Students Die In Providence College Dormitory Fire. *Fire Journal* 72(4):59–62, 103.

Egan, M. David. 1978. *Concepts In Building Firesafety.* Toronto: John Wiley & Sons, Inc.

Fires in Two Boarding Facilities Kill 34 Residents. 1982. *Fire Journal* 76(4):44–57, 106.

Hill, Steven. 1982, 19 Die in Chicago Hotel Fire. *Fire Journal* 76(2):53–55, 60–61.

Isner, Michael S. 1988. $80 Million Fire in Montreal High-Rise. *Fire Journal* 82(1):64–71.

Jones, B. K., and Hewitt, J. Ann. 1985. Leadership and Group Formation in High-rise Building Evacuations. In *Fire Safety Science-Proceedings of the First International Symposium,* Cecile E. Grant and Patrick J. Pagni, eds., pp. 513–522. New York: Hemisphere Publishing Corporation.

Klem, Thomas J. 1987. *Investigation Report on the DuPont Plaza Hotel Fire.* Quincy: National Fire Protection Association.

Life Safety Code Handbook. 3rd ed. 1985. James K. Lathrop, ed. Quincy: National Fire Protection Association.

Norton, Alison L. 1988. When Security Provisions Threaten Firesafety. *Fire Journal* 82(6):40–45, 76–77.

Pauls, J. L. and Jones, B. K. 1980. Research in Human Behavior. *Fire Journal* 74(3):35–41.

Sharry, J. A. 1974. South America Burning. *Fire Journal* 68(4):23–28.

Swartz, J. A. 1979. Human Behavior in the Beverly Hills Fire. *Fire Journal* 73(3):73–74, 108.

Uniform Fire Code, 1985 Edition. Whittier, California: International Conference of Building Officials and Western Fire Chiefs Association.

7
FIRE DETECTION
AND ALARM
SYSTEMS

People have always been the best and most reliable fire detectors. People have the ability to detect several aspects of the fire. They can see and smell the smoke and feel the radiated and convected heat of a fire. Their sensitivity to radiated heat provides people with a directional reference. After detecting fire, people can make judgments and take action. However, people have shortcomings. They are not always present which is detrimental when it is desired to continuously monitor for fire. People are not always awake or alert which is evident by the fire fatality statistics. Most of the civilian fatalities occur between the hours of 10 P.M. and 6 A.M. when people are generally asleep. In these situations, when there is a fire, by the time the people awaken, it is already too late. There may also be those areas in the industrial environment in which it is not appropriate for people to serve as monitors. Although people can make judgments and take action, they must be properly trained to make the appropriate decisions and to take proper actions.

Detection systems have been available for many years. From the very earliest, heat detector technology has produced detection systems for almost every conceivable application, and it is still the most reliable. The needs and demands of the marketplace have resulted in the development of systems of increasing reliability and complexity. These new developments meet the needs of large and high-value commercial and industrial operations. For example, the protection of high-rise buildings has necessitated the development of systems that detect fire very early in the fire development scenario, transmit alarms, and take remedial actions. Modern systems are field programmable which allows the system operating parameters to be changed easily without extensive rewiring. Detectors send analog signals to the control panel constantly, and the control panel decides which signal indicates an undesirable condition. Detectors are addressable, so that it can be determined which detector in the system has detected fire.

Technology can only produce detectors that sense some signature of fire, such as smoke, heat, or various radiation effects. Different fire conditions produce different fire signatures, and there is variation within the different fire signatures which will influence the type of detection system chosen. Therefore, the detection method selected must be matched to the hazards present and the expected fire signatures. Once a detection system has been selected and installed, a preventative maintenance program must be established and followed. Even the simple household smoke detector must be checked periodically. It is best to follow the manufacturer's recommendations regarding frequency and types of maintenance to be performed.

HEAT DETECTORS

Heat detectors were the first and are the simplest and least expensive form of automatic detection. They are very reliable and have the lowest false alarm rate of all detectors. But they are also the slowest to respond. There are two types of heat detectors, fixed temperature and rate-of-rise detectors.

Fixed-Temperature Detectors

Fixed-temperature detectors incorporate a device that becomes activated at some predetermined temperature. The most common fixed-temperature detectors are the fusible link and frangible glass bulbs used in sprinkler heads. Some other examples of fixed-temperature detectors include the following:

The bimetallic strip thermostat is a spot-type heat detector utilizing the different coefficient of expansion of two metals. When a bimetallic strip is heated, the different coefficients of thermal expansion of the two metals cause the strip to bend in one direction. At a predetermined temperature, this deflection is such that an electric circuit is completed causing an alarm. When cooled, the strip returns to its original position, reopening the circuit and the device is ready for the next alarm.

The snap-action disc thermostat is another spot-type device that utilizes the unequal expansion of a bimetallic assembly. The center of the disc is designed to toggle from concave to convex when a given temperature is reached [Figure 7-1(a)]. One beneficial feature of the bimetallic strip and the snap-action disc detectors is that when the ambient temperature drops below the operating point, the detectors reset themselves and they are ready for reuse. On the minus side, there is no indicator when either of these devices has activated. If, for some reason, one of the detectors activates and then resets, there is no way for responding fire protection personnel to identify where the problem might have been.

The thermostatic cable heat detector is an area detector that can extend over large areas. Thermostatic cable consists of two metal cables, under tension, which are electrically separated from each other by a heat-sensitivity covering applied directly to the wires. At the rated temperature, the covering melts and

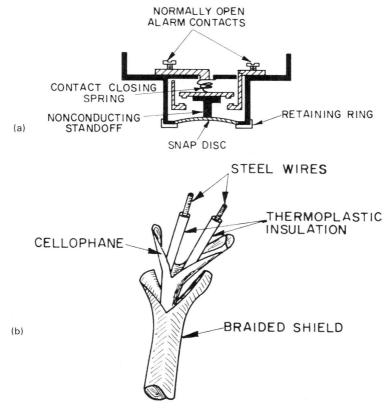

NORMALLY OPEN
ALARM CONTACTS

CONTACT CLOSING
SPRING

NONCONDUCTING
STANDOFF

(a)

RETAINING RING

SNAP DISC

STEEL WIRES

THERMOPLASTIC
INSULATION

CELLOPHANE

BRAIDED SHIELD

(b)

Figure 7-1. Fixed temperature detectors. (a) Bimetal snap-disc heat detector. (b) Thermostatic cable heat detector. (Source: Richard W. Bukowski)

the two wires make contact [Figure 7-1(b)]. In large area applications, it may be difficult to pinpoint the location where the thermostatic cable has activated.

A disadvantage with these devices is that fixed-temperature heat detectors have a certain amount of thermal inertia. They must, therefore, be exposed to some temperature above their rated operating temperature for a period of time before they activate. This difference between the operating temperature of the device and the actual air temperature is referred to as thermal lag. While they are slower to react than other detection methods, fixed-temperature detectors are extremely simple and reliable. Fixed-temperature heat detectors, like their sprinkler head counterparts, are classified as to the temperature of operation and marked with the appropriate color code.

When a fire occurs, the air above the fire is rapidly heated. Another type of heat detector, called the rate-of-rise detector takes advantage of this rapid temperature increase.

Rate-of-Rise Detectors

Rate-of-rise detectors are activated when the rate of temperature increase at the detector exceeds a stated rate (usually 12 to 15 degrees Fahrenheit per minute). Rate-of-rise detectors have the following advantages:

They can be set to operate more rapidly under most conditions than fixed-temperature devices.

They are effective across a wide range of ambient temperatures and are therefore good in low or high ambient temperature areas.

They recycle rapidly when the temperature returns to a stable condition.

They tolerate slow changes in temperature without giving an alarm.

Rate-of-rise detectors may have the following disadvantages:

They are susceptible to false alarm where a rapidly increasing ambient temperature is not the result of a fire.

They may fail to respond to a fire which propagates slowly and therefore has a slow temperature rise.

There are two types of rate-of-rise detectors, pneumatic and mechanical. Pneumatic-type detectors operate on the principle of the expansion of air heated in either a chamber (spot-type) or in a tube (area-type). Spot-type rate-of-rise detectors operate when the air in a chamber is heated and expands causing a diaphragm to move to complete an electric circuit. Pneumatic tube detectors consist of a tube containing air. It operates when the pressure rise caused by heating of the tubing causes the air to expand forcing a diaphragm to move to make an electric contact. There is a small vent in the system to accommodate a slow temperature rise (Figure 7-2).

Thermoelectric detectors are mechanical devices with two sets of thermocouples mounted in a single housing. One set of thermocouples is exposed to heat from convection air currents and radiation, while the other is shielded. A voltage is produced when a temperature difference exists between them. This type accommodates slow temperature changes because both thermocouples are heated equally. A rapid heat rise however, will cause the exposed thermocouple to be heated first.

Combined Rate-of-Rise and Fixed-Temperature Detectors

By combining the capabilities of the rate-of-rise and fixed-temperature detectors we benefit by being able to detect a slow growing fire (fixed) and a fast growing

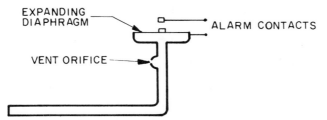

Figure 7-2. Pneumatic tube (rate-of-rise) heat detector. (Source: Richard W. Bukowski)

fire (rate-of-rise) and overcoming the shortcomings of either one individually. Of course, the combined devices have two ratings, a fixed-temperature and temperature rate-of-rise. This type operates as a vented air chamber containing either a bimetallic strip [Figure 7-3(a)] or a leaf spring that is soldered in place by a eutectic alloy [Figure 7-3(b)]. A mixture of two or more metals resulting in an alloy with a melting point that is lower than either of the two individual

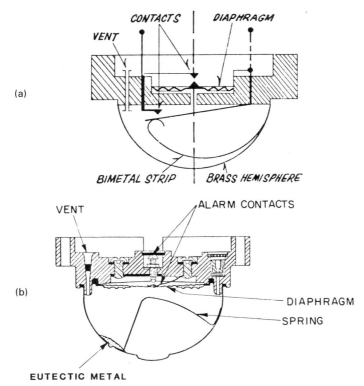

Figure 7-3. Combined rate-of-rise and fixed temperature heat detectors. (a) Using a bimetal element. (b) Using a eutectic solder. (Source: Richard W. Bukowski)

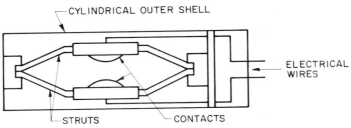

Figure 7-4.   Rate-compensation detector. (Source: Fenwal Inc.)

metals is defined as a eutectic alloy. These materials are commonly used where some device is required to operate at a specific predetermined temperature. The vented air chamber acts as the rate-of-rise portion and the flexing of the bimetallic strip or the spring acts as the fixed temperature device.

Another mechanical device that provides the characteristics of a combined rate-of-rise and fixed-temperature detector is the rate-compensation detector. This device consists of two metal struts under compression in the normally open position, contained in a metal cylinder (Figure 7-4). The outer shell is usually made of aluminum, a metal with a high coefficient of thermal expansion. The struts are usually made of copper, which has a lower expansion coefficient. When exposed to a rapid temperature rise, the shell expands, relieving the force on the struts and allowing them to close. When the temperature rises slowly, both parts expand and the contacts remain open until the cylinder, with its greater expansion rate, has expanded far enough to allow the contacts to close at the fixed temperature point of this detector.

The combustion process has been defined as, an exothermic gas-phase chemical reaction in which hot gases are produced which rise through convection. This rising column of hot gas and air carries with it smoke and other products of combustion. It is, therefore, desirable to locate heat detectors and other devices that detect products of combustion at high points above the protected area.

SMOKE DETECTION

Heat detectors have been around for many years, and they still have many applications in fire detection. They are dependable and reliable and require little maintenance. Unfortunately, heat detectors require substantial amounts of heat to operate, heat that is normally not produced until a fire is well developed. Smoke detectors were developed in response to a need to detect fire in the earlier development stages. Remember, smoke refers to solid or liquid particles that are released during combustion. Smoldering combustion generates smoke in the form of condensed vapors, and it appears light colored (liquid is largely water). Smoke produced during flaming combustion is darker (mostly from carbon). This also means that the particle size in smoke from smoldering fires is larger

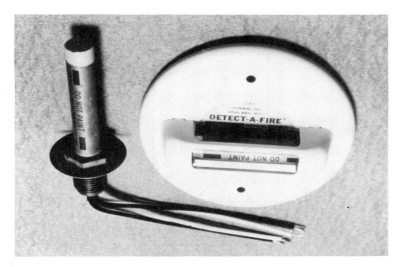

Figure 7-5. Rate-compensation detector for vertical installation (left) and horizontal installation (right). (Source: Fenwal Inc.)

than in smoke from flaming fires. Smoke detectors have been developed which are specific for each type of smoke. The type of smoke expected in a particular occupancy will dictate the type of smoke detector selected. The traditional methods for detecting smoke have been with either ionization or photoelectric smoke detectors. These detectors are more costly and require more maintenance than the heat detector, but they are considerably faster in their operation than heat detectors. Along with the greater sensitivity of smoke detectors goes a higher false alarm rate. Like heat detectors, it is also critical that they be properly located for optimum performance.

Ionization Smoke Detectors

Ionization smoke detectors are generally of the spot-type. They are more sensitive to the smaller particles that are produced by most flaming fires. These particles are less than 1 μm in size. A very simple ionization detector consists of a sensing chamber that contains two electrically charged electrodes, one positive and one negative. Between the two electrodes is a very small alpha or beta radiation source. Americium-241 is the commonly used alpha source and radium-226 is the commonly used beta source. The radiation source makes the air electrically conductive, or ionizes it, in the chamber creating positive and negative ions that are attracted to the oppositely charged electrodes. This creates a small ionization current between the two electrodes (Figure 7-6). When smoke particles in the size range of 0.01–1.0 μm enter the chamber, the ionization

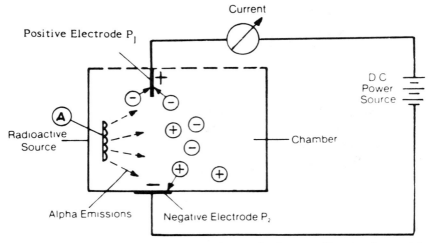

Figure 7-6. Principle of an ionization chamber smoke detector. The chamber contains minute quantities of a radioactive material (A). Alpha emissions from this material ionize the air between the plates (P_1 and P_2) in the chamber causing a small current to flow between the plates. Smoke particles entering the chamber will interrupt the current flow resulting in a drop in the current and an alarm condition. (Source: Fenwal Inc.)

current is interrupted, causing a drop in current in the electronic circuit. This explains why smoke from flaming fires, which is darker and contains carbon particles that are electrically conductive, is more readily detected by ionization detectors. When the current drop reaches a set point, the alarm is activated.

There are two kinds of ionization detectors based upon the placement of the alpha source. Placement of the ionization source may be used to create a unipolar or a bipolar chamber. In the unipolar chamber, a tightly collimated alpha source is located close to the negative electrode restricting its ionization effect to a small portion of the chamber [Figure 7-7(a)]. With most of the ionization taking place near the negative electrode, most of the positive ions are easily attracted to the cathode. The negative ions predominate in the rest of the chamber. The bipolar chamber detector has the ionization source centrally located so that the entire chamber space is subject to ionization [Figure 7-7(b)].

The unipolar chamber detector's performance is almost three times better than the bipolar chamber when exposed to smoke produced by a slow, smoldering fire. The reduced sensitivity of the bipolar chamber detector is probably due to recombination, or neutralization of ions of opposite signs, which occurs in the bipolar chamber. The predominance of negative ions in the unipolar chamber tends to preclude recombination.

There are two variations of the ionization detector based upon the number of chambers. In some detectors, there is a single ionization chamber which measures the current interruption and compares it to a reference circuit. In the dual

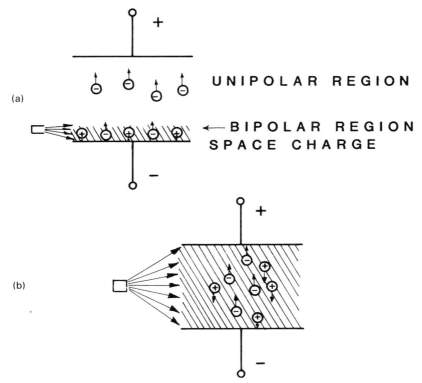

(a)

UNIPOLAR REGION

←BIPOLAR REGION
SPACE CHARGE

(b)

Figure 7-7. The unipolar ion chamber (a) and the bipolar ion chamber (b). (Source: Richard W. Bukowski)

chamber detector, ionization takes place in two chambers. One of the chambers is open to the atmosphere. The other chamber is restricted so that smoke particles cannot enter. This restricted chamber acts as the reference circuit by which the current drop in the exposed chamber is measured. One advantage in the dual chamber detector is its ability to accommodate to slow changes in temperature, pressure, and humidity.

Shortcomings. The shortcomings of the ionization detector are its susceptibility to low temperature, high humidity, and dirt or dust particles which may interrupt the current causing the detector to go into alarm.

Photoelectric Smoke Detectors

There are two spot-type photoelectric smoke detectors that operate on a light principle where smoke entering a light beam either obscures the beam's path to

Figure 7-8.   An ionization smoke detector. (Source: Cerberus Pyrotronics)

a photocell or reflects light into a photocell. Beam-type photoelectric detectors are also available as area devices to protect large open areas. Smoke detectors that look for attenuation of the light beam employ a light source, a light beam collimating system, and a photovoltaic or photoresistive cell [Figure 7-9(a)]. When smoke particles enter the light chamber or light beam, the light beam is blocked. The reduction in light alters the voltage output, and this change is detected by the detector circuit which initiates an alarm. Color of the smoke makes no difference to light obscuration detectors. The scattering of light onto a photocell is another, more common, photoelectric detection method. In this system, a photovoltaic or photoresistive cell is in the detection chamber, but it is not in the direct path of the light beam. Figure 7-9(b) shows two types of

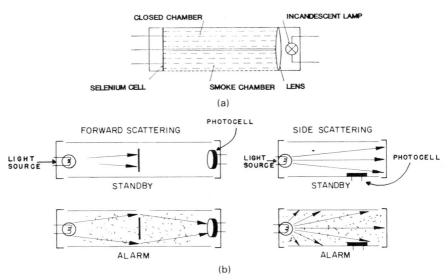

Figure 7-9.   (a) Spot-type light attenuation smoke detector. (b) Light-scattering smoke detectors. (Source: Richard W. Bukowski)

light-scattering chamber arrangement. When smoke enters the chamber, light is scattered onto the photocell. The operation of these detectors seems quite simple; however, their design parameters are really very complex. Light-scattering-type smoke detectors are more responsive to visible particles greater than 1 μm in size which are produced by smoldering fires. This smoke is commonly gray to white in color. The light color and larger sized particles help to scatter the light which makes this type of smoke detector effective.

The ionization detectors and spot-type photoelectric detectors may be used as single station, self-contained power devices similar to detectors used in the home, or they may be part of an integrated system with remote power supply, alarm, and zone-indicating hardware.

There is also an area-type photoelectric detector that utilizes a projected beam (Figure 7-11). This type of detector may be used to protect a large open area with the light source installed at one end of the area and the photoreceiver at the opposite end. This concept is ideal for high bay applications such as warehouses, atriums, convention centers, and sports complexes. One type of projected beam smoke detector projects an invisible beam of infrared energy across the protected space. A microprocessor analyzes the energy decrease caused by smoke obscuration. Area-type photoelectric detectors are not affected by the color of the smoke. The drawbacks of this type of system is that there can be no obstructions in the beam path, and since the beam is relatively narrow, smoke will not be detected until it migrates across the beam path. This problem can be overcome through the use of mirrors that reflect the beam back and forth across the protected space, or by employing multiple beams. Like the ionization detectors, the photoelectric detectors require more maintenance than heat detectors, but they are more sensitive and provide an earlier warning than the heat detectors.

Selection Criteria—Ionization Versus Photoelectric

Once the decision is made to install smoke detectors, it is necessary to determine the best detector for the application. Ionization detectors are considered to be superior to photoelectric detectors in detecting fast, flaming fires that produce combustion particles in the range of 0.01 to 3 μm. They are more sensitive to dark or black smoke. Photoelectric detectors on the other hand are more sensitive to smoldering fires that are characterized by larger particles in the range of 0.3 to 10 μm. They are more responsive to light gray smoke. It is difficult, in most situations, to determine in advance the type of fire and smoke that will occur. However, some generalizations may be made. Ionization detectors are preferred for protecting complex and costly equipment, such as computer rooms, because of their ability to detect invisible products of combustion. Ionization detectors are also recommended in occupancies containing plastics such as polyurethane and polystyrene, and combustible liquids such as gasoline

Figure 7-10. A photoelectric smoke detector. (Source: Cerberus Pyrotronics)

and fuel oil, since these products give off black smoke when they burn. Photoelectric detectors are preferred in areas containing internal combustion equipment such as trucks and forklifts and in areas where welding is performed, because these operations give off smaller sized combustion particles. They also may be used near kitchens or in areas in which slow smoldering fires are expected.

There is nothing wrong with mixing ionization and photoelectric smoke detectors in areas where the type of fire or fuel is mixed or unknown. The author once used ionization detectors to protect an area containing a quantity of polyurethane foam material. A false alarm and activation of a deluge sprinkler system occurred when the detectors became dust contaminated and simultaneously experienced a high humidity environment. In this case, the author cross-zoned, or paired, the ionization detectors with photoelectric to prevent inadvertent activation of the deluge system while retaining the ability to detect smoke from burning polyurethane.

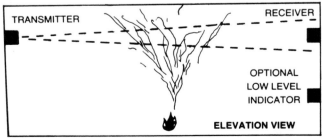

Figure 7-11. Operation of a projected beam smoke detector. (Source: Cerberus Pyrotronics)

Submicrometer Particle Counting Detectors

While the ionization and photoelectric detectors function to detect fires in the early smoldering, or thermal decomposition, stage of fire development, it still takes time for sufficient quantities of smoke to be generated to activate the detector. In areas of high airflow, where smoke may be diluted, the spot-type ionization and photoelectric detectors have a delayed response time. There is also a delay after a signal is sent while some response is initiated. In some applications such as clean rooms, anechoic chambers, telephone equipment rooms, and computer facilities, where high values or critical operations are performed, even earlier detection may be desirable. For example, clean rooms and computer facilities usually have considerable air movement to maintain cleanliness and to cool the heat loads generated by electronic equipment. A small fire in this type of facility may generate damaging quantities of corrosive fumes and smoke which will be spread throughout the facility by the air movement. If the fire can be detected in the incipient stage and air-conditioning systems shut down and suppression activities initiated, much of the damage can be reduced. For this reason, sampling-type submicrometer particle counting detectors have been developed.

During the incipient stage of fire development (pyrolysis or precombustion) while the fuel is being heated, submicrometer size particles are produced in vast quantities. Typically, heating of the combustible material will generate particles at the rate of 10^9 particles per second. The size of these particles ranges from 0.005 to 0.02 μm. An incipient fire raises the concentration of these particles sufficiently above background levels to be used as a fire signal. One type of incipient detector uses the submicrometer particles as condensation nuclei. When the particles are drawn through a humidifier, they pick up moisture and quickly reach a size where they can be detected by photoelectric means.

Another type of incipient detector uses a photoelectric principle of light obscuration of incipient particles. The particles must be slightly larger for this detector than those detected by the cloud chamber detector.

Since these are air-sampling-type detectors, they are unaffected by high air velocities, dust, humidity, vibration, and a wide range of temperatures. The tubes that make up the air sampling network can be plastic making them invisible for use in areas where RF radiation tests are conducted. Since the detection equipment can be located far away from the protected area, it is not affected by radiation. Activation by RF radiation has been a problem with spot-type ionization and photoelectric detectors.

Submicrometer particle counting detection systems, because of their complexity and reliability, are more expensive than any of the previously discussed systems, but the value of the protected property or requirement for earlier detection may well justify the expense. Additionally, the submicrometer particle counting detectors protect large areas and replace numerous spot-type detectors, resulting in some cost equalization.

Cloud Chamber Smoke Detectors

Cloud chamber smoke detectors are air sampling devices that employ cloud chamber particle detection technology. This type of detector is extremely sensitive to the very small particles (down to 0.002 μm) that result from material thermal degradation or combustion. These very small particles are generated during the incipient stage of a fire as the fuel source is beginning to decompose. Submicrometer products of combustion are referred to as condensation nuclei. This means that when exposed to high humidity, under the right conditions, the particles will pick up the water vapor and grow in size to about 15 μm. At 15 μm, the particles are optically visible and can be detected in a simple photoelectric detector.

An air sample is drawn through a filter to remove dust and other large particles, into a high humidity chamber within the detector. When the sample is in the humidity chamber, the pressure is lowered slightly. When submicrometer smoke particles are present, the moisture in the air chamber condenses on them, forming a cloud. The density of the cloud is measured by the photoelectric principle.

The currently available cloud chamber-type smoke detector consists of a four-zone control panel that collects air samples from a network of tubing. The sample network can sample up to four separate hazard areas for a total protected area of 36,000 ft^2 (Figure 7-12). Figure 7-13 shows a typical application of this device with one unit protecting equipment and storage areas, a laboratory, computer room (including a sensor within a piece of equipment), and an office area.

Photoelectric Incipient Fire Detector

There is an air-sampling-type photoelectric smoke detector that operates on the light scattering principle. It is highly sensitive to the submicrometer particles that are generated by the incipient fire before there is visible smoke. To achieve this high sensitivity, it utilizes an intense light source, a large scattering chamber, and a highly responsive photo receiver. The sample air is drawn through an 8-μm filter to eliminate large particles and dust. Air is sampled from a network of tubing that can be as much as 250 feet from the detector and can sample from an area up to 20,000 ft^2. Air is drawn through the filter and into the detection chamber where particles are illuminated by an intense xenon light source every 3 seconds (Figure 7-14).

An ultrasensitive photo receiver collects the light that is scattered off of the particles. This detector is available in three sensitivity ranges based upon obscuration. These three ranges are 0.003 to 0.03%/ft, 0.006 to 0.06%/ft, and 0.015 to 0.15%/ft. Like the cloud chamber detector, this detector has a similar response to gray and dark decomposition particles. The signal is processed to provide an analog smoke intensity reading that activates a 10 gradation bar

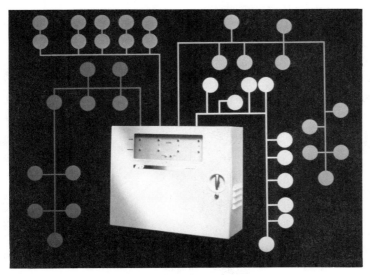

Figure 7-12. A cloud chamber incipient fire detector with symbols representing the capability to sample in four different zones of differing configurations. (Source: Environment One Corporation)

graph display from which three different programmable alarm levels may be activated. These three different levels of alarm can be programmed to provide different remedial functions from local alarm activation to activating a fire suppression system. There is an adjustable delay of from 0 to 60 seconds at each alarm level which can be used to delay activation of the response and

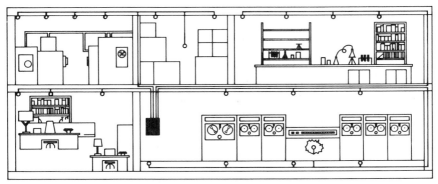

Figure 7-13. A typical application of the four-zone cloud chamber detector with one zone protecting equipment and storage areas (upper left), a laboratory (upper right), computer room with one sensor inside a piece of equipment (lower right), and an office area (lower left). (Source: Environment One Corporation)

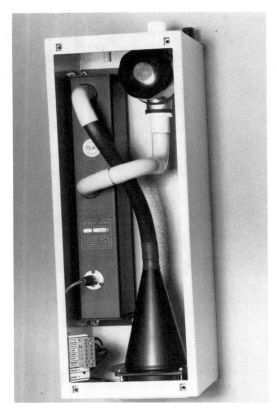

Figure 7-14. An air-sampling photoelectric smoke detector consisting of an air pump, filter, high intensity light source, and photo receiver. (Source: Fenwal Inc.)

prevent inadvertent activation. If smoke intensity drops during the delay, the alarm is cancelled.

FLAME DETECTORS

Another signature of the combustion process that can be detected is the flame. Some fires such as burning gases produce insufficient smoke for detection by other means. Flammable liquids may flash very rapidly before there is any smoke production, therefore a device that can detect flames would be preferred.

Flames radiate light energy over a broad spectrum. In addition to visible light, flaming fires emit ultraviolet (UV) and infrared (IR) radiation at wavelengths that are invisible to the human eye. Radiation in the visible and infrared region of the spectrum comes largely from thermal energy radiating from the carbon particles within the flame. This is why a hydrogen flame, which contains

Figure 7-15. The air-sampling photoelectric smoke detector with three different programmable alarm levels. (Source: Fenwal Inc.)

no carbon, is invisible. Ultraviolet radiation comes largely from OH radicals, and the thermally broadened OH radiation explains why alcohol flames and premixed gas flames appear blue.

Detectors that detect the light energy radiated from flames are called flame sensing fire detectors. Although it is possible to develop a detector that responds to energy in the visible spectrum, there are many other sources of visible light that could cause false alarms. For this reason, manufacturers of flame detectors have selected specific wavelengths in the IR or UV regions that are as unique to flame as possible. Although there are still sources of interference, the wavelengths chosen tend to minimize them. Flaming fire detectors are available in models that detect the IR, UV, or both IR and UV (Figure 7-16). IR detectors detect radiant energy in the range around 44,000 Ångstroms (4.4 μm). UV detectors detect radiant energy in the area of 2500 Ångstroms (0.25 μm) and less. With flame detectors, detection is almost instantaneous, because the light energy travels in a straight line and at the speed of light. Since the fire is radiating in all directions, the intensity falls off as the square of the distance from the fire to the detector and may be attenuated by any smoke particles in the

Figure 7-16. A UV/IR fire detector. (Source: Armtec Industries Inc.)

radiant beam. The key thing to remember about flame detection, especially when placing the detectors, is that the detector must be able to ''see'' the flame directly.

Because they are detecting light energy, flame detectors have the fastest detection times of any type of fire detector. Detection times for flame detectors are generally measured in milliseconds from fire ignition. Because of their high speed, flame detectors also have the highest false alarm rate of any of the detectors. There is an abundance of light sources that may imitate flame in the industrial environment. This shortcoming can be overcome when instantaneous reaction is not necessary. A time delay can be built into the alarm circuit to require the detector to ''see'' the fire signal for a period of time before alarming. A voting requirement may be incorporated which requires two or more detectors to ''see'' the fire signal. Similar to voting, the detectors may be cross-zoned or have a requirement for two electrically or mechanically separate zones of detectors to be actuated.

Flame detectors are generally only used in high hazard areas such as fuel loading platforms, industrial process areas, high ceiling areas, and any other areas with atmospheres in which explosions or very rapid fires may occur.

Infrared Flame Detectors

Infrared flame detectors respond to radiant energy outside the range of human vision (around 4.4 μm). Although infrared energy will reflect from surfaces at a reduced level, the primary mode of detection is line-of-sight. There are numerous sources of IR radiation found in nature and industry, such as sunlight and hot objects. For this reason, discrimination characteristics can be built into IR detectors, but speed of detection is sacrificed when this is done. To achieve high-speed response from an IR detector it must be carefully isolated from radiation sources other than those that originate from a fire. The detectors consist of a filter and lens system to filter out unwanted wavelengths and focus the incoming energy onto photovoltaic or photoresistive cells sensitive to infrared energy.

Interference from solar radiation in the infrared region can be a major problem in the use of infrared detectors, although filters can be added to partially resolve the solar interference problem. When detectors are used indoors, this filtering is not necessary. The detectors can also be made to respond to the light that is modulated at a frequency characteristic of the flicker of flame (5–30 Hz) in order to minimize false alarms. This is known as flicker discrimination. Even with these extra characteristics, IR flame detectors have been known to raise false alarms. In one case, a detection system that was located in a building went into alarm mode when a door to the outside was opened and a detector "saw" sunlight reflecting (flickering) off the ripples on a body of water.

Ultraviolet Flame Detectors

Ultraviolet flame detectors respond to high-energy radiation with wavelengths of 2500 Ångstroms and less. At this wavelength, they are essentially insensitive to sunlight, although gamma and x-radiation, welding flashes, and lightning can cause false alarms. They are not affected by adverse weather conditions such as wind, rain, snow, high humidity, or extremes of temperature or pressure. UV detectors are particularly suited for rapidly developing fires that emit flame, such as most hydrocarbons and munitions materials. The operation of UV detectors is very similar to the IR detectors and they can have the flame flicker discrimination incorporated.

UV/IR Fire Detection Systems

Flame sensing devices have been combined for special applications and where greater reliability is desired. These systems consist of one IR sensor and one UV sensor mounted adjacent to one another. These sensors are connected to a microprocessor-based controller which requires simultaneous actuation of both UV and IR sensors to produce a fire alarm. This system practically eliminates all false alarms since the IR and UV sensors have virtually no false alarm sources in common.

ADDRESSABLE ANALOG DETECTOR SYSTEM

With the availability of low-cost microprocessors smart, or intelligent, detection systems are now available. Any kind of detector or alarm may be incorporated, ionization, photoelectric, heat, or flame. Detectors can be combined with a microprocessor-based system control panel to form an addressable analog detector system, an intelligent system with virtually unlimited possibilities.

The detectors in this system are only sensors that are monitored or queried by the panel every 3 seconds. The panel questions their status, sensitivity, and any other information that is needed. The control panel analyzes the digital information returned and takes the programmed action. This programmed action can include any number of actions from transmitting an alarm, closing doors, activating ventilation systems, closing fire or smoke dampers, activating suppression systems, and printing out a permanent record. All of these activities can be programmed to take place in any priority sequence and based upon any desired combination of data received from the sensors.

Another capability of addressable analog detection systems is the ability of the system to analyze and automatically adjust the sensitivity of every detector in the system on a real-time basis to compensate for differences in the quality of the air at the protected site.

SELECTING THE DETECTION SYSTEM

An ideal detector is one that would recognize signals only from sources defined as potential fire hazards, sources that have a certain magnitude, signature, and persistence. The ideal detector would be able to detect and evaluate all of the fire signatures and reliably compare them to determine that a fire exists. The ideal detector, as described, is not possible, but the technology is available to create one that comes very close. Within each fire signature, high reliability can be achieved by installing detectors related to the type of environment being protected and the type of fire expected. Detectors are available for all of the fire signatures, and each type has different characteristics to discriminate the magnitude and persistence of the signature. Different types of detectors can be combined in a system with supervisory or self-checking circuits, flicker rate, and radiation frequency discrimination.

False Alarms

A false alarm is an alarm that is not caused by a source that could cause property damage or injury to personnel. False alarms are a troublesome problem to business and industry. They are time consuming, costly, and they lower the credibility of the detection systems. False alarms can be particularly costly when the alarmed detection system activates a fire suppression system such as deluge sprinklers or halon. When people experience too many false alarms, they tend to ignore them, or they have been known to disconnect alarms. When a fire really occurs, a disconnected alarm or the delay caused by people ignoring the alarm may result in significant property damage that should have been avoided.

The usual sources of false alarms are excessive air velocity, changes in humidity and temperature, condensation, dust, RF/EMI, transients, component failure, and marginal circuit design or poor installation.

The detection industry has been working on the problem of false alarms. Some newer systems have various alarm levels of which a significant level of alarm is necessary to cause the signal to be transmitted. Other systems have a built-in alarm verification capability in which the system resets itself after receiving an alarm. When the signal persists or reoccurs within a given time limit, the panel activates the full alarm.

Some of the major factors which the detection system must distinguish between sources of false alarms and genuine alarms include the nature, level, signature, and persistence of the source.

Nature of the Source. The detector must rule out all but actual indicators of overheating or burning, or all but actual potential fire sources. There are many sources that imitate fire-caused smoke, such as dust, condensation, and aerosols. Therefore, other discrimination characteristics must be built into the detection system or inspection and preventive maintenance activities must be incorporated to reduce the potential for false alarms.

Level or Magnitude of the Source. The detector must be designed to recognize a threshold below which the source is not considered to be a threat. For example, cigarette smoke, welding arc, and other ''noise'' or false sources must be excluded as fire indicators. The detection system should be installed and adjusted to the background. In other words, a detector in a normally smoky or dusty environment that may be normally on the verge of alarming should be adjusted to be less sensitive so that a real fire will create sufficient signature levels to provide an alarm.

Signature of the Source. The signal, or indicator, of the source at the point when it becomes a hazard is known as the signature of the source. For example, the flame detector looks for the signature of a fire to distinguish it from background radiation. It looks for a radiation frequency, or combination of frequencies to indicate fire. Signature recognition will not by itself prevent false alarm, since a short duration signal from a cigarette would satisfy the requirements for a detector that merely recognizes smoke.

Persistence of the Source. By testing for persistence of the signal within the detector, a means is provided to reject transient signals such as a gust of wind or a high voltage spike from causing a false alarm. Some detection systems are programmed to ''see'' the source for a certain period of time before signaling an alarm.

Methods of Reducing the Probability of False Alarms

There are characteristics that can be designed or programmed into the detection system to minimize the occurrence of false alarms, such as time delay, voting, cross-zoning, and sensitivity adjustment.

With time delay, the fire signal is required to be present for a predetermined amount of time before an alarm is activated. However, when time delay is incorporated, there is a tradeoff between high-speed detection and response and unnecessarily activating a suppression system.

When there is a requirement for more than one detection device to detect a fire signal before activating an alarm the system is said to ''vote.'' Voting eliminates false alarms caused by a single spurious source or an electronic failure of one device. With cross-zoning, two separate electrical or mechanical zones of detectors are both required to be actuated prior to the confirmation of a fire.

By adjusting the sensitivity of the detectors so as to require a greater signal strength to cause activation, false signals may be avoided. However, reducing the sensitivity compromises the detectors' ability to detect a small fire. When the system is finally activated, it may be too late.

LOCATION, INSTALLATION, AND MAINTENANCE OF DETECTORS

Location and Spacing of Detectors

The spacing and location of detectors must follow the manufacturer's instructions and should take into consideration the characteristics of the detection method used and the nature of the area protected. There are a number of variables to be considered when locating and spacing detectors, including the possibility of air currents, configuration of the ceiling, and burning characteristics of the combustibles that are present. Consideration must be given to the distance from the expected fire source and obstructions that might interrupt the desired fire signature.

Installation and Maintenance of Detectors

Regardless of the type of detection system selected, it must be properly installed to provide optimum protection. Design and installation of detection systems should be performed only by qualified individuals. It is beneficial to conduct fire tests of the system before placing it in service to ensure that detectors are located properly and can actually detect the fire signature for which they are intended.

All detection systems require some periodic maintenance in order to achieve optimum performance. Maintenance may include cleaning, testing, calibration, and replacing batteries, as necessary. Cleaning is important because, in some systems, dust or other contamination may cause false alarms. In other systems, contamination may obscure a real fire situation. Periodic testing is important to ensure that the system has the proper sensitivity and that the smoke can actually get into the sensing chamber. In all cases, the manufacturer's recommendations for maintenance and testing should be followed.

PROTECTIVE SIGNALING SYSTEMS

Once the detection system has identified a fire condition, it is necessary to transmit this information to alert the occupants for life safety purposes. Occupants may use this information to notify the fire department, or a signaling system could be incorporated to automatically perform this function. There are various systems that handle these signaling functions, each of which is adapted to different requirements of the protected property and the response activity.

Protective signaling systems have an extremely important function in the industrial fire protection program. From life safety notification of occupants to notification of the public fire department to activation of life safety and fire control systems, the signaling system must be reliable. To achieve reliability, the equipment used must be approved and the protective signaling service must meet the requirements of the applicable NFPA standard. The system should also be tested periodically to ensure that it is functioning properly.

Local Systems

With a local protective signaling system, the alarm or supervisory signal registers in the protected premises. A local alarm is for notification of occupants within the protected building, notification of the operation of protection equipment, the detection of smoke, or the detection of heat. The local system does not include provisions for notifying an outside, or off-site fire department. This function is the responsibility of the building occupants. Because the system is local, there is no protection during periods in which the premises is unoccupied. The local system must have a reliable power supply such as dependable commercial power service. It must also have a backup power supply such as an engine-driven generator or storage batteries.

Auxiliary Systems

With an auxiliary protective signaling system, signals are transmitted directly to the municipal fire alarm system. An auxiliary system utilizes the municipal fire alarm facilities to transmit an alarm to the municipal communications center. Alarms are received at the municipal communications center on the same equipment and by the same alerting methods as alarms that are transmitted from municipal fire alarm boxes. Equipment in the protected plant is owned and maintained by the property owner. As in the local system, the auxiliary system must have an adequate power supply and reliable backup power supply.

Remote Station System

A remote station protective signaling system is similar to the auxiliary system in that the alarm signal is received at a remote station. The receiving equipment may be at the fire department, police department, or an answering service. The alarm or supervisory signal is transmitted over leased telephone lines to the remote station. If the remote station is not the fire department, they notify the fire department. The remote station is common in small communities which have a volunteer, or unattended, fire department. The remote station, whether it is a police department or an answering service, has the responsibility to notify fire personnel. An adequate power supply and reliable backup power supply is required at the protected premises as well as the remote station.

Proprietary System

With a proprietary protective signaling system, signals are received at a central supervisory station which has trained and experienced operators on duty 24 hours a day. The proprietary system serves contiguous and noncontiguous property and is under the control of the owner or operator of the protected property. It is usually in or near that property. Operators of the proprietary system have the responsibility to notify the municipal fire department. They may have a number of other response functions, such as evacuation coordination, HVAC control functions, and communications with the building occupants. Newer systems for large industrial complexes and business occupancies may have very complex equipment in the proprietary system to monitor security, building HVAC systems, equipment parameters, and other alarm systems as well as the fire alarms. The many functions that may be incorporated into a proprietary system are often handled by signal multiplexing systems and built in minicomputer systems.

The receiving console to which the proprietary system transmits an alarm may be very complex. It may include individual lights, a digital display, or a CRT visual display. The panel also has an alarm to alert the operator and a printer to maintain a hardcopy of the activity. Of course, the proprietary system also requires an adequate power supply and reliable backup power supply.

Central Station Systems

The central station protective signaling system is owned and operated by a separate business entity that is in business for the sole purpose of operating the system for client businesses. Signals are usually transmitted to the independent central station agency over leased telephone lines. The central station, which is manned 24 hours per day is responsible for retransmitting fire alarms to the fire department and to take whatever action supervisory signals indicate is necessary. Central station personnel may also alert and confirm alarms with the protected property. The central station must also have an adequate power supply and reliable backup power.

SUMMARY

The automatic detection of fire is a major part of the industrial fire protection program. Automatic fire detection protects the facility during periods when the facility is unoccupied, and during working hours, it ensures that an alarm is given even before people have detected the problem.

There are many different kinds of detectors at many levels of sophistication to detect the different signatures of fire including heat, smoke, and flame. When selecting a detection system, it is important to consider the type of fire that is possible, the speed of detection that is required, the tolerance of false alarms, and the level of sophistication that is necessary.

Once fire has been detected, it is necessary to transmit the alarm to the appropriate emergency response activity. This is accomplished via a protective signaling system. Protective signaling systems are available to provide service depending upon the requirements, size, and capabilities of the facility, and equipment and type of notification required by the fire department.

All parts of the total system including the detectors, annunciators, and signaling system must be maintained according to the manufacturer's instructions, or more often when required by the local environmental conditions. The systems must also be periodically tested to determine proper function and response.

BIBLIOGRAPHY

Bertschinger, Susan. 1988. Smoke Detectors and Unwanted Alarms. *Fire Journal* 82(1): 43–53.

Bukowski, Richard W. 1986. Techniques For Fire Detection. Paper presented at Spacecraft Fire Safety Workshop, 20-21, 1986, at NASA Lewis Research Center, Cleveland, Ohio.

Fenwal Automatic Fire Detectors Application Engineering Manual (MC-402). Undated. Ashland MA: Fenwall Incorporated.

Fire Protection Handbook, 16th ed. 1986. Quincy: National Fire Protection Association.

NFPA 71-1987. Standard for the Installation, Maintenance and Use of Signaling Systems for Central Station Service. Quincy: National Fire Protection Association.

NFPA 72A-1987. Standard for the Installation, Maintenance and Use of Local Protective Signaling

Systems for Guard's Tour, Fire Alarm and Supervisory Service. Quincy: National Fire Protection Association.

NFPA 72B-1986. Standard for the Installation, Maintenance and Use of Auxiliary Protective Signaling Systems for Fire Alarm Service. Quincy: National Fire Protection Association.

NFPA 72C-1986. Standard for the Installation, Maintenance and Use of Remote Station Protective Signaling Systems. Quincy: National Fire Protection Association.

NFPA 72D-1986. Standard for the Installation, Maintenance and Use of Proprietary Protective Signaling Systems. Quincy: National Fire Protection Association.

NFPA 72E-1987. *Standard on Automatic Fire Detectors.* Quincy: National Fire Protection Association.

Skala, George F. 1989. The IFD—A New Generation Fire Detection System. Paper read at 9th International Conference on Automatic Fire Detection, 26 September 1989, at Duisburg, Federal Republic of West Germany.

8
FIRE EXTINGUISHING AGENTS

In Chapter 2, the Characteristics and Behavior of Fire, the fire tetrahedron was defined as being the four components necessary for a flaming fire to occur, namely oxygen, heat of ignition, fuel, and the chain reaction. These elements are all necessary for fire to occur. Conversely, the removal of any one of the elements will result in the extinguishment of the fire. In this chapter, the various extinguishing agents that are available to deal with the components of the fire tetrahedron will be discussed. When fire strikes, having the agent available that will attack the most vulnerable component of the fire tetrahedron will put the fire out easily. Can the fuel be reduced? Will water lower the temperature of the fuel? Should oxygen be removed by using an inert gas? These are examples of the evaluation process that must occur before the fire starts. When selecting an extinguishing agent there are a number of factors that must be evaluated including the type of fuel that is likely to be involved, the potential for adverse reactions with the agent, and the possible adverse effects of the agent itself. There are many types of fire extinguishing agents available for almost every fire situation. The firesafety professional must be familiar with all of them and ensure that the appropriate agent is available for use.

The fire extinguishing agents that are available include everything from simple and inexpensive water to complicated chemical formulations. When selecting extinguishing agents for first aid fire fighting or automatic fire control systems, the industrial fire protection specialist has the opportunity to evaluate the effectiveness of each agent with regard to the specific application. Agents can be selected that will be most effective, safest, and least damaging to the particular operation or equipment. Without this preplanning and equipment in place, fire fighters coming to fight a fire will not have the time to go through these evaluations and considerations, and they will use the most effective agent that is available to extinguish the fire. In many cases, further damage will result that may have been avoided had the proper agent been available and applied early in the fire scenario.

CLASSIFICATION OF FIRES

In most discussions of fire extinguishing agents and systems, types of fires are defined by class. The class definition is used extensively as a simple means to

169

identify the purpose of the fire extinguishing agent that is in portable fire extinguishers. The classification system is as follows:

Class A. Ordinary combustibles such as wood, paper, cloth, and plastics which, when burning, require the cooling and quenching effects of water, or solutions of water, or the blanketing effect of multipurpose dry chemicals.

Class B. Flammable liquid fires such as gasoline, oil, paints, and solvents which require blanketing, smothering, or chemical inhibition extinguishing agents.

Class C. Electrical fires which require a nonconductive fire extinguishing agent with cooling, smothering, or chemical inhibition characteristics.

Class D. Combustible metal fires such as magnesium (Mg), aluminum (Al), sodium (Na), potassium (K), sodium/potassium alloy, lithium (Li), zirconium (Zr), titanium (Ti), and uranium (U) which require special dry powder extinguishing agents which blanket the fire and exclude oxygen while being immune to the tremendous heat of a combustible metal fire.

WATER

The oldest and most common and abundant fire extinguishing agent that we have is water. It is inexpensive, readily available, and has excellent fire extinguishing properties. Another advantage of water is that it is easily transported, or moved, to the fire, although this has not always been the case in the history of American fire fighting. In the past, there was no uniformity in fire fighting equipment between one city and the next. The city of Baltimore suffered a major fire in 1904 in which 2500 buildings were destroyed. Fire companies were called to assist from Washington, D.C., Wilmington, and Philadelphia. But, their hose couplings would not fit the Baltimore hydrant connections; therefore, they had to pump water from the waterfront or haul it in barrels.

Following this fire, the fledgling National Bureau of Standards (NBS) published a standard for fire-hose coupling threads that could be followed by all manufacturers. In many older U.S. cities, especially in the East, fire fighters must still carry numerous adaptors in order to connect their hoses to older hydrants.

Characteristics of Water

Water is a heavy stable liquid. It is easily handled and applied through pumps, pipes, and hoses. The viscosity of water changes very little between its freezing point and its boiling point. Therefore, it can be easily pumped and conducted through hose and pipes at temperatures from slightly above its freezing point

(32 degrees Fahrenheit) to slightly below its boiling point (212 degrees Fahrenheit). It has excellent penetration capabilities when applied to ordinary combustibles. This characteristic can be enhanced through the use of chemical wetting agents. Conversely, water has sufficient surface tension to allow it to be applied in either a consolidated stream or in discrete water droplets as a fog or spray.

Water is normally applied to a fire in the form of the familiar stream, as from a fire hose, or as a spray. The stream is obviously more effective at reaching a distant fire area and at penetrating into burning ordinary combustible materials. The spray application of water, on the other hand, has a much greater heat absorbing capacity due to the large surface area presented by the water droplets.

There has been extensive research into the fire extinguishment capacity of water to include proper flow rates, droplet size, and its heat absorbing characteristics for various fire hazards. In the following chapter discussion of sprinkler systems it will be learned how the results of the research has been put to practical use to achieve the optimum sprinkler coverage, flow rates, and droplet size for each fire protection situation.

Extinguishing Properties

From a fire protection standpoint, the most useful characteristic of water is its ability to cool fuels below the temperatures required to sustain combustion. This characteristic applies to most solid fuels and combustible liquids. To change a 1-pound block of ice to water at 32 degrees Fahrenheit requires 143 Btu. To raise the temperature of this water from 32 to 212 degrees Fahrenheit requires 180 Btu. To change this 212 degree water to steam at standard temperature and pressure requires 970.3 Btu/lb.

When applied to a fire, water cools the surface of the fuel with which it comes into contact and interrupts the heat feedback cycle, retarding the further development of fuel gases and vapors. When applied to ordinary combustibles, water soaks into the fuel and prevents or slows further ignition, because it must be heated and evaporated before ignition can take place.

Water is a little less effective at cooling flammable liquids that can form combustible mixtures at, or below, normal ambient temperatures. Additionally, when water is applied to burning liquid fires, there is the possibility of further spreading of the fire by splashing. However, chemical foaming agents can be added to enhance the ability of water to extinguish liquid fires. It has been determined that small droplets of uniform size are the most effective in fire extinguishment, although in the discussion on sprinkler systems some applications will be discussed where larger droplet size is required. Sometimes, where penetration is necessary, a heavy water stream is necessary.

Another possible extinguishing property of water is by smothering through the action of steam. The expansion ratio of water to steam is about 1:1700. As water is applied to a fire and is changed to steam, and if the combustion zone is somewhat confined, the steam can displace enough air to produce a smothering action.

Fire in water soluble flammable liquids such as alcohol can be extinguished by diluting to the point where it no longer produces sufficient vapors to form an ignitable mixture. However, due to the large amount of water required, this method of extinguishment is only practical where facilities are capable of containing the resulting large volume of liquids.

Water Additives

There are various additives that are available to improve the effectiveness of water in order to meet various fire fighting situations. Included are those that lower the freezing point, increase the penetration capability, decrease the runoff tendency, and change the density of the water.

Antifreeze.   In climates where freezing of water in tanks, pipes, or portable fire extinguishers might be a problem, antifreeze materials may be added. Among the antifreeze agents that are available are calcium chloride for use in tanks and portable fire extinguishers and ethylene glycol, propylene glycol, and glycerine for the protection of wet pipe sprinkler systems. When fire suppression systems are connected to public water supplies, positive provisions must be made to prevent syphoning of the antifreeze solution back into the public water supply.

Wetting Agents.   Water has a high surface tension which is the characteristic that causes a droplet to bead, or form a convex shape. It is sometimes desirable to reduce the surface tension in water so that it will penetrate into the combustible materials. When dissolved in water wetting agents increase the spreading and soaking characteristics of the water, allowing it to soak in. The term for this solution is "wet water." Wet water is used on combustibles that are closely packed such as bailed or stacked cotton, cloth, hay, straw, and mattresses.

Thickening Agents.   Another additive for fire suppression water is one that makes it more viscous or thicker so that it does not run off as readily as plain water. The most common use for these materials is for wildland fires, which includes forest and brush fires, or where the fuel surfaces are oriented almost vertically. Treated water will adhere to the surface of combustibles rather than runoff and therefore, less water is required.

One type of water thickener is an organic gel-producing material that coats burning material or prevents its ignition. Another type produces a thick slurry. The slurry type mixtures are used primarily in wildland fire situations. Ammonium phosphates and sulfates are particularly good in these situations because of the added property of ammonium salts to retard flames and to halt glowing ignition.

Density Modifiers.   The density of water can be modified in two ways to enhance the fire extinguishing characteristics of water for certain situations. One method involves the addition of air to water to produce a foam that will float on the surface of flammable and combustible liquids. (See the section of this chapter entitled "Foam Extinguishing Agents.")

Synthetic detergents can be added to water to reduce the surface tension (similar to wetting agents). When these detergent solutions are applied to flammable or combustible liquids, they emulsify the fuel, or mix rapidly with the fuel, to produce a suspension of the liquid in the detergent solution. This froth has the effect of cooling the surface and lowering the vapor pressure of the fuel to the point that there are insufficient vapors for combustion. An example of emulsification is the application of solution of water and synthetic detergent to a heavy (No. 6) fuel oil.

Water and Electrical Fires.   It is well known that water contains impurities that conduct electricity and the rule of thumb is not to use it on electrical fires. Wet water, in particular, should not be applied to energized electrical equipment because it is sufficiently conductive to injure a fire fighter with an electric shock. Concerns about the electrical conductivity of water have led to much confusion with regard to the application of sprinkler systems in areas where there is electrical equipment. There is, of course, concern for the safety of occupants and fire fighters, but there is also concern about water increasing the damage to electrical, and particularly, electronic equipment. Here again, wet water, because of its penetrating characteristics, will have more harmful effects on electrical and electronic equipment.

Variables.   There are many variables concerning the application of water to live electrical equipment including the available voltage and current, the breakup of the water stream (droplets in air will be insulated by the air), purity of the water, and length and cross-section of the water stream. For the most part, these variables cannot be evaluated at the time of the fire. For this reason, it is recommended that employees and employee fire brigades follow the rule of thumb and not apply water to an electrical fire.

It is generally thought that there is not much danger to fire fighters directing a stream of water onto wires of less than 600 volts to ground from any distance encountered in normal fire conditions. However, when water must be used on or around energized electrical equipment, fire fighters should use a spray pattern rather than a solid stream. The spray provides better insulation than the solid stream. The big danger to fire fighters when working in the vicinity of energized electrical equipment is when they make direct contact with an energized source while standing in water and complete a circuit to ground.

Automatic Sprinklers and Electrical Fires.   Sprinkler systems are recommended in locations where electrical equipment is located. There is little danger of electric shock or of water causing damage to the equipment. The characteristics of the water spray pattern discharging from a sprinkler are such that there should be little danger of the transmission of hazardous current. It is also unlikely that personnel will be in the water discharge area when the sprinkler head activates, particularly with heat-activated systems.

Compared to the damage created by heat, flame, and smoke from a fire and to the physical damage caused by hose streams, there should be little concern regarding the water damage caused by automatic sprinklers. If cleaning is prompt, most electrical and electronic equipment is fully recoverable following water exposure. (See also Chapter 13 for protection of computer equipment.)

DRY CHEMICAL EXTINGUISHING AGENTS

Dry chemical extinguishing agents have been available and used for many years. They consist of dry powdered chemical formulations that are stored in moisture proof containers and applied to the fire pneumatically when the container is pressurized. They are stable at very low and at normal ambient temperatures, but at higher temperatures they may melt and become sticky. They are effective, nontoxic, and, since they are a dry powder mixture, they do not freeze. They provide only temporary extinguishing capabilities since they only provide instantaneous and momentary flame extinction.

Borax and sodium bicarbonate were the first chemical extinguishing agents developed. Later, sodium bicarbonate became the standard because of its greater effectiveness.

There are currently five basic varieties of dry chemical extinguishing agents, sodium bicarbonate, monoammonium phosphate based agents, ''purple-K'' potassium bicarbonate based agents, ''super-K'' potassium chloride based agents, and urea-potassium bicarbonate based agents. The ''purple K'' name comes from the fact that when this agent encounters the flame, it produces a purple color. The ''K'' is the chemical symbol for potassium. It is important to note that each agent formulation has unique properties for specific applications and they may not be compatible with one another. Therefore, dry chemical extinguishing agents should not be mixed. The dry chemical extinguishing agents are divided into two types, the dry chemical agents and multipurpose dry chemical agents.

Dry Chemical Agents

Dry chemical agents are those that are for use only on Class B and Class C fires. The bicarbonate dry chemical formulations are in this category. There are a number of fire extinguishing actions of dry chemical agents. It is thought that chemical powders such as ammonium or alkali metal salts or acid salts of carbonates, phosphates, or halides act, principally by chemical mechanisms to interrupt the chain reaction of the flames. In the combustion of hydrocarbon fuels, the H and OH free radical species exist in the flame. Dry chemical agents combine and remove these radicals as nonreactive water molecules. It is probable that the fineness of the powders results in greater reactive surface area to disrupt the flaming reaction. Heat is also absorbed from the reaction as the agents are volatilized. It is possible that the volatile decomposition products then enter into the flame chemistry. Radiation shielding caused by the powder cloud also helps the cooling process.

Dry chemical formulations containing potassium are superior to the sodium-based compounds because potassium is more reactive. Dry chemical agents are suitable for use on Class C electrical fires because the powder is not conductive and will not conduct electricity back to the operator.

Multipurpose Dry Chemicals

Besides the extinguishing characteristics of the dry chemical agents, multipurpose dry chemicals have the additional capability of being suitable for Class A fires. Monoammonium phosphate based agents are multipurpose and are particularly suited for combination Class A and B fires. It is thought that the flame extinguishing mode of action is similar to the dry chemical agents. There is an additional concurrent deposition of a coating of glassy metaphosphoric acid that provides a smothering action on the surface of Class A materials.

Uses of Dry and Multipurpose Dry Chemical Agents

The primary use of dry chemical agents is on flammable liquid fires. Because they are nonconductive, they are also valuable on electrical fires, although contamination of electrical contacts and delicate electronic equipment may be a problem.

The sodium bicarbonate agents are suitable for the protection of commercial food preparation equipment such as fryers, griddles, and range hoods because they produce no toxic effects.

The multipurpose dry chemicals are particularly useful in those situations where there might be fires involving mixed flammable liquids and ordinary combustibles.

Limitations. Some of the dry chemicals are corrosive and would have an effect upon delicate electronics. The residue from dry chemicals may coat electrical contacts making them inoperative. At any rate, when dry chemical agents have been used on electrical or electronic equipment, the equipment must be thoroughly cleaned as soon as possible when it is necessary to return the equipment to service.

On ordinary combustibles, multipurpose dry chemicals are limited to those situations where penetration of the fuel is not necessary. Because of its lack of penetration ability, where ordinary combustibles are protected by multipurpose dry chemicals, there should be a backup water-type extinguishing system.

CARBON DIOXIDE

Carbon dioxide has been effectively used for many years to protect flammable liquid and energized electrical installations. It is a noncombustible gas, which allows it to spread and penetrate throughout the fire area. It does not react with most substances, it is nonconductive, and it provides its own pressure for discharge.

Extinguishing Properties

Carbon dioxide extinguishes by cooling and by dilution of oxygen below the concentration necessary to support combustion. When it is discharged from a container, carbon dioxide converts to a mixture of vapor and fine dry ice particles.

Its cooling properties are best utilized when applied directly to a burning liquid in a tank. When the oxygen dilution capabilities have been exhausted, reignition of the fire may be prevented when the liquid has been cooled to the point where it is not generating sufficient flammable vapors.

Carbon dioxide is effective for extinguishing fires involving flammable liquids in open and closed tanks. It is effective for total flooding protection of rooms containing electrical equipment or flammable liquids. It is also an effective and nondamaging agent for the protection of furs, records, or sensitive electrical equipment that might be damaged by other agents.

Limitations. Carbon dioxide is not an effective extinguishing agent for use on ordinary combustibles because it does not penetrate the fuel and the cooling action is too brief and concentrated at the surface of the fuel to be of any value. Even when used on flammable liquid fires, carbon dioxide dissipates rapidly and reignition can occur.

Carbon dioxide is also not effective against fires involving chemicals such as cellulose nitrate that contain their own oxygen supply. It is not effective on fires involving reactive metals such as sodium, potassium, magnesium, titanium, zirconium, and the metal hydrides because these materials decompose carbon dioxide.

Effects on Personnel. One of the primary drawbacks to the use of carbon dioxide is its suffocating effects upon people. It is only mildly toxic, but at concentrations above 9 percent it is lethal by asphyxiation. Therefore, it cannot be used in confined spaces and total room flooding systems cannot be used where people might be present.

COMBUSTIBLE METAL EXTINGUISHING AGENTS

Some of the common combustible metals found in industry include magnesium (Mg), aluminum (Al), sodium (Na), potassium (K), sodium/potassium alloy, lithium (Li), zirconium (Zr), titanium (Ti), and uranium (U). Burning combustible metals are very difficult to extinguish because they burn extremely hot. Water is not acceptable as an extinguishing agent because of the severe reaction produced when the cool water meets the extremely hot metal and explosively turns to steam. Because of the extreme temperatures of burning metals, the extinguishing agent must be selected very carefully for the metal that is present.

Metal fire extinguishing agents are generally termed ''powder,'' or dry powder extinguishing agents, not to be confused with dry chemical extinguishing agents. They are intended to be applied as a powder either by pouring on the fire or expelled by pressure from an extinguisher.

Types of Dry Powder Agents

Because of the unique hazard of combustible metals, practice drills should be held using the appropriate powder on a small fire of the combustible metal.

G-1 Powder. ''Pyrene,'' or G-1 powder is composed of screened graphitized foundry coke to which an organic phosphate has been added. The graphite acts as a heat conductor and extinguishes the fire by absorbing heat and lowering the metal temperature to below its ignition temperature. The graphite powder also acts to smother the fire. Oxygen is further excluded by the organic material in the agent which forms a gas that penetrates between the graphite particles.

G-1 powder is listed by Underwriters Laboratories (UL) for use only on magnesium and magnesium alloys and is approved by the Factory Mutual System (FM) for use on magnesium, aluminum, sodium, potassium, and sodium–potassium alloy.

Met–L–X Powder. This powder is a sodium chloride base material with additives including tricalcium phosphate which is used to improve flow characteristics and metal stearates for water repellency. A thermoplastic material is added to bind the sodium chloride particles together when heated to form a solid mass. Met–L–X is suitable for fires involving magnesium, sodium, potassium, and sodium–potassium alloy. It is particularly useful for fires in solid metal pieces such as castings because of its ability to cling to hot vertical surfaces.

Na-X Powder. As its name implies, this powder was developed specifically for sodium fires. It has a sodium carbonate base plus additives to render the agent nonhygroscopic and easily fluidized for use in pressurized extinguishers.

Foundry Flux. Fluxes are used in magnesium foundry operations to form a protective crust on the surface of the molten metal to exclude air. They may also be shoveled onto spilled molten magnesium. These fluxes consist of various amounts of potassium chloride, barium chloride, magnesium chloride, sodium chloride, and calcium fluoride.

Lith–X Powder. This powder is specifically for lithium fires, but it is also used successfully on magnesium and zirconium chip fires, sodium, and sodium–potassium fires. Lith–X powder is composed of a graphite base with additives to facilitate free flow from an extinguisher.

FOAM EXTINGUISHING AGENTS

When aqueous solutions of foaming agents are applied through special applicators, a mass of foam or gas-filled bubbles are formed. Foam extinguishing agents are particularly noted for their ability to extinguish flammable liquid fires whether in tanks or spills. Since foam is lighter than the solution from which it was formed and is lighter than flammable liquids, it forms a cooling, smothering blanket on the surface of the liquid to extinguish the fire. If the foam blanket can be maintained on the surface, it will retard the generation of vapors to prevent ignition/reignition.

Foam agents are injected into water streams to produce foam for fire fighting, or they may be injected into fixed systems. Foams are characterized by their expansion ratio, which is the ratio of the final volume of foam to the original foam/water solution volume before air is added. There are three ranges as follows: low expansion foam with expansion ratios up to 20:1, medium expansion foam with expansion ratios from 20 to 200:1, and high expansion foam with expansion ratios from 200 to 1,000:1. The foam that is most suitable for flammable or combustible liquid spill or tank fires is the low expansion foam type. Low expansion foam provides a thick and consistent blanket across the surface of the liquid to cool and exclude oxygen while preventing the generation of vapors.

A frequent application for low expansion foams is to protect aircraft hangars where a fuel spill must be quickly covered with foam before it can be ignited or covered and extinguished if the spill is ignited.

The medium and high expansion foams are effective in filling enclosures such as the holds of ships or basements which are inaccessible or unsafe for manual fire fighting. These fires are controlled by the foam's cooling and smothering capabilities. The foam also halts convection currents and prevents air from reaching the fire. One particularly successful application of high expansion foam occurred in a fire in the basement of a Milwaukee furniture store several years ago. This fire was extremely hot and smokey and it was impossible to send fire fighters into the basement. The fire was effectively extinguished when the basement was filled with high expansion foam. Foam agents are generally suitable for use with either freshwater or seawater.

Types of Foam Extinguishing Agents

There are various types of foams available with characteristics for specific fire situations.

Aqueous Film Forming Agents (AFFF). As the name implies, these agents form an aqueous film on the surface of flammable hydrocarbon liquids. They operate through three fire fighting mechanisms. First, the aqueous film is formed which works to prevent the release of fuel vapor. Second, the foam blanket from which the film-forming liquid drains effectively excludes oxygen from the surface of the liquid. Third, the water content of the foam provides a cooling effect to further reduce vapor generation.

AFFF is intended for use on Class B hydrocarbon fuels having low water solubility such as crude oils, gasoline, diesel fuels, and aviation fuels.

Because it acts as a wetting agent, the solutions draining from AFFF have extremely low surface tension, making them suitable under both Class A and B fire situations where deep penetration of water is needed in addition to the surface spreading action of the foam.

Fluoroprotein Foaming Agents (FP). These agents contain fluorinated surface agents that give the foam a ''fuel shedding'' property. When applied beneath surface of a flammable or combustible liquid, they rise to the surface and shed fuel from the surface of the foam. This makes them particularly useful for subsurface application for tank fire fighting. They also act as barriers to vapor evaporation and resist burnback.

Film-Forming Fluoroprotein Agents (FFFP). These foam agents contain protein together with film-forming fluorinated surface active agents. This allows them the capabilities of AFFF and FP; they form aqueous films on the surface of flammable liquids and have a fuel shedding capability.

Protein Foaming Agents (P). These agents contain high molecular weight natural proteinaceous polymers. The polymers give the foam mechanical strength and water retention capability. They produce dense, viscous foams of high stability, high heat resistance, and good resistance to burnback.

Low-Temperature Foaming Agents. These agents may be of the AFFF type or protein-based foams, but they contain antifreeze materials making them suitable for use at temperatures as low as −20 degrees Fahrenheit.

Alcohol-Type Foaming Agents (AR). Special requirements are necessary for foams that are used on fires involving fuels that are water soluble, water miscible, or are polar solvents such as acetone, alcohols, isopropyl ether, methyl ethyl ketone, and thinners. These materials can quickly break down other fire fighting foams. Alcohol-resistant foaming agents are proprietary compositions that resist alcohol or other water miscible fuels to produce a floating gel-like mass for foam buildup.

Medium and High Expansion Foaming Agents. These agents are for control and extinguishment of Class A and some Class B fires and fires in confined spaces.

These foams have the unique capability of transporting wet foam masses into inaccessible spaces. They will displace vapor, heat, and smoke and, in the process, prevent air from reaching the fire and provide a cooling medium. The foam solution that is not turned to steam has low surface tension, allowing it to penetrate ordinary combustibles.

HALOGENATED AGENTS

When one or more of the hydrogen atoms of a hydrocarbon are replaced by halogen (fluorine, chlorine, bromine, or iodine) atoms, the resulting compound is not only nonflammable, but has excellent flame extinguishing properties. Halogenated agents, or halons, the generic name by which they are commonly known, act by chemical mechanisms to break the chain reaction that is flaming combustion. For example, Halon 1301 (CF_3Br) decomposes in flame and the chemical hydrogen bromide (HBr) is formed. It is believed that HBr reacts with the chain, propagating hydrogen (H) and hydroxyl (OH) radicals and forming water and free bromine as follows:

$$H + HBr \rightarrow H_2 + Br \text{ and } OH + HBr \rightarrow H_2O + Br$$

Therefore, the rate of the chain reaction is inhibited. It is also believed that HBr is regenerated when the Br ions remaining from the above reactions are recombined to form Br_2 and subsequently react with available H radicals. It is also possible that the fluorine (F) in CF_3Br acts to further remove H radicals through the formation of hydrogen fluoride (HF). Halons are probably the most important and, currently, popular fire extinguishing agents available. They are extremely effective agents in extinguishing flaming fires quickly, with no residue or damage to delicate equipment and they (in the case of Halon 1301) can be used safely in occupied areas. Not only is Halon 1301 safe to breathe in normal fire extinguishing concentrations, but the speed at which it acts results in minimization of the fire's production of toxic products of combustion.

Halogenated agents are also excellent agents for use in explosion suppression systems as described further in Chapter 10, Explosions.

There has been, and continues to be, some discomfort on the part of people in industry when halon, particularly a total flooding system, is proposed. This is because most people associate any gaseous agent with carbon dioxide. They believe that it displaces oxygen, and therefore is an asphyxiant. Although these systems are becoming quite common, there is still some education required when halon is discussed.

Types of Halogenated Agents

The halons are either methane or ethane based, with various arrangements of halogens replacing the hydrogen atoms. Each halogen atom that is added to the compound yields a product with differing degrees of toxicity and fire suppression capabilities. For simplicity, each halogenated compound in the halon series has been assigned a distinct number. The first digit of the number indicates the number of carbon atoms. The second digit indicates the number of fluorine atoms. The third digit indicates the number of chlorine atoms and the fourth digit the number of bromine atoms (Figure 8-1).

Carbon Tetrachloride (CCl4 or Halon 104). This was used as an extinguishing agent in the early 1900's. It had the advantages of being electrically nonconductive and it did not leave a residue after use. It was available in the familiar handpump-type of portable fire extinguisher (Figure 8-2). Its use as an extinguishing agent was discontinued in the 1960s, and it is no longer allowed because it is highly toxic.

Cl | Br — C — F | F	F | Br — C — F | F
Halon 1211 Bromochlorodifluoromethane	Halon 1301 Bromotrifluoromethane
F F | | Br — C — C — Br | | F F	F | Br — C — Br | F
Halon 2402 Dibromotetrafluoroethane	Halon 1202 Dibromodifluoromethane

Figure 8-1. The four common halogenated fire extinguishing agents.

Figure 8-2. A fire extinguisher from the 1930's containing carbon tetrachloride. (Photo: Charles Uebele)

Halon 1211 (BrCClF$_2$). Bromochlorodifluoromethane can be used in portable and local applications, but it is too toxic for use in total flooding systems. It is the halogenated agent of choice for portable fire extinguisher applications where the clean characteristics of halon are required. Human exposure at 4 percent for up to 5 minutes is the maximum allowable. Exposure should be minimized as much as possible.

Halon 1301 (BrCF$_3$). Bromotrifluoromethane is the least toxic and most effective of the halons. Halon 1301 is most commonly used in total flooding systems. It is relatively nontoxic, leaves no residue to damage equipment, is nonconductive, and is noncorrosive. Halon 1301 is particularly suited for the protection of high value electronic installations such as data processing, telecommunications, aircraft, ships, and vital defense installations. The real value of Halon 1301 is that it is safe for use in occupied areas. Personnel do not have to be evacuated before it is discharged. It is effective in concentrations as low as 4 percent and is normally used at 6–7 percent concentration. Study findings have concluded that exposure to Halon 1301 for 30 minutes did not produce sufficient adverse effects to harm, confuse, or debilitate healthy adults. Therefore, there is plenty of time, after the agent has been discharged, for personnel to evacuate. However, evacuation should not be unnecessarily delayed.

Halon 2402 (BrF_2CCBrF_2). Dibromotetrafluoroethane is a liquid at room temperature and is therefore used only for local application situations. It is currently only used in Europe and then, because of its toxicity, it is only used in unmanned locations.

Disadvantages of Halon

As is the case with most good things, there are certain disadvantages to the use of halon extinguishing agents. One minor disadvantage is its cost which limits its feasibility to high value protection where its unique characteristics are necessary. More importantly, from a personnel safety standpoint, is its production of toxic gases when heated. Its most significant disadvantage, however, is its detrimental environmental effects.

Decomposition Products. Halogenated agents decompose when exposed to flame or surface temperatures in excess of 900 degrees Fahrenheit. The main decomposition products of Halon 1301 are hydrogen fluoride (HF), hydrogen bromide (HBr), and free bromine (Br_2). Halon 1211 decomposition products are similar but include hydrogen chloride (HCl) and free chlorine (Cl_2) as well. In most situations, when halons are applied early in a fire scenario and in the recommended concentrations, the toxic decomposition products will not be significant. Also, the speed at which the material stops the flaming reaction results in minimal exposure to the flame. In most fire situations that have been evaluated, the levels of decomposition products generated do not exceed the irritant stage. When a fire is so large and so hot that excessive concentrations of decomposition products would be produced, personnel would have had to evacuate long before because the products of combustion generated by the fire would have already made the area untenable.

Environmental Effects of Halons. Since the 1970s, the issue of the depletion of the earth's protective ozone layer by chlorofluorocarbons (CFCs) has been increasing. As evidence of the damage to the stratospheric layer continues to mount, this concern has become worldwide. Halons, like CFCs, are fully halogenated hydrocarbons. Unlike CFCs, Halon 1211 and 1301 contain bromine which increases their effectiveness as extinguishing agents, but bromine is also more reactive than chlorine with ozone.

CFCs must be volatile in order to migrate through the troposphere into the stratosphere. The stronger ultraviolet radiation in the stratosphere breaks down the CFC molecule releasing the chlorine and bromine atoms. Chlorine reacts with ozone to produce oxygen. The destructive effects of chlorine can be summarized by the following equations:

$$Cl + O_3 \rightarrow ClO + O_2$$

$$ClO + O \rightarrow Cl + O_2$$

After reacting, the chlorine atom is regenerated as in the second reaction and is ready to react with more ozone. It is estimated that a single chlorine atom is capable of destroying approximately 100,000 ozone molecules during its lifetime in the stratosphere. Bromine atoms enter into similar reactions as chlorine but at a significantly faster overall rate. It is believed that fluorine plays an insignificant role in the destruction of ozone.

In 1987, an agreement, called the Montreal Protocol on Substances That Deplete the Ozone Layer, was signed by the United States and 23 other countries. The purpose of the Montreal Protocol was to limit the manufacture of ozone-depleting CFCs. Halons, because of their economic value, are treated differently than CFCs. As of 1992, production of halons will be frozen at 1986 levels. Effective on January 1, 1990, the United States government began an escalating tax on the production and use of CFCs. The 1990 tax rate is $1.37 per pound. By 1997, the tax rate will be $4.00 per pound. This disincentive to the use of CFCs will not apply to the halons until 1991.

The Future of Halon.   At the present time, there are no environmentally acceptable alternatives which are as effective as the halons in extinguishing fire. The manufacturers are studying alternatives and anticipate their availability before the turn of the century.

The halon industry, EPA, NFPA, and international organizations are all studying methods of reducing the amount of halons that are being released to the atmosphere, including studies to find alternatives to Halon 1301 discharge testing and enclosure integrity testing.

SUMMARY

Fire can be extinguished by interrupting, or removing, any of the four sides of the fire tetrahedron. There are many agents available that accomplish at least

Table 8-1. Fire Extinguishing Agent Application.

TYPES OF FIRE	TYPE OF HAZARDS	RECOMMENDED EXTINGUISHING AGENT	EFFECTIVE EXTINGUISHING ACTION
Class A	Ordinary Combustibles Wood Rubber Paper Many plastics Fabrics	Water AFFF ABC Dry Chemical Halon 1211	Quench, cool, penetrate Quench, cool, penetrate Chemical reaction, coat, cool Chemical reaction, quench, cool
Class B	Flammable Liquids and Gases Gasoline Oils Grease Paint Lacquer Tar Natural and Manufactured Gases	LIQUIDS: AFFF Regular Dry Chemical ABC Dry Chemical Purple K Dry Chemical Halon 1211, 1301 CO_2 GASES: Regular and Purple K Dry Chemical	Smother, cool Chemical reaction, smother Chemical reaction, smother Chemical reaction, smother Chemical reaction, smother, cool Smother, cool Smothering action preferred
Class C	Energized Electrical Equipment Wiring Generators Motors Panels Switches Appliances	Regular Dry Chemical ABC Dry Chemical Purple K Dry Chemical Halon 1211, 1301 CO_2	All are nonconductors of electricity

Table 8-1. (Continued)

TYPES OF FIRE	TYPE OF HAZARDS	RECOMMENDED EXTINGUISHING AGENT	EFFECTIVE EXTINGUISHING ACTION
Class AB	Ordinary Combustibles, Flammable Liquids, and Gases Combinations of A and B	AFFF ABC Dry Chemical Halon 1211, 1301	Smother, cool Chemical reaction, smother Chemical reaction, smother, cool
Class BC	Flammable Liquids and Gases Energized Electrical Equipment combinations of B & C	Regular Dry Chemical ABC Dry Chemical Purple K Dry Chemical Halon 1211, 1301 CO_2	Chemical reaction, smother nonconductor Chemical reaction, smother nonconductor Chemical reaction, smother nonconductor Chemical reaction, smother, cool, nonconductor Smother, nonconductor
Class ABC	Ordinary Combustibles, Flammable Liquids, and Gases Energized Electrical Equipment Combinations of A, B, and C	ABC Dry Chemical Halon 1211	Chemical reaction, smother, nonconductor Chemical reaction, quench, smother, cool, nonconductor
Class D	Combustible Metals and Combustible Metal Alloys	Dry powder agents depending upon type of metal	Excludes air, dissipates heat

186

one of these; agents that remove the fuel, remove the oxygen, cool the fuel, or interrupt the chain reaction. Fire extinguishing agents are available in any form including solids, liquids, and gases (Table 8-1).

While the major consideration in selecting a fire extinguishing agent is the type of fuel that might be involved in a fire, there are also considerations about the environment and effects of the agent on people and equipment. Agents have been developed to be compatible in almost every fire protection situation. The equipment and systems for applying these agents will be discussed in the next chapter.

BIBLIOGRAPHY

40 CFR Part 82. 1987. Protection of Stratospheric Ozone. Proposed Rules. *Federal Register* 52(239):47489–47523.

Dittman, Charles R. 1988. Selling Management the Best Fire Protection Available. *Professional Safety* 33(10):21–26.

Fire Protection Handbook, 16th ed. 1986. Quincy: National Fire Protection Association.

Friedman, Raymond. 1985. Some Unresolved Fire Chemistry Problems. In *Fire Safety Science— Proceedings of the First International Symposium*, Cecile E. Grant and Patrick J. Pagni, eds., pp. 349–359. New York: Hemisphere Publishing Corporation.

Godish, Thad. 1985. *Air Quality.* Chelsea, MI: Lewis Publishers, Inc.

Hoffman, J. S., and Gibbs, M. J. 1988. Future Concentrations of Stratospheric Chlorine and Bromine. USEPA, Office of Air and Radiation, Washington D.C. EPA 400/1-88/005.

Lyons, John W. 1985. *Fire.* New York: Scientific American Books, Inc.

Rasbash, D. J. 1985. The Extinction of Fire with Plain Water: A Review. In *Fire Safety Science— Proceedings of the First International Symposium*, Cecile E. Grant and Patrick J. Pagni, eds., pp. 1145–1162. New York: Hemisphere Publishing Corporation.

Tuve, Richard L. 1976. *Principles of Fire Protection Chemistry.* Quincy: National Fire Protection Association.

Zurer, P. S. 1988. Antarctic Ozone Hole. *Chemical and Engineering News* 66(22):16–25.

Zurer, P. S. 1989. Producers, Users Grapple with Realities of CFC Phaseout. *Chemical and Engineering News* 67(30):7–13.

9
FIRE EXTINGUISHING SYSTEMS AND EQUIPMENT

While there are many fire extinguishing agents that are available for almost every fire protection situation, they will be of little value if not applied properly and in a timely manner. The fire loss experience in industry would probably be much worse if it were not for the historical requirements for portable fire extinguishers. Many potentially disastrous fires have been extinguished in the incipient stage by a trained employee who acted in time using a fire extinguisher.

Likewise, when employees have not been available, or the hazard was too great, many other fires have been extinguished by automatic systems before the fires could reach damaging proportions. The statistics and reports on the value of automatic sprinkler systems are also indicative of the value of these systems in minimizing losses.

There are a diverse number of application systems and equipment that are available to apply fire extinguishing agents quickly and effectively. These systems range from portable hand-held extinguishers to large fixed automatic application systems. When fire does occur, there must be adequate numbers and types of manual extinguishers for use by building occupants who have been adequately trained. Besides manual fire extinguishing equipment, most industrial and business environments must have automatic extinguishing systems in place to stop fire before it can reach disastrous proportions. Experience has shown that appropriately designed and installed automatic extinguishing systems are instrumental in controlling losses when fire has progressed beyond the incipient stage. Industrial fire protection programs are becoming more and more reliant on the installation of fire extinguishing systems and equipment that are suited for the specialized hazards that are encountered in modern industry.

PORTABLE FIRE EXTINGUISHERS

Quick action in the use of portable extinguishers has mitigated many potentially damaging fires. The fire extinguishers were available, filled with an agent that was appropriate to the hazard, and were used by an individual who was properly trained. Portable fire extinguishers are defined as portable devices containing an extinguishing agent that can be expelled under pressure for the purpose of suppressing or extinguishing a fire. Portable fire extinguishers are available containing many different types of agents and in sizes from small containers for home and automotive use (Figure 9-1) to large wheeled units for industrial use (Figure 9-2). They are simple to use and can be used with little or no training. These extinguishers are much more effective when used by individuals who have had some hands-on training.

Portable fire extinguishers are classified A, B, C, or D for use on certain classes of fires on which they are effective, and their effectiveness is rated on a numerical scale. The numerical scale is based upon tests of an established size wood fire for Class A, 2-inch depth of *n*-heptane in square pans for Class B, and special tests on specific combustible metal fires for Class D. There is no test for Class C ratings as it would be impractical. Class C agents must be

Figure 9-1. A $2\frac{1}{2}$ pound Purple K Dry Chemical fire extinguisher. It has a 10B:C rating. (Source: Amerex Corp., Trussville, AL)

Figure 9-2. A 125-pound ABC Multipurpose dry chemical fire extinguisher. It has a 40A:240B:C rating. (Source: Amerex Corp., Trussville, AL)

nonconductors and the nozzle of a Class C rated fire extinguisher must also be nonconductive (Figure 9-3).

Water Extinguishers

Water-filled extinguishers are available as either stored pressure extinguishers, or hand pump operated extinguishers. The preferred extinguisher is the stored pressure extinguisher since it has a pressure gage and the pressure can be simply monitored during inspections Figure 9-4).

Obsolete Variations.   There are other variations of pressurization for water-filled extinguishers such as the soda-acid and cartridge operated. These types of extinguishers have become obsolete because of safety concerns over the deterioration of their shell and consequent possible explosion hazard when the extinguisher is pressurized. They were also awkward to operate because they had to be inverted.

The soda-acid extinguishers contained sodium bicarbonate dissolved in the water and a small amount of sulfuric acid in a container near the top inside of

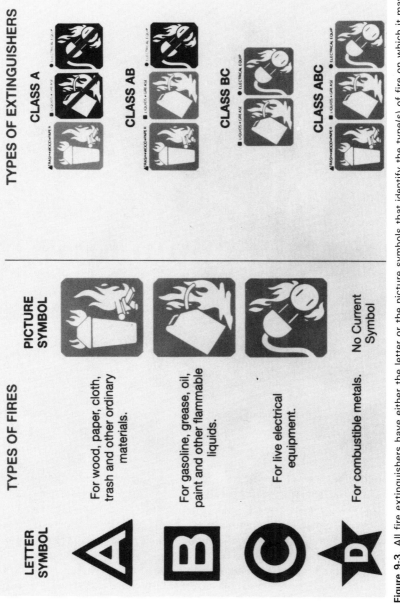

Figure 9-3. All fire extinguishers have either the letter or the picture symbols that identify the type(s) of fire on which it may be used. Picture symbols with a red slash indicate a potential hazard if the fire extinguisher is used on that particular type of fire. (Source: Amerex Corp., Trussville, AL)

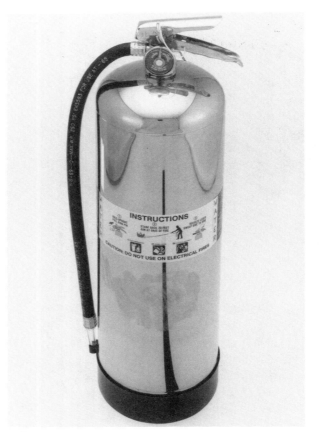

Figure 9-4. A $2\frac{1}{2}$-gallon stored pressure water fire extinguisher. (Source: Amerex Corp., Trussville, AL)

the extinguisher. When the extinguisher was inverted, the acid mixed with and reacted with the sodium bicarbonate producing carbon dioxide. The carbon dioxide provided the pressure to expel the water. There was no valve to stop the flow once the reaction was initiated. Cartridge operated extinguishers contained a small cylinder of carbon dioxide that was activated by striking a pin to release the pressure and expel the water. Like the soda-acid extinguisher, the flow of water could not be stopped once initiated.

Because of the possible explosion hazard, if any of these extinguishers are found, they should be removed from service, destroyed, and replaced with an approved type.

Uses.   Water-filled extinguishers are for use on ordinary combustible fires where cooling and wetting is required. They are easy to use, are capable of being operated intermittently, and are easy to maintain and recharge. The stream from a water-filled extinguisher is fairly long and can be used to penetrate burning ordinary combustibles.

Limitations.   Water-filled fire extinguishers are not recommended for use on electrical equipment because of possible damage to the equipment and the potential for electric shock. Although water extinguishers can be safely used on energized equipment in some situations, it is best to de-energize all equipment first or use a nonconducting agent and extinguisher. Most water-filled extinguishers are also not suitable for use on flammable liquid fires because of the tendency for the water stream to splash and spread the burning liquid.

Water-filled extinguishers must be protected from freezing which limits their use in cold climates or freezers. Although water-filled extinguishers may be treated with antifreeze solutions, some of these solutions are corrosive and they are good conductors of electricity which makes them unsuitable in any situation where there might be energized equipment.

Carbon Dioxide

Carbon dioxide extinguishers are Class B and C rated because they provide the cooling and smothering action that is necessary to extinguish flammable liquid and electrical fires. Additionally, the nozzles of these extinguishers are made of nonconducting plastic and carbon dioxide is a nonconductor of electricity. Liquid carbon dioxide is contained in a high-pressure cylinder at about 850 psi. When the operating valve is opened, the carbon dioxide flows through a siphon tube, the valve, and a small orifice at the base of the horn where it is transformed into gas and snow (Figure 9-5).

Use.   Carbon dioxide extinguishers are recommended for use on fires involving flammable liquids and electrical equipment.

Limitations.   Carbon dioxide is only expelled for a range of from 2 to 4 feet, making it difficult to approach a large fire. They will control only small fires in ordinary combustibles, and they are not recommended for this use. The reason that they are not recommended for deep-seated fires in ordinary combustibles is because they have no penetration capability and their cooling and smothering action is too short-lived. They are also not suitable for use on combustible metals because carbon dioxide reacts with some metals.

Although the carbon dioxide extinguisher is suitable for flammable liquid

Figure 9-5. A 5 pound carbon dioxide fire extinguisher. (Source: Amerex Corp., Trussville, AL)

fires, it produces no lasting blanketing effect and therefore, if a source of ignition is present, the fire could reignite.

Carbon dioxide fire extinguishers should not be used in a confined space because of the possible displacement of oxygen and asphyxiation hazard to personnel.

Air–Foam Extinguishers

This type of extinguisher is essentially a stored-pressure water-filled extinguisher that contains a foam concentrate and produces foam by passing a water–concentrate mixture through a special air aspirating nozzle. Different varieties of air–foam extinguishers are available that either contain the premixed water–

concentrate mixture in the extinguisher or pass water in the extinguisher through an external solid foam cartridge (Figure 9-6).

The agent used in air–foam extinguishers is an aqueous film forming surfactant.

Uses.   Air–foam extinguishers are recommended for use on flammable liquid fires where they form a very fluid foam that spreads over the surface of the fuel. The smothering action of the foam extinguishes the fire and, since a residual aqueous film remains, chances of reignition are minimized.

The effective range of air–foam extinguishers is approximately 20–30 feet making them effective without requiring the operator to approach too close to the fire. Another benefit of this type of extinguisher is that it is capable of being operated intermittently.

Air–foam extinguishers may also be effectively used on fires involving or-

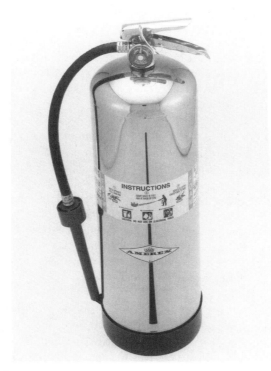

Figure 9-6.   A $2\frac{1}{2}$-gallon Film Forming Fluoroprotein (FFFP) fire extinguisher for use on fires involving alcohols, polar solvents, hydrocarbons, and combinations of these flammable liquids. (Source: Amerex Corp., Trussville, AL)

dinary combustibles because of the cooling and penetrating capabilities of the foam.

Limitations. Air–foam is not effective on materials such as alcohols, ketones, esters, or lacquer thinners that are miscible with water. These materials will break down the foam blanket or film.

Foam from hand extinguishers should not be applied to hot liquids such as oils, asphalt, tars, and waxes because the hot liquid may boil over.

Foam is also not recommended for fires in electrical equipment since foam is mildly corrosive and difficult to remove.

Foam extinguishers must be protected from freezing and anti-freezes must not be used because they are incompatible with the foam concentrate.

Dry Chemical Extinguishers

Dry chemical extinguishers are operated using either a carbon dioxide gas cartridge or stored pressure. Both are capable of intermittent use (Figure 9-2).

The dry chemical may be either the ordinary dry chemicals or the multipurpose dry chemicals described in the Chapter 8 section on dry chemical extinguishing agents. When selecting the agent to be used, consideration should be given to the possible fuels that are available and to the characteristics described for the various dry chemical agents.

Uses. The dry chemical extinguishers are extremely valuable with their diverse selection of chemical agents, and they are available in a wide range of sizes from $2\frac{1}{2}$-pound hand-held units to 300-pound wheeled units. They are not effected by freezing.

Dry chemical extinguishers are for use on flammable liquid fires including those in hot oils, asphalt, tars, and waxes where they do not cause boiling. They may be used on electrical equipment, but they are not desirable for use on delicate electronic equipment and relays. They may also be used for surface fires in textile fibers when there is a reserve extinguisher having a water spray capability for smoldering and deep seated fires.

Limitations. Some of the dry chemicals such as the potassium chloride based and ammonium phosphate in combination with moisture will cause corrosion on metallic surfaces. The ammonium phosphate agent in multipurpose dry chemical extinguishers will be difficult to remove because it hardens when it cools.

Dry chemicals do not produce a lasting blanketing effect on the surface of flammable liquids, making reignition a problem. Dry chemical fire extinguishers are ineffective for use on combustible metal fires.

Halon Extinguishers

Halon extinguishers have become popular in recent years, particularly in those situations where a clean, fast acting, safe, and noncorrosive agent is required. Most halon extinguishers use Halon 1211, although some may contain 1301 or a mixture of 1211 and 1301 for use in cold environments. Halon 1301 has a higher vapor pressure than 1211 and therefore, it would function better at temperatures below −40 degrees Fahrenheit. Halon extinguishers are intended primarily for Class B and C fires, but they are also effective on Class A fires. Halon 1211 has about twice the range of carbon dioxide extinguishers and, on a weight comparison, it is about twice as effective on Class B fires as carbon dioxide.

Uses.   Halon extinguishers are superior in computer rooms, telecommunications installations, electronics manufacturing operations, and on flammable liquids. The noncorrosive, clean, and nonabrasive characteristics are of benefit in reducing equipment damage and cleanup. Like carbon dioxide, halon extinguishers are appropriate in cold environments because they are not susceptible to freezing.

Limitations.   The primary limitation with Halon 1211 is its relative toxicity. The thermal decomposition products of Halon 1211, including hydrogen chloride, hydrogen fluoride, and hydrogen bromide, are also hazardous. However, their concentration is minimal when the fire is rapidly extinguished. In most cases, a large fire that would be capable of producing excess amounts of these products will be too large to fight with a portable extinguisher. When used in a confined space with no ventilation, the operator should avoid breathing the vapor and gases that are produced and should vacate the area as soon as the fire is extinguished. These decomposition products give off an acrid warning odor.

Dry Powder Extinguishers

Dry powder extinguishers containing proprietary dry powder agents are for use on combustible metal fires. They are available in sizes from 30-pound portable units up to 350-pound wheeled units. Both are gas cartridge type extinguishers.

Uses.   Dry powder extinguishers are intended for use on small fires in metals including magnesium, powdered aluminum, titanium, zinc, sodium, and potassium. They should be located in any locations where these metals may be present, such as laboratories, foundry, and machining operations.

As discussed in the section on fire extinguishing agents, dry powder does not have to be applied by extinguisher; it can merely be poured or scooped onto the fire. In small combustible metal machining operations or small laboratories, the agent is often kept in coffee cans ready for immediate application.

Limitations.   Dry powder agent is not effective or recommended for use on fires in materials other than the combustible metals for which they are intended.

The portable model dry powder extinguisher only has a range of 6 to 8 feet making it difficult to approach larger fires or those that are burning in chips containing water or water soluble lubricants which burn rapidly and violently.

Placement of Portable Extinguishers

Since portable fire extinguishers are intended to attack fire in its very early stages, they must be conveniently located. There are specified maximum travel distances for extinguishers, and it is generally advisable to locate extinguishers close to specific hazards. For example, when a welding or cutting operation is to take place, it is necessary to place a fire extinguisher nearby and not rely upon the nearest wall-mounted extinguisher. When placing extinguishers, there is a fine line between the minimum amount required and too many. In many industrial operations, the personnel who do the inspections and maintenance of fire extinguishers also do fire prevention inspections. When the operation has too many fire extinguishers, these people may have to spend all of their time with the extinguishers and the fire prevention inspections will suffer. It is generally necessary to begin with the minimum requirements for extinguishers and then using professional judgment, place additional extinguishers appropriately for specific hazards.

Travel Distance.   The maximum travel distance for fire extinguishers where the primary hazard is Class A fires is 75 feet.

The maximum travel distance for fire extinguishers where the primary hazard is Class B fires is 50 feet from the Class B hazard area.

Fire extinguishers for Class C hazards are distributed according to the existing appropriate Class A or B hazard distribution. The maximum travel distance for fire extinguishers where the primary hazard is Class D fires is 75 feet from the Class D hazard area.

In all cases, if the hazard is localized, it may be more appropriate to locate the fire extinguisher close to the hazard as long as the user would not be precluded from accessing it by the potential fire.

Use of Portable Extinguishers

Most portable fire extinguishers are simple to use and can be used by an untrained individual after reading the instructions on the extinguisher. However, with training, the use of fire extinguishers can be much more effective. Training will also add to the safety of the extinguisher user. In mixed hazard occupancies, training is required so that personnel will know which extinguisher may be safely used on which hazard.

Training.   In facilities that are subject to OSHAct, fire extinguisher training is required for all employees. This training should include the general principles of fire extinguisher use and the hazards involved with fighting fires in the incipient stage. This training is required on initial employment and annually thereafter. The training could be in the form of lecture, "tailgate session," or demonstration.

Designated first aid fire fighting employees such as plant fire brigades and emergency response teams must have more thorough training in the equipment that they may be expected to use. In the case of fire extinguishers, this would normally include "hands on" live-fire training. Most municipal fire departments will provide training in those facilities that do not have the inhouse capability to perform fire extinguisher training.

Training should include procedures to be followed when a fire is discovered such as notification of the public fire department and the plant emergency organization and making the decision to fight the fire or evacuate. Employees should also be trained to select the extinguisher that is appropriate to the type of fire. Training in use of the portable hand-held fire extinguisher should follow the following four steps of the Factory Mutual PASS method (Figure 9-7):

Pull the pin that is located in the handle of the extinguisher. When in place, this pin is to prevent inadvertent activation of the extinguisher. If the hose is clipped to the body of the extinguisher, unclip it.

Aim the nozzle at the base of the fire. This point should be emphasized be-

1	2	3
HOLD UPRIGHT. PULL RING PIN.	START BACK 10 FEET. AIM AT BASE OF FIRE.	SQUEEZE LEVER. SWEEP SIDE TO SIDE.

Figure 9-7.   Simple fire extinguisher "How To Use" instructions. All potential operators should be familiar with these instructions. (Source: Amerex Corp., Trussville, AL)

cause there is a tendency by untrained employees to aim the nozzle at the flames.

Squeeze the handle to discharge the agent. With most extinguishers, releasing the handle will stop the discharge.

Sweep the nozzle back and forth across the base of the flames. Continue to follow the base of the flames as they fall back until the fire is out. Watch for reignition.

Inspection and Maintenance

All types of portable fire extinguishers must be periodically inspected to determine that they are available and will work when needed. When a fire emergency occurs, there can be no doubt about the reliability of the fire extinguishers. They also may require an occasional hydrostatic test, maintenance examination, and repair.

Inspection. Portable fire extinguishers must be visually inspected monthly and have an annual maintenance check. The most important reason for the monthly inspection is to determine that fire extinguishers are in their proper location and have not been damaged or discharged. It is also important to note that the area immediately surrounding the extinguisher is unobstructed and that the extinguisher is available for immediate use. Other aspects of the inspection should include a check of the pressure gauge on those units that have them; a check of the condition of the extinguisher for signs of corrosion, damage, or deterioration; and ensuring that seals are in place. It is also important to note that the operating instructions and fire extinguisher rating information are legible.

Carbon dioxide fire extinguishers must be weighed every six months to ensure that they have the proper amount of carbondioxide. Should there be a weight loss of 10 percent or more, the extinguisher should be replaced.

Since the monthly inspection is a "quick check" and requires the inspector to have a limited amount of training, it can normally be performed by inplant personnel. A select group of reliable employees such as fire brigade members may be trained and assigned the monthly inspection duties. Inspection tags should be maintained on each extinguisher so that the inspector can initial and date when the inspection is performed.

Maintenance. Most of the maintenance requirements for portable fire extinguishers concern those that contain pressure. There are prescribed intervals for hydrostatic testing of pressure operated extinguishers. Most pressurized extinguishers require a 5-year hydrostatic test schedule. Some stored pressure extinguishers including most dry chemical, dry powder, and halogenated agents re-

Table 9-1. Fire Extinguisher Hydrostatic Test Interval.

TYPE OF EXTINGUISHERS	TEST INTERVAL (YEARS)
Cartridge operated water and/or antifreeze	5
Stored pressure water and/or antifreeze	5
Wetting agent	5
Foam (stainless steel shell)	5
Aqueous film forming (AFFF)	5
Loaded stream	5
Dry chemical with stainless steel	5
Carbon dioxide	5
Dry chemical, stored pressure, with mild steel, brazed brass, or aluminum shells	12
Dry chemical, cartridge or cylinder operated, with mild steel shells	12
Halon 1211 or 1301	12
Dry powder, cartridge or cylinder operated, with mild steel shells	12

Source: 29 CFR 1910, Occupational Safety and Health Standards, Section 157.

quire a 12-year hydrostatic test. The hydrostatic test intervals that are to be followed are provided in Table 9-1. Additionally, stored pressure extinguishers must be emptied and given a thorough maintenance check every 6 years.

Maintenance checks for extinguishers include disassembling the extinguisher, examining all of its parts, cleaning and replacing any defective parts, and refilling and repressurizing (if a pressure-type extinguisher).

It is normally necessary to use the services of a qualified fire extinguisher maintenance contractor to perform the maintenance inspections, tests, and services on portable fire extinguishers.

AUTOMATIC SPRINKLER SYSTEMS

Very early in the history of fire protection it was discovered that if water could be applied automatically and promptly to a fire, damage could be minimized. After some crude attempts at automatic sprinkler systems, the Parmelee sprinkler (named after its inventor, Henry S. Parmelee) was first installed in 1878. There have been continual improvements and new applications have been devised and implemented ever since. Automatic sprinkler systems have been perfected to the point that they are extremely reliable when properly maintained and supervised.

One factor that has accelerated the growth of the sprinkler industry was the reduction in insurance rates for property that had sprinkler protection. Sprinklers have now proven themselves to be major factors in loss control, and recently sprinkler installation has become mandatory in building codes and federal regulations.

The concept of sprinklers is to have water readily available in a piping system. Regularly spaced along the piping system are heat activated sprinkler heads to deliver the water to the fire. Unfortunately, this concept is feared by many uninformed individuals in today's high-technology industries as being too great a risk to allow into their facilities, even for fire protection purposes. One of the duties of the individuals who are responsible for fire protection is to convince these uninformed people that the benefits of water and sprinkler systems far out-weigh the risks.

The benefits of automatic sprinkler systems can be demonstrated through the statistics maintained by the National Fire Protection Association and the insurance industry. It can be shown that the majority of large-loss fires occur during off hours when people are not available to sound the alarm and take immediate remedial actions. While buildings may be of fire-resistant construction, the contents are normally combustible, and people are not very good at maintaining those contents in a firesafe manner. The sense of security that fire insurance seems to provide is lost when it is explained that insurance cannot guarantee complete restoration of operations, lost business, and most importantly, lost lives. This concept is difficult for many in business and industry to contemplate. The idea of having water suddenly discharged into their work environment is frightful.

This concept is further addressed in the Factory Mutual Engineering Corporation film *Sprinklers—the Myth and the Magic*. The myth is that sprinklers introduce a serious water damage hazard. The magic is that when the heat of a fire activates a head, and only when heat activates a head, it operates to discharge water. If the fire grows, more heads open to control it. But the real advantage of sprinkler systems is the fact that only the minimum amount of water to control the fire is discharged, at a time when only a minimum amount is required, minimizing the amount of water damage. With the fire controlled, early business interruption, or down time is reduced. On the other hand, when there are no sprinklers in service when fire breaks out, the fire damage will be greater by the time the fire department arrives. Then, hose streams will apply much more water to a greater area, and the force of the hose streams may add to the damage.

Value of Sprinklers

The real value of sprinklers is their ability to provide 24-hour-a-day automatic fire suppression capabilities. When properly installed, they cover all areas of the protected building and are able to promptly attack fire where it starts and continue to put water on the fire through thick smoke that might be obstructing the fire from manual fire fighting efforts.

Sprinklers have a psychological as well as physical value to life safety. Just the fact that automatic fire protection exists overhead provides occupants with a sense of security to say nothing of the effect that sprinklers operating over a fire have on the occupants. Operating sprinklers serve to provide a warning of the existence of fire, particularly in unoccupied or concealed spaces. Sprinklers operating over a fire will also help to control smoke thereby allowing better visibility for exiting occupants and advancing fire fighters.

Performance

Over the past 100 years that sprinkler systems have been available, they have demonstrated themselves to be the most effective and reliable form of fire protection. Statistics compiled by the National Fire Protection Association and Factory Mutual show that when fire occurs in an automatic sprinkler protected building, the fire is controlled or extinguished in about 96 percent of the cases. In the 4 percent of the fires where sprinklers have failed, the reason for the failure almost 30 percent of the time was due to the sprinklers being shut off; in 26 percent of the cases there was only partial protection; in 13 percent of the cases there was faulty construction; and other problems included inadequate water supply, obstructions, and improper maintenance. It hardly seems fair to blame the sprinkler system when people have left the supply valve shut off or have not properly installed the system. The personnel who are responsible for firesafety should be aware of these failure modes and guard against their occurrence. When these failure modes are eliminated, 100 percent fire protection is possible.

Sprinklers Impaired or Shut Off. Sprinkler systems are designed to activate and control a growing fire. Fire that occurs during the period that the sprinkler system is shut off, results in delayed discovery. By the time the system is activated, the fire may no longer be controllable. In almost 30 percent of the cases in which sprinkler systems fail, it is because the system was shut off. This may occur for maintenance purposes or for operational considerations. A common scenario occurs when a sprinkler system is shut off for maintenance or modifications and someone forgets to put it back into service. Most fire insurance companies have some form of sprinkler impairment system which requires the reporting of sprinkler valve closures (see Chapter 14). These systems force considerations of the necessity of the closure, duration of the closure, and contingency plans during the closure. This system also allows the insurance company to follow up to ensure that the system is placed back into service. The person who is responsible for fire protection should be involved in the decision to shut off the sprinkler system. When it is absolutely necessary to take a system out of service, the work should be planned in advance to minimize downtime. Work should proceed to completion, even if overtime is required. Temporary water supplies should be provided to the out of service portion of the system. It is also necessary to curtail hazardous operations during the outage and to provide a fire watch.

Incomplete Sprinkler Protection.   In about 26 percent of the cases in which sprinkler systems fail, it is because there was only partial sprinkler protection in the building. A classic example of incomplete sprinkler protection was in the MGM Grand Hotel Fire which occurred on November 21, 1980. Although the majority of the hotel was not sprinklered, there was automatic sprinkler protection in areas to the south and east of the casino and the Deli Restaurant, where the fire originated. The areas that had sprinklers were effectively protected. The fire burned uncontrolled through areas that were not protected (Figure 9-8). In many industrial occupancies, sprinklers are routinely omitted during renovations, in temporary structures, beneath mezzanines, and where there is an over-riding fear of water damage. In fact, one of the most frequently encountered arguments that firesafety professionals become involved in is convincing operating management that their fears of water damage are unfounded. Particular attention must be given to protecting concealed spaces, areas beneath ducts and shelves, vertical openings, hazardous processes, and under-roof areas of outside loading platforms (Figure 9-9).

The Arlington Racetrack in Arlington Heights, Illinois, suffered a $70 million fire on July 31, 1985. The fire originated in a two-story clubhouse where it spread through concealed ceiling spaces into the grandstand. The clubhouse had undergone remodeling at different times which resulted in many concealed spaces that were not protected by sprinklers.

Inadequate Maintenance.   Although automatic sprinkler systems provide the best fire protection available, they can become ineffective because of obstructions. Obstructions may be caused from rust and scale buildup, obstructions left in the piping during installation, or obstructions introduced to the system after installation (Figure 9-10).

Chemical reactions in nongalvanized steel piping may result in rust and scale buildup which is associated primarily with dry-pipe, deluge, and preaction sprinkler systems.

During installation of sprinkler systems coupons may be left in the pipe. Coupons are cut-out pieces of the pipe where holes are cut into the pipe for quick-connection sprinkler fittings.

After installation, obstructions in the form of sand, silt, and stones can get into the piping.

Routine water discharge tests will indicate obstructions in the form of discolored, silty or sandy water, or other foreign materials.

A 236,000-ft^2 plywood manufacturing plant in Nacogdoches, Texas burned to the ground during an April 16, 1984 fire resulting in an estimated loss of $32.5 million. Witnesses described ineffective sprinkler system operation and

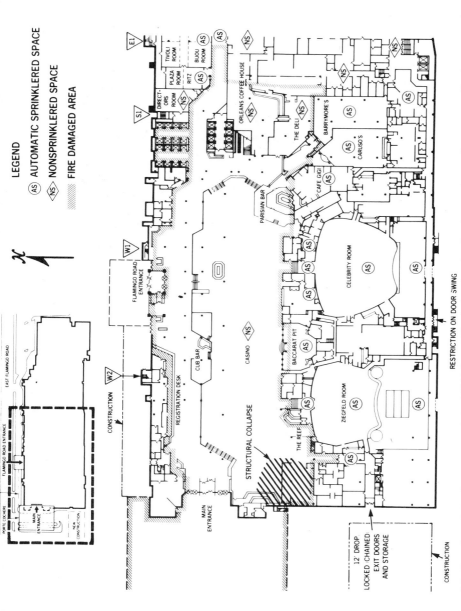

Figure 9-8. Drawing of the Casino area of the MGM Grand Hotel showing the fire damaged area that was confined to areas that were not sprinkler-protected. (Source: Reprinted with permission from the *Investigation Report on the MGM Grand Hotel Fire*, Copyright © 1982, National Fire Protection Association, Quincy, MA 02269.)

Figure 9-9. Sprinkler coverage must be extended down to cover areas that are obstructed by air ducts. (Source: Factory Mutual Engineering Corporation)

"muddy" and "rusty" discharges from the sprinklers. Investigation of the system after the fire revealed that a large number of the sprinklers were obstructed by rust and scale. Piping up to $1\frac{1}{2}$ inches in diameter was also found to be obstructed. There were apparently no flow tests performed on this system. If there were flow tests the condition may have manifested itself in the form of discolored water, scale and rust, or other debris in the water.

Improperly Designed Sprinklers. In many cases of sprinkler system failure, it is not that the system was designed improperly, but that the use exceeded the design capabilities of the system. Classic examples are some of the recent warehouse fires that have occurred. The sprinkler systems were properly designed for the storage when the warehouse was built, but then combustibility of the stored material changed or the designed capacity of the warehouse was exceeded. Some of the occupant-induced changes that exceed the parameters of sprinkler designs that lead to sprinkler system failure include increased storage heights, change or increase in the hazard of materials being stored, storage in aisles, and changes in storage configuration.

Sprinkler System Installation

It is very important that the design and installation of sprinkler systems be accomplished correctly so that the system will perform reliably under all expected conditions. NFPA #13 is very extensive and detailed in this regard and it must be followed explicitly. Only qualified contractors should be used for these very important functions.

Figure 9-10. Cross section of sprinkler piping that is almost totally obstructed with rust and scale. (Source: Factory Mutual Engineering Corporation)

The design and installation of sprinkler systems must take into account the building features including protection of openings, concealed spaces, and all parts of the building. The system should also be compatible and address the hazards of the occupancy such as high-piled storage, flammable liquids, dusts, chemicals, and other hazardous operations.

Types of Sprinkler Systems

There are basically six types of sprinkler systems, the wet pipe, dry pipe, preaction, deluge, combined dry pipe and preaction, and special types. Sprinkler systems include the piping and valves to get the water from a source of supply to the sprinklers in the area to be protected.

Wet Pipe Sprinkler System.   A wet pipe sprinkler system is one in which water is always present in the piping, under pressure, right up to the sprinkler head. Sprinkler heads are individually activated by the heat and water can flow immediately.

Obviously, a wet pipe system is used whenever there is no danger of water freezing and no special conditions that would dictate use of one of the other types. Antifreeze additives may be used in this type of system, however, a special valve is required to prevent syphoning into the public water supply.

Wet pipe systems are normally installed with a flow alarm to indicate when water is flowing through the system.

Dry Pipe Sprinkler System.   A dry pipe sprinkler system is just that; a system in which there is no water in the sprinkler piping. Rather, the piping contains air or nitrogen under pressure. This type of system is used only in areas that cannot be heated, such as unheated buildings in cold climates and large freezers. Unheated buildings may be converted to a faster acting wet pipe system during summer months. A dry pipe sprinkler system requires the use of a special valve that must be protected from freezing. Air pressure in the system keeps the valve closed. When fire occurs, individual sprinkler heads activate as in the wet pipe system, but there is a delay while the air runs out of the piping, allowing the valve to open.

There are two devices that can be incorporated to speed up the activation of the dry type valve in large systems. An *Exhauster* opens an auxiliary valve to let air out faster, allowing the water valve to open quicker. When the water valve operates, the exhauster valve closes automatically to prevent discharge of water. An *Accelerator* is a device that uses system air pressure to open the clapper of the water valve quicker, allowing the water pressure to force the remaining air out of the system.

Pre-action Sprinkler System. These systems are used primarily to protect properties where there is danger of serious water damage as a result of damaged automatic sprinklers or broken piping. This sprinkler system is different from a dry pipe system in that the preaction water supply valve is actuated independently of the open sprinklers. An automatic fire detection system such as smoke detectors actuates the water supply valve. The actuation of the sprinkler heads is an independent action caused by the heat of a fire.

This type of system is better than the dry pipe, because the valve is opened sooner by the detectors which, theoretically, will detect fire before the heat can fuse sprinkler heads. However, there is a delay in getting water to the fire that is similar to the dry type system. Another advantage to this system is its safety from waterflow if part of the system should be damaged. Water will still not be allowed into the system until fire is detected by the detectors.

Combined Dry Pipe and Preaction System. This system includes the essential features of both systems. The piping contains air under pressure as a dry pipe system. A supplementary heat detecting device can actuate the water supply valve and an exhauster allowing the system to fill with water. Should the supplementary heat detection system fail, the system can still function as a conventional dry pipe system.

Deluge Sprinkler System. A deluge sprinkler system is one that is capable of wetting down an entire area by admitting water to sprinkler heads that are open at all times. It may be used for extra hazard occupancies, such as flammable liquids, rocket propellants, aircraft hangars, or other areas that require immediate application of water. The deluge sprinkler system contains sprinkler heads that are always open. A deluge valve holds back the water until activated by some external signal, such as activation of a smoke or heat detector, or it may be activated manually.

Special Types of Systems.   A limited water supply system incorporates a 2000–3000 gallon pressure tank for systems where existing water supply or pressure may not be adequate.

AUTOMATIC SPRINKLERS

Automatic sprinklers are heat-sensitive devices that activate at a predetermined temperature to release a stream of water and distribute it in a specified pattern and quantity. Automatic sprinklers are available for many different temperatures and applications. Since their first introduction in the 1800s, automatic sprinklers have been studied and improved to the point where we now have sprinklers available for almost every conceivable application.

Because of their simple heat-activated mode of operation and simplicity, automatic sprinklers are extremely reliable. Instances of sprinkler failure are rare. When an automatic sprinkler has failed, it is usually due to some external factor such as physical damage or corrosion.

Standard Sprinkler Heads

The first classification of type of sprinkler head includes two types based upon the orientation of the head (Figure 9-11).

Figure 9-11.   An upright sprinkler head (left) and a pendant sprinkler head (right). (Source: Factory Mutual Engineering Corporation)

Upright Sprinklers. The upright sprinkler head is oriented upright on top of a branch line so that the water stream is directed upward against the deflector. It is used in spaces where the sprinkler piping is exposed. The distinguishing characteristic of the upright sprinkler is the shape of the deflector with the fins pointed down so as to direct the water pattern down.

Pendent Sprinklers. The pendent sprinkler head is oriented down below the branch line. The water stream is directed downward against the deflector. It is used in finished spaces where heads extend down through hung ceilings. The deflector of the pendent head has the fins flat so as to direct the water stream horizontally.

Special Application Sprinklers

There are many special application sprinklers that are available to protect most industrial applications. Some of the most common are described here.

Sidewall Sprinklers. These sprinklers have specially shaped deflectors that direct most of the water pattern away from a nearby wall while only a small portion of the pattern is allowed to discharge toward the wall. Sidewall sprinklers may be installed to provide special coverage in unique protection situations.

Early Suppression–Fast Response (ESFR) Sprinklers. The ESFR sprinkler is a relatively new type of sprinkler that was developed to respond quickly to a growing fire and deliver a high density of water in order to suppress the fire growth before a severe fire plume can be generated. The difference between the ESFR and standard sprinkler is the ability of the ESFR to suppress a growing fire rather than controlling it. Their primary application is in providing fire protection for warehouses by delivering water quickly before the fire plume can develop. The ESFR sprinkler responds rapidly because the temperature sensing element has significantly less mass than that of a standard sprinkler.

Although the ESFR sprinkler has a water discharge two to three times greater than that of standard sprinklers, the need for a larger water supply is probably unnecessary because fewer ESFR sprinklers will activate. Because of this, the relative costs of an ESFR system may be less than a conventional system.

Large Drop Sprinklers. Certain high challenge fires such as high hazard storage occupancies require water drops of large size and velocity to penetrate into the strong updrafts that are produced by such fires. Large drop sprinklers have a greater water discharge and a special deflector to produce the large drops with sufficient velocity to effectively penetrate high-velocity fire plumes.

Flush, Recessed, and Concealed Sprinklers. For protection of low-risk occupancies such as offices, it is sometimes desirable, for aesthetic reasons, to conceal the sprinkler heads. A flush-type sprinkler only has the heat sensing

Figure 9-12. A concealed-type sprinkler head in which the body of the sprinkler head is located above a concealing cover plate. When exposed to heat, the cover plate drops away. (Source: Factory Mutual Engineering Corporation)

element exposed. When heat of a fire activates the element, the deflector drops down into position and allows the water to flow.

A recessed sprinkler has part or most of the body of the sprinkler recessed within a housing. Operation of this sprinkler is similar to a standard pendent sprinkler.

Concealed sprinklers have the body, including the operating mechanism, located above a concealing covering plate. Heat of a fire causes the cover plate to drop, exposing the heat-sensitive assemble of the sprinkler (Figure 9-12).

Rack Storage Sprinklers.   Rack storage sprinklers are intended for use as in-rack sprinklers in rack storage arrays. In rack storage arrangements it is necessary to provide sprinkler protection in the rack to control a fire that may be remote and protected from ceiling-mounted sprinklers. On the other hand, operating ceiling sprinklers might cool in-rack sprinklers and prevent their operation. Therefore, the distinguishing characteristic of rack storage sprinklers is a disc that is mounted above the fusible element to protect the element from wetting from sprinklers above.

On–Off Sprinklers.   Cycling sprinklers turn on and off as needed for those environments where it is necessary to limit water damage. When the sprinkler is heated, it activates like a normal sprinkler. When the temperature of the device cools to about 100 degrees Fahrenheit it closes until it is again heated to the rated temperature.

Drop-Head Sprinklers. In environments such as anechoic chambers where sprinklers and their associated piping would interfere with RF radiation, drop-head sprinklers have been developed. For use in deluge and preaction sprinkler systems, drop-heads, or extendable head sprinklers are kept retracted in a telescoping pipe. When the system is activated by another detection means, water is allowed into the system and the water pressure is used to extend the heads into the protected area.

Wax-Coated Sprinklers. In corrosive environments such as laboratories, platting facilities, and exhaust ducts that may contain corrosive vapors, normal sprinklers can quickly degrade to the point of failure. In these applications wax-coated sprinklers are used. The wax coating must have a melting point that is slightly below the operating temperature of the sprinkler.

Operation of Automatic Sprinklers

Sprinkler heads are activated by the heat of a fire which results in the release of water. There are two main types of thermal response mechanism, the fusible link and the frangible glass bulb. There are some other types that will be occasionally encountered including the bimetallic disc, fusible alloy pellet, and chemical pellet.

The operating elements of the sprinkler head consist of a cap that is held in place over the orifice by a system of levers and links or a glass bulb, all of which are held in place by the struts or body of the head.

Fusible Link. The fusible link sprinkler head assembly is probably the most common. It consists of three pieces of metal that are soldered together with a eutectic solder. A eutectic solder is a blend of two metals, the resulting melting point of which is less than that of either one. Common metals used in eutectic solders include tin, lead, cadmium and bismuth (Figure 9-13).

Frangible Glass Bulb. The frangible glass bulb is a small glass bulb which holds the cap in place over the orifice. The bulb contains an amount of liquid which does not completely fill the bulb. As the bulb is heated the liquid expands and absorbs the bubble. As further heating increases the pressure, the bulb shatters, releasing the cap. The operating temperature of this head is set by regulating the amount of liquid and the size of the bulb when the bulb is sealed (Figures 9-14, 9-15).

Temperature Ratings of Automatic Sprinklers

Automatic sprinklers have a wide range of temperature settings to accommodate almost every operating environment. This temperature rating is stamped on the

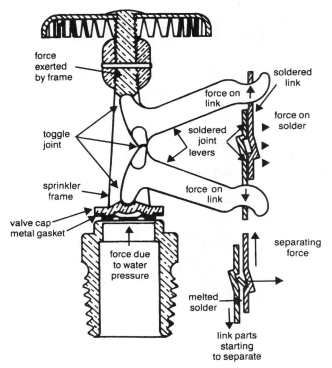

Figure 9-13.   Representative arrangement of a soldered link-and-lever automatic sprinkler showing how the closing force operates. (Source: Factory Mutual Engineering Corporation)

solder of soldered link-type heads; other types have the temperature stamped on one of the releasing elements. Additionally, the body struts of the head are color coded. The bulb of frangible glass bulb heads are color coded. NFPA 13 gives the temperature ratings, classification, and color codes.

STANDPIPE AND HOSE SYSTEMS

Standpipe and hose systems are provided for the manual application of water to fires by either employees or by fire department personnel. While they may be installed instead of a Class A portable fire extinguisher, they are not considered alternatives for automatic sprinkler protection.

Classification of Systems

Standpipe and hose systems are classified by the NFPA according to the size of the hose connection and the intended user.

Figure 9-14. A standard upright glass bulb sprinkler head. (Source: Factory Mutual Engineering Corporation)

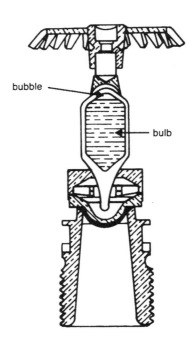

Figure 9-15. The Grinnell Quartzoid, Issue D, glass-bulb automatic sprinkler. The operating temperature is regulated by adjusting the amount of liquid and the size of the bubble when the bulb is sealed. (Source: Factory Mutual Engineering Corporation)

Figure 9-16. Without automatic sprinkler protection, there is usually little that fire fighters can do. (Photo: Factory Mutual Engineering Corporation)

Class I Systems.   Class I systems means a $2\frac{1}{2}$-inch hose connection for use by fire departments and those trained in handling heavy streams. These systems can provide the primary fire fighting water supply in high-rise buildings beyond the reach of fire department ladders.

Class II Systems.   Class II systems means a $1\frac{1}{2}$-inch hose system which provides a means for the control or extinguishment of fires in the incipient stage.

Class III Systems.   Class III systems contain both $1\frac{1}{2}$- and $2\frac{1}{2}$-inch hose connections for use by employees who are trained in the use of hose operations, and for use by those who are trained in the use of heavy streams in the advanced fire stages.

Water Supplies

Water supplies for standpipe and hose systems will depend upon the number of streams, the size of the streams, the potential hazard, and the other demands upon the systems such as automatic sprinkler systems. OSHAct requires a minimum supply of 100 gpm for a period of at least 30 minutes for those standpipe and hose systems which are provided for use by employees.

Water supplies may come from city water mains if pressure is adequate, or pumps may be incorporated to supplement the pressure. Another alternative for supplying water includes either gravity or pressurized water tanks on the roof of the building.

Types of Standpipe Systems

There are four types of standpipe systems depending upon their expected use.

Wet Standpipe. This is the most desired type of system because the water pressure is maintained in the standpipe at all times.

Dry Standpipe. This system is arranged to admit water to the standpipe system through manual operation of remote control devices that are located at each hose station.

Dry Standpipe in Unheated Building. This system is installed where there is a danger of freezing. A dry pipe valve is used to admit water automatically by means of a dry pipe valve or other approved means. There is a delay in this type of system during evacuation of the air as the system charges with water.

Dry Standpipe with No Permanent Water Supply. This type of system must be supplied and pressurized by the fire department. It is used to reduce the time involved for fire departments to put hose streams into action on the upper floors of tall buildings.

WATER SPRAY FIXED SYSTEMS

Water spray fixed systems are special systems to apply water spray to unique fire protection problem areas through a system of fixed nozzles. The water spray fixed system may be automatically or manually operated.

Water spray fixed systems are used to extinguish fire, to control burning, to protect exposures, and to prevent fire. Specific items that may be protected include flammable liquid and gas vessels, piping, and equipment such as transformers, oil switches, and motors. Exposure protection includes the protection of openings in walls or floors such as conveyor or escalator openings and the protection of walls from adjoining severe fire exposure.

Extinguishment. Water spray fixed systems may be installed to provide fire extinguishment of certain fire hazards such as cable trays and cable runs.

Control Burning. Water spray fixed systems may be installed to control fire spread in those situations where burning combustible materials are not susceptible to extinguishment by water spray, or when it is not desirable to extinguish the fire. An example of this application might be a flammable gas or liquid transfer areas where a fire at a leaking valve or pipe must be controlled until the flow can be shut off.

Protection of Exposures. Water spray fixed systems may be installed to protect buildings or structural members of buildings or process equipment that are exposed to a potential fire hazard.

Prevention of Fire. Water spray fixed systems may be used to prevent ignition of combustible materials from an exposing ignition source. The water spray is used to dissolve, dilute, disperse, or cool flammable or combustible materials. An example might be the application of water spray to stored wood logs.

FIXED FIRE EXTINGUISHING SYSTEMS

Fixed fire extinguishing systems are installed to protect special hazards where it is necessary to have more agent available than is practical with portable equipment, where people may not be in attendance, or the hazard is too great to expect people to control a fire with portable extinguishers. Fixed systems can also be automatically or manually activated so that a large quantity of agent can be applied directly to the problem area. Systems can be installed to protect inaccessible areas or areas where it is unsafe for personnel.

The primary fixed fire extinguishing systems that are in use and to be described here include foam, halon, dry chemical and carbon dioxide. It is not intended to completely describe each system because they are diverse and complicated. The reader should just be aware of the existence and application of each type of system.

Foam Systems

Foam extinguishing systems are for use on flammable liquid hazards that are large and may require immediate application of a large amount of foam to be effective such as refineries, flammable and combustible liquid storage and transfer facilities, and aircraft hangars.

Foam systems can be installed to provide automatic spot application through nozzles such as fixed nozzles which would apply foam under the wings of aircraft in airplane hangars. In flammable and combustible liquid storage facilities, foam systems can be installed to apply foam at the surface of tanks, below the surface, or through nozzles that are located on the ground or on towers. The system may just consist of the piping and nozzles to which the fire department can connect their foam equipment.

There are four basic types of foam systems including the fixed, semifixed, mobile, and portable.

Fixed Foam Systems. These are completed systems that are piped from a central foam station, discharging through fixed delivery outlets to the protected hazard. Fixed systems may be installed to protect a specific hazard such as aircraft hangars and storage tanks.

Semifixed Foam Systems. The protected hazard is equipped with fixed discharge outlets and piping that terminate at a safe distance. Necessary foam materials are transported to the scene after the fire starts. This system would be installed in areas where the hazard might change, necessitating different types of foam.

Mobile Foam Systems. Any foam system that is mounted on wheels, whether self-propelled or towed, is a mobile foam system. They may be connected to a suitable water supply or utilize a premixed foam solution.

Portable Foam Systems. Portable systems include those in which the foam producing equipment is transported by hand. It may include nozzles, hose, and portable extinguishers.

Halon Systems

Halon extinguishing systems may be of the local application or total room flooding variety. They are used on flammable and combustible liquid fire hazards and computer and other delicate electronic equipment installations.

One of the most common uses for halon systems is in high value computer rooms. It can be installed to protect under-floor areas that are not practical to protect with sprinkler systems. A halon system can also be installed as a total room flooding system when it is desirable to minimize or eliminate water damage. It should be noted that total flooding systems do not eliminate the necessity of a automatic sprinkler system, they increase the possibility of automatically extinguishing a fire before the sprinklers are required to operate.

Figure 9-17. A room-flooding halon system protecting a a tape storage room. (Source: Fenwal Inc.)

The under-floor halon system in computer rooms is a particularly useful application because it is a relatively confined space which takes advantage of and allows the full benefits of the halon gas to be realized. Other opportunities for halon systems exist in aircraft, ships, switchgear rooms, magnetic tape vaults, and processing and storage areas for flammable liquids.

Halon systems are applicable for some local applications where the hazard is concentrated in one area where the agent can flood the hazard area and maintain the flow for a period of time. Local applications include printing presses, spray booths, exhaust hoods, dip and quench tanks, and oil-filled electric power transformers.

Dry Chemical Systems

Dry chemical systems are appropriate for the protection of Class B and C fire hazards where quick extinguishment is desired. They are primarily installed to protect electrical equipment or areas where fires may involve liquids, gases, or grease. Systems containing multipurpose dry chemical agent may be installed to protect ordinary combustibles such as paper and wood.

Fixed dry chemical systems include a container of the agent, a gas pressure source to expel the agent, piping, and nozzles through which the agent is applied in the area to be protected. They may be installed for local application or, when the hazard to be protected can be totally enclosed, for total flooding or a combination of both. There is no lingering protection with dry chemical agents. Reignition sources in the area of the hazard must be controlled. The local application system is recommended for small area hazards such as open tanks of flammable liquids, dip tanks, deep fat fryers, and oil-filled electric transformers.

Total flooding applications for dry chemical systems would include flammable liquid storage rooms and electrical equipment vaults. In areas that are protected by a total flooding dry chemical system, provisions must be made to evacuate personnel prior to dumping the system. The dry chemical agents are not toxic, but they will cause temporary breathing difficulty and reduced vision.

Carbon Dioxide Systems

Carbon dioxide systems are particularly suited for extinguishing fires in flammable liquids, electrical apparatus, and high value occupancies such as fur or record storage areas that are susceptible to fire, smoke, and water damage. They may be of the total flooding, local application, and hoseline types.

Cylinders for a carbon dioxide system are normally stored outside the protected area. Cylinders are manifolded together to discharge piping and nozzles in the protected area. Because of the rapid dissipation of carbon dioxide, it is generally advisable to provide a reserve supply of the gas. The system may be activated either mechanically or electrically by almost any form of detection system.

There are two very important considerations for total flooding carbon dioxide systems. The protected space must be relatively confined so as to maintain the carbon dioxide concentration long enough to extinguish the fire. The protected space must be unoccupied or the system must have a predischarge alarm and time delay to allow personnel to evacuate the area.

SUMMARY

There are many types of systems and equipment available for the application of fire extinguishing agents. Equipment ranges from hand-held portable fire extinguishers to large fixed extinguishing systems.

Portable fire extinguishers have proven to be effective in controlling fires in the incipient stage when used by trained personnel. Automatic extinguishing systems have proven to be effective in controlling fires that have progressed beyond the incipient stage. A combination of portable extinguishers and automatic systems that are appropriate to the hazards and properly tested and maintained will usually prevent a small fire from growing to damaging proportions.

Whatever system is chosen, it must be reliable and be capable of quickly applying the proper agent for the hazard to the fire in adequate amounts to be effective.

BIBLIOGRAPHY

Best, Richard, and Demers, David P. 1982. Investigation Report on the MGM Grand Hotel Fire Las Vegas, Nevada, November 21, 1980. Quincy: National Fire Protection Association.

Code of Federal Regulations. 29 CFR 1910. 1987. Occupational Safety and Health Administration, Department of Labor. Washington, DC.

Dittman, Charles R. 1988. Selling Management the Best Fire Protection Available. *Professional Safety* 33(10):21–26.

Fire Protection Handbook, 16th ed. 1986. Quincy: National Fire Protection Association.

Industrial Fire Protection, First Edition. 1982. Stillwater, OK: Fire Protection Publications, Oklahoma State University.

Loss Prevention Data 4-1N. 1979. Water Spray Fixed Systems. Norwood, MA: Factory Mutual Engineering Corporation.

Loss Prevention Data 4-5. 1983. Portable Extinguishers. Norwood, MA: Factory Mutual Engineering Corporation.

Loss Prevention Data 4-7N. 1975. Foam Extinguishing Systems. Norwood, MA: Factory Mutual Engineering Corporation.

Loss Prevention Data 4-8N. 1978. Halogenated Fire Extinguishing Agent Systems. Norwood, MA: Factory Mutual Engineering Corporation.

Loss Prevention Data 4-10. 1976. Dry Chemical Systems. Norwood, MA: Factory Mutual Engineering Corporation.

Loss Prevention Data 4-11. 1976. Carbon Dioxide Extinguishing Systems. Norwood, MA: Factory Mutual Engineering Corporation.

Moore, Jeffrey. 1989. Why Sprinkler Systems Fail. *Fire Engineering* 142(4):36–40.

NFPA 10-1988. *Standard for Portable Fire Extinguishers.* Quincy: National Fire Protection Association.

NFPA 11-1988. *Low Expansion Foam and Combined Agent Systems.* Quincy: National Fire Protection Association.

NFPA 11A-1988. *Medium and High Expansion Foam Systems.* Quincy: National Fire Protection Association.

NFPA 12-1989. *Carbon Dioxide Extinguishing Systems.* Quincy: National Fire Protection Association.

NFPA 12A-1989. *Halon 1301 Fire Extinguishing Systems.* Quincy: National Fire Protection Association.

NFPA 13-1989. *Standard for the Installation of Sprinkler Systems.* Quincy: National Fire Protection Association.

NFPA 15-1985. *Standard for Water Spray Fixed Systems for Fire Protection.* Quincy: National Fire Protection Association.

NFPA 14-1986. *Standard for the Installation of Standpipe and Hose Systems.* Quincy: National Fire Protection Association.

NFPA 17-1985. *Standard for Dry Chemical Extinguishing Systems.* Quincy: National Fire Protection Association.

Redding, Donald, and Pauley, Richard, Jr. Large-Loss Fires in the United States During 1985. *Fire Journal* 80(6):34–39, 67, 70.

10
EXPLOSIONS

Explosions have always been a part of the industrial loss experience along with fires and other industrial accidents. Explosions are frequently spectacular and tragic. Because of the sudden release of energy, they usually result in extensive damage to property and may very well cause injury or death to personnel. Even with the many rules and regulations that govern potentially explosive operations, explosions still occur. There have been, and continue to be, explosions in the obvious industries such as the manufacturing and storage of explosives, blasting agents, and fireworks. One of the deadliest of these was the 1985 fireworks manufacturing plant explosion in Jennings, Oklahoma. On June 25, 1985, a series of explosions at the Aerlex Fireworks Manufacturing Corporation resulted in the deaths of 21 people and injuries to 5 others. Despite almost total destruction of the facility, investigators were able to determine that the explosion was the result of careless handling of pyrotechnic materials during the unloading of a truck.

There are also explosions in other industrial operations involving flammable liquids, chemicals, dusts, and lint. Grain milling and coal mining industries have also experienced many dust explosions (Figure 10-1).

The oil and chemical industries, in particular, have suffered many losses due to explosions. An example of a particularly tragic series of explosions occurred at the Petroleos Mexicanos, or PEMEX facility outside of Mexico City on November 19, 1984. This disaster was the largest LP gas explosion ever recorded, and it caused 500 fatalities and injured over 7000 people.

Also in 1984, a July 23 explosion and fire at the Union Oil Refinery in Romeoville, Illinois killed 19 people. The initial explosion was an unconfined vapor cloud explosion which occurred when propane gas escaping from a catalytic cracking tower ignited. This explosion resulted in numerous fires throughout the facility and impairment of the plant's fire protection water system. About 30 minutes later, a BLEVE occurred which resulted in further damage.

Industries that generate dusts such as mining and grain storage and milling operations have always been prone to dust explosions. The deadliest industrial explosion in United States history occurred in a 1907 coal mine explosion and fire that killed 361 people in Monongha, West Virginia. More recently, a 1984 coal mine explosion and fire killed 27 people in Orangeville, Utah. Grain dust explosions have been occurring as long as man has been grinding grain. In the

Figure 10-1. A grain dust explosion that extended through underground conveyor tunnel. (Source: Factory Mutual Engineering Corporation)

1970s, a series of devastating explosions rocked the grain handling industry. Two of these, which occurred in December 1977, were the most serious grain dust explosions in decades. In Westwego, Louisiana, 36 were killed in the Continental Grain Complex explosion on December 22. In Galveston, Texas, 18 were killed in the Farmers Export Grain Elevator explosion on December 27. These explosions resulted in an intense effort by the Occupational Safety and Health Administration and firesafety professionals to legislate better controls for this industry, and they resulted in the addition of section 1910.272 to OSHAct in December 31,1987.

In the storage and handling of flammable and combustible liquids, for industrial usage, the explosion possibilities are not always so obvious and a certain amount of complacency results. One of the biggest challenges to face the firesafety professional is to educate industry's employees and management to the hazards of the materials with which they work. When the hazards and risks involved with industrial materials and processes are understood, it is easier to convince management of the need for appropriate detection and suppression systems and equipment. Employees must be trained about the materials with which they work and the process safeguards and procedures that are incorporated for their protection.

On April 29, 1981, two workers in Newington, New Hampshire, were killed while cleaning an empty underground storage tank that had been used to store JP-4 jet fuel. The workers were using squeegees to remove sludge from the bottom of the 1.4 million gallon tank when flammable vapors exploded. The explosion lifted the 100-foot diameter steel deck roof that was covered with 9 inches of reinforced concrete and 4 to 6 feet of earth over 8 feet into the air.

In this chapter, the theory of explosions, how they occur, and how to prevent and protect against their destructive effects will be discussed. Although explosions may result from a variety of sources or mechanisms, this chapter will deal primarily with combustion explosions.

There are four methods of protecting against explosions which will be discussed in this chapter including prevention, suppression, venting, and containment. The ideal method is prevention, or eliminating those conditions that can cause an explosion. Suppression, the second method of protecting against explosions, is similar to extinguishment of fire, only much faster detection and suppression processes must take place. Suppression is simply the stopping or extinguishment of an explosion once it has been initiated. Venting, the third method, is a technique, usually through construction, to limit the damage by releasing some of the energy when an explosion does occur. Containment of the explosive forces, the fourth method, is only useful in certain process situations.

EXPLOSION DESCRIPTION

A simple and somewhat humorous but graphic definition of an explosion from an old book on powders and explosions written by Professor T. L. Davis, is as follows: "A loud noise accompanied by the rapid departure of things from the place where they have been."

The more technical definition, and the one to be used in this text, is as follows: "The effect produced by the sudden violent expansion of gases which may or may not be accompanied by shock waves, and/or disruption of enclosing materials."

The reader will notice that the terms fire or combustion are not included in this definition. There are numerous mechanisms or conditions that can result in a "sudden violent expansion of gases." Types of explosions that meet the conditions of this definition include: mechanical explosions, thermal explosions, nuclear explosions, and chemical explosions.

Mechanical explosions are those that result from such things as the rupture of a pressure vessel from excess pressure or failure of a component.

A thermal explosion results from overtemperature of a confined material such as water in a boiler that, if not relieved, will lead to the rupture of the boiler. An exothermic reaction that occurs in a process vessel and may lead to the rupture of the vessel is another example of a thermal explosion.

A nuclear explosion is one resulting from a nuclear detonation. In keeping with the objective of this text, we will concentrate on combustion reactions that occur in a confined space or with sufficient speed to build up enough pressure to meet the conditions of an explosion. Since combustion is a chemical reaction, these explosions are referred to as chemical explosions. This is not to imply that the other explosion types are to be neglected by the firesafety professional. These other types can also lead to damage to property and injury and death to personnel. In some cases, a mechanical explosion can cause chemical explosions as was the case on January 12, 1984, in Champaign, Illinois. A mechanical explosion of a nitrogen tank occurred that damaged adjacent hydrogen tanks. The leaking hydrogen ignited and caused a serious hydrogen fire and potential explosion hazard for responding fire fighters.

In a survey of explosion incidents conducted by Industrial Risk Insurers, and reported by John A. Davenport, explosion incidents were categorized as combustion, reaction, or metal failure. The survey found that combustion explosions accounted for 44 percent of the incidents. Reaction explosions, which included explosive liquids or solids and runaway chemical reactions, accounted for 39 percent of the incidents. Metal failure explosions, including corrosion, overheating, and accidental overpressure causes, accounted for 17 percent of the incidents.

As in other areas of fire protection, explosion prevention requires the close coordination of the firesafety professional, health and safety, environmental, and process personnel. Attempts to neutralize conditions or achieve compliance in these areas may result in increased explosion potential. For example, environmental protection requirements may necessitate the collection of flammable gases and vapors for incineration and increase the explosion potential. The environmental regulations may also require the collection of dusts in potentially explosive dry systems consisting of filters and electrostatic precipitators. The preferred method would be to collect dusts in wet scrubber devices; however, this creates wastewater disposal problems. Nitrogen dioxide is listed in the National Ambient Air Quality Standards (NAAQS) as a criteria pollutant. The Federal Clean Air Act requires the Environmental Protection Agency (EPA) to establish ambient ceilings for certain criteria pollutants. Nitrogen dioxide is one of six criteria pollutants for which the EPA established ambient levels of air quality necessary to protect public health. Nitrogen oxides (NO_x's) are emitted as a combustion product in boiler furnace operations. There are several methods to achieve reduced emissions of nitrogen oxides from boiler furnaces. Unfortunately, they may increase the explosion hazard and specific procedures and equipment are necessary to prevent explosions from occurring.

TERMINOLOGY

There are a number of other definitions that are pertinent to the discussion of explosions as follows.

Deflagration

An explosion may be described as either a detonation or a deflagration depending upon the speed at which it occurs. A deflagration occurs when the combustion process propagates itself through the unburned portion of the substance slower than the speed of sound. In a deflagration, no shock wave is produced. The unreacted material may be compressed by the deflagration, resulting in an increase in the reaction rate. When this continues, as in a pipeline, the rate may increase to supersonic and a detonation may result.

Because of the unique set of conditions for a detonation to occur, most of the explosions that occur are deflagrations. Therefore, references to explosions in this text are intended to be references to deflagrations.

Detonation

A detonation is a combustion process that proceeds faster than the speed of sound and produces a shock wave. A detonation is a unique explosion reaction which requires optimum conditions to occur. For one thing, the explosive range is narrower than the range of flammability. For example, hydrogen has a LFL of 4 percent and an UFL of 75 percent. The explosive range in which a detonation may occur in hydrogen is between 18 percent and 59 percent.

In a pipe or vessel, the diameter and length-to-diameter ratio is critical for detonation to occur. A length-to-diameter ratio of greater than 10 is conducive to detonation. Also, the pipe diameter must be greater than a critical diameter of 0.5 to 1 inch.

A detonation may occur when ignition occurs at one end of a closed pipe sending out a strong shock wave through combustible mixtures causing instantaneous compression, heating, spontaneous ignition, and reaction of those mixtures. Energy that is released is fed into and sustains the shock wave. Later waves traveling through unburned, compressed, and heated layers overtakes the earlier waves and a supersonic shock wave develops. An initial, very unstable shock wave is formed with pressures and speed in excess of the stable detonation that develops. Pressure in this initial shock wave is about 100 times the initial absolute pressure. It then settles into a stable shock wave with pressure about 30 times the initial absolute pressure. This high spike is normally undamaging because it happens so rapidly that it does not exist long enough to overcome the inertia of the pipe mass.

Explosive Limits

As with flammable liquids and gases, it is possible to identify explosive limits and an explosive range. The explosive limits are frequently used interchangeably with the flammable limits. The term explosive limit refers to the range of concentration of gas or mist or dust, with oxidant (or air) over which flame propagation can occur. The explosive range is referred to as the area between the upper explosive limit (UEL) and the lower explosive limit (LEL).

It should be recalled from Chapter 4, Flammable and Combustible Liquids, that increasing the temperature of a combustible/oxidant mixture widens the flammable range by reducing the lower and increasing the upper flammable limits (Figure 4-1). While changes in pressure have a minimal effect upon the LEL, increases in pressure greatly increases the UEL.

Changes in the pressure will have an effect upon the flashpoint of a liquid. An increase in pressure raises the flashpoint and a decrease in pressure lowers it (Figure 4-2).

Oxidant

An oxidant, or oxidizing agent, is any material or substance that can react with a combustible to produce burning or combustion, or an exothermic reaction. Oxidizing agents have the same considerations in explosions as in other combustion reactions. Oxygen in the air is the simplest and most prevalent oxidizing agent. Chemical oxidizers may very well increase the potential for an explosion instead of just a fire or they may cause a rapid exothermic reaction that results in an explosion. For example, the combination of chlorine (an oxidizer) and grease (a fuel) can result in an explosion.

FACTORS AFFECTING SEVERITY OF EXPLOSIONS

There are various factors that affect the severity of an explosion that the fire-safety professional and the process engineer should review. Ideally, explosive materials and the potential for explosive reactions should be eliminated from all processes. When this is not possible, attempts should be made to find a safer chemical or change some of the process parameters to achieve greater safety by reducing the severity of an explosion should it occur.

Chemical Composition

As the number of extra bonds in the molecular structure of a material increase, so does the reactivity. For example, as the number of bonds increases, from one bond in ethane to three bonds in acetylene, the reactivity increases.

H H	H H	
H C — C H	C = C	HC≡CH
H H	H H	
Ethane	Ethylene	Acetylene

Reactivity increases --------------------------------→

Ignition temperature (°F)	882	842	581
Reactivity	0	2	3

In NFPA 325, *Properties of Flammable Liquids*, Gases and Solids, ethane is listed as a flammable gas with an ignition temperature of 882 degrees Fahrenheit and a reactivity rating of 0. Ethylene is listed as a flammable gas with an ignition temperature of 842 degrees Fahrenheit and a reactivity rating of 2. Acetylene is listed as a flammable gas with an ignition temperature of 581 degrees Fahrenheit and a reactivity rating of 3. As additional bonds are added, the ignition temperature of the compound decreases and the reactivity rating increases. (Note: See Chapter 11 description of NFPA 704, for discussion of reactivity ratings.)

Concentration

The concentration of the fuel/oxidant mixture will have an effect upon the explosive potential and the explosion pressures that will develop. There is an optimum concentration between the UEL and the LEL called the stoichiometric mixture which is when the concentration of oxidant and fuel of a mixture is at a point where both are consumed equally during combustion. It is at, or near, the stoichiometric concentration of the mixture in air that the greatest explosion pressures occur.

Oxygen Content

The amount of oxygen that is available to the reaction will have an effect upon the explosive range and ignition temperature. Of course, too little oxygen will result in a fuel-rich mixture which will not ignite. This concept will be used later as a means of preventing explosions.

As the oxygen concentration of the mixture is increased, the range between UEL and LEL increases, with the UEL increasing markedly in oxygen-rich atmospheres. The presence of chemical oxidants has the same effect upon the range of flammability. Oxidants tend to lower the autoignition temperature of some fuel materials, increasing the possibility of spontaneous ignition at ambient temperatures.

Turbulence

Turbulence in stoichiometric gas/air mixtures causes only slight increases in the maximum explosion pressure. However, in mixtures that are nearer the LEL or UEL, there is a greater increase in the resulting explosion pressure. Another effect of turbulence is to increase the rate of explosion pressure rise.

Confinement

Confinement of the explosion reaction may result in an explosion of greater severity. Depending upon the degree of confinement, explosive pressures may build up before the confining vessel ruptures. Conversely, the area of vents that are available and the location of the vents will affect the severity of the explosion. Vents that are closer to the area of origin of the explosion will reduce the severity. In the following discussion on venting as a means of reducing the damage of a potential explosion, confinement will be further explained.

BOILING LIQUID, EXPANDING VAPOR EXPLOSION

The boiling liquid, expanding vapor explosion, or BLEVE, is an explosion that occurs, usually, when a container holding a liquefied flammable gas fails when exposed to fire. A BLEVE is a mechanical explosion. It occurs when the vessel containing a liquid fails due to the action of heat and the pressure of the boiling liquid and expanding vapors. The most common BLEVEs involve containers that hold a liquefied flammable gas. However, there have been occurrences where water heaters have BLEVE'd. On January 19, 1982, a hot water heater in a school in Spencer, Oklahoma BLEVE'd, killing 7 and injuring 33. Apparently the thermostat on this 85-gallon water heater failed and there was no pressure relief device. When the heater failed, the superheated water instantly expanded to steam creating the thrust that propelled tank pieces through the roof and up to 130 feet away. BLEVEs usually involve a liquefied gas. Liquefied gases are above their boiling point at normal temperature. They will remain in the liquid state as long as they are kept under pressure. When the pressure is suddenly reduced to atmospheric because of a container failure, the stored heat in the liquid causes rapid vaporization and tremendous expansion into the gaseous state. Should an ignition source be present, the rapidly expanding cloud creates a devastating explosion.

The most frequent scenario that results in a BLEVE occurs when an accident results in fire impinging on a tank containing a liquefied flammable gas. As the tank and its contents heat up, pressure is created inside the container causing the pressure relief valve to open releasing the gas which may ignite. At this point, the hazard is not apparent, a moderate fire impinging on a tank of liquefied gas which is venting satisfactorily. If the vented gas is ignited, a somewhat safer situation is created because it eliminates the possibility of a gas cloud forming. But this innocuous looking situation is misleading. As long as there is liquid within the tank, the liquid will provide sufficient cooling of the metal tank walls to prevent failure. However, as the gas vents off, the liquid level falls. When the liquid level falls below the point at which the tank is being heated, there is no longer any cooling action and the metal tank wall can heat up to the point where it weakens and fails from the internal pressures. When this occurs, the remaining gas is suddenly released to the atmosphere where it rapidly expands and ignites and a BLEVE occurs.

The most frequent BLEVEs are in transportation incidents such as a train derailment or a truck accident. Industrial BLEVEs have also occurred, such as the one at the Petroleos Mexicanos, or PEMEX facility outside of Mexico City on November 19, 1984. This disaster was the largest LP-gas explosion ever recorded and caused 500 fatalities and injured over 7000 people. At the time of the explosion, the plant's tanks were being filled with LP-gas which was being pumped through a 12-inch pipeline from a plant 250 miles away. It is estimated that the plant's tanks, consisting of spheres and horizontal cylinders, contained 2.9 million gallons of LP-gas at the time of the explosion. Although the exact cause of the explosion will probably never be known, it is thought that one of the filling pipelines failed resulting in a liquid pool that collected in a 3-foot high diked area beneath one the spherical tanks. When the gas cloud reached an ignition source and flashed back, it ignited the pool which, subsequently caused the sphere to BLEVE. Following the first BLEVE, a total of 15 violent explosions occurred within one hour and a half. Initial ignition of the cloud probably was by a ground-level flare used to burn off excess gas. Another contributing factor to this disaster was the diked area which allowed the liquefied gas to pool beneath a major storage tank. The high numbers of deaths and injuries were because of the close proximity of dwellings which consisted of several rows of relatively primitive houses that were, in some cases, just 45 feet from the plant.

UNCONFINED VAPOR CLOUD EXPLOSION

The Unconfined Vapor Cloud Explosion, or UVCE is another type of explosion that occurs when the vapor cloud of a combustible material is ignited. Unlike most deflagrations where the high-pressure gases that are produced are confined, a UVCE occurs when a flammable gas or vapor is mixed with air outdoors and is ignited. In this case, the gases that are produced are unconfined and most of the energy is released as heat. When there is a massive spill of combustible hydrocarbons or liquefied gas, one of four things can happen as follows: (1) the vapors may dissipate harmlessly, (2) the spill may ignite upon release, (3) the vapor cloud may disperse over a wide area and then ignite, and (4) the same scenario as 3, however, after ignition the flame propagates through the cloud and accelerates sufficiently to produce a dangerous shock wave. Similar to a BLEVE, the UVCE is a very spectacular and dangerous occurrence. The maximum rate of flame propagation occurs near stoichiometric concentrations and is generally enhanced by greater pressures, temperature, and turbulence.

Most UVCE incidents are the result of massive releases either at chemical plants, refineries, or facilities associated with transportation of flammable gases or liquids.

DUST EXPLOSIONS

Dust explosions are combustion reactions in which the dust is the fuel and the oxygen in the air is the oxidant. They are defined as the sudden release of heat energy through rapid combustion of airborne particulate matter in a confined or partially confined space. The potential for a dust explosion exists whenever combustible dusts accumulate, are handled, or are processed. Many of the same criteria involved in gas and vapor explosions apply to dust explosions such as explosive limits and concentrations. Dust explosions are similar to gas and vapor explosions when the particle size of the dust is less than 5 μm. The significant difference is that for a dust explosion, there must be turbulence. The dust must be suspended in air. Any process that produces dust that may be suspended in the air is subject to a dust explosion. As mentioned previously, some common examples are mining operations, all grain handling operations, and some plastics and metal operations.

The process of a dust explosion involves a high rate of combustion through the dust cloud. Flammable gases that are produced by the combustion of the dust result in an expanding flame front. As the flame front expands it produces a pressure wave which results in damage.

As in most other industrial explosions, most dust explosions are deflagrations. Tremendous energy is released during a dust explosion, and a detonation is possible. However, conditions are so strict for a detonation that they rarely do occur. A detonation might be possible in a coal mine, but only if initiated by a powerful ignition source. It can be assumed that most dust explosions are deflagrations.

In order to have a dust explosion, the dust must be combustible and must be capable of becoming airborne; the dust particle size and distribution must be capable of propagating flame; the concentration of the dust suspension must fall in the explosive range; an ignition source of sufficient energy must be present; and there must be sufficient oxygen present to support combustion.

Primary and Secondary Explosions

In a dust explosion, there is usually a primary and several secondary explosions. The primary explosion usually occurs in an enclosure or piece of material-handling equipment where dust is suspended in the air, oxygen is present, and ignition occurs. The expansion effect and resulting turbulence of the primary explosion causes additional dust to be suspended. One, or more, secondary explosions are ignited by the original ignition source or by combustion products of the primary explosion. The secondary explosions produce expansion effects that are transmitted throughout the facility causing structural damage and collapse (Figure 10-2). Flames propagate and may ignite dust fires far from the source of the primary explosion.

Factors Affecting the Severity of Dust Explosions

Many of the same factors affecting the severity of gas and vapor explosions are applicable to dust explosions. There are some additional factors that are applicable to the severity of dust explosions, including turbulance, particle size, and moisture content.

Turbulence.   In environments where combustible dusts are present, the effect of turbulence is much more dramatic than for explosions of gas or vapor. Whereas gas or vapor–air mixtures are already pretty well mixed with the air

Figure 10-2.   A grain dust explosion that has damaged exterior walls at different levels. (Source: Factory Mutual Engineering Corporation)

and turbulence has a smaller effect, dust requires turbulence to create the fuel–air mixture. Initial turbulence is necessary to suspend the dust in the air so that a primary explosion can result. The turbulence caused by the primary explosion helps to generate more dust particles in the air by disturbing them from beams, walls, and floor. This mechanism produces secondary explosions.

Particle Size. A cloud of small sized dust particles has a greater total surface area than larger sized particles. The greater surface area results in an increase in the reactive surface area of the fuel (dust) that is available to enter into the combustion reaction. Therefore, the smaller the particle size, the greater the severity of the resulting explosion. Additionally, smaller dust particle sizes are more readily dispersed in the air, and they remain in suspension longer, increasing the likelihood of explosion if an ignition source is present.

Moisture Content. Higher moisture content in the air results in a less severe explosion hazard. As in the combustion reaction described by the simple fire triangle, higher moisture content of the fuel, due to the higher moisture content of the air (humidity), tends to slow down the combustion reaction by requiring more heat for the reaction to proceed. It is also known that static electricity is a common source of ignition in dusty environments. Higher moisture content tends to retard the generation of static electricity.

EXPLOSION PREVENTION

Obviously, the best protection against the destructive effects of explosions is prevention, the application of whatever steps are necessary to prevent the explosion from occurring in the first place.

The first consideration should be to determine if there is a noncombustible replacement for the fuel in the potentially explosive mixture. This determination is normally only applicable for prevention of explosions in processes. When the presence of potentially explosive material is necessary, other prevention measures are required. There are three basic methods of preventing explosions from occurring including preventing or reducing the concentration of oxidant, reducing the concentration of combustibles, and eliminating ignition sources. There should not be total reliance upon any one of these methods, rather efforts at all three should be maximized.

Prevent or Reduce the Concentration of Oxidant and Fuel

As in fire prevention techniques, a principle explosion prevention technique is to prevent the formation of an explosive mixture. This is accomplished through elimination of the fuel or the oxidant or, when elimination is not possible, reducing fuel concentrations below the LEL.

Dust explosions frequently have occurred during material-handling processes. It would make sense then to concentrate explosion prevention activities around minimizing the dust near legs (bucket elevators), conveyor belts, cleaning, and milling equipment. The Panel on the Causes and Prevention of Grain Elevator Explosions reported in its 1982 report that the elevator legs are the most dangerous location with respect to primary dust explosions. This is probably because of the tremendous amount of dust that this equipment generates and the fact that it is subject to jamming which results in belt slippage. Additionally, the rapidly moving metal buckets may cause sparks when striking foreign objects.

Dust-generating product flows should be contained as much as possible to minimize the agitation and creation of dust. At openings where dust clouds are generated, vacuum collection methods should be employed.

Process Controls.   When potentially explosive materials are processed, that process must be thoroughly evaluated so that adequate safeguards may be incorporated. Safeguards should include controls of temperature, pressure, and the formation of fuel/oxidant mixtures. Where the failure of a process control could lead to an explosive condition, redundant controls should be incorporated. For example, when a runaway reaction could result in temperature or pressure excursions, redundant temperature controls or pressure relief valves should be incorporated.

Maintaining the process in a closed system so as to exclude air would be another form of process control. When flammable liquids are handled, for example, they should be in closed systems with minimal exposure to the air.

Grain handling operations should be conducted in such a manner so as to minimize dust generation. The more the grain is handled and agitated, the more dust will be generated. For, example, deeper layers of grain on conveyor belts will result in more product being moved and less dust being generated. It is also important to avoid long free-falls of grain from spouts.

Built-in dust collection systems with collection points that are located near the point of dust generation are also effective measures in any explosive dust generating process.

Housekeeping.   A preventative measure that has application in the areas of safety, health, and fire (and explosion) prevention is good housekeeping. Housekeeping is especially important in the prevention of dust explosions. Explosive dusts can be generated in grain handling and milling operations, mining operations, and combustible metal machining. In grain handling operations, the amount of floorspace that is taken up by the operations is very great compared to the number of workers that are required. Therefore, there are a lot of spaces for dust to accumulate and housekeeping becomes an important item.

Lint formation in operations that process fibers and fabrics can also lead to explosion hazards. Dust and lint collection systems are utilized that may include filters, cyclones, or wet scrubber systems. Regardless of the collection systems used, dust still accumulates on floors, walls, and equipment. Good housekeeping practices would include the frequent removal of these accumulations using vacuum or soft bristle broom. A past practice in these industries was to use compressed air to blow dust to one area of the room or building where it could be swept up. This created obvious explosion hazards by suspending the dust in the air so that a potentially explosive mixture was created. All that was necessary for an explosion to occur was an ignition source.

The control of combustible materials which may lead to fire hazards in potentially explosive operations is an important housekeeping function. Also, work areas must be kept neat and free of obstructions that prevent access to equipment, process controls, fire extinguishers and exits.

Control of smoking is another housekeeping item that is obviously important in those operations which may have explosion potential. Where there is potential for an explosive environment, positive controls on smoking are required. These controls include strict prohibition of smoking in hazard areas, to the extent that matches, lighters, and smoking materials are prohibited from the hazard area. This means that safe smoking areas must be provided with fixed lighters provided so that employees have no need to carry matches or lighters.

Maintenance.   Operations that have the possibility to generate an explosive mixture require extensive mechanical and electrical controls and safeguards on facility equipment. A thorough, periodically scheduled preventive maintenance program is essential to safe operations. Electrical grounding and bonding equipment must be inspected and maintained. Temperature and pressure controls and relief devices must be tested and cleaned periodically. Venting mechanisms must be cleaned and tested. Lubrication is important to prevent breakdowns and heat generating friction which may create ignition sources.

Maintenance is critical in dust generating operations because there is so much equipment that must operate properly. Dust generating operations require mills, cleaners, sieves, belt and screw conveyors, legs, vacuums, and other processing equipment. Breakdowns in the electrical power supplies, drive belts, or the equipment itself can result in sufficient heat from friction or sparks to be an ignition source. The operation of much of this equipment, particularly conveyor belts can generate electrostatic charges which could ignite a dust or vapor cloud. Provisions have to be made to bleed off static and these devices have to be maintained.

Purge Systems.   Explosive gas/air mixtures may be prevented by displacement of a gaseous oxidant or combustible by another gas to render the mixture noncombustible. This is a process called purging.

Purging an atmosphere to remove or dilute an oxidant concentration is usually accomplished when the possibility of an explosive fuel and oxidant exists in a closed container or vessel, such as a glove box, a process vessel, reaction chamber, or storage tank. Purging could be provided in room-sized areas, however, this is usually too costly and may present a hazard to personnel. A purge system must be capable of providing a sustained purge for the duration of the operation being protected; the system must be "tight"; the supply of purge material must be adequate; and alarms must be provided to indicate failure of the purge system. Since purge materials may result in the displacement of oxygen, the safety of personnel in the surrounding areas must also be considered in the event of a system malfunction that allows the purge material to leak. Also, it goes without saying, that the compatibility of the purge gas with the process and equipment being protected must be thoroughly evaluated. For example, if the purge gas is required to be inert, it must be remembered that only argon and helium are "truly inert." Other gases might react with the process materials, therefore compatibilities of the purge gas must be evaluated.

There are a number of types of purges, the review of which might offer the reader some insight into applications.

Batch purge. A one-time situation in which the purge gas is introduced to the vapor space as a liquid is drained off. A vacuum method is when a purge gas is introduced to break a vacuum (backfill). A pressure method is one in which the purge gas is introduced under pressure to act as a pump to remove the hazardous substance from the system.

Sweep through purge. The purge gas is introduced in one end of a system and allowed to exit at the other end of the system.

Continuous purge. A purge gas is allowed to flow continuously through a system. This type of purge can be at a fixed rate, or it can be at a variable rate. Variable rate purging is more complex and requires sophisticated valves and monitoring equipment.

There are a number of possible sources of purge gas including the following:

Commercially available inert gases such as nitrogen, carbon dioxide, helium, or argon are available commercially in high pressure tanks or cylinders.

Gas generator produced purge gas is produced by burning a hydrocarbon fuel, producing a purge gas that is oxygen deficient. The gas produced by a gas generators consist of the following: 87 percent nitrogen, 12 percent carbon dioxide, 0.5 percent carbon monoxide, and 0.5 percent oxygen.

Products of combustion from process furnaces or boiler furnaces may be collected and used as purge gas. Before these gases are used, they must be filtered to remove entrained dust, soot, and other foreign particles.

Steam may be used as a purge if it can be assured that the temperature can be maintained. If a steam producing system cools, the steam will condense and create a vacuum that may draw in oxygen and other purged materials resulting in the creation of an unsafe condition.

High purity nitrogen can be supplied by the air oxidation of ammonia for use as a purge gas.

When a fuel-rich atmosphere is desired, methane or natural gas may be used to purge air or oxygen from the system.

Elimination of Ignition Sources

Eliminating ignition sources is, understandably, a key part of explosion prevention considerations. Ignition sources are many and varied as discussed throughout this book. While elimination of ignition sources must play a big role in the explosion prevention progam, the program should not be based solely upon this method. The elimination of ignition sources should be one part of the overall program. The possibility of total elimination of ignition sources in a process can never be reduced to zero. There is always the possibility of an unforseen event occurring or of human error creating an ignition scenario. For example, failure of process controls can result in a mixture heating above the autoignition temperature of one of the components.

Electrical Ignition. Industrial loss experience indicates that electrical sources of ignition are the most prevalent. In operations where the possibility of an explosive mixture exists, there is usually some electrical equipment involved. Even with explosion-proof equipment, the possibility of equipment failure or operator error resulting in an ignition source exists.

The elimination or control of static electricity must be an important part of any explosion prevention program. Static can be generated in a variety of ways, any of which may exist in most industrial operations. Some of the common ways that static can be generated include moving belts (power and conveyor), the flow of liquids through pipes and hoses, the flow of gases from nozzles, stacks or leaking equipment, and static buildup on personnel.

Sparks. One of the most common sources of ignition in grain handling operations is the sparks that are produced by stones or tramp metal that contaminate the grain. These materials can generate sparks in handling equipment, grinding operations, and by striking against the sides of containers. Process controls should incorporate magnets and sieves to remove these objects.

Detonation Prevention

The geometry of the vessel will dictate whether or not a detonation can occur. In addition to the above explosion preventive measures, the geometry of vessels that are involved should be carefully evaluated. If a explosive mixture is possible, the vessels should be designed with the lowest feasible length-to-diameter ratio. Flat heads on a vessel will provide a favorable angle of incidence for pressure waves and should, therefore, be avoided. Dish curved heads, on the other hand, will survive the detonation better. When angles are required in a pipeline, two 45 degree bends are better than one 90 degree bend. A single 90 degree bend will reflect too much pressure. Finally, restrictions, such as orifices, in the pipeline may intensify a detonation by causing the pressure to build up. Flame arrestors, such as screen material which acts to trap a flame front may be installed. Flame arrestors should be installed as close to potential ignition sources as possible.

EXPLOSION PROTECTION

The combination of fuels and oxidants cannot always be eliminated. When an accident, or normal operations, could result in an explosive mixture, stringent ignition controls must be incorporated. As discussed previously, it is always best not to assume that all possible ignition sources have been controlled. Therefore, it is prudent to plan for the possibility of an explosion and take steps to protect against the destructive effects. Explosion suppression, containment, and venting are the three methods to accomplish protection.

Suppression

Explosion suppression is a technique by which burning in a confined mixture is detected and arrested during the incipient stages to prevent development of pressure which could result in the damaging effects of an explosion. Any equipment that is liable to contain and confine an explosive mixture, whether it be dusts, mists, or gases may be considered for an explosion suppression system. Most combustion explosions are slow enough so that they can be detected in the incipient stages and the use of a suppression system is feasible. Explosion suppression systems can typically function in 50–75 milliseconds which is rapid enough to prevent damaging pressures from being generated (Figure 10-3). Although explosion suppression systems may be used for rooms or equipment, they are seldom used to protect rooms because of limitations of wall strength, personnel safety, and room size. The utility of explosion suppression systems is also limited to combustion explosions having slow to moderate flame speed. Some materials such as metal dusts, hydrogen, and acetylene have very high flame speeds. This causes pressure buildup that is too rapid and will exceed the strength of the container before a suppression system could react. There are three main components that are required for an explosion suppression system. They include a detection system, a suppressant, and a power supply and activation system to release the suppressant (Figure 10-4).

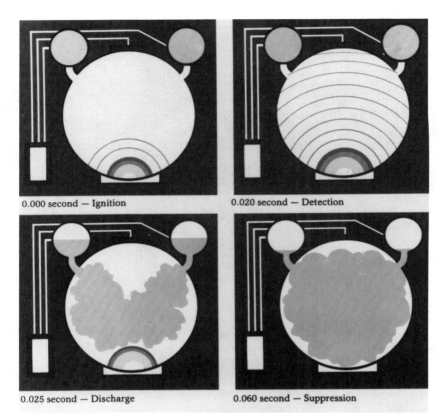

0.000 second — Ignition

0.020 second — Detection

0.025 second — Discharge

0.060 second — Suppression

Figure 10-3.   An explosion suppression system detects ignition, discharges a suppressant, and suppresses the explosion within 0.060 seconds. (Source: Fenwal Inc.)

Detection system.   Systems for detecting the incipient explosion are either pressure sensitive or radiant energy detecting devices. Pressure sensitive devices measure either static pressure or dynamic pressure. Static pressure measuring devices activate at a predetermined pressure level above atmospheric, usually 0.1 to 30 psi. The most common such detector is a highly sensitive, low inertia diaphragm-type pressure detector. This device is adjustible from 0.25 to 5.0 psi. Explosion pressures act upon a stainless steel diaphragm to close the detector electrical contacts. Dynamic pressure measuring devices react to a pressure change. They usually activate when the rate-of-rise of pressure exceeds 5–10 psi/sec.

In systems that are not adequately confined to allow sensitive pressure change determinations, or where there is a flash fire potential, radiant energy detecting devices should be prescribed. These devices measure the ultraviolet radiation given off by the combustion reaction.

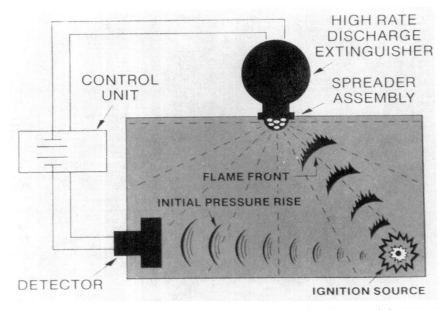

Figure 10-4. An explosion suppression system consists of a high speed detector, a control unit and power supply, and a high-rate discharge extinguisher. (Source: Fenwal Inc.)

Ultraviolet radiation detectors may also be used as part of a spark detecting and extinguishing system. They are used to detect sparks or embers as they pass through ducts that transport combustible dusts or solids. These devices require more maintenance and are generally less reliable than the pressure devices. They are subject to actuation by flames, electrical or mechanical sparks, glowing material, induced electrical currents, cosmic rays, and radioactive sources.

Suppressant.   The most commonly used suppressant material is one of the Halons, 1301, 1011, or 2402 discharged from a high rate discharge extinguisher. These materials inhibit the combustion chain reaction. High rate discharge extinguishers generally range in size from 5 to 30 liters and are strategically placed in the protected system. Each extinguisher has a 3-inch explosively actuated discharge opening at the bottom, piped into the enclosure to be protected. The extinguishers are pressurized with nitrogen gas to 360 psi to aid in delivery of the agent. Halon suppression systems are available with different nozzles and distribution heads to quickly release and disperse the gas, depending upon the configuration of the protected system.

Water may be used as a suppressant when it is necessary to absorb great amounts of heat, such as in areas containing solid propellants, nitrocellulose, or black powder. Water may also be used in closed vessels where dilution and

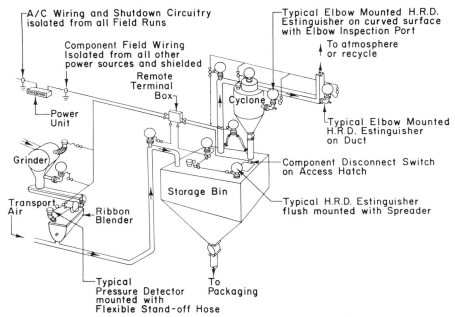

Figure 10-5. A skematic of an explosion suppression system installed to protect a dust explosion hazard system. (Source: Fenwal Inc.)

cooling are necessary to stop an incipient runaway reaction. To discharge the water, an explosively activated deluge valve will provide high-speed response.

Dolomite and limestone may be used for protecting processes involving combustible dusts, such as in coal mines. In a spark extinguishing system, the agent is usually water or halon that is discharged at a calculated distance downstream from the detector.

Power Supply and Activation System. The suppression system must have an adequate and reliable power supply to operate the detectors and release the suppressant. The suppressant is released by electrically fired initiators, or squibs. The wiring circuits for these devices must be continuously supervised. The electrical energy provided must be capable of firing the initiators according to the manufacturer's specifications.

Additional equipment may be required, depending upon the system being protected. In very large systems it is not practical or economical to flood the whole system with suppressant. High-speed isolators or dampers are installed. These devices are operated by initiators to close rapidly and isolate parts of the system and to shut down the equipment when the suppression system activates.

Containment

When the formation of flammable mixtures in a closed system is inevitable, containment of the explosion is a possible protective measure. When an explosion is to be contained, the strength and geometry of equipment must be evaluated. In order to contain the explosion, the equipment must be designed to contain 3.5 times the maximum explosion pressure expected. Attention must also be given to connecting piping and equipment. Sharp angles in equipment, vessel configuration, and piping should be avoided. When containment of a possible explosion is to be considered, the American Society of Mechanical Engineers (ASME) *Boiler and Pressure Vessel Code* should be consulted.

Explosion-proof electrical equipment is designed to contain an explosion resulting from flammable vapors that might leak into it. Explosion-proof equipment is classified by Article 500, NFPA #70, *The National Electrical Code* by group according to the characteristics of the substance to which it will be exposed.

Venting

Relieving the pressure of an explosion so as to minimize damage is an important part of explosion protection technology. Usually, venting is used to protect from the damage of deflagrations rather than detonations. This is the final protective measure since at the point that vents operate, the explosion and some damage and, possibly, injuries have occurred. In the case of operations that have dust explosion potential, secondary explosions will still occur, and therefore venting characteristics must be incorporated throughout the facility. Venting can be preaction, or activated by initiators, or more commonly, it can be activated by the pressures of the explosion itself. Size and arrangement of vent openings must be carefully studied for them to be effective. An undersized vent system will not adequately relieve the pressure and equipment and building damage will result. Likewise, the arrangement of vents and ducting, with relation to the source of the explosion, is also important to minimizing damage. A pressure rise will occur when an explosion occurs, regardless of the number and arrangement of vents, therefore construction of the structure that is intended to be protected must be adequate to accommodate this pressure rise.

SUMMARY

An explosion is the effect produced by the sudden violent expansion of gases which may or may not be accompanied by shock waves, and/or disruption of enclosing materials. Whether or not a shock wave is produced provides the definition of a detonation or a deflagration. A detonation is an explosion that proceeds faster than the speed of sound and a deflagration proceeds subsonic.

Explosions are not necessarily combustion reactions, but they can be the result of any release of energy due to a change in state of material or a chemical change in a substance. Other types of explosions are mechanical which result from the overpressure or failure of a vessel, thermal which result from overheating of a confined system, and nuclear detonations.

The severity of a combustion explosion is dependant upon its chemical composition, the concentration of fuel material, turbulence of the mixture, and the degree of confinement of the mixture.

There are various methods of preventing an explosion including activities to prevent or reduce the availability of fuel and oxidant and to prevent the formation of an explosive mixture. This activity includes the utilization of process controls, good housekeeping, maintenance, and purge systems. Ignition controls are another method of preventing an explosion. It is important that one not rely upon only one of these control methods. Should the possibility of an explosive mixture being formed exist, all possible prevention techniques should be incorporated.

Explosion protection to include suppression, venting, and containment should also be incorporated. Explosion suppression systems are designed to detect an incipient explosion and to activate a suppressing action to prevent destructive pressures from developing. Venting is the capability of relieving explosive pressures before they reach damaging proportions. In some cases, suppression and venting may not be practical. In these cases it may be feasible and preferrable to contain an explosion within the vessel in which it is initiated.

A good explosion protection program does not rely upon any one technique, but it incorporates prevention of the generation of explosive mixtures and ignition sources; it has suppression capabilities; and if an explosion does occur, its destructive effects can be vented or contained with a minimum amount of damage.

BIBLIOGRAPHY

Best, Richard, and Walls, Wilbur. 1982. Hot Water Heater BLEVE in School Kills Seven. *Fire Journal* 76(5):20–24, 104–105.

Brodurtha, Frank T. 1980. *Industrial Explosion Prevention and Protection.* New York: McGraw-Hill, Inc.

Code of Federal Regulations. 29 CFR 1910. 1988.

Occupational Safety and Health Administration, Department of Labor. Washington, DC.

Clark, David, and Straseske, James B. 1984. Nitrogen Tank Explodes. *Fire Command* 51(12):28–30.

Cote, Arthur, and Bugbee, Percy. 1988. *Principles of Fire Protection.* Quincy: National Fire Protection Association.

Davenport, John A. 1981. Explosion Losses In Industry. *Fire Journal* 75(1):52–56, 71–72.

Drysdale, Dougal. 1985. *An Introduction to Fire Dynamics.* Chichester: John Wiley & Sons Ltd.

Field, Peter. 1982. Dust Explosions. New York: Elsevier Scientific Publishing Co.

Fire Protection Handbook, 16th ed. 1986. Quincy: National Fire Protection Association.

Gugan, Dr. Keith. 1979. *Unconfined Vapor Cloud Explosions.* Houston: Gulf Publishing Co.

Hill, Steven. 1981. Two Killed in Underground Jet-Fuel Tank Explosion. *Fire Journal* 75(6): 26–28

Kyte, Greg. 1986. Oklahoma Fireworks Plant Explosion Kills 21, Injures 5. *Fire Journal* 80(4):58–65, 73.

Loss Prevention Data 7-0. 1981. *Causes and Effects of Fires and Explosions.* Norwood, MA: Factory Mutual Engineering Corp.

Loss Prevention Data 7-17. *Explosion Suppression Systems.* 1981. Norwood, MA: Factory Mutual Engineering Corp.

NFPA 69-1986. *Standard on Explosion Prevention Systems.* Quincy: National Fire Protection Association.

Palmer, K. N. 1973. *Dust Explosions and Fires.* London: Chapman and Hall.

Prevention of Grain Elevator and Mill Explosions. A Report of the Panel on Causes and Prevention of Grain Elevator Explosions of the Committee on Evaluation of Industrial Hazards, National Materials Advisory Board. 1982. Washington D.C.: National Academy Press.

A Short Course on Explosion Hazards Evaluations. 1979. San Antonio–Houston: Southwest Research Institute.

Union Oil Refinery Explosion, An Overview. 1984. *Fire Command* 51(10):32–33.

11
HAZARDOUS
MATERIALS

INTRODUCTION

On December 3, 1984, a runaway chemical reaction at the Union Carbide plant in Bhopal, India resulted in the deaths of 2500 people and injuries to another 200,000. This incident came at a time when there were growing concerns about the widespread industrial use of hazardous chemicals and the need for improved hazardous materials emergency response capabilities. Workers were becoming concerned about the adverse health effects of the hazardous materials that were used in their place of employment. At the same time, communities were becoming concerned about the hazardous materials used in local industries and were beginning to demand information.

Bhopal was the culmination of increasing public awareness of hazardous materials in the environment that began when President Carter declared the Love Canal in New York a federal emergency in 1978. This and other hazardous materials dump sites as well as other similar nationwide incidents of pollution, spills, and illegal hazardous waste activities had created concern across the country. There was also a growing belief that industry was not doing enough to inform workers of the materials to which they were being exposed and to inform public agencies and the public about the potential dangers of the materials being used.

Industry produces, uses, disposes of, and transports an ever-increasing inventory of exotic hazardous materials. As more hazardous materials found their way into the industrial inventory, the numbers of hazardous materials incidents increased. Greater use of hazardous materials by industry resulted in increased amounts of hazardous waste being generated. The handling, storage, shipping, and disposal of hazardous waste resulted in still more incidents. Public fire departments found themselves without adequate capabilities to deal with these emergencies. The old method of washing spilled chemicals away with water is not environmentally sound, and in some cases, created greater hazards.

In the mid-1970s, Congress began to address the environmental aspects of the hazardous materials problems with legislation that had far-reaching effects on industry and fire protection. During that same time period, safety and fire codes and standards also were expanded to address hazardous materials issues.

The gradual increase in the coverage of hazardous materials may be followed in earlier editions of the NFPA's *Fire Protection Handbook* beginning with the fourteenth edition in 1976. By the publication of the sixteenth edition in 1986, the NFPA was devoting a whole section to hazardous wastes and materials in addition to the traditional coverage in sections on fire hazards of materials, transportation fire hazards, and storage practices and hazards.

FEDERAL LEGISLATION

In addition to the existing OSHA, Department of Transportation, and local fire codes, new federal legislation came into being in the late 1970s and through the 1980s to deal with the growing hazardous materials problems. This legislation consisted of the Resource Conservation and Recovery Act (RCRA) of 1976, Toxic Substances Control Act (TSCA) of 1976, Comprehensive Environmental Response, Compensation and Liability Act (CERCLA) of 1980, Superfund Amendments and Reauthorization Act of 1986, and OSHA requirements dealing with hazard communications (1986) and hazardous waste operations and emergency response (1987).

Resource Conservation and Recovery Act (RCRA) of 1976

In the 1960s, the production of hazardous waste had grown in quantity and toxicity to the point where it could no longer be ignored. Surface and groundwater was being contaminated and wildlife and vegetation were being destroyed. Although much of the hazardous wastes generated in the United States were disposed of legally, the EPA estimates that the majority was illegally disposed of or, at least, cannot be accounted for in legal disposal sites.

Safe disposal of many hazardous wastes is very expensive, and attempts to avoid these high costs led to "midnight dumping." In other cases, generators of hazardous waste thought that they were paying for safe disposal, but haulers dumped illegally and pocketed the profits. Some legal dump sites and most illegal dumping has resulted in extensive contamination of soil and groundwater which has reached serious proportions in many areas of the United States.

In 40 CFR 260, EPA General Regulations for Hazardous Waste Management, the EPA established the objectives of RCRA as follows: The protection of human health and the environment and conservation of national and energy resources by:

Closing of existing open dumps and prohibiting further open dumping

Regulation of transportation, treatment, storage, and disposal of hazardous waste.

Establishing guidelines for solid waste management (SWM).

Recovery of energy and materials from solid waste.

State grants for development of SWM plans.

Research, development, demonstration, and information dissemination.

Under RCRA, the EPA established standards for the storage, treatment, transportation, and disposal of hazardous wastes. Probably the most significant provision of RCRA was the concept of "cradle-to-grave" or creation-to-destruction control of hazardous wastes. This responsibility was clearly established as the responsibility of the generator. The generator must ensure that hazardous waste is safely accumulated at the site of generation. The generator must ensure that the transportation of the hazardous waste is accomplished safely and by a licensed waste hauler. And finally, the generator must insure that the waste is properly disposed. Even then, the generator maintains liability for the hazardous materials that he has contributed to the disposal site. This provision was to encourage generators to eliminate hazardous waste or to find alternatives to land disposal such as recycling and recovery. All industrial operations that generate hazardous waste come under the RCRA requirements. There are more lenient requirements for small quantity generators.

As landfill disposal requirements become more restrictive and costs become prohibitive, other methods of disposal are increasing such as incineration, treatment, and recovery and recycling. These methods may increase the concerns of the firesafety professional as hazardous materials may be accumulated into economical lots for further processing or disposal, and they may be handled more which increases the possibility of an accident. For example, small containers of miscellaneous hazardous materials must be "lab packed" for safe disposal at an approved landfill. This requires that the materials be shipped to an approved hazardous materials storage area where they are accumulated. Then they must be packed by hand into barrels containing inert absorbent material and finally shipped to an approved landfill. Another example is the disposal of waste epoxy-resin systems. These materials are considered hazardous waste. In some cases, people have reacted the two to form a solid material which is not a hazardous waste. However, in some cases the materials do not react properly, or the resulting solid is chemically unstable and fire has resulted. A 1989 fire resulted when a Pennsylvania manufacturer reacted a polyvinyl resin to produce solid spheres for disposal. The liquid resin material which was outdated would have required treatment as a hazardous waste. The manufacturer thought that it could be reacted and safely disposed as a solid waste in the trash dumpster. In this case the fire did not result in high property loss, because it was confined to the trash bin. However, approximately $9000 worth of fire fighters' turnout gear was destroyed by the hydrochloric acid vapors that were produced. The opportunity for a much more serious loss certainly was present.

EPA Classification of Hazardous Wastes. In RCRA, the EPA established criteria for identifying the characteristics of and listing hazardous wastes. As with the other classification systems that are currently in use, the EPA classifies hazardous wastes according to their hazardous characteristics. Four characteristics were selected to classify hazardous waste as follows:

Ignitability. Materials that exhibit ignitability include the following: liquids with a flash point of less than 140 degrees Fahrenheit.; materials that are not liquid at standard temperature and pressure and are capable of causing fire through friction, absorption of moisture, or spontaneous chemical reaction, and, when ignited, burn so vigorously as to create a hazard; ignitable compressed gases; an oxidizer or material that yields oxygen readily to stimulate the combustion of organic matter.

Corrosivity. Corrosive materials are those that are aqueous and have a pH less than or equal to 2 or greater than or equal to 12.5; or liquids that corrode steel at a rate greater than 6.35 mm/yr (0.25 in./yr).

Reactivity. Materials are reactive if they exhibit any of the following: They are normally unstable and readily undergo violent change without detonating; they react violently with water; they form potentially explosive mixtures with water; when mixed with water, they generate toxic gases, vapors, or fumes; a cyanide or a sulfide bearing waste which, when exposed to pH conditions between 2 and 12.5, can generate toxic gases, vapors or fumes; and materials that are capable of detonation or explosive decomposition or reaction at standard temperature and pressure.

EP Toxicity. When a solid waste contains any of the contaminants listed in Table 11-1 in excess of the concentration shown, it is by definition an EP toxic waste.

Toxic Substances Control Act (TSCA) of 1976

It is estimated that approximately 1000 new chemicals are introduced each year. It became necessary to regulate the manufacture, processing, distribution, use, and disposal of these thousands of chemicals when they present an unreasonable risk to the public. In order to establish a uniform method of listing and controlling these chemicals and their hazards, congress charged the EPA, through TSCA, with the responsibility to:

1. Develop a uniform listing of all chemical substances.
2. Establish testing procedures for existing and new chemicals.
3. Determine the risk to health or the environment of these chemicals.

Table 11-1. Maximum Concentration of
Contaminants for Characteristic
of EP Toxicity.

EPA HAZARDOUS WASTE NUMBER	CONTAMINANT	MAXIMUM CONCENTRATION (mg/l)
D004	Arsenic	5.0
D005	Barium	100.0
D006	Cadmium	1.0
D007	Chromium	5.0
D008	Lead	5.0
D009	Mercury	0.2
D010	Selenium	1.0
D011	Silver	5.0
D012	Endrin	0.02
D013	Lindane	0.4
D014	Methoxychlor	10.0
D015	Toxaphene	0.5
D016	2,4-D	10.0
D017	2,4,5-TP Silvex	1.0

Source: 40 CFR 261.24

4. Prohibit or limit the manufacture, processing, use, application and concentration of chemicals that present too great a risk to health or the environment.
5. Recall or seize hazardous substances that are determined to be imminently hazardous to health or the environment.

With regard to number 4 above, the implementing regulations for section 6 of TSCA deal with the following materials:

Prohibits the addition of a nitrosating agent to a metal-working fluid containing mixed mono and diamides of an organic acid.
Prohibits the manufacture, processing, and distribution in commerce of fully halogenated chlorofluoroalkanes for aerosol propellant uses.

Establishes reporting requirements for asbestos manufacturers, importers, or processors. Requires abatement of friable asbestos-containing materials in school, and provides qualification guidelines for asbestos abatement contractors.

Establishes requirements for PCBs.

Polychlorinated Biphenyls (PCBs). PCBs, known generically as askarel, have been used for many years and may still exist in some applications in industry. They are addressed here because they are of concern in fire protection.

Chemically, PCBs contain two parts, a biphenyl molecule linked with up to 10 chlorine atoms. They are resistant to heat, nonflammable, and stable under a wide variety of conditions. These characteristics made them very useful in industry as heat transfer fluids, in hydraulic systems, machine tool cutting aids, and as specialized lubricants and plasticizers. They can still be found in transformers, power correction capacitors, motor capacitors, and fluorescent light ballasts. Because of the diversity of their application, the large amount that was used, and their long-term stability, PCBs may still be present in the soil, water, and air. They are recognized environmental pollutants, presenting potential risks to fish, animals, and humans.

The combustion products formed in high-temperature applications and during fires are more toxic than the PCBs. The PCB molecule decomposes into the extremely toxic dibenzofuran and dioxin families. Smoke from a fire involving PCBs can permeate a building, exposing personnel and contaminating the building and its contents. Two such fires occurred in the Binghamton State Office Building in Binghamton, New York, in 1981 and, two years later, in the One Market Plaza complex in San Francisco. The Binghamton building decontamination took more than 4 years and cost more than $20 million. The One Market Plaza decontamination took about 1 year and also cost more than $20 million.

The first regulations regarding PCBs were published in 1978 as a part of TSCA. In 1979, the EPA banned the manufacture, processing, distribution, or use of PCBs in other than a totally enclosed manner. In 1984, in recognition of the fire hazards of PCBs such as occurred in the Binghamton and One Market Plaza incidents, the EPA implemented new rules regarding the continued use of PCB-containing transformers. Owners were required to do the following:

Register PCB transformers with appropriate fire department response personnel.

Register PCB transformers serving buildings with the building owner.

Remove combustible materials within 16 feet (5 meters) of a PCB transformer enclosure or PCB transformer.

Visually inspect PCB transformers quarterly for leakage.

Replace PCB transformers that pose an exposure risk to food or feed by October 1, 1985.

Maintain inspection and maintenance records for at least 3 years after disposing of the transformer.

Mark all means of access to the PCB transformer using the EPA-designated label (Figure 11-1).

Figure 11-1. The EPA specified label for marking PCB items. (Source: U.S. Environmental Protection Agency)

Comprehensive Environmental Response, Compensation and Liability Act (CERCLA) of 1980

Late in the 1970s, it was perceived that a gap existed in RCRA. RCRA did not adequately cover inactive hazardous waste disposal sites and past disposal practices. In RCRA, there were no provisions to deal with closed disposal sites from which hazardous wastes were migrating into the groundwater and to the surface. CERCLA was established to extend the RCRA ''grave'' to include cleanup of waste sites or other contaminated facilities. To accomplish this, CERCLA established the superfund, a $1.6 billion fund, for EPA to use to clean up hazardous waste disposal sites. Additionally, CERCLA established reporting requirements, a requirement for EPA to develop a list of hazardous waste sites and methodology for their cleanup, and a liability scheme for cleanup.

In response to the requirement to list hazardous waste sites, the EPA came up with the National Priorities List (NPL), which listed the allegedly most serious sites in the country which are candidates for cleanup using the superfund, hence the term superfund sites. The NPL quickly grew to include hundreds of superfund sites across the country. The EPA also drafted the National Contingency Plan (NCP) which established procedures for cleaning up superfund sites.

The liability scheme is probably the most significant requirement for industry. CERCLA established potentially responsible parties (PRPs) which may be liable to pay for the costs of cleaning up sites from which there is a release or threatened release of hazardous substances. PRPs would include the current and past owners of the site, generators who arranged for transport of hazardous waste to the site, and transporters of waste to the site if the transporter was the one to select the site.

Superfund Amendments and Reauthorization Act of 1986

Probably the most important piece of legislation to deal with emergency planning and community right-to-know is the Superfund Amendments and Reauthorization Act (SARA), specifically Title III. Title III is referred to as the Emergency Planning and Community Right-to-Know Act of 1986 (EPCRA). Title III includes requirements for emergency planning and notification, community right-to-know reporting, and toxic chemical release reporting. Emergency planning and community right-to-know requirements of Title III are discussed in Chapter 12.

Toxic Chemical Release Reporting.   Not to be confused with emergency notifications are toxic chemical release reporting requirements found in Section 313 of Title III. Companies that use or produce certain specified amounts of more than 300 hazardous chemicals, or categories of chemicals, are required to report routine emissions to the air, land, or water. These emission reports to the EPA and appropriate state officials are required annually. The reported information will be available to the news media and the public via EPA's data base which is available to anyone with a PC and a modem. It is very important for companies to report accurately. However, caution must be exercised not to overestimate emissions as the data may come under public scrutiny. It also is necessary that the company's public relations personnel be involved in the contents of the reports so as to enable them to deal with inquiries that might be generated by the reports or by hazardous materials incidents. SARA has had the effect of causing municipal authorities to become aware of hazardous materials in their jurisdictions and to plan for possible emergencies. It has caused companies to do the same as well as to scrutinize their hazardous materials inventory and record-keeping techniques and emissions calculations.

OSHA, Hazard Communication Standard (29 CFR 1910.1200)

Although OSHA addressed specific hazardous materials and worker protective measures, it was really not sufficiently comprehensive to deal with the thousands of chemicals that were being introduced into industry.

In response to growing employee awareness and concern about the hazardous materials to which they may be exposed in the workplace, OSHA was amended in 1985, with Section 1910.1200, Hazard Communication. The Hazard Communication Standard is intended to ensure the flow of hazard information from producers of chemicals to the industrial user (workers). It basically requires that:

1. Manufacturers and importers of hazardous materials determine the hazards of chemicals that they produce or import, label them appropriately, and develop a material safety data sheet.
2. Employers must maintain labels on all hazardous materials containers.
3. Employers must maintain material safety data sheets on all hazardous materials and make them available to their employees.
4. Employers must train their employees about the hazardous materials that might be in the workplace and the location and availability of material safety data sheets.
5. Employers must prepare a written hazard communication program that details the program for compliance with this section.

Material Safety Data Sheets (MSDS). The MSDS has become a very important document in the industrial environment. It is provided by the manufacturer and must be maintained by the employer for each hazardous chemical on site. The industrial fire, safety, and medical personnel rely upon the MSDS for ingredients and guidelines regarding safe handling, storage, and disposal of the chemical. The employer has to make the MSDS available to employees for their reference, and the employer may also be requested to provide copies of the MSDS to the local municipal fire department. Fire departments use this information for preincident planning and as a reference when there is an emergency. The MSDS is required to provide the following information:

1. The identity of the material as described on the label.
2. The chemical and common name of all of the ingredients that might present a physical hazard.
3. Physical and chemical characteristics of the chemical such as vapor pressure and flash point.
4. Physical hazards of the chemical including the potential for fire, explosion, and reactivity.
5. The health hazards of the chemical.
6. Primary routes of entry of the chemical.
7. The OSHA permissible exposure limit, AGCIH Threshold Limit Value, or other exposure limits used or recommended by the manufacturer, importer, or employer.
8. Whether the chemical is listed in the National Toxicology Program (NTP) *Annual Report on Carcinogens* or has been found to be a potential carcinogen in the International Agency for Research on Cancer (IARC) or by OSHA.

9. Any generally applicable precautions for the safe handling and use of the chemical.
10. Any generally applicable control measures such as engineering controls, work practices, or personnel protective equipment.
11. Emergency and first aid procedures.
12. The date of preparation of the MSDS.
13. The name, address, and telephone number of the chemical manufacturer, importer, employer, or other responsible party preparing or distributing the MSDS.

CODES/STANDARDS REGULATING HAZARDOUS MATERIALS

There are numerous codes and standards that are used directly or indirectly to regulate hazardous materials or are available as references. As with fire codes and standards, hazardous materials requirements have evolved since the 1970s to meet the changing industrial environment. NFPA codes and standards and other model codes such as the Uniform Fire Code deal with hazardous materials, and like the fire codes, they must be adopted into law before they are enforceable.

Where OSHAct had been regulating hazardous materials in industry on the basis of hazards to employees, the fire regulations, such as the *Uniform Fire Code* and NFPA Codes and Standards, regulated hazardous materials on the basis of fire, explosion, and reactivity hazards. This is not to mean that the two are mutually exclusive. There has always been close coordination between fire and safety and health officials, and in fact, many NFPA codes have been adopted by the OSHAct.

As the numbers and severity of hazardous materials and hazardous waste incidents increased and society became more aware of the problems, legislative bodies began formulating regulations to deal with the problems.

Uniform Fire Code Hazardous Materials

The *Uniform Fire Code* (UFC) is one of several fire prevention codes that are in use in the United States. It is chosen for the discussion about hazardous materials because it addresses them completely.

In editions of the *UFC* prior to 1988, and other fire prevention codes, hazardous materials were addressed as to the fire or explosion hazard that they created or their properties that contributed abnormal dangers to fire fighting. Hazardous materials included flammable solids, corrosive liquids, poisonous gases, and highly toxic, radioactive, oxidizing, unstable or reactive, hypergolic or pyrophoric materials. With the growing use of increasing amounts and kinds of hazardous materials and the resulting increase in hazardous materials incidents, there was a need to expand Article 80 of the UFC. It was also necessary to incorporate nationally recognized terminology in addressing hazardous materials to come into agreement with EPA and OSHA regulations in this area.

Starting with the 1988 edition of the *Uniform Fire Code*, Article 80, Hazardous Materials, was rewritten and expanded. It now has more specific requirements with regard to the safe storage, dispensing, use, and handling of hazardous materials; and the terminology used is now consistent with existing EPA and OSHA requirements. It also provides for the availability of information needed by emergency responders.

Article 80 categorizes materials as, primarily, physical hazards or health hazards with the proviso that a material with a primary classification as a physical hazard can also be a health hazard and vice-versa.

HAZARDOUS MATERIALS DEFINED

There are several organizations that regulate, or develop model codes and standards or guidance concerning hazardous materials. Much of the legislation uses broad definitions of hazardous materials depending upon its purpose. For example, RCRA definitions deal with the environmental impact of ignitable, corrosive, reactive, or toxic hazardous wastes. OSHA definitions deal with health and safety effects of hazardous materials. Existing definitions were specific to the organizations such as NFPA and fire prevention codes which primarily pertain to fire hazards of materials. In the 1988 edition of the *Uniform Fire Code*, Article 80 was rewritten and now includes a very comprehensive set of hazardous materials definitions. The UFC has adopted OSHA, DOT, and NFPA definitions where appropriate. The definitions presented here will be primarily the UFC, Article 80 definitions. Variations with other organizations will be noted. The definitions that are used by the Department of Transportation to regulate the transportation hazards of chemicals will be discussed separately.

The *Uniform Fire Code* deals with hazardous materials by the hazard that they present, as physical hazards or health hazards as follows*:

Physical Hazards

Flammable Liquids.   For OSHA, NFPA, and UFC definitions see Chapter 4.

Combustible Liquids.   For OSHA, NFPA, and UFC definitions see Chapter 4.

---

*Source: 1988 edition of the *Uniform Fire Code*, copyright © 1988, with the permission of the joint publishers, the Western Fire Chiefs Association and the International Conference of Building Officials.

Explosives and Blasting Agents. Chemical compounds, mixtures or devices that are capable of exploding, as described in Chapter 10, are included in this category. Explosives are further divided according to the rate at which they react. For this category, OSHA has adopted the DOT definitions.

Class A explosives (OSHA), high explosives (UFC), primary or initiating high explosives, secondary high explosives (NFPA). These explosives present a detonating or maximum hazard.

Class B explosives (OSHA), low explosives (UFC), low explosives or propellants (NFPA). These explosives function by rapid combustion rather than detonation.

Class C explosives (OSHA), low explosives (UFC, NFPA). These explosives include certain types of manufactured articles which contain Class A or Class B explosives, or both, as components, but in restricted quantities.

Blasting agents (OSHA, NFPA, UFC). These are materials or mixtures that are designed for blasting, but they are not otherwise classified as explosives. Blasting agents are so insensitive that there is very little probability of accidental initiation of explosion.

Compressed Gases. These are gases or mixtures of gases having, in a container, an absolute pressure exceeding 40 psi at 70 degrees Fahrenheit. There are many compressed gases used in industry that are categorized as hazardous materials. There are representative materials of almost all of the physical and health hazard categories that are available and used in industry in the gaseous state, and they are further classified accordingly.

Flammable Gas. Any gas that will burn in the concentrations in air of less than 13 percent by (volume), or in the flammable range with air that is wider than 12 percent, regardless of the lower limit. NFPA defines flammable gas simply as any gas that will burn in the normal concentrations of oxygen in the air.

Oxidizing Gas. Oxygen and other gaseous compounds that contain oxygen in quantities greater than the oxygen–nitrogen mixture that comprises the air.

Corrosive Gas. (Only the UFC specifically refers to this term, other organizations include it under corrosive materials). Gases that, when brought into contact with living tissue, will cause destruction or irreversible alteration of the tissue by chemical action are termed corrosives. The primary hazard of corrosive gases is through damage to tissue upon contact or inhalation.

Highly Toxic Gas. Gases that are poisonous or irritating when inhaled or contacted and present a health hazard when they are released into the atmosphere.

Toxic Gas. Gases that are Class B poisons and pesticides and fumigants.

Inert Gas. Gases that are nonflammable and usually not reactive with other materials. Although inert gases are not fire hazards, they can all cause asphyxiation due to the displacement of air.

Pyrophoric Gas. A gas that will ignite spontaneously in air at a temperature of 130 degrees Fahrenheit or lower is called a pyrophoric gas.

Unstable Gas. Those gases that can enter into a hazardous chemical reaction with other stable or unstable materials or with themselves. They may vigorously polymerize, decompose, condense, or become self-reactive and undergo other violent chemical changes, including explosion. These reactions may be induced by heat, shock, the presence of contaminants, or exposure to incompatible materials.

Flammable Solid. These solids, other than blasting agents, are liable to cause fire through friction, absorption of moisture, spontaneous chemical change, or retained heat from manufacturing or processing, or can be ignited readily and when ignited burn so vigorously and persistently as to create a serious hazard. Flammable solids may be further classified as organic or inorganic solids, combustible metals, or combustible dusts.

Oxidizers. An oxidizer is any chemical other than a blasting agent or explosive that initiates or promotes combustion in other materials, thereby causing fire either of itself or through release of oxygen or other gases. Oxidizers promote combustion by decomposing to yield oxygen when heated or by reacting with other chemicals. Oxidizers may be solids, liquids, or gases. Oxidizers include the following groups of chemicals: nitrates, nitrites, inorganic peroxides, chlorates, chlorites, dichromates, hypochlorites, perchlorates, permanganates, and persulfates.

Oxidizers are further subdivided into four classes based upon their effect upon the burning rate of a combustible material and explosive hazard as follows:

Class 1. Oxidizing materials whose primary hazard is that they may increase the burning rate of combustible material with which they come in contact.

Class 2. Oxidizing materials that will moderately increase the burning rate or cause spontaneous ignition of combustible materials with which they come in contact.

Class 3. Oxidizing materials that cause a severe increase in the burning rate of a combustible material with which they come in contact.

Class 4. Oxidizing materials that can undergo an explosive reaction when catalyzed or exposed to heat, shock, or friction.

Organic Peroxides. An organic peroxide is an organic compound that contains a bivalent —O—O— structure and may be considered to be a structural derivative of hydrogen peroxide where one or both of the hydrogen atoms has been replaced by an organic radical (Figure 11-2). Organic peroxides are all combustible compounds and are subject to explosive decomposition. They may decompose when heated or exposed to shock or friction (NFPA). The rate of decomposition is dependent upon the temperature, and some of them have a temperature above which the decomposition accelerates. This is called the self-accelerating decomposition temperature (SADT). Diisopropyl peroxydicarbonate is an example of an organic peroxide that has a SADT of 51 degrees Fahrenheit. It must be shipped and stored in blocks of ice at less than 0 degrees Fahrenheit. Organic peroxides are available in the liquid, paste, or solid form. They are further subdivided into classes based upon their combustion and reactivity hazard.

Unclassified. Peroxides which are capable of detonation. They present an extremely high explosion hazard through rapid explosive decomposition and are regulated as Class A explosives.

Class I. Peroxides that are capable of deflagration, but not detonation. They present a high explosion hazard through rapid decomposition.

Class II. Peroxides that burn very rapidly and present a severe reactivity hazard.

Class III. Peroxides that burn rapidly and present a moderate reactivity hazard.

Class IV. Peroxides that burn in the same manner as ordinary combustibles and present a minimum reactivity hazard.

Class V. These peroxides do not burn or present a decomposition hazard.

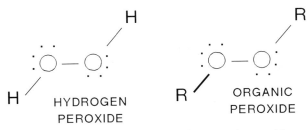

Figure 11-2.   The molecular structure of an organic peroxide.

Pyrophoric Materials. A chemical that will ignite spontaneously in air at a temperature of 130 degrees Fahrenheit or lower is called a pyrophoric chemical. They may be gases, liquids, or solids.

Unstable and Reactive Materials. Reactive materials are those materials that can enter into a hazardous chemical reaction with other stable or unstable materials or with themselves. Unstable materials are those materials, other than explosives, which will vigorously polymerize, decompose, condense, or become self-reactive and undergo other violent chemical changes, including explosion. These reactions may be induced by heat, shock, the presence of contaminants, or exposure to incompatible materials. Many unstable materials such as styrene, which is subject to polymerization, are shipped with inhibitors to prevent dangerous reactions. Polymerization is the process of forming very large, high-molecular weight molecules from smaller units. Since this reaction is exothermic, in some cases, as with styrene, the reaction can accelerate by its own heat. Vinyl chloride is a common toxic and flammable gas that may polymerize at higher temperatures. Unstable (reactive) materials are further subdivided according to their degree of instability as follows:

Class 1. Materials which in themselves are normally stable but which can become unstable at elevated temperatures and pressures.

Class 2. Materials that in themselves are normally unstable and readily undergo violent chemical change but do not detonate. This class includes materials that can undergo chemical change with rapid release of energy at normal temperatures and pressures and can undergo violent chemical change at elevated temperature and pressure.

Class 3. Materials which in themselves are capable of detonation or of explosive decomposition or explosive reaction but which require a strong initiating source or which must be heated under confinement before initiation.

Class 4. Materials that in themselves are readily capable of detonation or of explosive decomposition or explosive reaction at normal temperatures and pressures. This class includes materials that are sensitive to mechanical or localized thermal shock at normal temperatures and pressures.

Water-Reactive Materials. These materials explode, violently react, produce flammable, toxic, or other hazardous gases, or evolve enough heat to cause self-ignition or ignition of nearby combustibles upon exposure to water or water vapor. The NFPA includes air-reactive materials in this group with a similar definition. Water-reactive materials include the following groups of materials: alkalies, aluminum trialkyls, anhydrides, carbides, hydrides, oxides, and sodium. Water-reactive materials are further subdivided into three classes according to their degree of reactivity as follows:

Class 1. Materials that may react with water with some release of energy but not violently.

Class 2. Materials that may form potentially explosive mixtures with water.

Class 3. Materials that react explosively with water without requiring heat or confinement.

Cryogenic Fluids.   Fluids that have a normal boiling point below minus 150 degrees Fahrenheit. The NFPA defines these as a liquefied gas which exists in its container at temperatures that are far below normal atmospheric temperatures, but usually slightly above its boiling point at normal temperature and pressure (NTP), and at correspondingly low to moderate pressures (a cryogenic gas).

Health Hazards

Materials that are classified as health hazards by Article 80 of the UFC and by OSHAct include highly toxic materials, radioactive materials, corrosives, and other health hazard materials.

Highly Toxic and Toxic Materials.   These are defined as any material that falls within any of the following categories.

Highly Toxic Materials. A material that produces a lethal dose or lethal concentration which falls within any of the following categories:

a. A chemical that has a median lethal dose (LD_{50}) of 50 milligrams or less per kilogram of body weight when administered orally to albino rats weighing between 200 and 300 grams each.

b. A chemical that has a median lethal dose (LD_{50}) of 200 milligrams or less per kilogram of body weight when administered by continuous contact for 24 hours (or less if death occurs within 24 hours) with the bare skin of albino rabbits weighing between 2 and 3 kilograms each.

c. A chemical that has a median lethal concentration (LC_{50}) in air of 200 ppm by volume or less of gas or vapor, or 2 mg/l or less of mist, fume, or dust, when administered by continuous inhalation for 1 hour (or less if death occurs within 1 hour) to albino rats weighing between 200 and 300 grams each.

Toxic Materials. A material that produces a lethal dose or lethal concentration which falls within any of the following categories:

a. A chemical or substance that has a median lethal dose (LD_{50}) of more than 50 mg/kg but not more than 500 mg/kg of body weight when administered orally to albino rats weighing between 200 and 300 grams each.

b. A chemical or substance that has a median lethal dose (LD_{50}) of more than 200 mg/kg but not more than 1000 mg/kg of body weight when administered by continuous contact for 24 hours (or less if death occurs within 24 hours) with the bare skin of albino rabbits weighing between 2 and 3 kilograms each.

c. A chemical or substance that has a median lethal concentration (LC_{50}) in air more than 200 ppm but not more than 2000 ppm by volume of gas or vapor, or more than 2 mg/l but not more than 20 mg/l of mist, fume, or dust, when administered by continuous inhalation for 1 hour (or less if death occurs within one hour) to albino rats weighing between 200 and 300 grams each.

Radioactive Materials. These are defined as any material or combination of materials that spontaneously emit ionizing radiation (UFC) or material that emits, by spontaneous nuclear disintegration, corpuscular or electromagnetic emanations (OSHA). The types of radiation emitted includes alpha particles, beta particles, and gamma radiation. An alpha particle consists of two protons and two neutrons and has a charge of +2. The beta particle is identical in mass and charge to an electron. Gamma rays are photons of energy that have properties similar to those of X rays. They have no electrical charge and no measurable mass.

Materials that are radioactive have the same fire and explosion hazards as their nonradioactive forms. Under fire conditions involving radioactive materials, the smoke and products of combustion can be radioactive or carry radioactive particles, and these conditions can cause widespread contamination if not controlled.

Corrosives. Materials that, when brought into contact with living tissue, will cause visible destruction or irreversible alteration of the tissue by chemical action are termed corrosives. Their primary hazard is through damage to tissue upon contact, inhalation, or ingestion. Corrosives include such materials as acids, alkaline, or caustic materials. The halogens, including bromine, chlorine, fluorine, and iodine, are also corrosive materials. Some corrosive chemicals are also strong oxidizers or are water-reactive and are, therefore, physical hazards in addition to being health hazards.

Other Health Hazards. The UFC uses this category to address other OSHA definitions of health hazards that have not been specifically addressed in NFPA discussions of hazardous materials.

Carcinogens or Suspect Carcinogens. Substances that produce or are suspected of producing cancer. This group includes substances that are listed by the International Agency for Research on Cancer (IARC) or in the *Annual Report on Carcinogens* published by the National Toxicology Program (NTP) or are regulated by OSHA as carcinogens.

Target Organ Toxins. Chemicals that cause damage to a particular organ or system. This grouping includes the following examples:

Hepatoxins: Chemicals that produce liver damage.

Nephrotoxins: Chemicals that produce kidney damage.

Neurotoxins: Chemicals that produce their primary toxic effects on the nervous system.

Blood or hematopoietic system toxins: Agents that act on the blood or hematopoietic system to decrease hemoglobin function and deprive the body tissues of oxygen.

Pulmonary agents: Agents that irritate or damage the lungs.

Reproductive toxins: Chemicals that affect the reproductive capabilities including chromosomal damage (mutations) and effects on fetuses (teratogenesis).

Cutaneous hazards: Chemicals that affect the dermal layers of the body.

Eye hazards: Chemicals that affect the eye or visual capacity.

Irritants. These are chemicals that are not corrosive, but cause a reversible inflammatory effect on living tissue by chemical action at the site of contact.

Sensitizers. These are chemicals that cause a substantial proportion of exposed people or animals to develop an allergic reaction in normal tissue after repeated exposure to the chemical.

IDENTIFICATION OF HAZARDOUS MATERIALS

Each of the organizations that are involved in the regulation of hazardous materials has requirements for identification to meet their individual needs. The individual who is responsible for the industrial firesafety program must be familiar with all of the systems and the local requirements for identification.

Identification of Health and Safety Hazards of Materials

The primary regulation of health and safety is the Occupational Safety and Health Act (OSHAct) or the implementing state OSHA. OSHA's point of emphasis is at the area of employee use or exposure. Therefore, OSHA requirements deal mainly with labeling of containers, although other means such as signs, placards, process sheets, and procedures may be used. The information that is required in 1910.1200 includes the identity of the hazardous material and appropriate hazard warnings. Although this requirement is rather ambiguous, it was intended to be in order to maintain what OSHA terms the "performance-oriented" approach to the hazard determination and labeling requirements.

The term "appropriate" is defined in OSHA Instruction CPL 2-2.38A as that information that provides an immediate warning to employees and, through the chemical link, leads to more detailed information available through the MSDS. The warning should go beyond phrases such as "caution" and "danger" and define the specific hazard. Inplant labeling systems are acceptable if they are effective in conjunction with the plant's hazard communication program and MSDS procedures.

In addition, it should be noted that OSHA requires that chemicals that are known or suspected carcinogens must be so labeled. Any chemicals that are so listed by any of the following three references will be considered to be carcinogenic:

National Toxicology Program (NTP) Annual Report on Carcinogens (latest edition).

International Agency for Research on Cancer (IARC) monographs.

29 CFR 1910, Subpart Z, Toxic and Hazardous Substances, Occupational Safety and Health Administration.

Identification of the Fire Hazards of Materials

When fire fighters respond to a fire or other emergency in an industrial facility, storage location, or other occupancy where hazardous materials may be present, the hazards of the materials may not be readily apparent. It is important in these situations for the fire fighters to be able to quickly identify the hazards of the materials that they might encounter. For this reason, NFPA 704, *Standard System for the Identification of the Fire Hazards of Materials*, was developed. Although this system has some general application by industrial safety and health personnel, its primary function is to assist emergency response personnel. It

HEALTH HAZARD
4 — Deadly
3 — Extreme
    danger
2 — Hazardous
1 — Slightly
    hazardous
0 — Normal
    material

FIRE HAZARD
Flash Points
4 — Below 73°F
3 — Below 100°F
2 — Below 200°F
1 — Above 200°F
0 — Will not burn

REACTIVITY
4 — May detonate
3 — Shock and heat
    may detonate
2 — Violent
    chemical
    change
1 — Unstable if
    heated
0 — Stable

SPECIFIC
HAZARD

Oxidizer   OXY
Acid   ACID
Alkali   ALK
Corrosive   COR
Use No WATER W
Radiation Hazard

Figure 11-3. The diamond-shaped NFPA 704 symbol for the identification of the fire hazards of materials. (Source: National Fire Protection Association)

provides basic information regarding the health, flammability, reactivity, and unusual reactivity characteristics or special hazards of the hazardous materials that are present. The familiar diamond-shaped symbol of the NFPA 704 system (Figure 11-3) includes four diamond-shaped spaces for health, flammability, reactivity, and special hazards. Each category has a numerical rating ranging from "4," indicating a severe hazard to "0," indicating no special hazard. The fourth space is for an indication of any special reactivity to water or other special hazard. A "W" with a horizontal line through the center is used in this space to indicate that the material is reactive to water. Strong oxidizing materials might be identified by the letters "OXY" in this space. To further aid in the quick recognition of the symbol and the meaning of each of the spaces, there are color backgrounds assigned for the three categories. The health hazard space is blue, the flammability space is red and the reactivity space is yellow.

NFPA 325M, *Fire Hazard Properties of Flammable liquids, Gases, and Volatile Solids*, provides the suggested hazard identifications for listed materials. For materials that are not listed in NFPA 325M, the following guidelines or the actual discussion of the hazard identification system in NFPA 704 should be used to properly identify materials. However, the actual determinations of hazard identification should be made by someone who is technically competent and familiar with the properties of the materials being identified.

Health Hazards. The property of a material that may be detrimental to the health of responding fire fighters is categorized in the left-hand blue diamond. These materials are capable of causing injury from exposure by contact, inhalation, or ingestion. The numerical severity rankings in the health hazard diamond are based upon possible effects to fire fighters who are wearing their normal protective gear.

4—Materials that on very short exposure could cause death or major residual injury unless specialized protective equipment is worn. Examples in this category include acrylonitrile, cyanamide, hydrocyanic acid, and 3-methoxypropionitrile.

3—Materials that on short exposure could cause serious temporary or residual injury. Examples in this category include acrylic acid (glacial), ethylenimine, anhydrous hydrazine, hydrogen sulfide, and trichlorosilane.

2—Materials that on intense or continued exposure could cause temporary incapacitation or possible residual injury. Examples in this category include acetic acid (glacial), benzene, ethylene oxide, methylene chloride, trichloroethylene, and vinyl chloride.

1—Materials which on exposure would cause irritation but only minor residual injury. Examples in this category include acetone, butyl acetate, ethylene glycol, isopropyl alcohol, and silane.

0—Under fire conditions, these materials offer no hazard beyond that of ordinary combustible material. Examples in this category include amyl propionate, camphor, denatured alcohol, fuel oils, and vegetable oils.

Flammability Hazards.   The degree of burning hazard of materials is characterized in the top red diamond of the symbol. The numerical severity rankings again are based upon the four-point scale with number 4 being the most severe hazard.

4—Materials that will rapidly or completely vaporize at standard temperature and pressure or which are readily dispersed in air. Examples in this category include flammable gases and Class IA flammable liquids.

3—Liquid and solid materials that can be ignited under almost all ambient temperature conditions. Examples in this category include Class IB and IC flammable liquids and dusts and fibers which may burn rapidly.

2—Materials that can be ignited only after moderate heating or at high ambient temperatures. Examples in this category include combustible liquids and solids and semisolids which readily give off flammable vapors.

1—Materials that must be considerably preheated before ignition can occur. Most ordinary combustibles are included in this category.

0—Materials in this category will not burn when exposed to a temperature of 1500 degrees Fahrenheit for a period of 5 minutes.

Reactivity Hazards.   This category deals with the capability and susceptibility of materials to rapidly release energy by self-reaction, polymerization, or
by reaction if contacted by other materials. This category is identified in the
right-hand yellow diamond on the symbol.

4—Materials that by themselves can detonate or decompose explosively at
standard temperature and pressure. These materials are sensitive to mechanical or thermal shock. Examples in this category include nitroglycerine and
propargyl bromide.

3—Materials that like those in category 4 can detonate or decompose explosively but, in category 3, a strong initiating source is needed. This category
includes materials that are sensitive to mechanical and thermal shock but only
at elevated temperatures and pressures. Examples in this category include
acetylene, dynamite, TNT, nitrocellulose, and nitroethane.

2—Materials that are normally unstable and readily undergo violent chemical
change but do not detonate. These materials can undergo chemical change
with rapid release of energy at normal temperatures and pressures or can
violently react at elevated temperatures and pressures. Examples in this category include acetaldehyde, acrolein, acrylonitrile, hydrazine (anhydrous),
styrene, and vinyl acetate.

1—Materials which are normally stable, but which can become unstable at
elevated temperatures and pressures as in a fire exposure or a runaway chemical reaction. Examples in this category include acetic acid (glacial), allyl
chloride, ethoxyacetylene, methyl ether, and vinyl chloride.

0—These materials are normally stable even under fire exposure conditions.
Examples in this category include acetone, amyl alcohol, benzene, fuel oils,
gasoline, vegetable oils, and xylene.

Special Hazards.   This category addresses other unique hazards that a material may have such as reactivity with water, radiation or oxidizing properties.
Special hazards are denoted in the bottom white diamond of the symbol. Materials that are unusually reactive with water such as acetic anhydride and acetyl
chloride are noted by the letter W with a horizontal line through the center.
Materials that have radioactivity hazards are noted by the standard radioactivity
symbol. Materials that are strong oxidizers such as amyl nitrate and propyl
nitrate are noted by the letters OXY.

---

*The above material has been reprinted with permission from NFPA 704–1985, *Identification of
the Fire Hazards of Materials*, copyright © 1985, National Fire Protection Association, Quincy,
MA 02269. This reprinted material is not the complete and official position of the National Fire
Protection Association, on the referenced subject which is represented only by the standard in its
entirety.

STORAGE OF HAZARDOUS MATERIALS

Proper methods of storage of hazardous materials must be considered whether the storage is a warehouse, storage yard, waste storage area, or ready storage in the area of use. Items to be considered include housekeeping, hazard identification using the NFPA 704 system, chemical compatibilities, fire protection, personnel protection, and incident mitigation. Specific storage requirements are provided in the OSHAct, applicable fire prevention code, NFPA standards, RCRA Hazardous Waste Requirements, and individual Material Safety Data Sheets.

Housekeeping

As in other areas of fire prevention and efficient industrial operations, housekeeping is an important aspect of hazardous materials storage. Hazardous materials must be stored in a neat and orderly manner so that materials are accessible for normal operations and for possible emergency operations. Combustible debris that is allowed to accumulate may provide a fuel source for a fire. Accumulations of debris in hazardous materials storage areas can also clog drainage facilities and be possible reactants if there is a spill. In many storage arrangements, a drainage pit or basin is located beneath the stored hazardous materials. This area will accumulate dirt and debris, and it must be cleaned periodically.

Segregation

Hazardous materials are classified depending upon their unique characteristics. For the most part, the characteristics that differentiate hazardous materials are also characteristics that make them incompatible with one another. For example, oxidizers are incompatible with and must be stored separately from flammable and combustible materials; acids should be stored separately from bases and cyanides.

Segregation of hazardous materials may be achieved by special storage cabinets, storage rooms, firewalls within the same structure, open space between incompatible groups, or intervening space filled with inert or nonhazardous storage.

Many jurisdictions require the overall storage area to be identified using, as a minimum, the hazard identification system described in NFPA 704. When there are materials of different hazard classifications present, the sign should indicate the most severe health, flammability, and reactivity hazard that is present. When the storage facility is designed to store different hazardous materials in segregated rooms or areas, each storage area should have specific identification of the hazard that is present. The DOT label that may be on the chemical container is not adequate since it only classifies the material's hazard for transportation purposes. The NFPA system for identification includes health, flammability, and reactivity information, and it is required in many jurisdictions. In many cases, it is appropriate and beneficial to include specific signs that specify characteristics, hazards, and first aid actions for individual chemicals.

Fire Protection

The fire extinguishing agent selected for use where hazardous materials are used or stored is dependent upon the characteristics of the hazardous materials. Water, particularly an automatic sprinkler system, is generally the preferred method of fire protection for hazardous materials storage areas. However, the reactivity of the materials with water must be considered. One would not want a water system in a location where water-reactive chemicals are used or stored. Another factor when water is being considered is containment of runoff. If water used to fight a chemical fire may be contaminated and have detrimental effects on the environment, containment of the runoff will have to be considered. When containment of the runoff is not possible, it may be necessary to allow the building to burn. This is what occurred at a 1985 fire in an agricultural store in Westbrook, Maine. The store-warehouse contained 7756 pounds plus 670 gallons of pesticides and herbicides when fire fighters arrived to find heavy smoke, high heat, and small explosions. Because of the heavy heat, toxic smoke, and concerns of contaminated water entering the sewage treatment system and a river, the decision was made to let the fire burn. This decision was similar to the situation that was faced by fire fighters at the Sherwin-Williams warehouse fire in Dayton, Ohio (see Chapter 13).

Spill Control/Drainage

Most hazardous materials storage areas have provisions for containment and drainage of spills to a holding area. In some cases, it may be feasible to provide a large enough holding area to contain water from sprinklers or dilution of a spill. On a very large scale, NASA contains contaminated water runoff that occurs during the launch of the space shuttle from the Kennedy Space Center in Florida. During the launch of the shuttle, as much as 280,000 gallons of water are expended through a deluge system to suppress noise and to provide cooling of the tremendous amount of heat that is generated by the shuttle's main engines and solid rocket motors (Figure 11-4). Although much of this water is changed to steam during the launch, some is contaminated in the process and is collected in two 500,000-gallon holding basins for neutralization and disposal (Figure 11-5).

Figure 11-4. Test of the Space Shuttle launch pad 39A sound suppression system at Kennedy Space Center, Florida. During the launch of the Space Shuttle, nearly 300,000 gallons of water are dumped onto the pad during a 30-second period. (Source: National Aeronautics and Space Administration)

On a smaller scale, most regulations governing the storage of hazardous materials, whether waste or supply, specify containment facilities to include at least 6-inch high curbs or dikes. Storage areas may also be sloped to a containment area or trench or the storage area may be located on grates over a pit which serves to catch spills and contain spills plus dilution or sprinkler water.

Unique Requirements

Oxidizing Chemicals. When storing oxidizing chemicals, it must be remembered that although they are not combustible themselves, they do support combustion. Therefore, they must be separated from ordinary combustible materials, flammable and combustible liquids, greases, oils, and other materials, including other oxidizers, that could react with the oxidizer. A common oxidizer that has been responsible for many fires is calcium hypochlorite and the other forms of chlorine for use in swimming pools. This material is stored and

Figure 11-5. Kennedy Space Center's Launch Complex 39B showing the water tower supply for the sound suppression system (upper center) and one of two 500,000 gallon wastewater holding basins (left of the water tower). (Source: National Aeronautics and Space Administration)

used in all types of occupancies from large distribution warehouses to single family dwellings.

Frequent scenarios include sweeping spilled oxidizer and dumping it into a container that contains other reactive materials; or the swimming pool owner who inadvertently mixes two incompatible oxidizer chemicals in the same dispenser.

The hazards of oxidizing chemicals range from those that merely increase the burning rate of combustible materials to those that can undergo an explosive reaction when catalyzed or exposed to heat, shock, or friction.

Organic Peroxides. These materials have hazards ranging from Class I, those that are capable of deflagration to Class V, those which do not sustain combustion and which present no reactivity hazard. They must be stored separately from other chemicals and must be appropriately identified.

Some organic peroxides are temperature sensitive and must be appropriately identified and provided with temperature-controlled storage. Where specific temperature controls are required, high-temperature alarms and backup cooling systems such as sprinklers should be installed.

Radioactive Materials. There are stringent regulations for the safe use and storage of radioactive materials that are enforced by OSHA and other state and federal agencies. Under fire conditions involving radioactive materials, the smoke and vapors (including vaporized fire suppression water) that are produced could spread radiation throughout the building of fire origin or outside to adjoining areas. On a large scale, the explosion and fire at Chernobyl, Russia on April 26, 1986, demonstrated the widespread contamination that can occur when radioactive materials are involved in a fire and cannot be contained to the building of origin.

TRANSPORTATION OF HAZARDOUS MATERIALS

The United States government has been regulating the shipping, handling, and transportation of hazardous materials since late in the 1800s. Early emphasis was on the shipping, handling, and transportation of explosives as addressed in the Transportation of Explosives Act of 1909. This act authorized the Interstate Commerce Commission (ICC) to carry out the provisions of the act utilizing the services of shippers and carrier associations. In the Department of Transportation Act of 1966, the U.S. Department of Transportation (DOT) was created to assume the ICC's functions, powers, and duties relating to explosives and dangerous articles.

During the first year of its existence, the DOT formed the Hazardous Materials Regulation Board (HMRB) to handle all matters relating to regulations issued under the ICC authority and under the authority of the Federal Aviation Act of 1958 for the shipment and transportation of hazardous materials. Also under the DOT, the Office of Hazardous Materials was established to act as the principle staff advisor and to represent the Assistant Secretary for Safety and Consumer Affairs in all matters relating to the transportation of hazardous materials. The Office of Hazardous Materials was also charged with administering the hazardous materials safety program and promoting uniformity in the regulations of the operating administrations with hazardous materials responsibilities including the Federal Aviation Administration, Federal Railroad Administration, federal Highway Administration, and the U.S. Coast Guard.

The Office of Hazardous Materials developed and recommended regulations governing hazardous materials for all modes of transportation; coordinated research in the area of hazardous materials, containers, and transportation facilities; and provided technical advice and training in the hazardous materials regulations.

The Transportation Safety Act of 1974 assigned to the secretary of transportation the authority to promulgate and enforce hazardous materials regulations for all modes and aspects of transportation. The secretary was authorized to establish criteria for all aspects of packaging hazardous materials for shipment, handling of hazardous materials, training requirements, monitoring shipments, and registration of hazardous materials transporters. The law also established strict civil penalties for violations of the DOT regulations.

In 1975, the Materials Transportation Bureau (MTB), consisting of the Office of Hazardous Materials Regulations and the Office of Pipeline Safety, was established. The MTB was made responsible for exercising the authority of the secretary of transportation for all aspects of hazardous materials transportation. In 1985, the MTB was abolished and its functions and responsibilities were divided between the Office of Pipeline Safety and the Office of Hazardous Materials.

Responsibility for enforcement of the hazardous materials regulations remains vested in the operating administrations, including the Federal Aviation Administration, the Federal Highway Administration, the Federal Railroad Administration, and the U.S. Coast Guard.

Dot Hazardous Materials

The Transportation Safety Act of 1974 defines hazardous materials as "a substance or materials in a quantity and form which may pose an unreasonable risk to health and safety or property when transported in commerce." Title 49, CFR further categorizes and defines hazardous materials similar to the NFPA, UFC, and OSHA systems that were discussed previously. The following general definitions are used by the regulations, with more specific definitions in the specific regulations for each category.

Explosives. These include any chemical compound mixture, or device, the primary or common purpose of which is to function by explosion.

Class A Explosives. These explosives present a detonating or maximum hazard.

Class B Explosives. These explosives function by rapid combustion rather than detonation.

Class C Explosives. These explosives include certain types of manufactured articles which contain Class A or Class B explosives, or both, as components, but in restricted quantities.

Blasting Agents. These are materials designed for blasting and are so insensitive that there is very little probability of accidental initiation of explosion.

Compressed Gases. These include any material or mixture in a container having a pressure which exceeds 40 psia at 100 degrees Fahrenheit. Compressed gases are further defined as flammable or nonflammable.

Flammable Compressed Gas. Generally considered to be any flammable mixture that meets the definition of a compressed gas. More specifically, the DOT definition specifies either a mixture of 13 percent or less (by volume) with air forms a flammable mixture or the flammable range with air is wider than 12 percent regardless of the lower flammable limit.

Nonflammable Compressed Gas. Any compressed gas that does not meet the definition as a flammable compressed gas is considered to be a nonflammable compressed gas. It is worth noting that ammonia (anhydrous) is classified by DOT as nonflammable due to its high LFL; however, it is in fact flammable.

Flammable Liquids. A flammable liquid is considered to be any liquid having a flash point below 100 degrees Fahrenheit, except those liquids which meet the definition of a compressed gas, or a mixture having one or more components with a flash point of 100 degrees Fahrenheit or higher that makes up at least 99 percent of the total volume of the mixture.

Flammable Solids. A flammable solid is defined as any solid material, other than an explosive, which under conditions incident to transportation is liable to cause fires through friction, retained heat from manufacturing or processing, or which can be ignited readily, and when ignited, burn so vigorously and persistently as to create a serious transportation hazard. This class includes spontaneously combustible and water-reactive materials.

Combustible Liquids. These are defined as liquids that do not meet any other classification definitions of hazardous materials and have a flash point at or above 100 degrees Fahrenheit. An exception is any mixture having one component or more with a flash point at 200 degrees Fahrenheit or higher, which makes up at least 99 percent of the volume of the mixture.

Organic Peroxides. These are organic compounds which contain the bivalent —O—O— structure and which may be considered a derivative of hydrogen peroxide where one or more of the hydrogen atoms have been replaced by organic radicals.

Oxidizing Material. A substance that yields oxygen readily to stimulate the combustion of organic matter is considered an oxidizing material.

Poisons. Poisons are divided into three groups based upon the degree of hazard posed in transportation.

Poison A. These are extremely dangerous poisons. They are gases or liquids such that a very small amount of the gas, vapor of the liquid, mixed with air would be dangerous to life.

Posion B. These are not considered to be as dangerous as Class A poisons. Included are those substances, liquid or solid, other than Class A or irritating material which are known to be so toxic to man as to provide a hazard to health during transportation, or which in the absence of adequate data on human toxicity, are presumed to be toxic to man based on results with test animals.

Irritating Materials. These are liquid or solid substances which upon contact with fire or when exposed to air give off dangerous or intensely irritating fumes, but do not include any material classed as poison Class A.

Corrosive Material. This is a liquid or solid that causes visible destruction or irreversible alterations in human skin tissue at the site of contact, or in the case of leakage from its packaging, a liquid that has severe corrosion rate on steel.

Etiologic Agents. These agents are viable organisms, or their toxins, which cause or may cause human disease.

Radioactive Materials. These are any material or combination of materials which spontaneously emits ionizing radiation, and has a specific activity greater than 0.002 microcuries per gram. The definitions provided in the regulations include further classification according to "fissile" groupings, identified as small or large quantity, and so on.

Other Regulated Materials. These are materials that do not meet the definition of a hazardous material, other than a combustible liquid in packaging having a capacity of 110 gallons or less, and are specifically listed in the Table of Hazardous Materials as an Other Regulated Material (ORM).

Part 172 of 49 CFR contains the Hazardous Materials Table which lists many hazardous materials and provides their DOT hazard class, UN/NA identification number, required labels, packaging references, and information and requirements for water shipments. UN identification numbers are numbers assigned by the United Nations Classification System. This international system was established by the United Nations to provide a uniform regulatory control system over the transport of dangerous articles by all modes of transportation and to improve the capability of emergency personnel to quickly identify hazardous materials and to ensure accurate transmittal of information to and from the scene of accidents. NA numbers are not recognized internationally except on shipments to and from Canada. The UN and NA class numbering systems are referenced in the Hazardous Materials Table and found on hazardous materials warning labels (Figure 11-6).

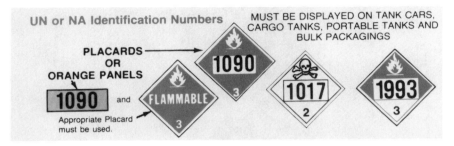

Figure 11-6. UN (United Nations) or NA (North American) numbers, as found in the Hazardous Materials Tables (49 CFR, Section 172.101 and 172.102) are to be displayed on placards or orange panels when hazardous materials are transported in tank cars, cargo tanks, portable tanks, or bulk packagings.

Packaging of Hazardous Materials

The regulations provide guidance and requirements for the preparation of hazardous materials for transport. Specifications for container design and packaging methods are all intended to minimize the possibilities of an accident during transportation whether by air, rail, water, or highway. Packaging requirements are specific to the material being shipped. There may be, depending upon the material, restrictions on the quantity of the hazardous materials that can be in a container or in a shipment. The person who offers a hazardous material for transport must ensure that the material has been properly packaged and prepared for shipment. Appropriate containers should be used and they must be properly packaged, labeled, and manifested.

Labeling/Placarding of Hazardous Materials for Shipment

The DOT hazardous materials warning labels and placards are the familiar diamond-shaped and color-coded materials shown in Figure 11-7. The Hazardous Materials Table in Part 172 provides the proper label to be used for listed materials. For materials that are not listed, the shipper must make the determination based upon the definitions for the hazard classes.

The shipper has the responsibility to determine the proper label(s) for the materials being shipped, multiple label requirements, affixing the label(s), the number of labels required, and the location on the package. Carriers of hazardous materials must not accept packages for shipment unless the proper labels are affixed.

Placards are larger, but they correspond very closely with the shape, color, and design of the hazardous materials warning labels. The purpose of placards is to alert personnel to the potential dangers associated with the particular haz-

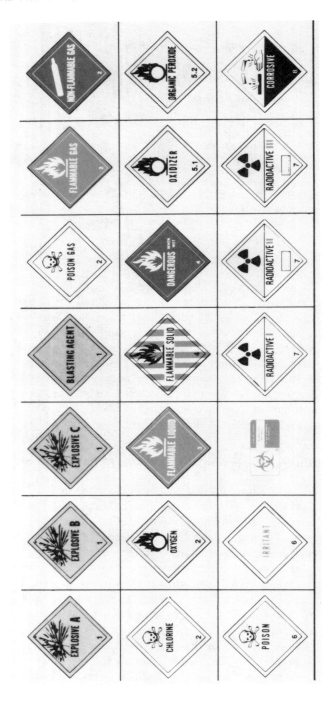

Figure 11-7. DOT domestic labels (upper) and domestic placards (lower) as specified in 49 CFR, Transportation, Parts 100-177.

ardous materials contained therein and to serve as a guide to emergency response personnel who might be responding to an incident involving the carrier. Regardless of the mode of transportation, the person who offers a hazardous material for shipment is responsible for providing the carrier with the appropriate placard(s). No carrier of hazardous materials may transport the material unless the appropriate placards are affixed to the vehicle, rail car, freight container, or tank.

Documentation of Hazardous Materials Shipments

Each shipment of hazardous materials must be accompanied by properly completed and certified documentation to include a bill of lading, waybill, manifest, or other shipping papers. In addition to the shipping papers, there are requirements for paperwork which reflects the nature of the hazardous materials shipment. This documentation is important, not only to the shipper, but to the carrier as well. The carrier must be concerned with placarding and procedures that are appropriate to the material being shipped. In the event of an accident, emergency responders must have ready access to the documentation concerning the shipment.

Each shipping paper that describes hazardous materials must include the proper shipping name of the material, the hazard class of the material, the UN/NA identification number and the total quantity by weight, volume, or as otherwise appropriate for the hazardous material. All of the above information may be referenced in Part 172, 49 CFR, the Hazardous Materials Table.

SUMMARY

As far as fire protection is concerned, the person who is responsible for fire-safety must be concerned with the materials that provide fuel for fires, including flammable and combustible liquids, flammable gases, and flammable solids. Also of concern is the large category of materials that are known as oxidizers which do not burn, but can support combustion. There are also many other materials that are classified as hazardous that deserve the attention of the fire-safety people. Many have fire and explosion considerations, health hazard, and life safety implications, and require special handling, storage, and fire fighting procedures.

There are many systems for classifying and identifying hazardous materials including the following: the OSHA definitions which are concerned with health hazards; the NFPA 704 system which is concerned with fire fighting hazards; the fire prevention codes which address the fire or explosion hazard or the properties of hazardous materials that contribute abnormal dangers to fire fighting; and the DOT regulations which deal with transportation of hazardous materials. Fortunately, the various classification systems are fairly consistent, but the firesafety person should be familiar with each system as it applies to the situation. An important part of any industrial fire protection program is to ensure that hazardous materials are properly marked, stored, used, and disposed and that employees and the local emergency response agencies are informed of their hazards and safe handling.

BIBLIOGRAPHY

Casaccio, Ellen K. 1985. *Applying the New Federal PCB Regulations*. Record 62(4):3–10.

Code of Federal Regulations. 29 CFR 1910. 1987. Occupational Safety and Health Administration, Department of Labor. Washington, DC.

Code of Federal Regulations. 40 CFR 260. EPA General Regulations for Hazardous Waste Management.

Code of Federal Regulations. 49 CFR, Parts 100-199. Transportation. 1988. Washington, D.C.

Fire, Frank L. 1986. *The Common Sense Approach to Hazardous Materials*. Fire Engineering, New York.

Fire Protection Handbook, 16th ed. 1986. National Fire Protection Association, Quincy, MA.

Isner, Michael S. 1988. $49 Million Loss in Sherwin-Williams Warehouse Fire. *Fire Journal* 82(2):65–73, 93.

NFPA 43A-1980. *Code for the Storage of Liquid and Solid Oxidizing Materials*. National Fire Protection Association, Quincy, MA.

NFPA 43B-1986. *Code for the Storage of Organic Peroxide Formulations*. National Fire Protection Association, Quincy, MA.

NFPA 43C-1986. *Code for the Storage of Gaseous Oxidizing Materials*. National Fire Protection Association, Quincy, MA.

NFPA 325M-1984. *Fire Properties of Flammable Liquids, Gases, and Volatile Solids*. National Fire Protection Association, Quincy, MA.

NFPA 704-1985. *Standard System for the Identification of the Fire Hazards of Materials*. National Fire Protection Association, Quincy, MA.

OSHA Instruction CPL 2-2.38A. 1986. Inspection Record for the Hazard Communication Standard, 29 CFR 1910.1200. Washington, D.C.

Public Law 99-499, Superfund Amendments and Reauthorization Act, 1986. Washington, D.C.

They Let It Burn, 1985. Report compiled by the NFPA Fire Analysis Division. *Fire Command* 52(10):40–42.

Uniform Fire Code, 1988 ed. Whittier, California: International Conference of Building Officials and Western Fire Chiefs Association.

42 U.S. Code Sections 6901-6991. Resource Conservation and Recovery Act (RCRA), 1976. Washington, D.C.

42 U.S. Code Sections 9601-9675. Comprehensive Environmental Response, Compensation and Liability Act (CERCLA), 1980. Washington, D.C.

12
HAZARDOUS MATERIALS EMERGENCIES

Along with the increasing quantities and types of hazardous materials that are used in industry came an increase in the number of hazardous materials emergencies. Industries and public fire departments were not prepared for these emergencies. In the past, the fire department response to most hazardous materials spills would be to flush the spill with large quantities of water. Fires involving hazardous materials were still handled as fires with suppression being the first priority. In most cases water was applied with little regard to runoff of the contaminated water.

Chief Glenn E. Alexander of the Dayton, Ohio Fire Department, speaking about hazardous materials incidents at the 1988 Fall Meeting of the National Fire Protection Association, said that fire fighters have traditionally put water on fires, or in the vernacular of fire fighters, "put the wet stuff on the red stuff." Chief Alexander said that there are increasingly severe environmental impacts resulting from fires involving hazardous materials. He was speaking specifically about the Sherwin-Williams Warehouse fire that occurred in Dayton on May 27, 1987. In this fire, Chief Alexander recognized that the flammable liquid fire was not going to be easily extinguished and excessive water was only going to carry out large amounts of contaminants which would endanger the groundwater, so he directed that water only be applied to protect exposures. While there was some groundwater contamination, Chief Alexander's actions minimized the damage to the aquifer underlying Dayton. The damage that did occur was contained and controlled by the timely installation of a groundwater purification and vapor recovery system. The environmental contamination would have been much more severe if the fire department had not curtailed the application of water to the fire.

Contaminated water runoff is only one of the environmental consequences that is involved in a fire involving hazardous materials. Toxic vapor and gas clouds can form and injure fire fighters and the public. When chemicals are involved in the fire, fire fighters face the potential of violent reactions when containers rupture and there is commingling of chemicals. Corrosive materials in the smoke and runoff water can have harmful effects on people and equipment, and the problems can be compounded should radioactive materials be involved.

It is likely that future fires that involve hazardous materials and are nonlife-threatening, such as the Sherwin-Williams fire, will be allowed to burn in order to reduce damage to the environment as well as to protect fire fighters from exposure to toxic smoke. This possibility raises serious concerns for industrial loss control personnel.

When not controlled, hazardous materials incidents have the potential for complex interactions. The characteristics of a particular material that make it hazardous are but one dimension in an emergency. There are also the possible adverse interactions with other materials and with the environment. When fire is involved in the hazardous material incident, the potential for severe effects is enormous. Fire greatly increases the hazard and the dilemma faced by the emergency responders. When the fire is allowed to burn, the property loss could be greatly increased. On the other hand, cleanup costs resulting from a fire-related environmental incident can be astronomical. In retrospect, in those situations where fires involving hazardous materials have been allowed to burn, there has been agreement among the loss control, insurance, and fire fighters that the decision was proper.

The prospect of a total fire loss or astronomical environmental cleanup costs reinforces the importance of the industrial spill control program and fire prevention efforts in areas where hazardous materials are used or stored.

In the late 1970s and throughout the 1980s, it was recognized that improved information sharing and preplanning was required between public officials and industry to deal with hazardous materials emergencies. This resulted in the institution of hazardous materials response capabilities in many public fire departments and in industry. Legislation was enacted to require sharing of information, preplanning activities, and protective measures for emergency response personnel.

THE DEVELOPMENT OF RESPONSE CAPABILITIES

Public Fire Departments

It was not until the early 1980s that public fire departments began acquiring specialized vehicles and equipment and began training firemen to deal with hazardous materials incidents. The Los Angeles City Fire Department was one of the first in the United States to form a specialized hazardous materials response capability in the form of a mobile laboratory (Figure 12-1) in 1976. The creation of this unit followed a January industrial fire involving chlorine gas cylinders and two June fires, one at a swimming pool supply facility and the other involving a pipeline. The later two fires occurred within 12 hours of one another and served to emphasize the critical need for a better response capabil-

Figure 12-1. The first hazardous materials response unit operated by the Los Angeles City Fire Department in 1976. (Source: Los Angeles City Fire Department)

Figure 12-2. This June, 1976 gas pipeline fire in Venice, California, emphasized the growing need for a hazardous materials response capability in the Los Angeles Fire Department. (Photo: Mike Mullen)

ity. Initially, the van was operated by two fire department inspectors who had chemistry degrees. At the scene of a hazardous materials incident, fire fighters utilized the equipment from the van. The city's capabilities grew with the need for hazardous materials response. In 1982, the city placed three hazardous materials squads into service (Figure 12-3) to provide hazardous materials response for a city of approximately 470 square miles. Each squad is manned by an officer and three fire fighters who have received special training. The squads are housed in a task force station (an engine company and a truck company), and when there is a call for a hazardous materials incident, the whole task force responds with a total of 14 fire fighters. Los Angeles also maintains two motor home-type hazardous materials command vehicles (Figure 12-4) for use at major incidents.

The Fire Department of New York City had limited capabilities to respond to serious hazardous materials incidents prior to 1980. After 1980, a rescue company was equipped to operate in a dual function concept which included hazardous materials response. It was not until 1984 that a dedicated hazardous materials response unit was established. The city still maintains only this single unit for hazardous materials emergencies. Six firehouses have been designated as hazardous materials equipment locations. When needed at the scene of a hazardous materials emergency, these materials are delivered by fire department apparatus.

The city of Chicago Fire Department acquired a step-van in 1982 for hazardous materials response. This equipment was not manned solely by hazardous

Figure 12-3. The current hazardous materials response unit operated by the Los Angeles City Fire Department. (Source: Los Angeles City Fire Department)

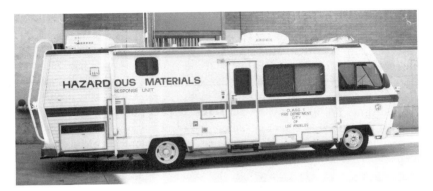

Figure 12-4. Hazardous materials response command vehicle operated by the Los Angeles City Fire Department. (Source: Los Angeles City Fire Department)

materials specialists, but it was used by fire suppression personnel as required. In 1985, Chicago began to operate the unit with a full-time officer and driver who were specifically trained for hazardous materials response. The program has since evolved to larger crews and better equipment for hazardous materials response. Chicago still has only one hazardous materials unit for the city covering 226 square miles. Chicago operates its hazardous materials response task force in a manner similar to the Los Angeles task force. Any time that there is a call for the hazardous materials unit, an engine company and a truck company respond for size up and to perform necessary rescues. There are also four heavy rescue squads in the city with limited hazardous materials response capability.

Industrial Hazardous Materials Response

At about the same time that public fire departments were developing their response capabilities, industry also recognized the need for rapid internal response to hazardous materials incidents, and they began staffing and equipping for this activity. Most industrial operations always had some form of first aid hazardous materials response capability, but like the public fire departments, they came to realize the need for better equipment and better training for their personnel.

Depending upon the size of the operations, the upgrading of hazardous materials response ranged from the acquisition of supplies of absorbent material and laboratory spill kits to large step-van units similar to public fire departments (Figure 12-5). Much of this activity was disorganized, and when public authorities responded to hazardous materials incidents there was confusion over reporting and command responsibilities which compounded the dilemma over identification of the involved materials and proper remediation procedures.

Figure 12-5. A well-equipped industrial hazardous materials response unit. (Source: Hughes Aircraft Company El Segundo North Fire Department, El Segundo, California)

LEGISLATION

Much of the legislation that was discussed in Chapter 11 included provisions to cause hazardous materials operations to be conducted in a manner that would minimize emergencies or would enhance and make safer the response to hazardous materials incidents. Some of the legislation will be discussed again here with respect to its effects upon the emergency response activity.

Resource Conservation and Recovery Act (RCRA) Of 1976

The transportation, treatment, storage, and disposal of hazardous waste is regulated under RCRA. One of the requirements is the preparation of an operating plan for a RCRA permitted facility for storage, treatment, or disposal of hazardous wastes. The plan must include contingency plans that include procedures and equipment for dealing with emergencies that may occur in the facility.

Superfund Amendments and Reauthorization Act (SARA) Of 1986

SARA, Title III, is also referred to as the Emergency Planning and Community Right-to-Know Act of 1986 (EPCRA). Title III includes requirements for emergency planning and notification, community right-to-know reporting, and toxic chemical release reporting.

Title III's requirements to report hazardous materials inventories, which may include material safety data sheets, to the public fire department is intended to assist the fire department and other public authorities in planning for possible emergencies.

Emergency Planning.   Title III requires the establishment of a state emergency response commission and local emergency planning districts and planning committees for each district.

Emergency Notification.   Businesses are required by EPCRA to immediately notify appropriate state, local, and national emergency response entities of any release into the environment of specified amounts of some 721 reportable hazardous materials. Reports must include the identity and amount of the chemical released, possible health effects, and safeguards that are necessary to protect the community. There has been much confusion in industry over "reportable quantities" and "release to the environment." However, because failure to report may result in substantial penalties, the recommendation that most of industry is following is to report all questionable releases. This responsibility frequently falls upon the industrial fire response unit or the safety, health, or environmental personnel. The responsibility and procedures for reporting of hazardous material releases should be documented in the company's emergency response plans.

Community Right-to-Know Reporting.   The purpose of community right-to-know reporting is to inform the local fire department of the existence of hazardous materials in their jurisdiction to enable them to properly respond to an emergency. EPCRA requires annual reporting of the identity and quantities of hazardous materials stored. Quantities include maximum amounts stored and daily averages on hand. Additionally, the local fire department must be provided with material safety data sheets for each chemical stored on the plant site. Update reports are required within 3 months of adding chemicals.

OSHA, Hazardous Waste Operations, and Emergency Response

29 CFR 1910.120, Hazardous Waste Operations and Emergency Response, was issued as an interim final rule in 1987, with the final rule going into effect March 6, 1990. This rule was mandated by SARA to cover employers and employees working on hazardous substance response operations under CERCLA, cleanup operations under RCRA, operations involving hazardous waste storage, disposal, and treatment facilities under RCRA. It also covers emergency responders to hazardous materials incidents. The important aspect of this rule is

that it specifies stringent training requirements for personnel who respond to hazardous materials incidents including all police officers, fire fighters, EMS personnel, and industrial fire brigades.

OSHA has established five levels of responsibilities to determine training requirements for personnel who might be involved in hazardous materials emergencies. These levels are similar to the four levels established by the NFPA in NFPA 472, *Standard for Professional Competence of Responders to Hazardous Materials Incidents*. The five OSHA levels including first responder awareness level, first responder operations level, hazardous materials technician, hazardous materials specialist, and on-scene incident commander are described as follows:

First Responder Awareness Level. This group includes those individuals who, in the normal course of their duties, might be the first on the scene of a hazardous materials emergency. In the industrial facility, this group would include truck drivers, employees who work in hazardous materials operations, and plant fire brigade members. The only response that is expected of these individuals would be to initiate an emergency response procedure by notifying the proper authorities and to evacuate employees. Training for people in this group of first responders is, as the term implies, to create a basic awareness about hazardous materials emergencies. It is similar to but more in depth than OSHA's Hazard Communication Standard. In addition to information about hazardous materials and their associated risks, awareness first responders must learn to recognize the presence of hazardous materials in an emergency, to make appropriate notifications, and to properly isolate the incident site.

First Responder Operations Level. The "operational" level of first responder includes those individuals whose duties include responding to the scene of emergencies that may involve hazardous materials. This level would include fire fighters in the public as well as private sector and any employees who might be involved in initial response or rescue activities. In addition to the awareness level of training, these individuals must be able to assess the hazard and risk, determine when their normal personnel protective equipment is adequate protection for the particular hazardous material, understand basic hazardous material terms, understand decontamination procedures, be able to perform basic recordkeeping, and be able to expand the Incident Command System until a responder at the next higher level arrives.

Employers must certify that all responders at this level have received at least 8 hours of specialized training or have had sufficient experience to demonstrate competency in the above areas.

Hazardous Materials Technician. These individuals are members of specialized teams who accomplish the incident mitigation. In addition to meeting all of the first responder training requirements, the technician must have at least

24 hours of additional training. The technician must have a basic understanding of chemical, biological, and radiological terms and their behavior. The technician is trained to operate using at least Level B protection, in those cases in which high-level respiratory protection if required, but a lesser level of skin and eye protection. Technician level personnel should be able to classify, identify, and verify materials using basic monitoring equipment, to perform advanced hazardous materials control operations, and select and implement appropriate decontamination procedures.

Hazardous Materials Specialist.   The specialist is similar to the technician but is more highly trained and equipped. Personnel in this classification may also be specialists in handling only certain hazardous materials and, in other situations, would be classified as technicians. Specialists have the ability to select and use Level A protection in addition to other specialized personal protective or hazardous materials equipment.

On-Scene Incident Commander.   This level includes all personnel who may be expected to assume control of an incident. It includes all public fire department officers and may include line fire fighters who might be expected to assume command. It would also include industrial fire suppression officers, supervisors, or fire brigade officers who might be expected to supervise mitigation activities.

Potential incident commanders must have at least 24 hours of training beyond the first responder operations level to be able to implement the incident command system, know how to implement the local and state emergency response plans, know the hazards and risks of employees working in specialized chemical protective clothing, and understand decontamination procedures.

NFPA STANDARDS

As the numbers of hazardous materials incidents increased, the fire services were struggling with formulating response capabilities, equipment, and training needs. At the same time, the National Fire Protection Association was expanding its involvement in the area of hazardous materials emergencies. In 1989, at the request of the fire services, the NFPA published two documents that establish levels of competence for responders and provide detailed criteria for responding to hazardous materials incidents.

Both documents very clearly make the point that they are not intended solely for use by fire departments. They are intended for any entity that may use hazardous materials and respond to emergencies.

Competence Levels for Hazardous Materials Responders

Prior to 1988, any specialized hazardous material response training that was provided to public fire departments was based upon locally established criteria.

There was no uniform curriculum for these individuals. In 1988, at its fall meeting in Nashville, Tennessee, the National Fire Protection Association adopted NFPA 472, *Standard for Professional Competence of Responders to Hazardous Materials Incidents*. This standard was developed in response to requests from the fire fighter community to clarify necessary competence levels and training for those individuals who respond to hazardous materials emergencies. While primarily intended for public agency emergency responders, NFPA 472 also provides excellent criteria to develop the industrial hazardous materials response capability.

NFPA 472 establishes three levels of competence, including first responder, hazardous materials technician, and hazardous materials specialist. These levels of competence are very similar in name and function to the levels that were established by OSHA in 1910.120, but the NFPA standard deals specifically with fire fighter responders as follows:

First Responder Level.   This level contains two sublevels based upon the type of responder, including a basic, or awareness, level of response and a more highly trained operations level.

The awareness level includes those personnel who in the normal course of their duties may be the first on the scene of a hazardous materials incident. The awareness level personnel are not expected to take any actions other than to recognize that a hazard exists, call for trained personnel, and secure the area. These personnel will include truck drivers carrying hazardous cargo, train crews, and police officers.

The operations level includes those personnel whose duties include responding to the scene of emergencies that may involve hazardous materials. This is the main difference between awareness and operational level first responders. Where the awareness level was defined as those who *may* be the first on the scene of a hazardous materials incident, the operations level individuals are those whose duties *include* responding to the scene of an incident. The operations level person would not be expected to use specialized chemical protective clothing or control equipment. Operations level personnel would include fire service, state police, and EMS personnel.

Hazardous Materials Technician.   The technician is a person who is trained, equipped, and officially designated as a member of a hazardous materials response team. The technician has met all of the training requirements for first responder, and in addition, is able to mitigate hazardous materials incidents including implementation of a safety plan, using at least Level B protection plus other specialized personnel protective equipment, performing advanced hazardous materials control operations, and implementing decontamination procedures.

Hazardous Materials Specialist. The specialist is similar to the technician but is more highly trained and equipped. The specialist may also be a specialist in handling only certain hazardous materials and, in other situations, would be able to function as a technician. Specialists have the ability to select and use Level A protection in addition to other specialized personal protective equipment or hazardous materials equipment.

Responding to Hazardous Materials Incidents

Because of the wide diversity and the complexity of hazardous materials incidents, the fire services requested specific and uniform operating guidelines for such response. The NFPA responded with NFPA 471, *Recommended Practice for Responding to Hazardous Materials Incidents.* NFPA 471 provides guidelines that are suitable for all hazardous materials incidents and are applicable to any organization that may be involved in response activities. This practice provides a basis around which a training program could be designed for any level of responder.

TYPES OF HAZARDOUS MATERIALS EMERGENCIES

There are three types of hazardous materials emergencies, a spill, a leak, reactions, and fire involving hazardous materials.

Spill. A spill occurs when a material has escaped its container and has entered the environment. A spill may be the release of a liquid, powder, or solid form of hazardous material. Evaluating the spill includes consideration of the type and physical form of the material, the environmental media being contaminated, and the surface media or material in which the hazardous material is in contact.

Leak. A leak is considered to be the inadvertent release or generation of a liquid or gas in a manner that poses a threat to the environment or to the health and safety of personnel.

Evaluation of a leak also requires consideration of the hazardous characteristics of the material, the threat to the environment or people, and possibilities of containment.

Reactions. There are any number of reactions that are possible depending upon the hazardous materials that are stored. When incompatible chemicals mix as a result of an accident, they could react violently producing an explosion, fire, or toxic cloud. Some chemicals are water reactive, others react on exposure to air. It is necessary for personnel at facilities that use and store hazardous materials to be familiar with the possible reactions that might occur. This information should be incorporated into contingency plans and imparted to responder personnel.

Fires. When a hazardous materials incident involves fire, the decision must be made whether to allow it to burn or attempt to extinguish it. Fire fighting water may become contaminated, as discussed previously, resulting in runoff problems. Should the material be water reactive, attempts to extinguish the fire may result in a more serious situation. It may be preferable in some situations to allow the fire to burn and consume the hazardous materials.

Site Safety

The imperative in dealing with hazardous materials incidents is to establish site safety. The initial activity of the responders is to ensure the safety of potentially exposed personnel and to establish a safe working environment for the responders.

NFPA 471 establishes procedures to ensure site safety which are in accordance with 29 CFR 1910.120 and EPA requirements. It encourages implementation of an incident command system and designation of a safety officer who reports to the incident commander. Safety of response operations can be maximized through an incident commander who is in overall charge of the incident and a safety officer who is capable of recognizing, evaluating, and controlling hazards and assuring that safe practices are carried out and observed.

THE INDUSTRIAL HAZARDOUS MATERIALS EMERGENCY PROGRAM

While the public fire department usually has the responsibility for the initial response to hazardous materials emergencies, the industrial plant that stores or uses hazardous materials must also be prepared to take initial response actions. Most cities that have hazardous materials response capabilities have a limited number of units for this activity. For example, as indicated above, the city of Chicago and New York City have only one unit. While other fire suppression units in these cities play support roles and have training as first responders, the response time of trained technicians and specialists may be greater than for a fire emergency. It is, therefore, necessary that industrial operations that use and store hazardous materials maintain some form of capability to take first aid measures such as containment of the spill, or application of absorber materials.

Planning

Hazardous materials emergencies require advance planning of industry, the media, and public agencies. These organizations cooperate in preplanning, coordinate their efforts, and maintain close communications. This means that when the emergency is beyond the capabilities of industrial hazardous materials first aid, contingency plans must be in place for the public fire department to respond rapidly and effectively. To do so, they must have advance information about the industrial activity, the types, quantities, and location of hazardous materials that are present, and knowledge of how they are used. Community right-to-know legislation requires some of this interchange, but the proactive industrial program will go beyond the requirements to ensure that the local fire department is well informed of the hazards that are present.

Personnel.   Hazardous materials emergencies require fast response by personnel who are properly trained and equipped and are protected with personal protective equipment that is appropriate to the hazards. One of the first decisions to be made in the hazardous materials planning stage is whether to form an in-plant hazardous materials emergency response team. Facilities with full-time fire suppression forces should provide the additional training and equipment to help their fire fighters deal with chemical incidents (Figure 12-6). Companies who rely upon employee emergency organizations such as fire brigades, should provide necessary training and equipment to these individuals. When the decision is made to provide a company response team, the guidelines found in NFPA

Figure 12-6. Hazardous materials response capabilities must be well rehearsed. (Source: Hughes Aircraft Company El Segundo North Fire Department, El Segundo, California)

471 and 472, and the requirements in OSHA Section 1910.120 may be used to help determine to what level the in-plant responders will be trained.

Equipment.   When the decision is made to have trained personnel in the plant who will respond to hazardous materials emergencies, appropriate equipment must be selected. When equipment is procured, it must be dedicated and maintained to ensure its availability for emergency response activities. The types of hazardous materials emergencies that are expected and the level of response to be maintained will dictate the type of equipment that will be required. Again, the NFPA 471 and 472 and OSHA Section 1910.120 should be used for guidelines and requirements.

Communications.   The planning process must consider both passive and active communications. Passive communications include such things as the hazardous materials inventories that are provided to the private and public fire department, signs such as NFPA 704 system signs, placards, and labels. Active communications include telephones, radios, alarms, and employees who are well informed about the nature of the chemicals and procedures in their work area as well as emergency communications procedures.

Notification.   Among the activities that can be preplanned is notification. Emergency procedures must include responsibility for notifying the public emergency responders. Additionally other agencies, organizations, groups, and individuals including emergency response contractors may be needed to assist in emergency response activities. These entities and their telephone numbers should be listed in the plan.

EPCRA and some state requirements mandate notification of various governmental agencies in the event of a release of specific types and quantities of chemicals. This information should be part of the plan as well as responsibility for determining the need for notification and making the notification.

Facility Evaluation.   The preincident planning effort is used to determine possible failure points and to make key decisions before the incident. The planning effort should include a complete facility hazardous materials evaluation conducted by the planners and the public fire department response unit. The inventories will provide the information concerning types, quantities, and locations of hazardous materials as well as the storage means. The evaluation can be used to predict flow patterns, direction of spread, possible dispersion zones, identification of evacuation routes, key control points, access points, and unseen conduits. This information can be used to determine the location and amount of preplaced remediation equipment such as absorbent materials, containers, shovels, personal protective equipment, and other remediation equipment. Emergency actions can be preplanned for a variety of possible scenarios such as vapor release, spill, leak, or fire involving hazardous materials.

Passive Controls

The facility evaluation and other planning activities may result in the identification of facility modifications and other actions that will eliminate hazardous materials incidents or help to minimize the effects when they do occur. Some fire prevention codes contain information and requirements that might be useful in identifying passive control measures for hazardous materials storage and operational facilities.

One form of passive control that might be utilized includes facilities to confine and control spills and leaks.

Confinement and Containment.   Facilities should be designed to contain possible spills or leaks in areas where chemicals are used or stored. This is the very important first line of defense to minimize risk to life and the environment until response forces or contracted cleanup personnel can respond.

Confinement and containment include the provision of curbed and diked areas where hazardous materials are used or stored. Another safeguard is the storage of absorption materials in these areas. There are many absorbent materials that are available for use including powder and granular absorbers, and absorbent pillows. Sand, sawdust, clay, and charcoal may also be used. It is most important to ensure that the absorbent material selected be compatible with the materials that are likely to be spilled.

Hazardous Materials Emergency Response Personnel

When the planning process has determined that the industrial facility will form a hazardous materials response team, and the level of response that will be achieved, provisions must be made to train and equip the personnel.

Training

OSHAct requires basic hazardous materials training for all employees who use or may be exposed to hazardous materials in their workplace. This training includes information about the physical and health hazards of the chemicals in the work area, methods and observations that may be used to detect the presence or release of hazardous chemicals in the work area, measures that the employees can take to protect themselves from these hazards, and details of the employer's hazard communications program. When employees are expected to take some form of remedial action, their training will have to be more extensive. It may be desirable to train the plant fire brigade to respond to hazardous materials emergencies or, if the plant has its own fire suppression organization, it may be desirable to train them to be hazardous materials emergency responders.

Once the extent of the response capability is determined, the training program can be established. The following are suggested training programs for each of the OSHA 1910.120 competency levels:

First Responder Awareness.   In the industrial plant, these employees would be those who work in areas where hazardous materials are used or stored. Their duties and work areas are such that they "may be" first on the scene of a hazardous materials incident. Training for these individuals is primarily for recognition of hazardous materials and hazardous materials emergencies. The number of hours of training at this level is not established but will depend upon the experience and prior training of first responders at the awareness level. Suggested classes include:

Basic definition and understanding of hazardous materials including types, effects, and hazards.

Identification of hazardous materials, including OSHA requirements, NFPA 704 system, DOT identification system, and the plant labeling system.

Familiarity with the site hazardous materials program and emergency response plan including notification procedures and requirements.

First Responder Operational.   These employees might be expected to respond to a hazardous materials emergency on the plant site. They would include plant-site fire suppression personnel, plant fire brigade members, or selected employees in the area where hazardous materials are used or stored. The most important part of the training of first responder personnel is the ability to recognize those situations that are beyond their capabilities in terms of training and equipment. These individuals must receive at least 8 hours of training or demonstrate competence at the awareness level as well as in the following additional areas:

Basic hazardous materials hazard recognition and evaluation to include recognition of substances involved and possible impact on the responders, public health, and the environment.

Hazardous materials definitions including physical properties, and those associated with the hazards of toxic materials, flammable and combustible materials, corrosives, reactive materials, compressed gases, explosives, etiologic/infectious materials, and radiation.

Personal protective equipment including familiarity with the equipment that is provided for individuals at this level. Equipment might include air-puri-fying respirator (only if the type and quantity of the possible contaminant is known in advance and an appropriate cartridge respirator is available), hard-hats, safety glasses/goggles/faceshields, gloves, boots, and coveralls.

Control and containment of spills. This training will depend upon the type of materials that are expected to be involved in an incident, the individual's evaluation of the hazard, and the type of personal protective equipment that is available. Training will include such things as closing of valves, replace cover, tightening fittings, repositioning of containers, and placement of ab-sorber materials.

Basics of decontamination. The need for decontamination of personnel and equipment and the procedures to be followed.

Familiarity with the site operating procedures.

Hazardous Materials Technician. These individuals are to be trained to respond to a hazardous materials release or potential release for the purpose of stopping the release. In the industrial plant, the plant-site fire department may be trained to this level. Industrial fire brigade members may be trained to this level, but only in unique operations, such as chemical plants or refineries. Their training must be at least 24 hours, equal to the first responder operational train-ing, plus include the following additional areas:

Implementation of the site hazardous materials emergency response plan. This training will include details of the plan, responsibilities, procedures, equip-ment, and systems.

Chemical hazards, reactions, and handling methods with emphasis on the materials that are normally on site. This training will include compatibilities, possible adverse reactions, and handling of various possible chemical emer-gencies.

Description, uses, and shortcomings of air monitoring equipment. This train-ing should include at least oxygen monitors, combustible gas monitors, and sample tube techniques as well as any other monitoring equipment that is maintained on the site.

Protective clothing and equipment. Technicians must be capable of deter-mining and using the appropriate protective clothing and equipment to in-clude the type of environmental suit that is required for the level of hazard. Training should include exercises in donning and decontamination of the clothing and equipment.

Self-contained breathing apparatus (SCBA). This training should include, types, uses, limitations, and inspection of SCBA. As with protective clothing, exercises in donning, fit checking, and use of the SCBA should be conducted.

Chemistry and toxicology of hazardous materials to include terms and reactions.

Hazard and risk assessment techniques. This training is to allow the technician to assess or characterize the situation, and it should include exercises in hazard evaluation.

Advanced control, containment, and/or confinement to include adsorbents, diking, overpacking, covering, and plugging and patching. Technicians must know the proper method to contain all types of accidents involving solids, liquids, and gases. This training will be in accordance with the equipment and personal protective clothing that is available to the technicians.

Decontamination procedures and exercise. This training should include donning and removal of protective clothing, setting up a decontamination area, decontamination solutions, and effectiveness of decontamination. Possible injuries should be included such as heat stress, chemical exposure, and other medical emergencies.

Hazardous Materials Specialist. These specialists have training and duties that are similar to the technician. Their duties require a more specialized knowledge about substances that they may be called upon to contain. For example, a plant that manufactures chlorine products may train specialists who are trained to handle chlorine emergencies. They would normally respond with and assist technicians as part of a response team. Specialists must have at least 24 hours of training equal to the technician level and must have additional training in the following:

Knowledge and implementation of the local and state emergency response plan. The specialist should be familiar with both plans and the proper notification procedures. The specialist should be able to develop a site safety plan.

Classification, identification, and verification of known and unknown materials. This training will be more in depth regarding air monitoring and survey instruments and involve more complex instruments than the training at the technician level. For example, a specialist in radiological incidents will have detailed training in radiation detection instruments and personal dosimetry. Training will include familiarization with various reference materials and outside sources of information and assistance.

Selection and use of personal protective equipment. This training may be more advanced than at the technician level or may include specialized equipment for unique hazards.

Advanced hazard and risk assessment techniques involving multiple hazards.

Advanced control, containment, and/or confinement to include adsorbents, diking, overpacking, covering, and plugging and patching. This training may be more specialized than at the technician level for particular materials or using particular equipment and techniques.

Decontamination procedures and exercise. This training may be specialized for particular materials or circumstances and should include donning and removal of protective clothing, setting up a decontamination area, decontamination solutions, and effectiveness of decontamination. Possible injuries should be included such as heat stress, chemical exposure, and other medical emergencies.

Medical Surveillance

Personnel who are expected to respond to hazardous materials emergencies at the technician or specialist level must be on a medical surveillance program. First responders may be required to be on such a program depending upon potential exposures in their normal work assignment. Additionally, employees who must wear a respirator in the course of their duties must be on the medical surveillance program.

Medical surveillance provisions dictate a medical examination upon assignment to one of the positions described above and at least annually thereafter. Examinations are also required at termination from a job assignment that requires medical surveillance, when the employee reports signs or symptoms that indicate a possible overexposure, or when an unprotected employee has been exposed in an emergency situation.

The extent of the medical examination will be determined in consultation with a physician based upon the type of hazardous materials to which the employee might be expected to be exposed. As a minimum, the examination should include a medical and work history with emphasis on the symptoms related to handling hazardous materials. The employee's fitness to wear any required personal protective equipment and to function under adverse conditions such as temperature extremes must also be ascertained.

Personal Protective Equipment

When establishing a hazardous materials response capability, one of the prime considerations is the protection of the responders. In the industrial facility where the inventory of hazardous materials may be limited, this job is simpler than for a public fire department that has to be able to respond to a diverse group of hazardous materials. Consideration must be given to the physical, chemical, and thermal hazards that might be encountered by the responders. These considerations must be incorporated into respiratory protection and protection against skin contact.

Respiratory Protection. The best respiratory protection is the self-contained breathing apparatus (SCBA). This equipment can be used in toxic environments as well as where oxygen levels are unknown or below 19.5 percent. SCBA should be the minimum level of respiratory protection in situations where the contaminant is unknown.

Air purifying respirators are devices that filter particulates and contaminants from the air. Filter cartridges must be selected based upon the type of contaminant. Therefore these devices can only be used where the type and quantity of contaminants are known. There must also be sufficient oxygen present in the air.

Chemical Protective Clothing. When selecting chemical protective clothing, careful consideration must be given to the expected chemicals that may be involved in an emergency, mechanical strength of the material, flexibility, temperature resistance, and size. No material provides satisfactory protection against all chemicals. Therefore, protective clothing selection is based upon the chemical substances involved and the manufacturers' recommendations. Not only must the clothing material be compatible with the expected chemical exposure, but it must resist penetration and permeation of the contaminant. Protective clothing is rated in terms of permeation rate and breakthrough time. Permeation rate is the quantity of chemical that will move through an area of protective garment material in a given period of time. Breakthrough time is the time required for the chemical to be measured on the inside surface of the fabric. Protective clothing must also be evaluated in terms of penetration of the chemical. Penetration can occur through zippers, buttonholes, seams, flaps, and as a result of physical damage to the material.

Thermal protection must be considered when the protective clothing will have to be used in conjunction with fire fighting operations. There are various types of thermal protection suits available that may have to be worn in conjunction with chemical protective clothing.

Levels of Protection. There are four categories of personal protective equipment based upon the degree of protection provided.

Level A. This equipment provides the greatest level of protection to skin, respiratory, and eyes. This ensemble includes pressure-demand, full face-piece, self-contained breathing apparatus (SCBA), or pressure-demand supplied air respirator with escape SCBA for respiratory protection. For skin protection, a totally encapsulating chemical-protective suit is required. Chemical-resistant steel toe and shank boots and two-way radio (worn inside the encapsulating suit) are also required.

Level B. This equipment provides the highest level of respiratory protection, however, a lesser level of skin protection than Level A equipment. The same respirator protection as the Level A ensemble is required for Level B. For skin protection, hooded chemical-resistant clothing is required. This could include coveralls, one or two-piece chemical splash suit, or disposable chemical-resistant overalls. Level B protection also includes gloves, chemical-resistant, steel toe and shank boots, hard hat, and two-way radio.

Level C. This equipment is for use when the type and concentration of contaminants is known and the criteria for using air purifying respirators are met. The only difference from level B protection is that a full-face or half-mask air purifying respirator (with appropriate NIOSH approval) may be worn instead of SCBA.

Level D. This is the lowest level of protection and consists of a work uniform. It is only used for nuisance contamination. Level D protection includes coveralls, chemical-resistant steel toe and shank boots, safety glasses or chemical goggles, and hard hat.

The Hazardous Materials Emergency Plan

Companies that are involved in the use, storage, processing, or manufacturing of hazardous materials should be prepared for emergencies that may arise during the course of business. Just as the 1970s found public fire departments ill-prepared for hazardous materials emergencies, many companies have not been prepared when disaster strikes.

A hazardous materials incident can result in serious injuries to employees as well as people outside the borders of the plant and damage to facilities, equipment, and the environment. Incidents can result in lawsuits and fines. Hazardous materials incidents are newsworthy and often result in bad publicity for the company. The key to effectively dealing with hazardous materials emergencies is the emergency plan. To be effective, the preparation of the plan must be assigned to a knowledgeable individual, have the support of top management, and be coordinated with the public emergency responders.

The completed plan should be the subject of training sessions with all affected employees, not only the responders. Area supervision should have a copy of the plan and all employees should know how to respond to any incident involving any of the materials that are used.

The plan should be documented in ready-reference format and adequately distributed so that anyone in the plant who might be involved in a hazardous materials emergency will have access to a copy.

Hazardous Materials Emergency Plan Components

Some of the basic components of an industrial hazardous materials emergency plan are provided. Each plan will vary depending upon the types of materials that are likely to be involved, the capabilities of the plant and public responders, and the location of the plant.

Objectives. The objectives of the hazardous materials emergency program and plan must be described.

Description. The plant-site emergency plan should be described to include the types of incidents and facilities that are covered by the plan, the composition and level of training of the team, the authority of the plan and team members, and the command structure of the response team. Also to be described are the resources available from other public agencies, private mutual aid industrial organizations, and cleanup and waste hauler contractors who are either under contract or on retainer.

Incident Classification. The expected types of incidents and materials that will be involved should be classified according to degree of hazard. This will include the level of response to each classification of incident. For example, the lowest level of incident may be so minor as to be handled by the personnel in the area without mobilizing the plant-site response team. The highest level of incident would be one that is beyond the capability of the plant-site team and will require response by several public agencies.

Incident Command Procedures. Procedures must be established for management of the scene of each hazardous materials incident. This portion of the plan should follow NFPA 471 as well as incorporating incident command procedures followed by the public response agency.

Hazardous Materials Response Team. The composition of the plant-site response team should be described in the plan. This portion should include others who may be involved such as health and safety, medical, operations, maintenance, management, and public relations personnel.

Emergency Controls. This section is used to describe the methods for controlling the scene of the incident including the use of control zones, barriers, and the use of security personnel. This section includes the establishment of a decontamination area.

Evacuation Plans.   The emergency plan must have an evacuation plan that accounts for all employees in the area of hazardous material usage as well as peripheral areas. The evacuation plan must accommodate changes in wind direction. As with the rest of the plan, the evacuation plan must be rehearsed.

Many companies and local emergency responders have teamed together to implement emergency planning and to conduct hazardous materials emergency drills. Companies that come under EPCRA requirements would be well advised to develop in-house plans as well as preincident plans with the local fire department. In-house planning must involve, as a minimum, the plant firesafety, safety and health, and public relations personnel. In the preplanning effort, do not overlook the facility's operations and technical personnel. The operations employees must be trained regarding the materials that they work with and immediate response activities when there is an incident in the area in which they work. Technical personnel may be able to provide technical advice during an emergency. The emergency plan should incorporate instructions for them to be available.

Notification.   Procedures must be established for notification of every employee and agency that might be involved in an emergency. Telephone numbers and responsibility for notification should be included.

Postincident Recovery.   Procedures that will maximize plant recovery are important. Arrangements and contracts should be established with hazardous waste cleanup and hauler entities so that this part of the recovery effort can be accelerated. Alternate operations areas and raw materials should be identified and listed in the plan.

TECHNICAL ASSISTANCE IN HAZARDOUS MATERIALS EMERGENCIES

There are numerous governmental agencies, industry associations, and private contractors that can provide assistance in an emergency. The facility hazardous material emergency program should list the resources that are available or that might be required to provide support in an emergency.

Chemtrec

The Chemical Manufacturers Association established the Chemical Transportation Emergency Center as a public service to provide information and/or assistance to hazardous materials emergency responders. CHEMTREC has the ability to track and cross-reference names, identification numbers, and contacting chemical manufacturers and shippers to assist in dealing with emergencies. They also maintain close contact with the Department of Transportation and other public and private organizations that are involved in responding to hazardous materials emergencies. CHEMTREC is available 24 hours a day, 7 days a week at (800) 424-9300. Another response organization that may be called into service by CHEMTREC is CHLOREP.

Chlorep. The Chlorine Emergency Plan is a voluntary program that is administered and coordinated by the Chlorine Institute to aid in chlorine emergencies occurring during transportation or at user facilities.

Chlorine producers provide personnel to provide advice and assistance for chlorine emergencies when notified by the CHEMTREC dispatcher. CHLOREP is available 24 hours a day, 7 days a week.

Community Awareness and Emergency Response (CAER)

CAER is a program that was initiated by the Chemical Manufacturers Association in 1985 in response to growing concerns of its members regarding the image of the chemical industries and preparation for chemical accidents. Its objectives were to increase public understanding of the chemical industry and to provide industry and local government with a proactive approach to engage in coordinated emergency response planning activities. CAER's objectives formed a foundation for EPCRA requirements in 1986, by establishing an interchange of information, planning, and training between industries and between industry and community emergency responders.

Industries that are involved in the CAER program in a community and the community itself benefit by sharing in hazardous materials response training, equipment, expertise, and technical information. The end result is improved fire and hazardous materials incident mitigation resources.

Other Sources

Various industry associations and most major chemical manufacturers provide emergency technical information and assistance. Material safety data sheets will provide the manufacturer's emergency contact person and telephone number. The preincident planning and participation in organizations such as CAER will identify other similar industries in the area that may be interested in forming mutual aid teams and equipment.

SUMMARY

As the inventories of hazardous materials in the workplace increase, the need for continued coordination and preincident planning becomes ever greater. Industrial fire protection officials must be aware of the hazardous materials in the workplace and be capable of dealing with emergencies or coordinating emergencies with the municipal authorities. They must also have a close working relationship with the industrial safety and industrial hygiene personnel who can provide technical advice.

Industrial facilities that use or store hazardous materials or may somehow be involved in hazardous materials emergencies must have an established program that is documented in a plan. When a plant-site emergency response team is to be formed, there are extensive requirements for training, equipping, and medical surveillance.

BIBLIOGRAPHY

Alexander, Glenn E. 1988. Environmental Consequences of Hazardous Materials Fires. Paper read at 1988 Fall Meeting of the National Fire Protection Association, 14–16 November 1988, at Nashville, Tennessee.

Code of Federal Regulations. 29 CFR 1910. 1987. Occupational Safety and Health Administration, Department of Labor. Washington, DC.

Daneker, James L., Captain, Los Angeles City Fire Department. Interview with author, Los Angeles, California, February 10, 1990.

Eversole, John M., Chief, Hazardous Materials Coordinator, Chicago Fire Department. Telephone conversation with author, December, 1989.

F.D.N.Y. Haz-Mat. 1989. Booklet published by the Fire Department, City of New York.

Fire Protection Handbook, 16th ed. 1986. National Fire Protection Association, Quincy MA.

Franklyn, Steve G. 1989. Mandatory Haz-Mat Emergency Response Training: OSHA's Final Rule. *Fire Engineering* 142(8):31–36.

Henry, Martin F., ed. *Hazardous Materials Response Handbook.* Quincy, MA. National Fire Protection Association, Quincy, MA.

Lesak, David M. 1989. Incident Estimation and Strategic Goals at Haz-Mat Incidents. *Fire Engineering* 142(8):89–96.

Martens, Keith. 1988. Responding Properly to Hazardous-Waste Spills. *Chemical Engineering* 95(1):87.

NFPA 471-1989. *Recommended Practice for Responding to Hazardous Materials Incidents.* National Fire Protection Association. Quincy, MA.

NFPA 472-1989. *Standard for Professional Competence for Responders to Hazardous Materials Incidents.* National Fire Protection Association. Quincy, MA.

Stringfield, W. H. The Final Rule. 1989. *Fire Command* 56(5):14–19.

Uniform Fire Code, 1988 Ed. Whittier, California: International Conference of Building Officials and Western Fire Chiefs Association.

13
INDUSTRIAL FIRE PREVENTION AND PROTECTION

INTRODUCTION

Many of the large-loss fires that occur in the United States every year are in manufacturing and industrial occupancies. As of the National Fire Protection Association's 1987 report of large-loss fires in the United States, large-loss fires were those that resulted in a loss of over five million dollars. During 1987, losses in manufacturing and industrial, storage and stores, offices, and public assembly occupancies accounted for about 69 percent of all direct dollar losses for large-loss fires. In 1988, manufacturing and industrial occupancies alone accounted for 61 percent of all direct dollar losses.

Fire losses in storage occupancies were particularly high during 1987 and 1988. During those years, fire losses for storage occupancies accounted for 20 percent of the total direct dollar losses for large-loss fires. There are increasing numbers of very large warehouses in the United States resulting in large concentration of values and very large loss when fire does occur. The warehouse fire loss problem will be discussed later in this chapter.

While industrial and manufacturing facilities may experience large property damage from fire, the number of fire-related deaths in these occupancies is correspondingly low. In the United States, there were 48 large-loss fires in 1987 and 54 in 1988 which resulted in a total of 23 fatalities. The deadliest industrial and manufacturing fires that occur usually involve an explosion. In 1907, 361 persons were killed in a coal mine explosion in Monongha, West Virginia. In the five years 1984 to 1989, there were four deadly explosions and fires in this property class, including a 1984 coal mine explosion and fire in Orangeville, Utah that killed 27; a 1985 fireworks manufacturing plant explosion in Jennings, Oklahoma that killed 21; a 1984 oil refinery explosion that killed 17, and a 1989 explosion and fire in a Texas polyethylene plant that killed 23.

While many large-loss fires occur in properties that have no fire suppression or detection systems, there are also those major fires that result from deficiencies in the suppression and detection systems which are present. In many instances, these deficiencies resulted from impaired sprinkler systems. There are also many cases where the fire load or hazard level of an occupancy has changed, but the suppression and detection systems have not been upgraded to meet the new demand. One such example occurred in a retail warehouse in Garland, Texas on October 8, 1987. The warehouse was heavily loaded with merchandise in racks 20–24 feet high. The fire, which was deliberately set, quickly burned out of control because the storage arrangement defeated the warehouse's sprinkler system.

SOURCES OF IGNITION

In order to prevent fires in any environment, it is necessary to eliminate one of the three sides of the fire triangle, or provide an environment in which the chain reaction cannot exist. Because there is usually enough oxygen in the air, it is difficult to control this side of the fire triangle. Fuels can be controlled in most situations; in some cases, though, it is not always possible to eliminate this side of the triangle. It is possible to identify causes, or ignition sources that initiate most industrial fires. This information can provide a basis for the industrial fire prevention program. By understanding common ignition sources, an evaluation can be made to determine the highest ignition risk areas on which to concentrate fire prevention activities. Probably the best source of information about fire ignition sources in industry is the insurance industry. Table 1-2 shows the causes of fires and explosions based upon data compiled by Factory Mutual over the period 1983–1987. It is fairly obvious from this data that a good portion of the industrial fire prevention program should be devoted to the detection and elimination of electrical deficiencies, smoking within buildings, and areas that might be susceptible to incendiarism. These three areas account for over 50 percent of all sources of ignition in industrial fires.

Electrical

There are three common ways in which electricity causes fires. These are circuit overloading, sparks and arcing, and electrostatic discharge.

Overloading. Electrical circuits are overloaded when the conductor is too small for the current demand. Increased demand on a circuit that is too small results in the production of heat. This definition implies that the conductor is defective, or at fault. Actually, the opposite is usually true. Most overloading incidents occur because someone misuses the system, resulting in the overload condition. Most electrical insulator materials are combustible at some temperature, so when a wire is overloaded and heats up, either the insulation will melt and begin to burn or combustibles in the vicinity of the wire may ignite. A common example occurs in the office environment when portable space heaters are used to supplement the building heating system. That practice may overload a circuit that is already loaded with other office equipment. Extension cords are another source of overloading. Extension cords frequently have multiple outlets that may result in overloading of the building circuits or of the cord itself. Extension cords may not be sufficiently heavy for the loads that are encountered in the industrial environment. In the 1974 fire in the Joelma Building in Sao Paulo, Brazil, the fire was ignited by an overloaded extension cord to a window air conditioner.

Resistance heating also occurs when electrical connections are loose or when corrosion buildup at a connection causes higher resistance and overheating. This condition can be avoided through preventive maintenance programs that include inspection, cleaning, and proper tightening of connections.

Electrical transformers are also subject to overloading and overheating to the point where fire or explosion may occur. Transformers are used to change the high electricity distribution voltages, as provided by the power company, to lower voltages that can be used by the consumer. Many industrial operations require onsite transformers. These transformers must be monitored, maintained, and protected against failure and fire. A fire in a transformer can not only result in damage to the transformer, but it may damage surrounding unprotected exposures and result in extensive business interruption. Even with fire protection, fire in a transformer will result in 75–85 percent damage to the transformer. Therefore, the major concern is to prevent secondary damage to surrounding equipment and structures. Transformers should be protected by circuit breakers, the load and temperature should be monitored, and the oil (in oil filled transformers) should be analyzed periodically. While transformers are generally under the control of the power company, in many larger industrial occupancies, the company may own and maintain the transformers.

Transformers should be separated from other exposures by fire walls, and they should be protected by fixed water spray systems.

Sparks and Arcing.   When current-carrying conductors are abruptly separated, when there is a short circuit, or when there is a ground fault, sparks may result. A common example of sparking occurs when an electrical switch is opened. Sparks can ignite the conductor insulation material or nearby flammable or combustible material.

Arcing is very similar to sparking. It occurs when electrical energy discharges across an air gap due to a break in electrical continuity in the connection to an appliance, or in switches and fuse blocks. When there is a poor electrical connection or there is poor metal to metal contact between conductors, arcing and heating takes place at the joint. When there is damage to the insulation on a current-carrying conductor current may arc across to a grounded object. If the ground return path is poor, an arcing ground fault may be created which may persist for a considerable amount of time. This results in excessive heating and the expulsion of hot metal particles, both of which can be sources of ignition.

Probably the most dramatic fire caused by sparks and arcing occurred in the November 21, 1980 fire at the MGM Grand Hotel in Las Vegas, Nevada. In this incident, flexible metal conduit, which was to serve as a ground, pulled away from the box connector at a junction box resulting in an ungrounded electrical circuit conductor. Sparking and arcing occurred when the ungrounded circuit conductor came in contact with the flexible metal conduit which shorted to metal structural members. Wooden structures within a concealed space were ignited and the stage was set for one of the most deadly fires in recent history. Sparks and arcing can also provide the ignition source for flammable vapors and gases and combustible dusts.

Cables. A particularly troublesome electrical fire hazard that has resulted in some large-loss fires involves wires and cables. There are many installations in which wires and cables are grouped together including junction boxes, cable trays, manholes, cable trenches, motor control centers, and similar installations. Usually, there is an insulation breakdown as a result of mechanical damage, excessive temperatures, vibration, moisture, poor connections, or surface deposits. Breakdown of the insulation results in arcing and overheating and ignition of the insulation. Most insulation materials produce a hot smokey fire which is damaging to electric and electronic equipment with which it is associated. An added hazard is produced by some insulation materials that consist of polyvinyl chloride (PVC) which produces hydrogen chloride gas during combustion. This, in turn, reacts with available moisture to produce corrosive hydrochloric acid. Fires are usually difficult to find because of the inaccessible nature of most cable installations.

The May 8, 1988 fire at the Hinsdale, Illinois Telephone Central Office of the Illinois Bell System is thought to have started in grouped cables. Although flames were contained to a small area, there was extensive damage to equipment from smoke. In addition to the estimated 40 to 60 million dollars damage to the building and equipment, there was extensive interruption of telephone service.

The fire is thought to have been caused by an electrical fault. An armored cable sheath became energized when it contacted a damaged dc power cable.

As is common in this type of fire, very thick smoke filled the building making finding and extinguishing the fire extremely difficult. The fire was further spread as burning cable insulation melted and dripped into burning pools.

In addition to the smoke, there were a number of factors that contributed to this fire. Although there was a smoke detection system in this unmanned facility, the alarms were misinterpreted resulting in a delay in fire department notification. Because of the critical nature of this facility, it had an uninterruptible power supply with no simple means of emergency shut down. This resulted in continuous power to the fire area and further shorting of cables.

Protection for grouped cables should include considerations of the following:

Protection for grouped cables should include automatic sprinklers. Where enclosures can be made air tight, halon or carbon dioxide room-flooding systems may be used as an alternative or in addition to sprinklers.

Smoke detection systems should be provided.

Power cables should be installed in cable trays separate from control, signal, and instrumentation wiring.

Where trays are stacked, the cables with highest voltage should be on top.

Dust, debris, and other accumulations should be kept out of the trays and away from other cable groupings.

Where conductors penetrate floors or fire cutoffs, provide fire stops.

Control and power cables for emergency equipment and systems should be separate from control and power cables for other equipment in order to maintain the integrity of the emergency equipment.

Electrostatic Sparks.   Sparks that are caused by electrostatic energy differ from the sparking described above, in that they are high-voltage discharges of very short heating duration. Heating duration in this case may be as little as a fraction of a microsecond. But the sparks are hot enough to ignite flammable gas, vapor, or dust–air mixtures.

Electrostatic sparks are formed when the electrical charge of a conductor is sufficient to bridge the gap to another conductor or nonconductor. Electrostatic charges are also generated through the movement of liquids through pipes, or when liquids are poured, and during the movement of finely divided or pulverized solids. Upon discharge, these static charges can cause ignition of airborne dust or flammable vapors. This is the reason that bonding and grounding, as discussed in Chapter 4, are so important in areas where flammable liquids are used, stored, and dispensed. Electrostatic ignition sources are also an important factor in operations that are capable of generating explosive dust concentrations as discussed in Chapter 10.

Spray applications of flammable and combustible liquids, as discussed later in this chapter, create possible static electricity hazards.

Many other industrial processes are capable of generating static electricity and must be protected, especially when flammable gases or liquids, dusts, or fibers may be present. Some of the processes include the movement of belts on pulleys; conveyor belts, especially those that transport very dry materials; coating, spreading, and impregnating operations; printing and lithographing; paper industry operations such as paper running through presses and over rollers; film casting and extrusion; and powder and dust handling or generating operations.

Smoking

Concerns about the health hazards of smoking are gradually reducing the numbers of smokers. Local ordinances and workplace restrictions are beginning to curtail the smoking activity in industry. But, until smoking is totally eliminated, it is going to be a major source of ignition.

In industry, there are fire and explosion hazard areas where smoking must be restricted such as flammable and combustible liquid usage and storage areas. Rules are violated by disgruntled or poorly trained employees and fires often result. Many times during firesafety inspections, evidence of smoking has been found in clearly posted "no smoking" areas. To combat this, some high hazard areas, such as propellant and explosive storage areas have requirements for employees to deposit matches, lighters, and smoking materials in a holding area before they are allowed to enter the high hazard area.

However, there will always be the accidental or deliberate incident of smoking in high hazard areas, making it equally important to emphasize control of the fuels that create the hazard.

Arson

In industry, many arson fires are set by employees or former employees. Frequently, revenge is the motive in employee-involved arson. Employees and exemployees are a particular problem because they are familiar with plant layout, critical operations, and the location and operation of protection systems. Storage and mercantile properties have been the most frequent targets in nonresidential cases of deliberately set fires. Storage occupancies offer large amounts of potential fuel in areas where there are seldom very many employees. The 1987 fire in a retail warehouse in Garland, Texas, described above, was an incendiary fire. Mercantile occupancies offer large amounts of combustibles in areas that are open and where it is simple for the arsonist to mingle with shoppers.

Probably the best protection against arson is a properly designed and installed automatic sprinkler system. Sprinkler control valves should be locked in the wide open position using sturdy locks and chains. Other safeguards include a well-trained internal emergency organization and a security system that includes roving guards. Automatic smoke, heat, and fire alarm systems are also helpful in protecting against incendiarism.

INDUSTRIAL FIRE HAZARDS

As one reviews the annual reports of large-loss fires that are published by the NFPA, there are common elements in the summaries of detection and suppression systems. In 1987 and 1988, there were a total of 102 large-loss fires in the

United States, not counting the 10 forest fires that resulted in large losses. In only 25 of these fires was there some type of automatic detection system present. In only 33 cases was there some type of automatic suppression system present. In most of the large-loss fires, these systems are either nonexistent, exist but are defective, or they exist but only provide partial coverage. This data, from NFPA's annual reports of large-loss fires in the United States would indicate the value of having automatic fire detection and suppression systems. It should be essential for all high-hazard or high-loss potential operations to be thoroughly protected by detection and suppression systems that are appropriate to the hazards. These systems must be well-maintained and frequently reviewed for adequacy.

Another common element in large-loss fires is the sources of ignition, as previously discussed. This information provides emphasis areas for the industrial fire protection program. Finally, after detection and suppression concerns are addressed and programs are in place to minimize ignition sources, it is necessary to address the unique high hazard or high loss potential areas.

COMPUTER ROOM PROTECTION

Automation has evolved to the point where almost every industrial and business operation has some form of data processing operation, from small personal computer (PC) applications to large mainframe computer operations that are housed in computer rooms or data centers. The applications for automation have also increased to the point where almost all aspects of business and industrial operations are automated. Many aspects of industrial operations such as payroll, inventory, design, planning and scheduling, process control, and quality assurance tests rely totally on computer equipment.

As the number and size of computer operations increased, the losses involving damage to electronic data processing equipment also increased. These losses are usually high while the actual damage to property may be quite minor. The reason for the high losses is twofold. Computer equipment is generally high value, and it is concentrated in environmentally controlled areas. The loss of computer equipment also represents substantial associated losses. Besides the loss of equipment, there are two other fire loss potentials including lost data and business interruption. The data generated by, or necessary for, operations is frequently stored with the hardware. A fire in the computer room will usually result in the loss of data. As automation applications have grown in industry, so has the potential for business interruption as the result of a fire involving data processing centers.

According to data reported to the NFPA and the National Incident Reporting System for the years 1981–1985, there was an average of 80 fires per year involving computer and data processing centers resulting in an average direct property damage loss of just over one million dollars.

Location

It is noteworthy that only about 37 percent of the fires reported in the NFPA report originated in the electronic computer or data processing area. This would indicate that fire prevention and protection efforts are concentrated in the high-value area but that peripheral support and adjoining areas may be neglected. For this reason the computer facility should preferably be located in a separate one-story building. Second choice would be on the ground floor or close to the ground floor of a multistory fire-resistive building. Computer facilities should not be located in the basement unless the building is adequately flood-protected.

The computer room should not be located adjacent to areas where hazardous processes are located unless positive protective measures are provided.

FIRE CAUSES

There were three major groupings of fire causes in computer room fires. These include electrical distribution system fires, other equipment fires (a category that includes computer equipment and could include other electrical causes), and incendiary or suspicious fires. These data pretty much follow the fire cause data for all fires, and provide areas for concentrated protection activities.

Many computer operations include battery backup power sources known as uninterruptible power supply (UPS) systems. There have been frequent fires recorded in these installations because of short circuiting of the batteries. These fires involving plastic battery cases and wire insulation and acidic electrolyte are, typically, smoky and corrosive. In situations where UPS systems are not provided with suitable fire separation and exhaust systems, the damage to computer equipment has been severe. Since the rate of incendiary-caused fires is high, most computer facilities should incorporate stringent security provisions.

Construction

Computer equipment is susceptible to damage from fire, water, smoke, and corrosive gases, therefore construction must attempt to minimize these contaminants. Although computer equipment contains some combustible parts and some fires have occurred in the equipment, most of the fires that affect computer rooms occur outside of the computer room in adjoining areas.

Computer rooms should be separated from other areas by fire-resistance rated walls and floors and ceilings having a rating of not less than 1 hour.

Special attention should be given to openings in floors and walls for cables and other penetrations that might allow the transmission of smoke and fire into the computer area from a fire in another area. These openings should be fire-stopped with a suitable material that has a rating equal to the fire-resistance rating of the penetrated structure.

Floor openings contributed to a $6 million loss to a data processing company in Massachusetts. Fire struck the four-story building in which this company was located in April 1976. Holes were cut in the floor slabs between the first, second, and third floors for the passage of electrical cables in steel conduit to serve the computer company. The holes were not properly sealed. When fire occurred in a first floor storage room, heat and smoke traveled up through the openings and caused extensive damage in the computer area.

Heating, Ventilating, and Air Conditioning

Several different types of air conditioning arrangements are used in computer rooms. The space under the raised floor may be used as a plenum chamber, carrying conditioned air for distribution up through floor openings, into each unit, and out into the room. Or, the opposite arrangement may be in place. Air may be drawn from the room, through the equipment and down into the plenum. A third arrangement includes an air conditioning unit built into a separate compartment of the computer equipment from which cooling air is circulated directly through adjacent sections of the computer and into the main room.

The computer facility should not share HVAC systems with other occupancies. If sharing is necessary, provisions should be in place to detect fire or smoke in adjacent areas and to activate isolation devices. Air ducts serving other areas of the building should not pass through the computer area.

Fire Detection

Normally, either ionization or photoelectric detectors are provided in computer rooms and in the under-floor spaces. Some very high-value facilities·are now incorporating the more sensitive incipient fire detectors.

It is generally necessary to provide detection systems for the space under raised floors, particularly if it is a large high-value computer room, if the raised floor material is combustible, or if there are many cables under the floor. This system, as a minimum, should provide audible and visual alarms. If an under-floor suppression system is provided, of course, it will be activated by the detection system.

The under-floor spaces are particularly susceptible to dust and dirt contamination necessitating periodic cleaning of the smoke detectors to minimize false alarms. To facilitate location of the smoke detectors for cleaning or maintenance, the floor panel section above each detector should be plainly marked. It is also recommended to locate floor-pullers around the facility in plainly marked locations.

Fire Suppression

All areas of buildings that house computer operations should be protected by an automatic sprinkler system. The necessity of automatic sprinkler protection in computer rooms is frequently disputed by those who are responsible for the equipment. However, it must be explained to these people that the sprinkler system is intended to control a fire to the site of origin, and without sprinklers, a small fire may turn into a major high-loss incident ultimately destroying not only the computer but the rest of the occupancy. It should also be pointed out that water-damaged equipment can, and has been cleaned and put back into service following a water-damage incident, whereas fire-damaged equipment is generally a total loss. There are numerous companies who specialize in cleaning and restoring water-damaged electronic equipment. Part of the prefire planning for a computer operation should include identifying such restoration companies that are nearby and are able to respond in an emergency.

It must also be ensured that sprinkler protection is provided in adjoining and support areas and that it be adequate to the occupancy.

Portable fire extinguishers should be provided in the computer room for control of incipient fires. Normally, carbon dioxide or Halon 1211 extinguishers are used because they would present minimum damage to electronic equipment. Support rooms that are used to store paper supplies should be provided with appropriately sized Class A fire extinguishers.

In computer facilities that are very high value, it is sometimes advisable to install a total room-flooding Halon 1301 system. Or, it may be preferable to provide only in-cabinet Halon systems for very high-value pieces of equipment. At any rate, all of the environmental considerations concerning CFC's, as outlined in Chapter 8, apply.

Most computer facilities are constructed on a raised floor. The area below the raised floor is used for running cables and wires and may be used as an air plenum to provide cooling for equipment. This area must have separate protection because it is shielded from the sprinklers by the floor. Raised floors are considered to be concealed spaces and, in buildings such as high rises where sprinkler systems are required, the raised floor area is required to be protected. In the past, halon systems have been provided for the underfloor area, particularly when the room contains high-value equipment, performs a critical function, or the underfloor space contains lots of cables. It must be ensured that openings to the under-floor area are sealed or can be automatically closed at the time of halon application so as to maintain the halon concentrations necessary to extinguish the fire.

Arrangement

As much as possible, the support functions necessary for computer room operations should be separated from the computer room enclosure. These support functions include offices, maintenance operations, stationery supplies, work stations, mechanical and electrical equipment, and data storage.

The extent of consolidation of these support activities in the computer room is dependent upon the value of the computer equipment and the criticality of the operation. Support activities all represent potential ignition sources or loss multipliers that must be separated from high-value or very critical operations.

Training/Operational Requirements

Personnel who work in computer facilities should be periodically trained and drilled in emergency procedures. Training should include the fire detection and suppression systems and operational requirements of the facility. Personnel must be informed of the detection system characteristics and their expected response should an alarm sound. Portable fire extinguisher training is especially important for computer facility personnel. When a halon fire suppression system is installed, personnel should be trained concerning operation of the system, and they must be informed about halon and its physiological effects upon people. Training must also include de-energizing of the computer system, closing of doors and salvage, including the use of waterproof covers.

There should be stringent rules regarding housekeeping, smoking, eating, and other activities that may degrade fire prevention efforts in the facility. One particular problem that arises during computer room operation is the removal of raised floor panels. Floor panels are occasionally removed to clean the underfloor spaces, to rearrange cabling, or perform other maintenance work. Personnel must be trained to replace these panels as soon as possible. In the event of a fire, halon concentrations below the floor cannot be maintained if floor panels are removed. There is also the personnel hazard that occurs when floor panels are left open and there is not proper barricading.

WAREHOUSE PROTECTION

Warehouses for industry and the consumer marketplace have had to grow in size and complexity, resulting in a wide variety of materials stored under one roof that may cover acres. As the size of warehouses has increased, so has the fire hazard and the lost potential. And, predictably, there have been an increasing number of major warehouse fires since 1977. These fires have been the result of changes in storage, new packaging concepts, increasingly hazardous storage, and the evolution of huge regional distribution centers. Table 13-1 lists some of the major warehouse fires that have occurred, the tremendous size of the warehouses, and dollar loss of the fires.

Major Warehouse Losses

A brief description of the warehouse fires in Table 13-1 will help to clarify some of the consistent problem areas.

Table 13-1.   Recent Major Warehouse Fires.

WAREHOUSE	DATE	SIZE (ft^2)	LOSS ($M)*
Ford Depot Cologne, West Germany	October 20, 1977	800,000	100
Montgomery Ward Chicago, IL	September 21, 1978	360,000	21
Supermarket General Edison, NJ	January 17, 1979	270,000	40
K-Mart Distribution Center Falls Township, PA	June 21, 1982	1,200,000	100
MTM Partnership Elizabeth Port, NJ	February 21, 1985	3,600,000	150
Sherwin-Williams Dayton, OH	May 27, 1987	800,000	50
Service Merchandising Co. Garland, TX	October 8, 1987	201,730	27
Safeway Richmond, CA	July 11, 1988	506,000	50

*Loss values are estimates for property and contents as reported at the time of the loss.

Ford Depot.   Fire in this automobile parts and accessories depot was caused by careless smoking. Storage was too high and sprinkler density was too low for the plastics and oils that were stored there. Other factors included sprinkler orifice sizes that were too small and temperature ratings that were incorrect, temporary storage that blocked aisles, and the lack of flue spaces between racks.

K-Mart Distribution Center.   This fire was caused by a carton of carburetor and choke cleaner that fell from pallet storage after a forklift truck had entered the aisle. Ignition was probably caused by the electric powered forklift which ignited spilled cleaner fluid. Although the warehouse was fully sprinkled and divided into four fire areas by fire walls, the high fuel load and exploding aerosol cans resulted in the fire spreading to all areas and overcoming the sprinkler system.

MTM Partnership.   The exact cause of ignition of this fire is unknown, although the fire is thought to have originated near an electrical panel in an area of the warehouse that contained 20-foot-high racks of aerosol products. The fire completely overwhelmed the sprinklers which were installed throughout the facility. Early loss of power to an electric fire pump also contributed to the loss.

Sherwin-Williams.   This warehouse was designed for the storage of paints and related flammable liquids. This fire resulted when 8 to 10 gallons of flammable liquid spilled while stock was being moved by a forklift truck. Ignition

Figure 13-1. Debris, including many ruptured flammable and combustible liquid containers, following the Ford Depot fire in Cologne, West Germany. (Source: Factory Mutual Engineering Corporation)

was from a spark from the lift truck. In spite of automatic sprinkler systems and emergency response of employees, the fire grew out of control. A major factor to the fire development was exploding aerosol cans.

Service Merchandizing Co. This distribution warehouse containing small appliances, sporting goods, toys, and baby furniture was destroyed by a fire that was of incendiary origin. The sprinkler system was of little value in controlling the fire due to the storage arrangement (too high) and the excessive amount of combustibles which were probably not anticipated in the design of the sprinkler system.

Safeway. The grocery warehouse at the Safeway complex was totally destroyed in a fire that was probably ignited by an overhead light fixture. It has not been established whether the light fixture had been damaged by forklift operations or the light malfunctioned. Although the warehouse was sprinkled, the fire overcame the system. A contributing factor in this fire was the height of the stock which prevented the sprinklers from getting to the seat of the fire.

Causes and Contributing Factors

There are some reoccurring causes and contributing factors of the major warehouse fires and other causes and factors that will provide some direction for warehouse fire prevention and protection. Some of the major problems include increasing fuel load brought about by changes in the type of commodity stored; exceeding the designed storage capacity of the warehouse, and inadequate fire protection which may or may not have resulted from the other two factors.

Changes in Commodity.   In many of the major warehouse fires, the composition of the products being stored had changed from the time that the facility had been designed. Metal, wood, cloth, and glass products have been replaced by plastic materials which introduce a greatly increased fire load. Metal products are being replaced by plastics. Cotton and wool fabrics are being replaced by more hazardous synthetic materials. Packaging materials are also changing to more hazardous materials. Paper packaging materials are being replaced by polystyrene foam and foamed-in-place packaging materials. Other packaging practices such as the use of plastic containers, shrink-wrap, and foam cushioning materials add to the fire load.

When the fires described in Table 13-1 occurred, the Safeway warehouse was over 30 years old, the Ford warehouse was 15 years old, and the K-mart Distribution Center was 10 years old. It is certainly conceivable that storage arrangements and commodity compositions changed during the life of these facilities.

Large multicommodity distribution centers can contain many materials of differing hazard levels including flammable and combustible liquids, tires, plastics, polyurethane foam materials, and paper products. A practice that is adding to the hazard of warehouse storage of flammable and combustible liquids is the increasing use of plastic containers. It is becoming more common to find bulk quantities of flammable and combustible liquids in polyethylene or polypropylene drums. Smaller packages of flammable and combustible liquids that are used at home and in industry are now stored and shipped in plastic containers. Tests have demonstrated that when exposed to fire, these containers soften, melt, and release their contents. This develops into a flammable liquid spill fire which is a severe, hard-to-control, flowing fire.

In some of the large fire losses, the fire protection was not designed for the highest hazard commodity and the high hazard commodities were not segregated into separate protected areas of the warehouse. Flammable and combustible liquids must be separated from other less hazardous storage into specially designed and protected buildings or rooms. These areas should have adequate sprinkler protection, noncombustible construction, and drainage to handle product spill and water from fire fighting. The storage height of these materials should also be restricted to levels that can be managed by the sprinkler system.

Exceeded Capacity.   Another problem facing the fire protection professional in protecting warehouses is the practice of increased storage capacity of the warehouse. Warehouse operators occasionally increase the storage capacity of the warehouse by adding additional tiers of storage or by storing materials in the aisles between the rows of main storage. These practices can severely challenge the effectiveness of a sprinkler system that was adequate for the designed storage arrangement. An added tier of storage has been demonstrated by fire tests and by loss experience to add significantly to the fuel load. Storage height was listed as a contributing factor in the Safeway warehouse fire. Because of the height of the stock, the sprinklers could not reach the fire and the fire grew beyond the capabilities of the sprinkler system. Height of storage was also listed as a factor in the Service Merchandise fire. In addition to adding to the fuel load, aisle storage aids in the spread of fire across aisles and can result in fire spreading ahead of the sprinkler system to the point where the system is overloaded. Aisle storage also impedes manual fire fighting and salvage operations.

Forklift Trucks. It is noteworthy that forklift trucks have been involved in the ignition scenario of several warehouse fires. In these incidents the trucks have not necessarily been defective, but they do present an ignition source which must be carefully controlled. Like so many other things, forklift trucks are necessary to warehouse operations, and since they present certain hazards, they must be protected accordingly. Driver training is as important as any operation involving forklifts. The Safeway warehouse fire is thought to have been caused by damage that was caused to a light fixture by a forklift. Witnesses indicated that it was a common occurrence in this facility for lights to be struck.

In Chapter 5, it was pointed out that the guide channels for rollup fire doors must be protected from being damaged by forklift trucks. A damaged guide channel will prevent the door from closing properly resulting in the spread of a fire from one fire area to another.

Aerosols. Further compounding the flammable and combustible liquid storage problems in warehouses is the use of aerosol containers. Again, there is dramatic evidence available from large-scale fire tests and severe loss experience from fires involving aerosols. There are numerous accounts of aerosol containers rupturing explosively, rocketing considerable distances with a trail of burning product and causing multiple fires. In the Sherwin-Williams, Supermarket General, and the K-Mart warehouse fires, aerosol containers of flammable liquids were listed as contributing factors to the fire severity and rate-of-spread.

Recently, because of environmental considerations, the use of nonflammable chlorofluorocarbons as a propellant has declined and the use of flammable propellants such as propane and butane has increased. Since as much as 90 percent of the product may contain propellant, this development is of considerable concern to fire protection professionals. As with flammable liquids, the safeguards for the storage of flammable aerosols includes isolation of these products in specially protected areas or rooms, reduced storage height, and adequate sprinkler protection that includes in-rack sprinklers for rack storage situations.

Warehouse Fire Protection

To properly protect a warehouse, it is vitally important for the warehouse manager to understand what is stored in the warehouse. This understanding must go beyond knowledge of the product. Warehouse managers must understand the fire hazard of each commodity in the warehouse including how it is packaged and arranged. When the fire hazards of the materials are understood, the protection that is provided should be evaluated. This evaluation should include such things as the storage arrangement, sprinkler system, and manual fire fighting capabilities. The way that materials are arranged in the warehouse will have an effect on the fire hazard. When materials are stacked solidly, the fire hazard will be lessened because there will be less surface area exposed to the air. Sprinkler water can easily reach exposed surfaces. Palletized storage, on the other hand, increases the fire hazard because the pallets create a horizontal air space which is more difficult for sprinkler water to reach. Solid and palletized storage arrangements are also more likely to collapse during a fire which is beneficial because it reduces the stack height, scatters the pile, and exposes more of the materials to sprinkler water and hose streams.

The greatest fire hazard is created by rack storage because the stored materials are surrounded by air and fire can travel in any direction. Racks allow much greater height of storage than palletized or solid arrangements. Racks are also much less likely to collapse in the early fire stages, thus the fire hazard is maintained longer in the fire scenario. All of the major warehouse fires listed in Table 13-1 involved rack or mixed rack and palletized storage.

Probably the most important fire protection element for warehouses is the proper design and installation of a sprinkler system. The sprinkler system must be compatible with the type and arrangement of the materials in the warehouse. This element must be reviewed periodically to ensure that neither stored commodities nor arrangements have changed to the point where the sprinkler system might require upgrading to meet the changing demands. Most of the large warehouse fire losses in the recent past have been the result of changing storage practices that exceeded the capacity of the sprinkler system.

There has been extensive study concerning sprinkler systems for warehouse protection. In-rack sprinklers have been developed to provide protection in the spaces within rack storage. Early Suppression-Fast Response (ESFR) sprinklers can be beneficial in warehouse fire protection because they discharge a large volume of water very early in the fire scenario to suppress the fire rather than control it.

First aid fire fighting may be beneficial in controlling a warehouse fire in its developmental stages. Employees must be trained in the use of fire extinguishers and small hoses. Many small fires have been extinguished by employees before the fires have reached damaging proportions. As in any other industrial occupancy, there should be documented emergency plans and an emergency organization. Extinguishers and hoses should be conveniently located, clearly marked, and maintained.

SPRAY FINISHING AND COATING OPERATIONS

The spray application of coating materials is common in many manufacturing industries. These operations are frequently conducted within a spray booth which is used to control vapors and overspray.

Paint spray operations involving the use of flammable or combustible materials present a significant fire hazard, whether the operation is conducted inside or outside of a spray booth. The vapors that are produced and the overspray materials that adhere to walls, ducting, and filter media create the fire hazard.

Spray Application Processes

Many coatings are suspended in organic solvents which generate volatile organic compounds (VOC). VOCs are frequently regulated by environmental air quality authorities requiring the use of application processes that minimize the amount of overspray. When the coating is a flammable or combustible material, the firesafety people are also interested in minimizing overspray. This is one area in industry where the goals of environmental compliance and firesafety are compatible.

When discussing the overspray and environmental concerns with spray coating operations, the term transfer efficiency is frequently used. Transfer efficiency refers to the amount of the coating that sticks to the object being coated versus the amount that evaporates into the air or is lost as overspray. Obviously, a process that gives high transfer efficiency is most desirable.

Air Spray. The most commonly used application process is the air spray. In this process, a flow of compressed air is used to atomize a fluid. Air is supplied by an air compressor at the point of spray application or by plant air. Since the air compressor may be a source of ignition, plant air is the preferred source. This process has always been the greatest producer of overspray since it is difficult to control the stream of coating material with the high pressures that are generally used.

With concerns for air quality, many operations are changing to a high-volume low-pressure (HVLP) application process which, because of lower pressures will result in higher transfer efficiencies.

Airless Spray. In the airless spray, high-velocity fluid flowing through a nozzle generates a fine spray. The high velocity of the fluid generates the spray rather than compressed air resulting in the generation of less VOCs, but still fairly excessive overspray.

Electrostatic Spray. Electrostatic spray operations may incorporate air and airless atomizers. In this process, a spray gun is provided with a high-voltage electrical discharge input. An electrostatic charge is imparted to the coating particles causing them to be attracted to the grounded conductive or conductive-coated workpiece. This type operation results in less overspray than common air and airless applications.

Another electrostatic application utilizes a disc or bell rather than a spray nozzle. The electrostatic disc is a sharp-edged disc that is electrically charged. During operation, the disc spins at high speed while fluid is slowly poured onto the surface. The centrifugal force spreads the fluid into a thin film. The film is disrupted by electrostatic forces and distributed in a 360 degree pattern. The electrostatic bell uses a bell-shaped applicator rather than a disc.

Powder Coatings. Another process involves the application of dry organic powder coatings. In this process, the powder is suspended in air and then electrostatically charged. The powder is directed onto the workpiece and held in place by electrostatic forces. The workpiece is then passed through an oven which melts the powder into a continuous coating. In this process no organic solvents are used to carry the coating and there is no overspray. The leftover coating powder is recoverable and reusable.

Spray Booths

Although a spray booth is easier to protect, fires still can and do occur in this controlled environment. While a spray booth is usually built with sufficient exhaust to prevent the buildup of flammable mixtures in the air, the filters that are intended to collect overspray can become a major fuel source when not replaced frequently. Interior surfaces of the booth and ducts must also be cleaned frequently to prevent accumulations of overspray from becoming a fuel source.

The booth and areas where paint spray operations are conducted must have electrical equipment that is approved for Class I, Division 1 locations. This includes lighting that may be provided inside the chamber. When lighting fixtures are built into the walls of the chamber so as to avoid the higher cost of explosion-proof fixtures, they must be inspected frequently to ensure that they are adequately sealed to isolate the light from the flammable vapors in the booth. Areas adjacent to the booth must be evaluated for possible electrical ignition sources for flammable vapors that may escape the booth. The rules for bonding and grounding must be carefully followed in the area of paint spray operations.

Sparks from metal tools that may be used in the booth are another source of ignition that must be protected.

An automatic sprinkler system must be provided in the booth. Spray booth sprinkler heads are protected from paint overspray with thin clear plastic wrap or ordinary sandwich bags. Unprotected sprinkler heads will accumulate paint overspray, rendering them either inoperable or, at least, slowing their operation time.

One person was killed in a 1988 fire that flashed through a paint spray booth where automatic electrostatic spray finishing of ignition coils took place. The paint that was used was a mixture of lacquer-based paint with a flash point of 74 degrees Fahrenheit and a thinner with a flash point of 54 degrees Fahrenheit. The booth had been shut down and work was in progress to install sprinkler heads in the exhaust ducts. When holes were drilled through the duct, enough heat was generated to ignite paint residue which had built up inside the exhaust duct. There were also paint residues on the spray booth, roof vent, and filters which accounted for the rapid spread of the fire.

This incident emphasizes the need for frequent and thorough cleaning of the interior of paint spray booths and duct work and changing of filters, particularly in situations where flammable materials are used.

Plastic Duct Work. Reinforced plastic ducts present a fire hazard when used in any industrial operation. Plastic is generally used whenever corrosive gas, dust, or mist must be exhausted from a building. Plastic is the most cost-effective substitute for corrosion-resistant metal alloys. Unfortunately, plastic duct work is combustible, and depending upon the installation, may introduce combustible materials into concealed spaces where there are no other combustibles. Duct work may penetrate fire-rated walls or floors. This duct work adds considerable fuel to a fire and enhances fire spread. Exhaust fans and blowers in the duct work further accelerates fire spread.

The best protection for plastic duct work is sprinklers that are both internal and external to the system. If the diameter of the duct materials is too small for internal sprinklers, they may be omitted; however, external sprinkler coverage must be complete.

METAL AND METAL PRODUCTS

The NFPA 1987 report of large-loss fires lists occurrences in metal and metal products facilities as accounting for 20 percent of the industrial and manufacturing incidents and 16 percent of the property damage. While fires in metal and metal products occupancies account for a large percentage of the losses, a review of the reports of these and other related losses reveal few causes and contributing factors that are unique to these occupancies. The sources of ignition in these occupancies follow similar frequencies as presented earlier (see

Figure 13-2. Plastic ductwork is susceptible to fire. It must be cleaned periodically and provided with automatic sprinklers. (Source: Factory Mutual Engineering Corporation)

Sources of Ignition). The fires caused by sparks from cutting and welding and from heating devices such as plating, heat treating, and melting operations are higher. As in most occupancies, housekeeping is frequently listed as a contributing factor in most reports of losses in metal and metal products facilities.

Machining

The cutting and shaping of metals is referred to as machining. Power-driven machine tools are used in all segments of industry. Although metal machining appears to be a rather innocuous operation, this perspective is misleading. Some metals are categorized as combustible (Chapter 3) and almost all metals will burn in air depending upon their size, shape, and quantity. The machining of combustible metals such as magnesium presents a fire hazard. Metal chips may be ignited by the machining process itself, or chip accumulations on the floor may be ignited by a dropped cigarette. Burning magnesium produces a very hot and smoky fire that, when not extinguished immediately, is very difficult to control. In a machining operation, chips may accumulate under machines and in other hard-to-reach places making a fire difficult to attack with combustible metal extinguishing agents. Burning metals generate a tremendous amount of heat, and they will quickly ignite other combustibles. The fire may burn through hoses containing hydraulic fluid and compressed air which will contribute to the severity of the fire. Housekeeping is particularly important in operations that work with combustible metals to minimize accumulations of ordinary combustibles in the area as well as chips and scrap that could contribute to the severity of a fire. An automatic sprinkler system is also necessary to control ordinary combustible fires that may be ignited by the burning metal.

The small particles that metal machining generates are called chips and fines. Fluids that are used as lubricants and coolants during machining operations may also be combustible. Heat generated by friction during machining processes can ignite the coolant/lubricant and small metal particles. Spontaneous ignition also may occur under certain conditions in which waste materials and oils are combined.

Most metal machining involves mechanical operations; however, there are some electrical machining processes known as electrical discharge machining (EDM) and electrochemical machining. In the EDM process an electrode and the workpiece are submerged in a dielectric fluid. The electrode is positioned very close to the workpiece and a direct current is pulsed resulting in a spark which melts and dislodges a metal particle. An EDM machine was responsible for a 1986 fire in Harrisburg, Pennsylvania, that resulted in a $65 million loss to a manufacturer of high-quality turbine blades for aircraft. The oil level in the EDM got too low and overheating occurred which led to ignition of the oil and the devastating fire.

There are a number of fire hazards that are inherent in machining operations including the following:

Chip fires at the machine, where ignition may be caused by the heat of the metalworking process, smoking materials, or electrical malfunctions. Chip fires are generally associated with poor housekeeping practices.

Spontaneous oxidation of cuttings or other oil-contaminated materials.

Fines that have accumulated in exhaust of vacuum systems or are due to poor housekeeping.

Reaction of some specialty metals that may react with water generating hydrogen and heat.

Combustion of hydraulic fluids that are used to operate some machining tools and equipment.

Combustion of oil vapors that have deposited on building structure or oil-saturated floors. This fire hazard can be minimized by proper housekeeping.

Housekeeping programs in metal working facilities must include control of cuttings and chips that may accumulate on and around machines. They should be collected periodically and placed in noncombustible containers. Metal dusts and chips also tend to accumulate on building structures and equipment surfaces and must be periodically cleaned.

Oil mists and vapors also tend to accumulate on building structures, equipment, and the floor and should be cleaned. Oily waste and rags must also be treated as a potential source of spontaneous combustion. Metal self-closing containers should be used to collect these materials.

Cutting and Welding. Cutting operations are defined as those that involve the use of a high-intensity thermal source to cut metals. Welding is the use of intense thermal energy to melt metal parts together. Cutting and welding operations have provided the ignition source for many industrial operations in the form of sparks and slag that are generated and are capable of traveling great distances. In recognition of this fact most insurance and industrial firesafety programs include some form of cutting and welding permit system and training for employees who are involved in these operations (Figure 13-3). Even with the training and permit systems, fires resulting from cutting and welding operations still occur on a regular basis.

Operations that are stationary and normally include cutting and welding are easier to control and consequently the fire incident rate is usually lower. Nonroutine cutting and welding operations such as maintenance and construction operations, on the other hand, are much more difficult to control and are the sources of most of the fires. Outside contractors and others who might be performing cutting and welding operations are the most difficult to control. Outsiders are unfamiliar with the facility and the inherent hazards of the facility. They are also not included in the facility training program. It is these operations that need the dedicated application of a permit system. Permit systems force the review of the work area by a third party. The person who is designated to issue cutting and welding permits is very important to the safety of the operations. Usually this person is a fire brigade member or a firesafety person. This is to ensure that a fire extinguisher is available, a fire watch is maintained, the area is free of combustibles, and holes through walls and floors or ignitable materials are adequately covered. Some of the precautions that must be considered when cutting and welding operations are to take place include the following:

Cutting and welding areas should be specifically designated and appropriate safeguards provided. When these operations must take place in other areas, a qualified person should be designated to authorize the operation (issue the permit).

Cutting and welding must not take place in flammable atmospheres, in close proximity to readily ignitable materials, on metal parts that have combustible coverings, or on metal with combustible sandwich-type construction.

Floors and nearby area should not be combustible. If it is necessary to perform the operations over a combustible floor or near combustible material, the combustibles should be wet or otherwise protected/shielded from the heat and hot sparks (Figure 13-4).

Openings in floors, walls, or ducts should be covered if they are within 35 feet of the operation.

A charged and operable fire extinguisher that is of appropriate size and class for the hazard should be in close proximity to the operation.

Trained fire watchers should observe during the operation and maintain the check of the area at least 30 minutes after the operation. If a fire watch was not required, the area should be checked at least 30 minutes after the operation.

WOOD, PAPER, AND RELATED PRODUCTS

The NFPA 1987 report of large-loss fires lists occurrences in wood, paper, and related products as accounting for 20 percent of the industrial and manufacturing incidents and 17 percent of the property damage. While occupancies containing wood, paper, and related products account for a large percentage of the losses, a review of the reports of these and other related losses reveal few causes and contributing factors that are unique. The sources of ignition in these occupancies follow similar frequencies as presented earlier (see Sources of Ignition, Chapter 1). The fires caused by sparks from cutting and welding, arson, and from heating devices such as furnaces and ovens are higher.

Fires are frequently ignited by cutting and welding operations in wood and paper products industries. This fire hazard is enhanced by the ready availability of ignitable fuels, particularly if the plant's housekeeping program is substandard. A good closely supervised cutting and welding program that utilizes training and a permit system is vital in these industries.

Housekeeping

As in most occupancies, housekeeping is frequently listed as a contributing factor in reports of losses in wood, paper, and related products facilities.

On April 16, 1984, fire caused an estimated $32.5 million damage to International Paper Companies' plywood manufacturing plant in Nagcogdoches, Texas. The source of ignition in this fire was an arc welding operation. Sparks ignited deposits of oil, pitch, and wood dust that had accumulated on equipment, catwalks, and wood structural members of the roof assembly. These accumulations allowed the fire to spread rapidly both above and below the automatic sprinklers.

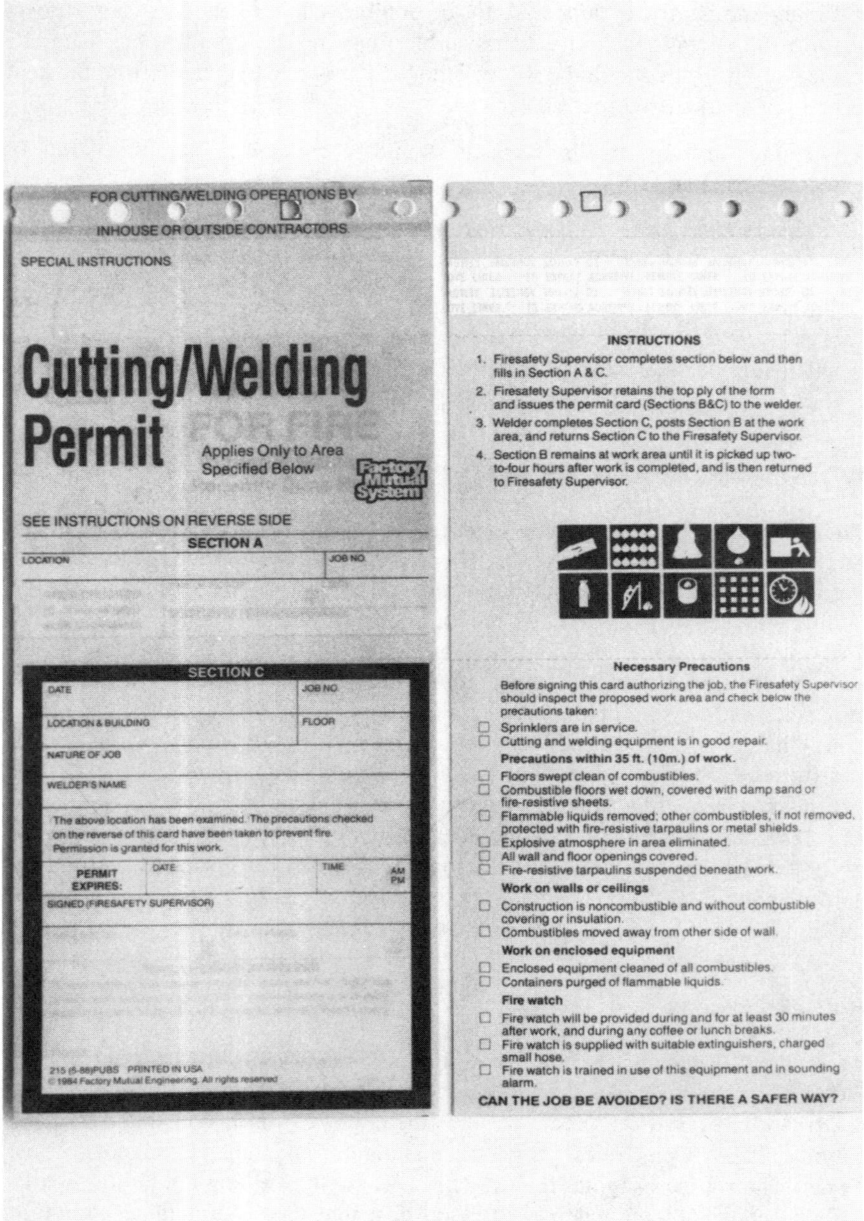

FOR CUTTING/WELDING OPERATIONS BY
INHOUSE OR OUTSIDE CONTRACTORS

SPECIAL INSTRUCTIONS

Cutting/Welding Permit

Applies Only to Area Specified Below

Factory Mutual System

SEE INSTRUCTIONS ON REVERSE SIDE

SECTION A

LOCATION	JOB NO.

SECTION C

DATE		JOB NO.
LOCATION & BUILDING		FLOOR
NATURE OF JOB		
WELDER'S NAME		
The above location has been examined. The precautions checked on the reverse of this card have been taken to prevent fire. Permission is granted for this work.		
PERMIT EXPIRES:	DATE	TIME AM PM
SIGNED (FIRESAFETY SUPERVISOR)		

215 (5-86)PUBS PRINTED IN USA
© 1984 Factory Mutual Engineering. All rights reserved

INSTRUCTIONS

1. Firesafety Supervisor completes section below and then fills in Section A & C.
2. Firesafety Supervisor retains the top ply of the form and issues the permit card (Sections B&C) to the welder.
3. Welder completes Section C, posts Section B at the work area, and returns Section C to the Firesafety Supervisor.
4. Section B remains at work area until it is picked up two-to-four hours after work is completed, and is then returned to Firesafety Supervisor.

Necessary Precautions

Before signing this card authorizing the job, the Firesafety Supervisor should inspect the proposed work area and check below the precautions taken:

☐ Sprinklers are in service.
☐ Cutting and welding equipment is in good repair.

Precautions within 35 ft. (10m.) of work.

☐ Floors swept clean of combustibles.
☐ Combustible floors wet down, covered with damp sand or fire-resistive sheets.
☐ Flammable liquids removed; other combustibles, if not removed, protected with fire-resistive tarpaulins or metal shields.
☐ Explosive atmosphere in area eliminated.
☐ All wall and floor openings covered.
☐ Fire-resistive tarpaulins suspended beneath work.

Work on walls or ceilings

☐ Construction is noncombustible and without combustible covering or insulation.
☐ Combustibles moved away from other side of wall.

Work on enclosed equipment

☐ Enclosed equipment cleaned of all combustibles.
☐ Containers purged of flammable liquids.

Fire watch

☐ Fire watch will be provided during and for at least 30 minutes after work, and during any coffee or lunch breaks.
☐ Fire watch is supplied with suitable extinguishers, charged small hose.
☐ Fire watch is trained in use of this equipment and in sounding alarm.

CAN THE JOB BE AVOIDED? IS THERE A SAFER WAY?

Figure 13-3. A three-part cutting and welding permit that includes identification of the job, signature requirements for the welder and the firesafety supervisor, and precautions. (Source: Factory Mutual Engineering Corporation)

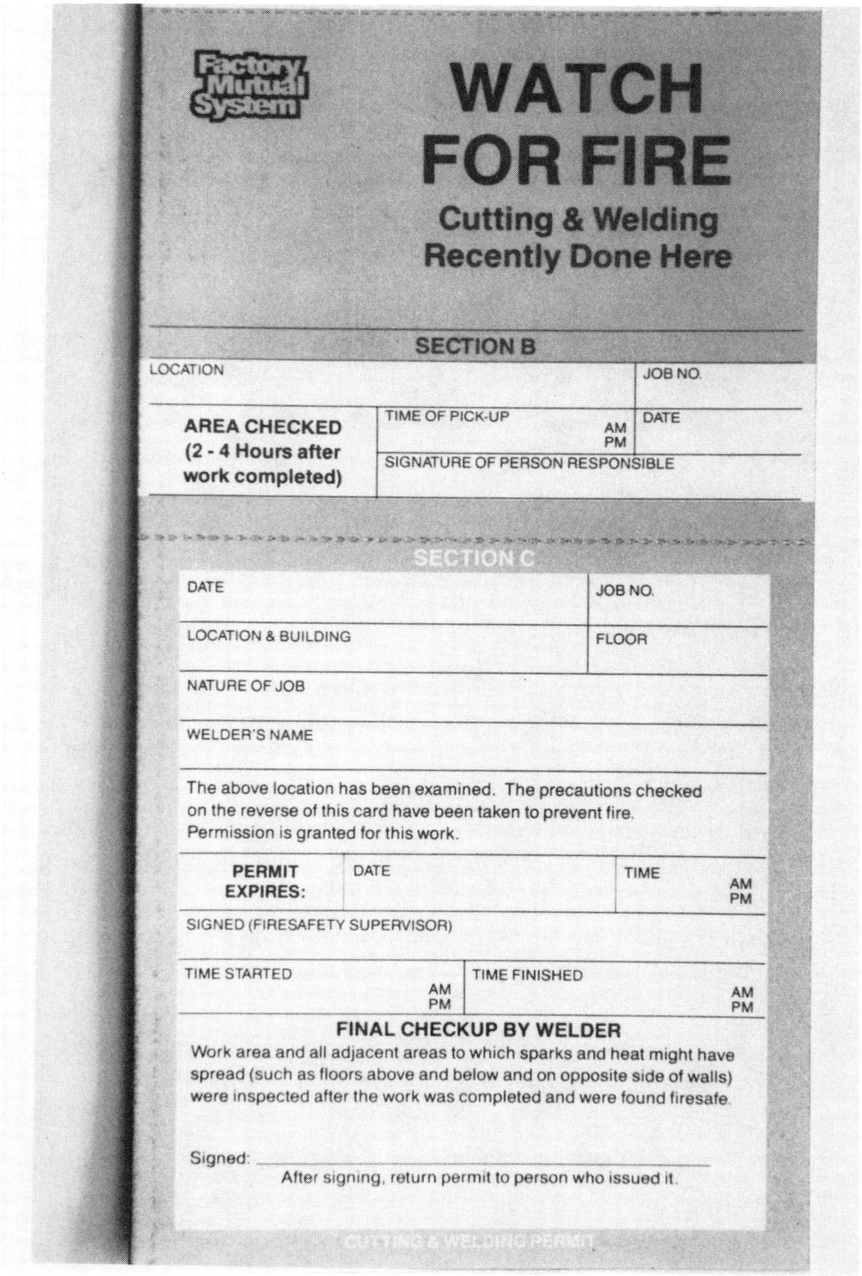

Factory Mutual System

WATCH FOR FIRE

Cutting & Welding Recently Done Here

SECTION B

LOCATION			JOB NO.

AREA CHECKED (2 - 4 Hours after work completed)	TIME OF PICK-UP	AM PM	DATE
	SIGNATURE OF PERSON RESPONSIBLE		

SECTION C

DATE	JOB NO.
LOCATION & BUILDING	FLOOR

NATURE OF JOB

WELDER'S NAME

The above location has been examined. The precautions checked on the reverse of this card have been taken to prevent fire. Permission is granted for this work.

PERMIT EXPIRES:	DATE	TIME	AM PM

SIGNED (FIRESAFETY SUPERVISOR)

TIME STARTED	AM PM	TIME FINISHED	AM PM

FINAL CHECKUP BY WELDER

Work area and all adjacent areas to which sparks and heat might have spread (such as floors above and below and on opposite side of walls) were inspected after the work was completed and were found firesafe.

Signed: _____

After signing, return permit to person who issued it.

CUTTING & WELDING PERMIT

Figure 13-3. *(Continued)*

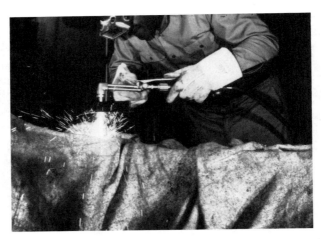

Figure 13-4. The areas surrounding cutting and welding operations must be protected from flying sparks. (Source: Factory Mutual Engineering Corporation)

In the wood products industries housekeeping programs are necessary to reduce the hazards of fire and explosions. A good housekeeping program should include the following:

Removal of dust accumulations from equipment, facility structural members, and floors using sweepers or vacuum cleaning equipment that is approved for Class I, Division 1, Group G locations as defined in NFPA 70, *National Electrical Code*.

Removal of loose bark, sawdust, and waste wood from the vicinity of generating equipment. The under-floor area in the vicinity of waste conveyors is an area that is prone to accumulations of combustibles.

Removal of metal scrap such as nails, band iron, or any wood containing metal from wood handling or processing equipment, the dust collection system, or the scrap wood hog.

Control of combustible hydraulic fluids, and sources of ignition in the vicinity of fluid use, by regular maintenance programs and cleanup of spills.

Frequent removal of oil and resin residue from board curing ovens and other equipment and facility structures.

Control of flammable and combustible liquids in accordance with Chapter 4 and NFPA 30, *Flammable and Combustible Liquids Code*.

The category wood, paper, and related products covers many industries and operations that are too numerous to elaborate in this text. However, certain similar operations occur in these industries which present common hazards.

Dusts. The various processes involving woodworking, and particularly wood pulverizing operations, produce dusts and chips that, if not adequately controlled, provide a ready fire or explosion fuel source. Dusts are generated by grinding, cutting, pulverizing, machining, sanding, and conveying operations, all of which are inherent in wood processing operations. Protective measures are the same as in other dust generating operations, including maintenance of equipment, magnetic separators, and dust control measures (see also Chapter 10, Explosions).

Ignition Sources. The wood and paper processing industries include numerous operational ignition sources such as ovens, heaters, and dryers and accidental ignition sources such as spark generating materials, electrostatic sparks, malfunctioning machinery, and cutting and welding operations.

Flammable and Combustible Liquids. Other factors that contribute to the fire loss problems in the wood and paper processing industries include flammable and combustible liquids such as paints, varnishes, adhesives, inks, and oils.

Hydraulic fluids may be present in presses that are used in the forming of particle board and fiberboard and plywood manufacturing and in mechanical handling machinery. Even if high flash point fluids are used, a severe fire hazard could result should these fluids leak under pressure and be exposed to a source of ignition.

A 1987 Oregon fire in a wood products mill began in a compressor room where it ignited hydraulic oil and sawdust and resulted in a $7 million loss.

Paints, varnishes, adhesives, and other finish materials may be flammable liquids and present a fire hazard. Although water soluble finishes are being developed and used to reduce the fire hazard as well as for environmental considerations, there are still many flammable materials being used. Finish materials are usually applied using a spray process which presents added fire possibilities (see section Spray Coating Operations).

Fire Protection

Automatic sprinkler protection is necessary for all parts of the wood and paper products industries. Areas that are subject to freezing may require dry pipe sprinkler systems. High-hazard areas such as hot presses and forming boxes used in particle board and fiberboard plants should be protected by deluge sprinklers systems. Roll paper storage areas require sprinkler protection. Special attention must be paid to the proper density depending upon the type of roll paper and the storage configuration. Water-type fire extinguishers and small hoses should be provided throughout wood and paper products facilities. Special extinguishing systems may be necessary for individual operations. For example, in areas where lumber is stacked, particularly when horizontal layers of stacked lumber are separated (stickered), an extreme fire hazard may exist in the form of horizontal flues which will result in a burrowing fire. This type of fire is very difficult to control. Large hose streams and powerful water supplies are required for fire control.

Special extinguishing systems are also necessary in some paper printing operations where flammable inks are used and electrostatic sparks may be generated. In these operations, automatic carbon dioxide systems are sometimes installed, and carbon dioxide extinguishers are necessary.

SUMMARY

In this chapter, some of the basic firesafety information that was discussed earlier in the book has been applied to some common industrial fire problems. This chapter is not, by any means, all inclusive in dealing with industrial fire hazards, but it is intended to get the reader started and help identify firesafety problem areas that will need further research and assistance. The firesafety person in any industry must become familiar with the fire hazards in that industry. Armed with a knowledge of the industry-specific fire hazards, the firesafety person can apply basic and specific firesafety guidelines to achieve fire protection. Additionally, the loss experience information that is available from the insurance industry and the National Fire Protection Association is valuable in identifying common sources of ignition and common sources of fire loss. This information will supplement the known fire hazards of the particular industry in providing emphasis areas for the fire prevention program.

BIBLIOGRAPHY

Anatomy of a Fire. 1979. 16 Pages, Booklet Item No. 7906. Factory Mutual Engineering Corp, Quincy, MA.

Best, Richard L. 1982. Investigation Report K Mart Corporation Distribution Center Fire Falls Township. PA June 21, 1982. National Fire Protection Association, Quincy, MA.

Best, Richard, and Demers, David P. 1982. Investigation Report on the MGM Grand Hotel Fire Las Vegas, Nevada November 21, 1980. National Fire Protection Association, Quincy, MA.

CFR 1910.107, Spray Finishing with Flammable and Combustible Liquids.

Cooper, W. Fordham. 1978. *Electrical Safety Engineering.* Butterworth (Publishers), Inc., Boston.

Giarmita, Richard. 1988. Report of Building Fire No. 7105, Safeway Warehouse, July 11, 1988. Richmond Fire Department, Richmond, CA.

Hall, John R. 1988. Selections from The U. S. Fire Problem Overview Report through 1987, Leading Causes and Other Patterns and Trends, Industrial and Manufacturing Facilities. National Fire Protection Association, Quincy, MA.

Industrial Fire Hazards Handbook, 2nd ed. 1984. National Fire Protection Association, Quincy, MA.

Isner, Michael. 1989. Fire Investigation Report, Telephone Central Office, Hinsdale, Illinois, May 8, 1988. National Fire Protection Association, Quincy, MA.

Isner, Michael. 1987. Investigation Report, Flammable Liquid Warehouse Fire Dayton, Ohio, May 27, 1987. National Fire Protection Association, Quincy, MA.

Loss Prevention Data 5-31. 1976. Cables and Bus Bars. Norwood, MA: Factory Mutual Engineering Corporation.

Loss Prevention Data 5-32. 1978. Electronic Computer Systems. Norwood, MA: Factory Mutual Engineering Corporation.

Mullen, Ronald R. 1988. Flash Fire During Sprinkler System Alteration. *Fire Command* 55(4):43–36, 41.

NFPA 75-1989. *Standard for the Protection of Electronic Computer/Data Processing Equipment.* National Fire Protection Association, Quincy, MA.

NFPA 77-1988. *Recommended Practice on Static Electricity.* National Fire Protection Association, Quincy, MA.

NFPA 664-1987. *Standard for the Prevention of Fires and Explosions in Wood Processing and Woodworking Facilities.* National Fire Protection Association, Quincy, MA.

Sotis, Louis P. 1989. Commodities and Storage Arrangements. *Record* 66(3):13–18.

Sotis, Louis P. 1986. Ignition Sources: Recognizing the Causes of Fire. *Record* 63(3):11–18.

Sotis, Louis P. 1986. Warehouse Storage: Old Problems and New Challenges. *Record* 63(2):3–10.

Standard for Fire Protection of DOE Electronic Computer/Data Processing Systems. 1984. Prepared for: U.S. Department of Energy Assistant Secretary, Policy, Safety, and Environment Office of Operations Safety, Washington, D.C.

Standard Practice for the Fire Protection of Essential Electronic Equipment Operations. 1978. U.S. Department of Commerce National Fire Prevention and Control Administration, Washington, D.C.

Taylor, K.T. 1988. Special Report on Computer and Data Processing Centers, 1981–1985 Fire Experience. Quincy: National Fire Protection Association.

Taylor, K.T., and Norton, L.L. 1988. Large-Loss Fires in the United States During 1987. *Fire Journal* 82(6):24–38

Taylor, K.T., and Tremblay, Kenneth. 1989. Large-Loss Fires in the United States During 1988. *Fire Journal* 83(6):58–81.

Thomas, Susan. 1984. Arson: Not Only for Profit. *Record* 61(3):14–20.

Tuve, Richard L. 1976. *Principles of Fire Protection Chemistry.* National Fire Protection Association, Quincy, MA.

14
THE INDUSTRIAL FIRE PREVENTION AND PROTECTION PROGRAM

Many companies lack a formal fire protection program. Fire protection concerns are frequently delegated to someone as an additional duty. Since there are fire prevention requirements in OSHA, the responsibility for firesafety frequently falls to the safety organization. When these companies do have a fire emergency, their losses are usually greater because they are not adequately prepared.

There is a growing need for every industrial operation, regardless of the size and complexity, to have some form of fire prevention and protection program. This is necessitated by the concentration in industry of expensive machinery, equipment, processes, and stock and by the need to protect employees. Provisions must be in place for fire prevention and fire protection. Fire prevention includes those activities to eliminate fire hazards by housekeeping, training, and preventive maintenance activities. Fire protection includes those activities aimed at controlling fire once it occurs: fire suppression systems and equipment, prefire planning, and training.

The primary goal of the industrial fire protection program is to minimize those conditions and situations that may result in a fire. Other goals include preparing the organization for those other occurrences that may result in losses. The broad objective of the program is to provide optimum protection of life, property, production base, and vital records. The degree of protection is consistent with the value at risk, operational effectiveness, and reasonable cost. To achieve these goals and objectives, the fire prevention and protection program must be integrated into all operations and functional areas of the organization.

The program seeks to identify and correct those situations through an inspection and corrective action program and a workforce that is trained to recognize and correct hazardous conditions. Another part of the program is the establishment of a plant site emergency organization that is trained and has the necessary equipment to react to emergencies in the plant. The overall program creates a firesafety awareness in all employees so that they can all participate in the program.

By definition, the industrial fire protection program has goals that are similar to the safety program and the two have joint legal requirements to provide a safe work environment. In fact, in many organizations, the two functions of occupational safety and firesafety are combined. Whatever the organizational structure, the two functions require very close coordination and communications.

Ultimate responsibility and accountability for the program rest with the chief operating official. Based upon information and recommendations provided by middle management, executive managers determine the scope of the fire protection program. Once the executive official has determined the level of protection to be maintained, the amount of risk to be insured, and the acceptable operating risk, responsibilities must be delegated to each level of management. Each manager must be held accountable for the fire prevention and protection programs in their area of responsibility. This is probably the most important requirement of the program, that it have the full support and involvement of all levels of management.

The industrial fire protection program should be established based upon the individual plant site. It should address those hazards and possible emergencies that are applicable for that site. It should address the operations and materials that are indigenous to that industry, location of the site, and the availability of outside emergency support.

INDUSTRIAL FIRE PREVENTION

The purpose of the industrial fire prevention part of the program is to minimize or eliminate fire hazards and therefore fire by engineering firesafe operations, increasing the firesafety awareness of everyone in the plant site, and incorporating inspections and procedures to identify and correct fire hazards. The fire prevention program requires a coordinated program that incorporates these three elements and is integrated into all aspects of the operation. This coordinated program should be one that fosters communications between all parts of the organization as well as the involvement of every employee.

Engineering

The engineering aspect of the firesafety program includes the consideration of firesafety in facility design and construction, process reviews, materials and equipment procurement, and maintenance activities. Engineering is the basis of the firesafety program, as it provides basic facilities, processes, materials, and equipment for the operation.

Facility Design Reviews. The design of the basic facility as well as modifications are required to meet applicable codes. However, it must be recalled that codes are minimum requirements; they do not ensure firesafety. It is necessary for a firesafety professional who is familiar with the particular industrial operation to review the facility designs to ensure that, not only the code requirements are met, but that where necessary, the designs go beyond the codes to ensure optimum firesafety. The person who is charged with this responsibility must be familiar with and incorporate all of the applicable fire codes and regulations, including local and state building and fire codes and standards, NFPA standards, OSHA regulations, insurance carrier requirements, and company policies.

Process Controls.   Many of the fire hazards that are faced by an industrial operation may be inherent in the processes that take place in that operation. Processes may involve fire hazardous materials, toxic chemicals, ignition sources, or these three together. The organization's technical staff who establish the materials and processes to be used must include firesafety considerations as they do quality, product requirements, and employee health and safety, and they must implement controls accordingly. These considerations must be made in coordination with the person who is responsible for firesafety. Process controls may include procedural controls, material substitutions, and equipment controls.

Many times the processes that a company uses are documented in engineering instructions, protocols, plans, or procedures. These documents must include not only materials and process instructions, but safety and fire safety controls and precautionary instructions. Contingency plans should also be documented, and they should be compatible with existing site emergency/prefire plans.

In many cases, it may be appropriate to substitute materials in a process or operation to achieve greater firesafety. Substitution is frequently a consideration in achieving employee safety, health, and environmental compliance. Firesafety must be included in these considerations. This activity may result in a dilemma. Materials that are selected to achieve employee safety, health, and environmental compliance may be flammable or combustible. If the overriding concern is safety, health, and environmental, then procedural or equipment controls will be necessary to achieve firesafety.

Procedural controls will include handling precautions, storage and quantity-on-hand limitations, and contingency plans. Equipment controls must also be included in the development of materials and processes. Equipment controls include such things as electrical ignition safety, over-temperature and pressure devices, spill control and containment, and automatic detection and suppression equipment.

Procurement Controls.   Procedures must be established to include the evaluation of firesafety in the procurement of materials and equipment. This should be an integral part of the procurement function. The procurement function includes purchasing, procurement, and materials management. The important elements of procurement which impact firesafety include quality, quantity/inventory control, pricing, and receiving inspections. Materials and equipment of the appropriate quality are necessary to firesafety. Inferior quality machinery parts may cause premature breakdown and possible fire hazards. Materials that are purchased as "fire retardant treated" must be properly treated so that the intended fire-resistant characteristics may be relied upon. This may require the procuring organization to conduct source testing or receiving inspection and testing to validate the appropriate levels of fire retardant.

Control of inventory is important to the firesafety of the organization. When excess quantities of fire hazardous or combustible materials are purchased and storage capabilities are exceeded, existing fire protection systems will not be adequate. When shortages occur due to inadequate inventories, inferior substitute materials may be used which have different burning characteristics and may contribute to fire hazards.

Cost-benefit decisions are key to the purchasing function and firesafety considerations should be integrated into this decision-making process. Lower prices may result in more hazardous materials and substandard equipment. Fire protection systems may be purchased that are inexpensive, but they may not have the appropriate characteristics for optimum performance that a more expensive system would provide.

Inspection of incoming material and equipment is an important part of the procurement function. Fire hazards may be created when hazardous materials are improperly received and unpacked. Some hazardous materials such as in glass bottles are best left in their shipping packages until used.

Maintenance.   Once firesafety has been designed and constructed into the facility, it is necessary to maintain the facility and equipment to its intended level of firesafety. Fire detection and suppression equipment must be maintained so that it will function reliably when fire occurs. Over-temperature and pressure devices must be checked and maintained periodically as well as liquid level sensors.

A good preventive maintenance program will not only keep production equipment operating, but help to avoid fire ignition sources such as burned out drive belts, overheated bearings, and failed hydraulic fluid hoses. A preventive maintenance program should include documentation of organization, equipment inventories, maintenance schedules, and actions. As any other organization, the maintenance function requires specific assignment of responsibilities and accountability and controls to ensure completeness, timeliness, and effectiveness of the program. With the high rate of electrically caused industrial fires, it should be obvious that electrical preventive maintenance requires a high priority.

The maintenance department needs to have a certain amount of authority to intercede when conflicts arise between production schedules and the accomplishment of preventive maintenance activities.

Training

The majority of losses that occur in industry are either caused by, or contributed to by the human element. These are cases where the actions or inactions by employees are a significant factor in the loss scenario. The second part of the fire prevention program is increasing the level of awareness in the organization in order to minimize the human element in the fire loss scenario.

Training programs are a method of creating a greater awareness on the part of people in the organization. Training must stress housekeeping, equipment maintenance and operation, and employee emergency response activities. Firesafety should also be integrated into other training programs such as new employee orientations, safety, equipment operation and maintenance, process, and quality. Specific firesafety training should include fire extinguisher handling, use of fire suppression equipment, response to emergencies, and special hazard procedures. Not only does the training teach employees specific actions, but it has ancillary value in increasing awareness of fire hazards, both on and off the job. The purpose of the training program is to create a firesafety awareness in all employees and an attitude that firesafety is a part of their jobs and necessary to protecting their lives and livelihood.

Training programs should not neglect management and supervision. These people can be much more effective in contributing to the plant's firesafety program if they have some basic loss control training.

Training materials and instructional assistance is generally available through the property loss insurance carrier, workers' compensation insurance carrier, NFPA, National Safety Council, and commercial sources. Many municipal fire departments can also provide assistance in training employees.

Enforcement

The plant's firesafety program will include a certain number of rules that employees are expected to follow such as smoking, use of safety/firesafety equipment and safeguards, and rules regarding acceptable behavior.

Inspections. Inspections are an integral part of the firesafety program. Large plants may have full-time fire inspectors or fire professionals who conduct firesafety inspections. Smaller plants may integrate firesafety into the safety inspection program. Inspections may also be conducted by the members of the firesafety committee, or jointly with each member supporting his or her supervisor on an inspection. Firesafety can also be integrated into other inspection programs, such as quality, production operations, and management inspections. The person who is responsible for firesafety may want to initiate a program of periodic management firesafety and housekeeping inspections. It is generally helpful for the firesafety professional to prepare an inspection checklist for use by inspectors who do not have full-time firesafety responsibilities. Items to be covered by a checklist would include as a minimum, the following:

Building conditions
Unprotected openings in vertical or horizontal structures
Condition of fire doors and automatic closing devices

Life safety
Adequacy of exits
Accessibility of exits
Condition of exit facilities such as panic hardware
Existence of evacuation procedures and diagrams
Operation of emergency lights

Common firesafety hazards
Heating, ventilating, and air conditioning
Housekeeping
Smoking practices
Condition of electrical equipment including cords, plugs, and outlets

Special process hazards
Flammable and combustible liquids and flammable gases
Dust and lint producing operations
Paint spray operations
Welding and cutting operations
Other hazardous materials

Fire alarm and detection systems
Evacuation alarm systems
Smoke and heat detection systems
Alarm systems

Fire extinguishing systems and equipment
Automatic sprinkler systems
Special extinguishing systems
Portable fire extinguishers
Standpipes and hose systems

Inspections may also be made by outside organizations including the property loss insurance company, the municipal fire department, state or federal OSHA, or outside consultants. All of these can be helpful as expert reviews, or just another pair of eyes that may look at things a little differently. OSHA compliance officers may issue citations when they find life threatening or serious deficiencies.

Whoever does the inspection, the results must be documented, distributed to the responsible parties and management, and corrective actions initiated. Then, there must be followup to ensure that corrective action is adequate, complete, and that the problem does not reoccur. Without this followup, should an accident occur, management could be criminally responsible for failure to correct the problems.

Housekeeping

Fires cannot burn without fuel. If unnecessary combustibles are removed and all employees are encouraged to support the housekeeping program, fire may not occur even when an ignition source is present. Like any other program, the housekeeping program requires the involvement of all levels of management and supervision. The manager who condones poor housekeeping, and the supervisor who allows poor housekeeping in his area can destroy the housekeeping effort in a plant and cause severe fire hazards.

The housekeeping program must address the removal of accumulations of combustibles from work areas, storage areas, offices, and outside areas of buildings. The buildup of lint, dust, and oil on machinery can provide fuel for a stray spark. Operators must be encouraged to keep their work areas and machinery clean.

A smoking policy must be in place that clearly defines those areas where smoking is not allowed, such as flammable and combustible liquid storage areas, warehouses, and other areas where excessive combustibles are present.

The housekeeping program must also address the storage of equipment and materials so that obstructions are not created in front of emergency equipment such as fire extinguishers and hoses, sprinkler systems, and exit aisles and doors.

Investigation

The investigation of fire incidents is as important to the firesafety program as accident investigations are to the safety program. An investigation program that identifies causes and establishes corrective actions will support the overall fire prevention effort. The purpose of the fire investigation is to identify the origin, or place where the fire began, and the cause of the fire. The cause of the fire includes such factors as the fuel involved in the ignition sequence, the form of heat of ignition, the source of heat of ignition, and human interactions that caused or contributed to the severity of the fire. The causes of fire can be one of four classifications including acts of God, accidental, undetermined, and incendiary. An act of God fire would include those that were caused by lightning or as a result of an earthquake. An accidental fire would include those that are unintentional and explainable. An undetermined fire is one in which the cause is unknown or unidentifiable. An incendiary fire is one that is intentionally set.

The results of the investigation will provide information concerning the cause or need for further investigation as in the case of undetermined and incendiary

Figure 14-1. Poor housekeeping was a factor in the loss of this industrial facility. (Photo: Alan Simmons)

fires. The investigation will also result in recommendations for corrective actions to prevent reoccurrence of the fire incident, or similar fire incidents, will highlight requirements for training, and will indicate other necessary changes to the firesafety program. There are basically three types of fire investigations including the basic, technical, and arson investigation.

Basic Investigation. A basic investigation is conducted following every fire incident. As the name implies, it addresses the basics of cause resulting damage and injuries, and recommendations for corrective actions. The basic investigation is generally conducted by the municipal fire department in order to fulfill necessary reporting and recordkeeping requirements. The facility that suffered the incident should assist in, or supplement, the basic investigation so as to provide pertinent operational and procedural information and to determine in-house corrective actions. In most cases, the basic investigation is the only investigation in which the plant will have the capability to participate.

Regardless of who does the formal investigation, there are some things that the plant fire personnel can begin doing during the fire and immediately after the fire that will facilitate the investigation. These initial investigative actions include recording observations, photography, gathering witness statements, and review of records.

Recording of observations includes appearance of the fire scene during the fire such as appearance of the fire and smoke, position and status of plant equipment, status of doors and windows, operation of automatic fire suppression equipment, actions of plant personnel, and anything else that may be out of the ordinary. Much of this information will also be developed through the witness interrogation process. When the plant has a photography capability, pictures will greatly assist in the fire investigation process. Photography should begin as soon as possible after discovery of the fire. Pictures should include all aspects of the fire, fire fighting efforts, and post-fire damage and cleanup activities. During the investigation, pictures of evidence and other critical items will be necessary. When arson is a possibility, pictures of onlookers are essential to the investigation.

Pictures are indispensable during the investigation for validating witness statements, demonstrating fire spread, and showing the position of doors and equipment that might later be moved by fire fighters or during salvage efforts.

The interrogation of witnesses should begin as soon as possible. This process should begin even as fire suppression is underway. Safety personnel and security personnel who are trained in investigation techniques can be utilized for this process. As time passes, the witnesses will forget, will collaborate with other witnesses, and will begin to interpret what they saw. Therefore, the best information will be that which is collected immediately after the incident.

The investigation will include a review of the records to determine such things as processes and machinery that were in operation, maintenance data, training records, and other operational data.

Technical Investigation.   The technical investigation is an in-depth investigation that is usually performed by experts from outside the organization. Experts may be provided by the insurance carrier or they may be fire protection consultants. Technical investigations are usually performed when there has been a major incident resulting in excessive property damage, many injuries, or fatalities. In some cases, it may not be possible to determine the cause of the fire with the capabilities of the basic investigation. Experts may be required in such areas as electrical engineering, metallurgy, or thermal engineering. Additionally, the services of an analytical laboratory may be necessary.

Arson Investigation.   The basic or technical investigation may reveal the possibility of the fire having been deliberately set. In fires that are incendiary in origin, local or state officials or insurance companies may get involved or be requested to investigate since arson is a deliberate criminal act.

Communications

Communications are a necessary part of the industrial fire protection program. Internally, there must be good communications between staff and line functions and with all levels within the organization.

Externally, communications are necessary with the public fire department, property loss insurance organizations, and other governmental agencies. Probably the most important external communications for the fire protection program are with the public fire department. These communications include the preparation and review of prefire plans, business plans, facility and operational changes, and joint drills. The public fire department will be much more effective when the company's plan calls for early notification of the fire department and when there is a comprehensive, rehearsed preincident plan. The municipal fire department must also have advance knowledge of the hazardous materials and operations that are on the premises which includes amounts and locations of hazardous materials.

Committees. Safety and firesafety committees are effective methods of promoting communications in the plant's firesafety program. An employee firesafety committee should be formed in each industrial facility or, as a minimum, firesafety should be integrated into the employee safety committee. Employee safety committees are excellent means of creating firesafety awareness in employees. They can be used as employee training forums, and they provide excellent feedback for the firesafety professional. Committee members should be recognized for their efforts, encouraged to solicit suggestions from their coworkers, and should help supervision with the local work area firesafety program.

Firesafety should also be integrated into other committees on the plant site such as management committees, safety/firesafety/facilities committees, and other specialty committees that may exist. The firesafety professional should be a member, or at least be invited to participate in these other committees. Firesafety committee meetings can be devoted to training, discussing current firesafety issues, and processing employee suggestions. A portion of each meeting can be utilized for training and a firesafety curriculum should be established for this purpose. Membership can rotate periodically to involve more employees in the firesafety program. Firesafety issues affecting the plant or relating to the training can be discussed. Employee suggestions and concerns must be discussed at each meeting. This is an area, however, where many employee committees flounder. Management must encourage employees to voice their concerns and suggestions and must reward employee initiative. At the same time, management must follow through on employee concerns and suggestions and take action or provide the employee with some type of response concerning the action or reason that action does not take place.

INDUSTRIAL FIRE PROTECTION

While a good fire prevention program will help to prevent fires and other emergencies, there are instances where emergencies will occur, and plans must be in place for that eventuality. Acts of God and incendiary fires are two instances where the organization may have little control. An organization can assure early control of the situation, even in these instances, when a fire protection program is in place. This will result in minimization of injuries, damage, and downtime.

The industrial fire protection program should include an organization to deal with emergencies, a plan that describes the fire protection program, procedures that address emergency response, and equipment to respond to fires and other emergencies.

Fire Protection Systems and Equipment

A necessary part of the industrial fire protection program is the provision of detection, suppression, and alarm systems and the equipment that is necessary for emergency response. These systems must be well planned and integrated into the program as appropriate for the type of occupancy and the operations. Fire protection systems must be designed, installed, and maintained in accordance with Chapter 9 and the manufacturer's instructions.

The industrial fire protection program should include regularly scheduled inspections of the fire protection systems and equipment and training in its use.

THE FIRE PREVENTION AND PROTECTION ORGANIZATION

The organization for fire prevention and protection will vary depending upon the size of the company and the complexity and degree of hazard involved in the operations of the supported unit. For example, a facility that uses or stores large amounts of flammable and combustible liquids or hazardous chemicals will necessarily have a larger and more sophisticated emergency organization. A warehouse operation with a large amount of space and relatively few employees may require that all employees be trained to become members of the emergency organization. Other organizations, due to their size or the criticality of their operations, may require a full-time plant fire protection organization. In most cases, the plant site emergency organization will be composed of selected employees who are trained to respond from their work stations to accomplish some basic emergency actions. Very small companies will likely have just one individual designated with the responsibility. In the small company, the fire responsibilities are likely to be an "additional duty," and not a primary function. This additional duty is likely to be assigned to the safety person, the plant manager, plant engineer, or administrative officer.

The larger company is likely to have a person or staff designated with fire as a full-time responsibility plus a staff of fire inspectors and/or suppression personnel.

Even companies that have an in-house full-time fire protection organization will also need to consider an emergency organization composed of selected employees who are able to respond in times of emergency. This would include electricians and other maintenance personnel who may be needed to monitor fire pumps, shut off gas mains, or operate HVAC equipment. For the purpose of this book, the discussion will center on the company without a full-time fire protection staff. It should be noted that there are very detailed requirements in OSHAct that apply to fire brigades, and particularly to those fire brigades who have an interior structural fire fighting capability. The part-time organization that is formed in many companies to provide emergency response is frequently referred to as the fire brigade.

Emergency Organization Composition

The composition of the plant site emergency organization will vary depending upon the size and type of the operation and the availability of public fire fighting services. A basic organization is described here.

Emergency Organization Director.   Usually one management level person will be charged with the responsibility and authority for the company's emergency response. It may be the plant manager, safety manager, security manager, or someone in the management chain. This person will have to analyze the possible emergencies that confront the organization as well as the availability of assistance from the municipal fire department and build the brigade around that analysis. Although fire brigades are generally designed to respond to fires, there are other possible emergencies to which they will have to respond such as earthquakes, tornadoes, hurricanes, floods, and power outages. The head of the emergency organization will have to appoint a chief of the organization.

Fire Brigade Chief.   The chief of the fire brigade must be someone who is very familiar with the facility and any inherent hazards. The chief should be familiar with the facility's operations, production equipment, and fire protection equipment. He or she should also have some training in fire fighting, salvage, and rescue operations. The maintenance manager or superintendent frequently meets these requirements, but there may be others in the organization who should be considered. The chief is responsible for appointing brigade members, training the organization, maintenance of the organization's fire protection equipment, and directing the brigade's activities during an emergency.

The fire brigade chief is also responsible for preplanning fire and other emergencies that are possible for the plant site. It should be noted that in most jurisdictions, regardless of the level of training and experience of the industrial fire brigade chief, when the municipal fire department arrives on the scene of an emergency they assume command of the situation. The duties of the chief and the brigade do not end with the arrival of the public fire department. They will assist the fire department and provide information as necessary, serve as guides, and begin salvage operations.

Fire Brigade Members. Because many of the duties of the fire brigade may be strenuous, the chief must ensure that employees who are selected are physically capable of performing their duties. The numbers and type of employees who are selected for the fire brigade will vary depending upon the type and size of the facility. Frequently, the core of the fire brigade is composed of maintenance employees because they are usually familiar with the whole facility and their normal job specialties are needed during most emergencies. All parts of the facility should be represented on the brigade including offices and warehouses, with special emphasis in high-hazard operations. There are several basic functions that must be addressed by the fire brigade including monitoring of sprinkler valves, fire pumps, and emergency generators. Additionally, the brigade fights incipient fires, assists with evacuation, and monitors production equipment. Specific brigade functions should provide for alternate coverage.

The sprinkler valve monitor is responsible for checking that the sprinkler valves for the fire area and adjacent areas are open and remain open until the brigade or municipal fire chief orders them closed. This is a duty that requires the assignment of alternates.

The fire pump monitor ensures that the fire pump is operating, or starts it should it be manually operated. He then ensures that the pump continues to run during the fire. This assignment also requires alternates.

The facility's electricians must be a part of the brigade. Their expertise is required in most emergencies for such things as providing temporary power, shutting off power as directed, and checking for damage before restarting power after the emergency. Other brigade members will fight incipient fires until the arrival of the municipal fire department, initiate salvage operations, act as runners, escort emergency officials, and provide whatever assistance the fire department may require.

Fire Brigade Training

Although there are extensive training requirements for fire brigade members, the training will result in payoffs to the organization. Not only will solid training provide a plant emergency organization that can assist and minimize the loss during most emergencies, but it will create a group of employees who have a high degree of fire prevention awareness which will be useful in their day-to-day job-related activities as well as off-the-job activities. Part of the training of the brigade can even include having members participate on fire prevention inspections of the facility. Training programs should be worked into an annual schedule with a minimum of 1 hour of training per month. Training will ensure that proficiency is maintained and that new members get worked into the program.

The following are basic industrial fire brigade subjects that should be considered for the program, as appropriate.

Program Description.   The brigade members should be familiarized with the fire protection program, to include management commitment, organizational structure, job descriptions, and responsibilities.

Basics of Fire Science.   All brigade members should be familiar with the fire tetrahedron, the basics of flame spread, methods of extinguishment, classes of fire, flammable and combustible liquids, and other hazardous materials that are unique to the operation.

Fire Prevention.   One of the benefits of training fire brigade members is the resulting firesafety awareness that is created in these individuals. This benefit can be enhanced by providing fire prevention training that includes housekeeping procedures, sources of ignition that are common in industrial fires and are present in the plant's operations, and cutting and welding procedures.

Fire Suppression.   Basic training must include fire extinguisher and small hose stream handling which includes drills with the equipment. Fire extinguisher training should include familiarization with the four classifications of fire and appropriate extinguishing agents and live fire exercises.

Notification.   Another important function is to train members in the proper procedures for sounding the alarm for the brigade and notifying the municipal fire department.

Detection and Suppression Systems.   Training must include familiarization with all of the facility's fire protection systems and equipment and location of valves and monitoring panels. They must know how to determine that a valve is open and the importance of ensuring that the valve remains open.

Special Hazards of the Facility.   Special characteristics of the facility's processes and materials, with particular emphasis on hazardous materials, radioactive materials, and high-energy sources are important training subject areas. The brigade must also know how to limit the damage during an emergency by applying salvage techniques.

First Aid. All fire brigade members should receive a basic first aid training. Cardiopulmonary respiration (CPR) training may also be given, but not at the expense of training that directly relates to fire protection activities. The need for CPR during a fire emergency is remote when compared to all of the other things that must be accomplished.

Drills. Joint facility tours and training exercises with the municipal fire department have proven to be very effective in preparing both organizations to deal with an emergency.

THE EMERGENCY PLAN

The industrial facility should have a written plan that describes the organization and the responsibilities that the organization has assigned to deal with emergencies. OSHA standards may require a written emergency action plan. For example, when a plant site emergency organization is established a plan is required. Even without OSHA requirements, an emergency plan is beneficial to the loss control program of any industrial facility.

Some of the emergencies that should be considered for the plan include fire and explosion, bomb threat, civil disturbance, environmental release, earthquake, flood, tornado, and hurricane. This plan must address membership on the brigade, detailed training provisions, and functions that the members will be expected to perform. Other items covered by the plan include other emergency situations that the plant might encounter. Preparation of the plan should be closely coordinated with the municipal fire department since that organization will need to be familiar with all of the elements of the company's emergency response program.

To be effective, the plan should be periodically reviewed and practiced after it is prepared. Post drill critiques should be held to discuss problems with the planned procedures and appropriate corrections made to the plan. It goes without saying that following every plant emergency, the plan should be critiqued and adjusted accordingly.

Elements of the Emergency Plan

The following are basic elements of a plant site emergency plan. Each plan will be modified to meet the needs and address the special characteristics of the organization.

Charter. The emergency plan should start with a charter statement that is signed by the chief operating officer of the organization. The charter establishes the program and the organization that will implement the program. Accountability and responsibilities are assigned for the program.

Organizational Structure.   The emergency organizational structure should be spelled out in the plan. It should include organizational charts and complete descriptions of each participant's responsibilities. Among the organizations that will be addressed in this part of the plan are site management, safety and health, security, fire protection, medical maintenance, plant engineering, transportation, and public relations.

Emergency Notifications.   The emergency plan must provide for the notification of appropriate personnel during emergencies. One of the most frequently overlooked activities during an emergency is the notification of the fire department. Employees get involved in fire extinguishment and evacuation activities, and notification is easily overlooked. This portion of the plan must define the procedures for the prompt notification of appropriate municipal authorities for various emergencies. As discussed previously, there are numerous federal, state, and local reporting requirements, especially for environmental incidents. The plan should assign specific responsibility for making these notifications.

The plan must provide a procedure for notifying the plant fire brigade and appropriate management personnel both during work hours or off hours. Notification rosters should be made and updated periodically. Consideration should be given to making a billfold-sized notification list with telephone numbers of key people in the emergency organization.

Emergency Evacuation Procedures.   This section of the plan affects everyone on the plant site. It will describe the evacuation routes and procedures for every location and building on the plant site. Emergency evacuation procedures should include evacuation diagrams, or route maps, that are posted in the buildings as well as being included in the plan. Evacuation diagrams should follow the exiting and travel distances that are provided in NFPA 101, the *Life Safety Code.*

One of the most important parts of this portion of the plan is a provision for accounting for all employees following an evacuation.

Evacuation drills should be conducted at least annually, with revisions made to the plan to reflect the critiques of these drills.

In some circumstances, it may be necessary to assign certain employees to remain in the facility to operate critical equipment, safely shut down hazardous processes, or perform other critical operations before they evacuate. The plan must thoroughly define these conditions, the employees who will remain, and how their safety will be assured.

Emergency Operations Procedures.   In this section of the plan the various emergencies that the plant may experience are described as well as the plan to respond to each. Duty descriptions and responsibilities are provided for each member of the brigade. The plan should specifically assign and describe rescue and first aid/medical duties for those employees who are to perform them. Various contingencies are discussed and preplanned including the establishment of alternative operations to be utilized if a portion of the plant's operations are lost. Also to be preplanned are methods for procurement of replacement stock and any other recovery efforts that might be necessary.

Special Hazards. This part of the plan should describe the special hazards that exist in the plant such as flammable liquids, toxic chemicals, radioactive materials, and high-pressure sources. Special protection systems that are installed for these hazards should be described. When special tools or protective clothing or breathing apparatus is required to deal with these emergencies, they should be described in this section. Necessary procedures for incidents that may involve these special hazards should be described, such as spills of toxic chemicals or flammable liquids, or fires exposing radioactive materials.

FIRE PREVENTION AND PROTECTION PROGRAM AUDIT

Just the fact that an industrial plant has a firesafety program in place does not ensure that it is adequate or that all of the functions are being performed satisfactorily. A periodic program audit can be an effective way of evaluating the program's adequacy and effectiveness.

Changes in personnel, processes and materials, facilities, and external factors will bring about the need to continuously modify the fire protection program.

An audit is a thorough review of the entire program that is performed, preferably, by an outside auditor. It is preferable to have a firesafety professional from outside the organization perform the audit. The audit will encompass compliance with what is referred to as command media, or published rules and regulations that apply to the fire protection program. Command media include plant, company, governmental, and contractual requirements. Not only will the audit look at compliance with command media, but it should look at the adequacy of the plant and company command media to ensure that it is current with external regulations.

The audit will not be just a plant fire inspection, but it will look at overall program elements. For example, it will review the plant's fire inspection program to determine that inspections are taking place, that deficiencies are documented, that corrective actions are assigned, and that there is followup. The audit will review the training program to determine that it is adequate, it is taking place with appropriate frequency, and that it is effective. The audit should also evaluate the support and involvement of upper management that is so important to any program.

To be effective, the results of the audit should be reviewed by the top management of the organization and a corrective action plan developed. Responsibilities for corrective action should be assigned as well as milestones and projected completion dates. Finally, periodic status reviews should take place until all actions are complete.

SUMMARY

The industrial firesafety program is one that establishes activities to prevent fire from occurring in the industrial facility as well as institutes programs to effectively control the fire and minimize the damage when fire does occur. Like any other industrial program, the success of the fire protection program depends upon the total support and active involvement of the organization's top management.

The size of the industrial fire protection organization may vary depending upon the size of the organization and the degree of hazard that is associated with its operations. The industrial fire protection organization will range in size from one or two people with firesafety as an additional duty to a full-time fire suppression unit and staff fire protection engineers.

The industrial fire protection program must be well documented with responsibilities and accountability assigned to all levels of management in the organization.

Documentation must include an emergency plan that provides structure and responsibilities of the plant site emergency organization and describes emergency actions that are the result of extensive preplanning.

A periodic audit of the effectiveness of all parts of the program will help to point out areas for improvement. Improvement is key to the continued success of the program. Changes in personnel, processes and materials, facilities, and external factors will necessitate continued development of the program.

BIBLIOGRAPHY

Code of Federal Regulations. 29 CFR 1910. 1987. Occupational Safety and Health Administration, Department of Labor. Washington, DC.

Fire Protection Handbook, 16th ed. 1986. National Fire Protection Association, Quincy, MA.

Industrial Fire Protection, 1st ed. 1982. Fire Protection Publications, Oklahoma State University, Stillwater, OK.

Mackie, J.B., and Kuhlman, R.L. 1981. *Safety and Health in Purchasing.* Institute Press, Loganville, GA.

NFPA #600-1986. *Recommendation for Organization, Training and Equipment of Private Fire Brigades.* National Fire Protection Association, Quincy, MA.

O'Connor, John J. 1987. *Practical Fire and Arson Investigation.* Elsevier Science Publishing Company, Inc., New York.

15
LOSS PREVENTION RESOURCES

INTRODUCTION

It is understood that not every industrial organization may be able to afford its own fire protection engineer or fire suppression unit. The size and complexity of the particular operation will dictate fire protection staffing requirements. There are many outside organizations with the expertise and desire to assist with the industrial or business fire protection program. Some sources of assistance are free, others are nominally priced. However, everything is available to the industrial organization that is interested in providing a firesafe operation and protecting the organization's assets. Regardless of the level of technical training or education possessed by the person who has firesafety responsibility, he or she will, at some time, require some outside assistance in providing fire safe operations. Even large companies that have fire professionals on staff frequently require the assistance of outside experts.

Some of the sources of firesafety assistance that are available will be discussed in this chapter.

FIRE INSURANCE COMPANIES

Very few companies rely solely upon insurance coverage for loss control. They recognize that there are many intangibles that are not covered by insurance such as time, customers, good will, and market position. Many insurance companies now assist companies in aggressively practicing total risk management. They help their insureds to identify risks, and they provide advice on methods to eliminate or minimize risks so as to reduce potential losses.

Almost every company will have some form of fire or other loss insurance. Other occurrences besides fire that may be insured include explosion, flood, windstorm, earthquake, building collapse, liquid damage, theft, and arson. Most insurance companies offer their insureds a wide variety of services that are intended to eliminate or minimize these potential losses. While some of the services provided by the insurance company are required by them such as inspections and water flow tests, they should not be viewed as punitive, but as part of the plant's overall loss control program.

Inspections

One of the primary services of the industrial insurer is the periodic inspection of the insured's facilities. Inspections of the insured's property are for the purpose of identifying those hazards that may result in a loss and making suggestions to mitigate the hazards. Even if the insured has a fire protection staff, it is always beneficial to have an outside expert periodically review the facilities. Insurance companies' engineers are usually trained to recognize other loss potentials besides fire that may affect a plant's operations. Besides their own training and experience, insurance engineers can draw upon the data that their employer has accumulated and the results of research and testing performed by such laboratories as the Factory Mutual Research Corporation.

Education and References

Most insurance companies are able to assist their insureds with reference materials and training programs to further their loss control programs. Most of them maintain libraries of films that are available to insureds, or they have agreements to provide films through film rental libraries. Films and videos are available in many loss control subject areas including management training, fire extinguisher usage, storage and handling of flammable and combustible liquids, prefire planning, and others. Films and videos are an excellent and inexpensive training media for training employees and industrial fire brigades.

Some insurance companies such as Factory Mutual, Industrial Risk Insurers (IRI), and Kemper operate training facilities in which they offer nominally priced property loss prevention and control courses. These facilities are used to train their own personnel, and for a fee, they train insureds, engineers, architects, and fire marshals.

Posters, pamphlets, and slide/cassette programs are also available for use in management, employee, and fire brigade training programs.

Engineering Services

Many insurance companies provide professional loss control engineering services for their insureds. The loss control services include advice on specific loss control programs and review of proposed construction, fire protection installation plans, and new equipment. Loss control engineers help the insured to manage change through plan review, site visits, and consultations on new construction, proposed changes in facility use, contents, arrangement, or equipment. They also provide advice on protection of fire related hazards.

Personnel who are responsible for industrial fire protection programs would be well advised to utilize the available loss control engineering services to review construction drawings and planned fire protection system installations.

They can evaluate plans for adequacy of proposed fire protection systems, ensure proper approvals by the authority having jurisdiction for proposed systems and equipment, and provide suggestions for optimizing overall loss control measures. Of particular concern to the insurance carrier and the facility owner are hazardous operations involving such things as flammable and combustible liquids, explosives, and other hazardous materials. Also of concern are high-value operations that are sensitive to fire-related damage such as computers, switching equipment, and electronics manufacturing. There are also those operations that are both high hazard and high value such as semiconductor facilities that require special attention.

New Construction and Facility Modifications. The insurance company's loss control engineers can also provide design review for new construction or modifications of existing facilities. It is particularly useful to have them review the designs of fire protection systems to ensure that adequate coverage is provided. It is very important to conduct design reviews early in the design process. Thorough reviews and incorporation of suggestions for loss control can save the property owner money. It is much more costly to try to incorporate changes after the facility is constructed, or even during construction.

Loss Recovery. Another service of the property insurance carrier occurs after a facility has suffered a loss. The insurance carrier's engineers can assist with investigations, loss analysis, and recovery and cleanup activities. They can provide advice on salvage techniques and can recommend organizations that specialize in these activities.

Specific Loss Control Programs

Many insurance companies have programs that address specific problem areas that experience has shown to contribute to losses. Some examples of these programs include IRI's RSVP (Restore Shut Valves Promptly), PEPlan, and OVERVIEW and Factory Mutual's FPP (Fire Protection Programs) including valve supervision, hot work permits, and regular facility inspections.

Overview. The OVERVIEW program, developed and used by Industrial Risk Insurers, is a program to demonstrate to insureds the interaction among people, hazards, and protection equipment. OVERVIEW is worthy of discussion here because it provides a summary of all of the important aspects of an industrial loss control program. OVERVIEW is a concept based upon the six characteristics of a highly protected risk as follows:

1. A concerned management with the determination to minimize the probability of loss.
2. Substantially constructed and maintained facilities that are approved for the type of property.

3. Interior protection, where necessary, with automatic sprinklers and/or water spray systems.
4. Special hazards that are properly protected in accordance with uniform standards.
5. Exterior protection including an adequate public or private water supply.
6. Proper surveillance in the form of watchman or alarm service or continuous occupancy.

Valve Supervision.   Most insurance companies have a program for supervision of fire protection control valves. Experience in large property loss fires have shown that closed or partially closed valves have been a significant factor in the size of the loss. Insurance company programs, like IRI's RSVP (restore shut valves promptly) and Factory Mutual's Valve Supervision program, if enforced, will ensure that valves that feed the automatic sprinkler system are open and ready when fire occurs. Valve supervision programs emphasize consideration of the necessity to inspect all valves, lock valves in the open position, and to use reminders, such as tags, labels, and the insurance company notifications, when valves must be closed.

Factory Mutual's valve supervision program incorporates a 12 step "Red Tag Alert System" as follows:

1. Contacting the Factory Mutual Engineering Association District Office to discuss the impairment and methods to minimize the impact of the impairment. When notified, the insurance carrier can review the precautions with the ensured to make sure that the effects and duration of the impairment will be minimized.
2. Use of the Red Tag Alert System kit which includes red tagging of the shut valve (Figure 15-1), recording the closure on a record of valve closure card, and use of a fire protection out of service card (Figure 15-2). This system serves to remind all people involved that an impairment exists and to expedite a return to full protection.
3. Preparing in advance so that the duration of the impairment is minimized.
4. Working without interruption, in order to minimize the duration of the impairment. It is cheaper to pay overtime than to take the risk of a loss.
5. Working during idle periods such as nights, weekends, and holidays when fewer sources of ignition are present.
6. Shut down hazardous processes which may increase the risk during the impairment.
7. Notify the public fire department of the nature and duration of the impairment.
8. Post someone at the closed valve throughout the period of impairment.
9. Patrol areas of the facility that are affected by the impairment.

Figure 15-1. The "Red Tag" is placed on a fire water supply valve when it is necessary to close the valve. (Source: Factory Mutual Engineering Corporation)

10. Provide temporary protection such as a charged hoseline in the areas affected by the impairment.
11. Reinspect the valve after the work is finished to insure that it is fully open.
12. Recontact the Factory Mutual Engineering Association Office to report reopening and locking of the valve.

Cutting and Welding.   In the discussion of frequent ignition sources in industrial fires (Chapter 1), cutting and welding sources were high on the list. IRI reports that in a recent period, three industrial facilities together sustained over $37 million worth of property losses due to cutting and welding activities. In approximately one-third of cutting and welding related losses, outside contractors were at fault. For this reason, it is advisable to include requirements in the contract that assigns the contractor responsibility to conduct the work in

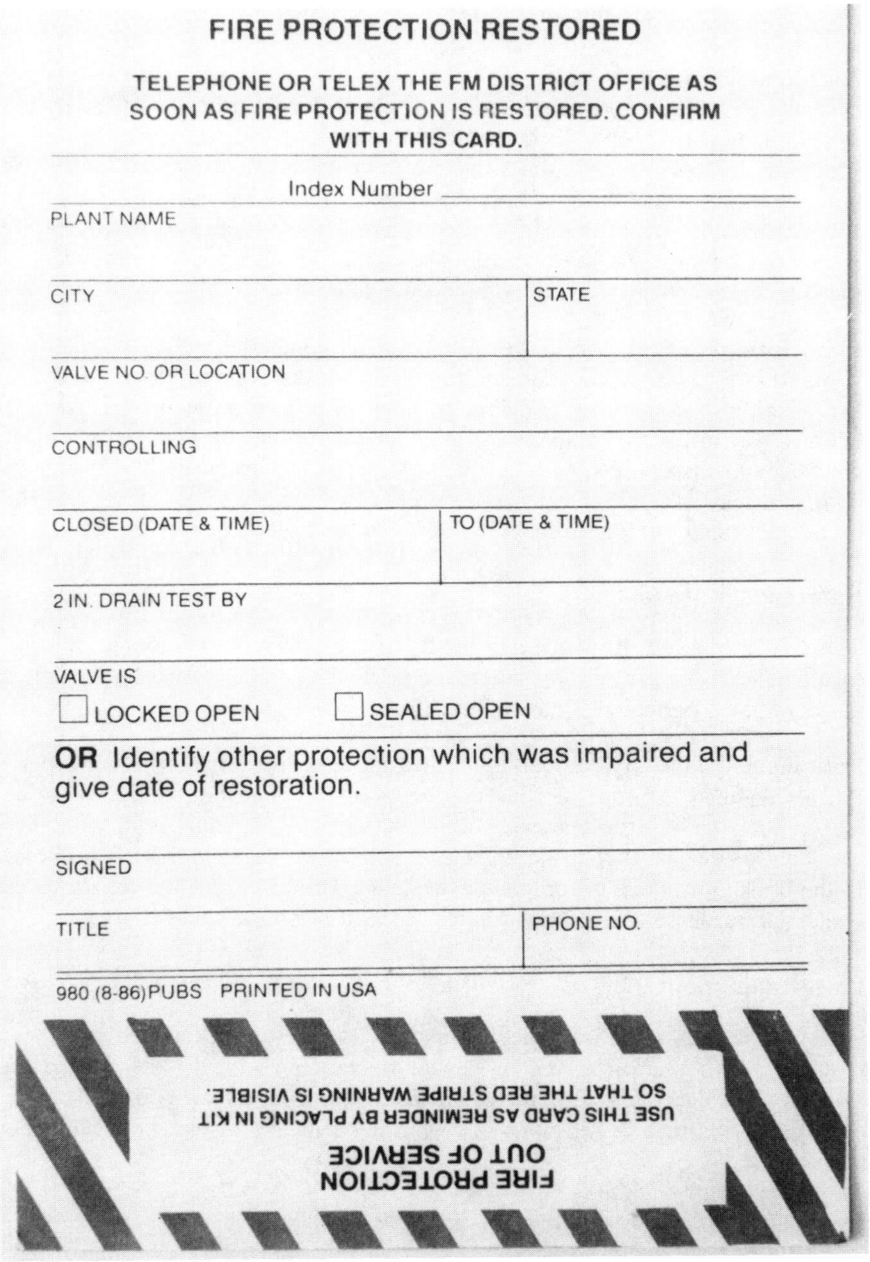

FIRE PROTECTION RESTORED

TELEPHONE OR TELEX THE FM DISTRICT OFFICE AS
SOON AS FIRE PROTECTION IS RESTORED. CONFIRM
WITH THIS CARD.

Index Number _____

PLANT NAME

CITY | STATE

VALVE NO. OR LOCATION

CONTROLLING

CLOSED (DATE & TIME) | TO (DATE & TIME)

2 IN. DRAIN TEST BY

VALVE IS

☐ LOCKED OPEN   ☐ SEALED OPEN

OR Identify other protection which was impaired and
give date of restoration.

SIGNED

TITLE | PHONE NO.

980 (8-86)PUBS   PRINTED IN USA

FIRE PROTECTION
OUT OF SERVICE
USE THIS CARD AS A REMINDER BY PLACING IN KIT
SO THAT THE RED STRIPE WARNING IS VISIBLE.

Figure 15-2. The "Out of Service Card" is used as a reminder that a fire protection
system is out of service. (Source: Factory Mutual Engineering Corporation)

accordance with the safety provisions of the National Fire Codes pertaining to such work.

Cutting and welding loss prevention programs are based upon the loss experience with these types of operations. Most of the programs involve a permit system like Factory Mutual's cutting/welding permit system (Figure 13-3). The programs require preoperation inspections to check on the condition of the equipment, removal of possible fuel sources, and sealing openings within 35 feet of the work. A fire watch is usually required as well as a postoperation inspection 2 to 4 hours after work is completed. Permits provide reminders of these requirements as well as a signoff procedure.

Fire Protection Program Inspections. Each industrial facility should have some form of internal fire inspection program for determining the existence of fire hazards, documenting deficiencies, and ensuring followup on corrective actions. The insurance company can assist in determining areas to be inspected, frequency of inspections, and coverage of special hazard areas. The insurance company may also be able to provide checklists that can be adapted to the particular operation and used by in-plant personnel who conduct inspections.

Reference Materials

The larger property loss insurers publish many reference materials that are available to insureds as well as others at a nominal charge. There are such things as data books, periodicals, pamphlets, and approval guides.

Periodicals. Factory Mutual and Industrial Risk Insurers both publish periodicals devoted to property conservation. *Record* is the bimonthly magazine that is published by the Factory Mutual System. *The Sentinel* is the property loss control magazine that is published quarterly by Industrial Risk Insurers. Both publications contain comprehensive loss control information that provides a valuable resource to the industrial loss control person.

Loss Adjustment

Following a loss, most insurance companies do not stop at establishing a settlement, but they are involved in salvage operations, advising the insured on sources of replacement equipment and facilities, and assisting in getting the operation back on line and otherwise working with the insured to reduce the loss.

NATIONAL FIRE PROTECTION ASSOCIATION

The National Fire Protection Association (NFPA) is the preeminent fire prevention and protection organization in the United States. Its mission is the safeguarding of people and their environment from destructive fires, by using scientific and engineering techniques and education. The primary technical activity of the association involves the development, publication, and dissemination of codes and consensus standards. The association's educational activities are directed at people of all ages and are intended to teach the importance of firesafety as a way of life. There are many NFPA publications that are directed specifically at industrial fire protection. These publications provide direction for fire protection activities in many industries. They provide training materials for industrial fire protection programs as well as off-the-job training programs, and they provide technical information that is necessary for the engineering aspects of the industrial fire protection program.

There are 13 sections within the association based upon the functional interests of the voting membership. The following are the 13 sections:

Architects	Fire Service
Aviation	Industrial Fire Protection
Education	Lodging Industry
Electrical	Railroad
Engineers and Building Code Officials	Research
Fire Marshals	Wildland Fire Management
Fire Science and Technology	

NFPA *Fire Protection Handbook*

The NFPA *Fire Protection Handbook* is a single-source handbook that has been prepared to provide state-of-the-art fire prevention and protection practices for the fire protection community. The first edition was published in 1896, and it has evolved through 16 editions to almost 1800 pages in the sixteenth edition. This growth has been necessary to keep pace with the increases in the body of knowledge and complexity that has proliferated in the fire prevention and protection field. The handbook is an edited volume that includes the participation of many experts from within as well as outside the NFPA organization.

Specific NFPA Handbooks

The NFPA also publishes some specific handbooks on certain subjects to clarify individual NFPA codes. Some specific handbooks have been referenced in this book including the *Life Safety Code Handbook* (Chapter 6), the *Flammable and Combustible Liquids Code Handbook* (Chapter 4), the *Hazardous Materials Response Handbook*, and the *National Electrical Code Handbook* (Chapter 5).

Other code specific handbooks include the *Automatic Sprinkler System Handbook*, the *Liquified Petroleum Gases Handbook*, the *National Fuel Gas Handbook*, and the *Fire Alarm Signaling Systems Handbook*.

The *Industrial Fire Hazards Handbook* (Chapter 13) is not a code specific handbook, but it is intended as a fire protection guide for industry. This handbook focuses on the fire hazards and control methods that are associated with major industries and industrial processes.

Standards and Codes

The NFPA and its standards and codes grew out of the insurance industry's need to standardize the design, installation, and maintenance of sprinkler systems. These standards and codes have evolved to the point where there are currently about 260 covering a broad range of fire related topics. They are widely used as the basis of legislation and regulation at all levels of government. There are currently about 200 NFPA committees representing a balance of interests that develop standards and codes using a democratic process.

The standards and codes are available either individually in pamphlet form or in the multivolume set of *National Fire Codes*. The most widely used documents are NFPA 70, the *National Electrical Code;* NFPA 101, the *Life Safety Code;* NFPA 30, the *Flammable and Combustible Liquids Code;* NFPA 13, the *Automatic Sprinkler Standard;* NFPA 58, the *Liquified Petroleum Gases Standard;* and NFPA 99, the *Health Care Facilities Standard.*

Educational Materials

The NFPA produces an abundance of educational materials for all age groups and all levels of competence from firesafety materials for children to fire ground tactics for professional fire fighters. The NFPA materials include pamphlets, slides, movies, videos, posters, and books.

The personnel who are responsible for the industrial firesafety program can find educational materials for themselves, regardless of their level of expertise. There are educational materials for training the general employee population, the plant fire brigade, and for employee off-the-job firesafety education.

Periodicals

The NFPA publishes three informative periodicals that may be of use to the industrial firesafety people, including the *Fire Journal*, *Fire Command*, and *Fire Technology*.

Fire Journal.   NFPA members receive an automatic subscription to *Fire Journal*, a bimonthly magazine for firesafety professionals. The industrial firesafety person will find it an informative source of information on the latest code developments, current topics in fire prevention and protection, and reports on significant fire incidents; to name a few of the key areas.

Fire Command.   This publication is written for fire service leaders, but it is also informative for the industrial firesafety specialist and the industrial fire suppression unit, in particular. *Fire Command* is published monthly and provides information about new fire fighting techniques, equipment, and products. Reports are provided about fire suppression efforts during fire incidents and lessons learned.

Fire Technology.   This publication is published four times a year to provide a forum for fire researchers, scientists, and engineers. It provides detailed information on current research and applied engineering topics, the very latest developments, book reviews, and technical topics.

CONSULTANTS

Another source of help for the industrial fire prevention and protection program is the fire protection consultant. In cases where the fire insurance carrier does not provide loss control services, the company may consider using a property protection consultant. Even when the carrier does provide these services, consultants may be useful to supplement or coordinate the carrier's activities. Where the property insurance carrier is concerned primarily with property loss, the consultant can provide the added dimension of life safety expertise. Consultants have a greater motivation to serve the client's best interests, whereas the property loss insurance companies might be more parochial.

There are several large consulting organizations available in the United States, some of whom also function internationally. There are also many smaller independent consultants. From this selection, the right consultant can be found to meet the needs of most any industrial operation. Consultants can provide registered professional fire protection engineers when that level of expertise is required, and they can provide specialists for individual applications.

Some of the many services for which consultants may be considered include technical reviews of operations to identify and evaluate risk to life and property, developing a total loss control program, auditing an existing program, investigating losses, evaluating and establishing training programs, and providing consultation regarding special or unusual hazards.

Consulting Services

Hazard Analysis.   Consultants can be used to perform general fire and life safety hazard evaluations of an entire facility, a building, or an operation or process. They may be needed to conduct computerized fire and smoke spread modeling. Operations that involve special hazards or special protection systems such as chemical plants, refineries, computer operations, and nuclear facilities may consider the services of a consultant to perform a special hazard analysis.

Program Audits. Consultants may be used to conduct comprehensive audits of a company's fire protection or total loss control program. Consultants can provide a comprehensive audit by serving as unbiased experts. The audit may include interviews with top management, middle management, and line personnel. Auditors should also review policy statements, documentation, and procedures, and they should review facilities and operations. The purpose of the audit is to identify, analyze, and recommend solutions to fire hazards or other areas of potential property loss. Additionally, audits may be used to identify target areas for the company's loss control efforts, staffing needs, organizational structure adjustments, and program documentation.

Project Reviews. In the design and construction of new buildings, fire protection engineering consultants can provide a valuable service by reviewing the project at every stage.

During property planning, consultants can provide preliminary code reviews and review the initial design concepts for major fire protection or life safety issues.

During the beginning design phase, consultants can prepare detailed code summaries that outline the fire protection requirements for the specific building being designed. Consultants would also review the building design for code compliance, identify items that may require a variance, outline the fire safety features required, and act as an interface with the building code officials.

During the design development phase, the consultant will review designs, continue to act as the interface with building code officials concerning variances, perform exit calculations, prepare performance specifications for fire protection systems, and prepare preliminary design drawings for fire protection systems.

During the construction documents phase, the consultant will finalize and document negotiations with building code officials, prepare final drawings and specifications for fire protection systems, conduct the bidding for fire protection systems, review design documents for compliance, and perform general consulting. During the construction process, the consultant will review shop drawings, assist the owner in responding to change order requests or new code requirements, conduct site inspections to review fire protection system installation, and witness final testing and approval of fire protection systems.

For existing buildings, the services of a fire protection consultant will be valuable for retrofitting and rehabilitation of the building or fire protection systems. Professionals are capable of assuring that current code requirements are satisfied, and to assure that building modifications do not jeopardize life safety or fire protection. This is accomplished through design review, code negotiations, inspections, and testing.

Emergency Plans. Consultants could help the industrial facility to prepare emergency plans for life safety as well as operational emergencies such as fire and explosion, earthquake, hurricane, and environmental emergencies. They could also help to devise detection, alarm, and protection systems to deal with these emergencies.

Training Programs. Many fire protection consultants include training capabilities in their repertoire and others specialize in training. They may develop and present practical training seminars or workshops to meet specific needs, or they may provide stock training programs. The consultant should have the ability to evaluate the particular operation and recommend pertinent training needs.

Engineering Investigations. Most industrial facilities do not have the ability to do a complete investigation following a fire or an explosion. Consultants are available who have this expertise. It is important for whoever does the investigation to begin early before evidence is destroyed and witnesses forget what they have observed. A fire investigation may include reconstruction, data collection, and analysis, and testing of material and equipment. The investigation report will include an unbiased analysis of the facts, description of the cause, and recommendations to prevent additional losses.

Consultants can also provide assistance in litigation and expert testimony.

Research and Analysis. Occasionally, a special fire protection problem will be encountered that is not addressed by existing information or codes. In these cases, professional fire protection consultants can provide assistance in the form of analyses, mathematical and computer-based analysis and modeling, arranging and witnessing tests, and code research.

FIRE PREVENTION CODES

Fire prevention codes are published as model codes by three regional organizations. These organizations, which also publish various model building codes are the International Conference of Building Officials (ICBO), the Southern Building Code Congress International (SBCCI), and the Building Officials and Code Administration (BOCA). These model codes are not law until they are adopted as such by a jurisdiction.

Uniform Fire Code (UFC)

The UFC is a model code that has been developed and is amended by the International Commission of Building Officials (ICBO) and the Western Fire Chiefs Association (WFCA). These two organizations have correlated the UFC and the Uniform Building Code (UBC) so that there is no conflict between them. The UFC is not intended to be a stand-alone document and it is only a model.

It is intended to be part of a package of codes such as the UBC, Uniform Mechanical Code, and the National Electrical Code.

The UFC prescribes regulations that are intended to safeguard life and property from the hazards of fire and explosion and from conditions that are hazardous to life or property in the use or occupancy of buildings or premises.

The UFC and UBC are primarily used in the western United States, and they are published at the headquarters of the ICBO and WFCA which is located in Whittier, California.

Standard Fire Prevention Code

The *Standard Fire Prevention Code* was developed by the SBCCI and is intended for use with the *Standard Building Code*. As of 1988, this code has been updated by the Southeastern and Southwestern Association of Fire Chiefs.

The *Standard Fire Prevention Code* references many NFPA standards to prescribe regulations for the protection of life and property from the hazards of fire and explosion. It deals with fire or explosion which might result from the storage, use, or handling of hazardous materials, substances, and devices, and from conditions hazardous to life or property. The code applies to the use or occupancy of buildings or premises, other than one- and two-family dwellings.

The SBCCI is located in Birmingham, Alabama, and it has regional offices in Austin, Texas and Orlando, Florida. Its codes are used primarily in the southern United States.

National Fire Prevention Code

The *Fire Prevention Code* is one of the *national codes* published by BOCOA. Like the others, it is intended to be used in conjunction with other *national codes.*

BOCA is located in Country Club Hills, Illinois, and it maintains regional offices in Columbus, Ohio, Tulsa, Oklahoma, and Trevose, Pennsylvania. Its codes are used primarily in the midwestern and northeastern states.

OTHER CODE-RELATED AND STANDARD SETTING ORGANIZATIONS

There are other organizations that establish standards and test criteria that may be adopted into the regulations of a jurisdiction. These organizations may also be used as references and should be understood by the firesafety personnel.

American National Standards Institute (ANSI)

The American National Standards Institute is the nonprofit coordinator of the voluntary standards system in the United States. The system coordinates the efforts of industry, standards development organizations, and public and consumer interests in the development of national consensus standards.

Underwriters Laboratories (UL)

Underwriters Laboratories is an independent, not-for-profit organization dedicated to the investigation of devices, systems, and materials with respect to hazards affecting life and property. For over 95 years, UL successfully pursued the goals of reducing or preventing bodily injury, loss of life, and property damage.

The principal business of UL is safety investigations of electrical and electronic equipment and products, mechanical products, building materials, construction systems, fire protection equipment, burglary protection systems and equipment, and marine products.

UL develops many of its own standards to conduct its investigations. Many of these standards become nationally recognized and receive approval as consensus standards through the ANSI process.

UL listing is the most widely recognized of UL's services. Listing of a product by UL means that samples of the product have been tested and evaluated, and they comply with UL requirements. Another service of UL is the classification and identification of products. Industrial or commercial products may be classified with respect to the properties of the product, a limited spectrum of hazards to life and property, suitability for certain uses, and other special conditions. Once classified, products may be identified by a classification marking which includes UL's name and a statement to indicate the extent of UL's evaluation. UL safety-tested and listed products are identified with the familiar UL logo and listing mark.

American Society of Testing and Materials (ASTM)

The American Society of Testing and Materials is the world's largest source of voluntary consensus standards on characteristics and performance of materials, products, systems, and services. ASTM standards represent a common viewpoint of those parties concerned with its provisions (consensus). They are intended to aid industry, government agencies, and the general public. Their use is purely voluntary, and it is recognized that under varying conditions or requirements, they may be modified.

THE INDEPENDENT TESTING LABORATORY

The number of independent testing laboratories has grown significantly in the past 20 years because of the demands of four major areas in American industry.

There are heightened concerns about the environment, there is new emphasis on product quality, there are increasing health and safety issues, and there has been an increase in governmental regulations in these areas and at all levels of government. Of particular interest to the firesafety professional has been the recent concentration of the testing laboratories on the changing aspects of combustion with respect to smoke and toxic products of combustion. There is concern about toxic products of combustion that may jeopardize the ability of occupants to safely evacuate a building fire. There is also increasing concern about the effects of smoke and corrosive products of combustion on delicate electronic equipment.

The independent testing laboratory provides a valuable tool to the individual who is charged with the responsibility for the industrial fire protection program. The laboratory plays an important role in helping the firesafety professional select safe building materials, systems, and products. The laboratory conducts unbiased evaluations to ensure that these items conform to established performance standards and building codes. Armed with test data, the firesafety professional can make the proper product selection that will ensure suitability, reliability, and safety.

The manufacturer can also use the independent testing laboratory in the area of product development to determine if manufactured products are safe enough to be marketed.

Most jurisdictions have specific code requirements for equipment that is used in business and industry. For example, permanently installed equipment must meet standards that have been established by the American Society of Testing and Materials (ASTM), National Electrical Code (NEC), National Fire Protection Association Fire Codes (NFC), and others. In the past several years, there is increasing quantities of machinery and equipment being introduced into American industry that is manufactured abroad. Foreign-built equipment may not have been designed and manufactured according to codes and standards that are applicable in the United States. In most cases, the foreign standards to which the materials were manufactured are adequate, but occasionally, there are deficiencies that could ultimately result in accidents or fire. For example, electrical wiring or components may be installed that are not heavy enough for the loads that will be placed upon them during industrial usage. When foreign-made machinery and equipment is being purchased, the vendor should be required to provide certification that the equipment meets or exceeds applicable U.S. standards. To accomplish this, the vendor will have to have the equipment, or a sampling of the equipment evaluated and tested by an independent testing laboratory. Should equipment or machinery find its way into the factory without proper certification, it becomes the responsibility of the plant operator to secure the necessary certifications. Independent testing laboratories are available to provide this service.

An independent laboratory is a non-tax-favored proprietorship or corporation that is not affiliated with any academic or governmental institution or with any outside industrial company or trade group in any manner which might affect its ability to conduct investigations, render reports, or give professional counsel objectively and without bias.

Independent engineering and scientific laboratories must have an in-house quality control program to verify the validity and accuracy of their own results. This is accomplished by an in-house program that outlines standards for personnel as well as equipment and establishes standard reference materials. Additionally, there are a number of outside organizations that monitor and inspect these laboratories to ensure standardization and provide comparative evaluation techniques throughout the industry. These organizations include the following: the American Society of Testing and Materials (ASTM), the National Voluntary Laboratory Accreditation Program (NVLAP) sponsored by the National Bureau of Standards, the International Conference of Building Officials, and the National Research Council. The Defense Contractors Administrative Services (DCAS) is involved in witnessing tests to assure the government of quality in testing, evaluation, and conformance to military standards and specifications. The Federal Aviation Administration (FAA) also provides inspectors to guarantee conformance to the high-quality standards required for the aviation industry.

THE PUBLIC FIRE DEPARTMENT

The local public fire department should not be overlooked by the facility that is concerned about its fire protection program. The public fire department may be able to provide training programs, inspections, and program guidance. Not all public fire departments have the same capabilities, but as a minimum, they should conduct joint familiarization tours of the facility. When the fire department responds to an emergency, they should be familiar with the operations and processes of the facility; they should be aware of the special hazards that may exist and their location; they should be aware of the location of very high-value equipment and materials; and they should know who are the key people in the facility and how to contact them.

Public fire departments frequently provide training programs, particularly fire extinguisher training, for companies in their jurisdiction. Joint training exercises with the plant fire brigade are also valuable. They should also monitor and assist in evacuation exercises.

Many public fire departments are required by law to conduct periodic inspections of the facilities that are within their jurisdiction. These inspections aid the fire department in its familiarization with the facility and it can aid the industrial program by identifying potential problem areas.

VENDORS AND MANUFACTURER REPRESENTATIVES

The industrial fire protection program management should not overlook the vendors and representatives of fire protection systems and equipment manufacturers with which they do business. These people can be invaluable with information and training regarding, not only their products, but unique hazards and applications for fire protection systems and equipment.

Many vendors and manufacturers' representatives have training and experience in analyzing special fire protection problems and recommending solutions. For example, when dealing with a flammable liquid handling concern, the manufacturers of flammable liquid handling equipment can be helpful in studying the problems and identifying solutions.

Many manufacturers of fire protection systems, agents, and equipment offer training materials and programs free of charge. And, of course, they will train users of the equipment that they supply. To ensure that this training takes place, it should be included in the purchase and/or installation contract.

SUMMARY

Since the person who is assigned responsibilities for the fire protection program in the business or industrial operation may not have adequate training and experience, it is important to know that there is assistance available. Even the fire protection professional will require assistance in the conduct of the fire prevention and protection program.

Property protection insurance companies provide extensive assistance, usually at no additional cost to the insured. Their costs are included in the insurance premium.

The NFPA has available codes and standards as well as a wealth of educational materials and training programs that can be used to supplement the industrial firesafety program.

There are many consultants available who specialize in fire safety and life safety. They can be utilized to supplement existing expertise in the industrial facility or to provide expertise that is not readily available through other sources. The public fire department should be involved in the facility's fire prevention and protection program. They can assist in training, drills, and hazard evaluation.

Vendors and manufacturers of fire protection systems and equipment can also be helpful to the industrial fire protection program.

BIBLIOGRAPHY

Cote, Arthur, and Bugbee, Percy. 1988. *Principles of Fire Protection*. National Fire Protection Association, Quincy, MA.

Fire Protection Handbook, 16th ed. 1986. National Fire Protection Association, Quincy, MA.

Gage-Babcock & Associates, An Independent Consulting Engineering Service. Promotional brochure. Elmhurst, IL.

IRI Advertorials, Hartford, CT: Industrial Risk Insurers.

Loss Control Resource Catalog. The Factory Mutual System, Norwood, MA.

McCullen, Patrick V. 1986. The Role of the Independent Testing Laboratory in Safety Engineering. Paper presented April 1986, at the University of Southern California, Los Angeles, California.

M & M Protection Consultants. Professional Hazard Control Consulting Services. Promotional materials. Chicago, IL.

NATLSCO, National Loss Control Service Corporation. Property Loss Control Consulting Services. Promotional brochure. Long Grove, IL.

The NFPA Catalog. National Fire Protection Association, Quincy, MA.

Rolf Jensen & Associates, Fire Protection Engineers Building Code Consultants. Promotional brochure. Deerfield, IL.

GLOSSARY

Accepted. The insurance company may accept equipment of materials as installed at a specific location. Accepted equipment or materials may be, but are not necessarily, approved. It is merely an indication that the equipment or materials are suitable for their intended use.

Aerosols. A material that is dispensed from its container as a mist spray or foam by a propellant under pressure.

Approved. A commonly used term that generally means acceptable to the authority having jurisdiction. Approval refers to listings or tests by organizations concerned with product evaluations. These organizations determine if a particular item or product meets certain established test criteria.

Arson. The crime of setting an incendiary fire.

Askarel. (ASTM definition) A generic term for a group of synthetic, fire-resistant, chlorinated aromatic hydrocarbons used as electrical insulating liquid. They have a property under arcing conditions such that any gases produced will consist predominantly of noncombustible hydrogen chloride with lesser amounts of combustible gasses. Askarel does not necessarily contain PCBs.

Asphyxiant. A gas that is essentially nontoxic, but it can cause unconsciousness or death by lowering the concentration of oxygen in the air or by totally replacing the oxygen in breathing air.

Authority Having Jurisdiction. The organization or office having statutory responsibility for approving equipment, an installation or procedure.

Backdraft. A type of explosion caused by the sudden influx of air into a mixture of gases, which have been heated to above the ignition temperature of at least one of them.

Blanketing (or padding). Maintaining an inert, or fuel rich, atmosphere in the vapor space of a container or vessel.

BLEVE. Boiling Liquid Expanding Vapor Explosion. An explosion in which a container containing a liquefied fuel gas that is exposed to fire suddenly fails, releasing a vapor cloud which is immediately ignited.

Boiling Point. The temperature at which the vapor pressure of liquid equals atmospheric pressure.

Bonding. The process of connecting two or more conductive objects together by means of a conductor.

Breakthrough time. During the evaluation of chemical protective fabrics, breakthrough time is the time required for the chemical to be measured on the inside surface of the fabric.

British thermal unit. A Btu is the amount of heat required to raise the temperature of 1 pound of water 1 degree Fahrenheit at 60 degrees Fahrenheit.

Calorie. The amount of heat required to raise the temperature of 1 gram of water 1 degree Celsius at 59 degrees Fahrenheit (15 degrees Celsius).

Combustible Liquid. A liquid with a flash point greater than 100 degrees Fahrenheit.

Combustion. A rapid chemical combination of a substance with oxygen, usually accompanied by the liberation of heat and light.

Compartmentation. The design and construction of a building into firesafe compartments for the purpose of containing a fire when it occurs.

Composites. A composite material is a macroscopic combination of two or more distinct materials, a reinforcement material such as fibers or particles supported by a binder (matrix) material.

Conduction. Conduction is the transfer of heat through solid objects such as through metal, which is a good conductor and through wood which is not a good conductor.

Convection. Convection is the transfer of heat through air or through a fluid.

Corrosive. A chemical that will attack and destroy, by chemical action, any living tissue with which it comes into contact.

Cross-zoned. An expression used in activating fire suppression systems when more than one detection circuit alarm is required for a release to occur.

Cryogenic gas. A liquefied gas that has a boiling point of less than -150 degrees Fahrenheit.

Deflagration. A combustion reaction that proceeds much faster than ordinary combustion but slower than the speed of sound.

Detonation. A combustion reaction that is propagated by a shock wave and proceeds faster than the speed of sound.

Endothermic. The absorption of heat.

Eutectic alloy. A mixture of two or more metals resulting in an alloy with a melting point that is lower than either of the two.

Exit. That portion of a means of egress which is separated from all other spaces of the building or structure by construction or equipment as required in this code to provide a protected way of travel to the exit discharge. The simplest is a door to the outside. It may be a corridor or a stairwell if it is adequately enclosed.

Exit access. That portion of a means of egress which leads to an entrance to an exit. Maximum travel distances to exits are provided in the occupant chapters of the code.

Exothermic. The generation, or liberation, of heat.

Explosion. The effect produced by the sudden violent expansion of gases which may or may not be accompanied by shock waves, and/or disruption of enclosing materials.

Explosion proof. Refers to electrical equipment which is enclosed in a case that is capable of withstanding an explosion of a specified gas or vapor which may occur within it and of preventing the ignition of a specified gas or vapor surrounding the enclosure by sparks, flashes, or explosion of the gas within, and which operates at such an external temperature that it will not ignite surrounding flammable atmospheres.

Explosion suppression. A technique by which burning in a confined mixture is detected and arrested during the incipient stages to prevent development of pressure which could result in the damaging effects of an explosion.

Fire. A rapid, self-sustaining oxidation process resulting in the evolution of heat, light, and smoke.

Fire point. The temperature at which an ignitable vapor/air mixture will continue to burn after ignition (usually 5 to 10 degrees above the flash point).

Fire resistant. An expression of the ability of a material, structure, or assembly to resist the effects of a large-scale severe fire exposure. Fire resistance is usually expressed in units of time, in minutes, or hours, that materials or assemblies have withstood a fire exposure.

Fire retardant. Signifies a material that has been treated with chemicals, coatings, paints, or other materials to reduce its degree of combustibility. Fire retardant is a lesser degree of fire protection than fire resistant.

Flame. The burning gas or vapor of a fire, usually seen as a flickering light of various colors.

Flame arrestor. A passive device that is intended to prevent the transmission of flame from one point to another by absorption of heat energy.

Flame spread. The rate at which fire will spread from the point of ignition to involve an ever-increasing area of combustible material.

Flammable gas. Any gas that will burn in the normal concentrations of oxygen in the air.

Flammable liquids. Liquids that have a flash point greater than 100 degrees Fahrenheit.

Flammable range. The concentration in air between the upper and lower flammable limits in which all flammable gas or vapor mixtures are ignitable.

Flashover. A situation in which heat from a fire is radiated back into the room from the hot air and smoke at the ceiling. This heat raises the temperature of all combustible materials in the room to their ignition temperature. Flashover occurs when there is a sudden and dramatic simultaneous ignition of most of the combustible materials and gases in the room or space.

Flash point. The lowest temperature at which a liquid will give off enough vapors to form an ignitable mixture, which will momentarily flash across the surface of the liquid.

Fusible link. Two pieces of metal that are held together by low-melting point solder.

Grounding. The process of connecting one or more conductive objects to earth or to some conducting body that serves in place of the earth.

Halogens. The elements of group VIIA of the periodic table of the elements: fluorine, chlorine, bromine, iodine, and astatine.

Halon. A halogenated extinguishing agent in which one or more of the hydrogen atoms has been replaced by atoms from the halogen series.

Heat conductivity. The heat conductivity of the material is a measure of the rate at which absorbed heat will flow through the mass of the material.

Heat of combustion. A measure of the maximum amount of heat that can be released by the complete combustion of a unit mass of combustible material.

Hydrocarbon. A compound containing hydrogen and carbon.

Ignitable mixture. A vapor–air, gas–air, or dust–air mixture or combinations of these mixtures in concentrations that are within the flammable limits and can be ignited by a static spark.

Ignition temperature. The minimum temperature to which a substance in air must be heated in order to initiate self-sustained combustion.

Incendiary fires.   Fires that are deliberately set including those that are motivated by fraud, vandalism, spite, politics, and crime coverup.

Incipient.   In describing a fire, an incipient fire is one that is starting. An incipient fire may be one in which the fuel is just beginning to pyrolize, or has just been ignited.

Inert gas.   A noncombustible, nonreactive gas that renders the combustible material in a system incapable of supporting combustion. Inert gases including helium, neon, argon, krypton, xenon, and radon are also known as the noble gases.

Intrinsic safety.   An intrinsically safe system is one which is incapable of releasing sufficient electrical energy to cause ignition of a specific hazardous atmosphere under normal and abnormal operating conditions.

Intumescent coatings.   Paints that, when heated, swell to form a thick foamy insulating barrier to retard thermal decomposition of the protected material.

Lower flammable limit.   The minimum concentration of gas or vapor in air below which it is not possible to ignite the vapors.

Means of egress.   A continuous and unobstructed way of exit travel from any point in a building or structure to a public way and which consists of three separate and distinct parts: (a) the way of exit access, (b) the exit, and (c) the way of exit discharge.

Occupant load.   The total number of persons who may occupy a building or portion thereof at any one time. Occupant load is based upon the allowable square footage per occupant in each specific type of occupancy.

Oxidant.   Any gaseous material that can react with a gas, dust, or mist to produce combustion. Oxygen in air is the most common oxidant.

Oxidation.   A chemical reaction that takes place with oxygen, or when a substance combines with oxygen.

Oxidizing agents.   Materials that contain oxygen that is available for reaction, plus the halogens. Halogens are included in the definition because they will support combustion.

Padding (or blanketing).   Maintaining either an inert or a fuel rich atmosphere in the vapor space of a container or vessel.

Permeation rate.   Permeation rate is the quantity of chemical that will move through an area of protective garment material in a given period of time.

PCB (polychlorinated biphenyl).   Any chemical substance that is limited to a biphenyl molecule that has been chlorinated to varying degrees or any combination of substances that contains PCBs greater than or equal to 500 parts per million (ppm).

Plenum.   An air compartment or chamber to which one or more ducts are connected and which forms part of an air distribution system.

Purge gas.   A gas that is continuously added to a system to render the atmosphere nonignitable by displacement of a gaseous oxidant or combustible.

Pyrolysis.   The chemical decomposition of matter through the action of heat.

Pyrophoric.   Possessing the ability to react in air.

Radiation.   The transfer of energy in the form of rays of light and heat by electromagnetic waves.

Reactivity hazard.   An expression of the degree of susceptibility of materials to release energy either by themselves or in combination with other materials.

Reduction reaction.   Reduction is a reaction involving the removal of oxygen from a substance containing oxygen.

Smoke.   Airborne solid and liquid particulate products of combustion.

Stack effect. The natural movement of air vertically through a high-rise building caused by differences in temperature and air density between the inside and outside air.

Suppressant. The chemical agent used in an explosion suppression system to extinguish the incipient explosion.

Thermal lag. The difference between the operating temperature of a heat detecting device and the actual air temperature at which the device is activated.

Thermoplastics. Resins of compounds that may be formed over and over again upon applying heat and pressure.

Thermosets. Resins or compounds that may be formed and cured once; any subsequent heat will cause the plastic to degrade or burn.

Toxicity. The ability of a material to cause bodily harm by chemical action.

Unit of exit width. Means of egress are measured in units of exit width of 22 inches. 22 inches of width is considered to be the minimum required for the orderly movement of a single file of people along a passageway.

Upper flammable limit. The maximum concentration of gas or vapor in the air above which it is not possible to ignite the vapors.

Vapor density. The ratio of the relative weight of a volume of vapor or gas to the weight of an equal volume of air under the same conditions of temperature and pressure.

Vapor pressure. The pressure exerted by molecules in a liquid, when in equilibrium in the vapor space in a *closed* system. Vapor pressure is given in millimeters (mm) of mercury or pounds per square inch (psi) (atmosphere = 14.7 psi or 760 mm Hg).

Vertical opening. An opening through a floor or roof. In buildings, vertical openings include stairwells, elevator shafts, service chaises, laundry chutes, and air shafts.

Wet water. A solution of water and a wetting agent that has reduced surface tension which increases the penetration capabilities of the water.

INDEX